IN THE CASTLE OF MY SKIN

Portrait of the Author
by Denis Williams

IN THE CASTLE

OF MY SKIN

GEORGE LAMMING

Foreword by Sandra Pouchet Paquet

Ann Arbor Paperbacks

THE UNIVERSITY OF MICHIGAN PRESS

2010   2009   16   15   14

Library of Congress Cataloging-in-Publication Data

Lamming, George, 1927–
    In the castle of my skin / George Lamming ; foreword by Sandra
Pouchet Paquet.
        p.   cm. — (Ann Arbor paperbacks)
    Includes bibliographical references.
    ISBN 0-472-06468-1 (Ann Arbor paperbacks : alk. paper). — ISBN
0-472-09468-8 (cloth : alk. paper)
    I. Title.
PR9230.9.L2515   1991
813—dc20   91-42068
                                                        CIP

ISBN 978-0-472-09468-4 (cloth : alk. paper)
ISBN 978-0-472-06468-7 (Ann Arbor Paperbacks : alk. paper)

To
MY MOTHER
&
FRANK COLLYMORE
whose love and help
deserved a better book

'Something startles where I thought I was safest'

WALT WHITMAN

Foreword

> In the desolate, frozen heart of London, at the age of twenty-three, I
> tried to reconstruct the world of my childhood and early adoles-
> cence. It was also the world of a whole Caribbean reality.
>
> GEORGE LAMMING, from the Introduction (1983)

In the Castle of My Skin is an autobiographical novel of childhood
and adolescence written against the anonymity and alienation from
self and community the author experiences in London at the age of
twenty-three. It is a narrative of reconnection and repatriation that
seeks to position the written self as a developing sensibility within
native community and to fuse that sensibility anagogically with
native community.[1] The text recreates the world of childhood from
the artistic perspective of a writer in exile and also a child's understanding of that world. In this highly politicized narrative, the elaboration of a myth of childhood reveals the underlying attitudes,
thought systems, and ideals of a whole society. The past is situated
in a network of values that reveals the sociocultural processes of
the colonial Caribbean as facets of childhood and, by the same
token, gives that childhood mythic status as evidence and symbol of
those sociocultural processes at work. Childhood is a destination in
art arrived at by way of art.[2] It is a place of writing and renewal
where artistic consciousness and historical conscience are formed.

In the Castle of My Skin recreates the author's childhood and
adolescence in Barbados from the age of nine to the eve of his
departure for the neighboring island of Trinidad at the age of
seventeen. The narrative is both singular and collective; it is about
one boy among other boys and the village community in which
they are raised. From the outset, personal history is linked to major
upheavals in the community that are cumulatively of disastrous
proportions: a devastating flood on his ninth birthday, an island-

wide strike and riots not long after, and the sale of the village land
to speculative interests shortly before he leaves his mother and
friends for his first job in Trinidad.[3] A parallel between the child's
world and the world of the village is established at the outset and
sustained unevenly to the end. Autobiographical time is linked to
village and island history embryonically and anagogically. At the
end of the narrative, the village is dismantled just as the author and
subject of the narrative leaves the island. Though the autobiographical novel is by its very nature open-ended, the boundaries of childhood and adolescence in this autobiographical novel give a certain
degree of structural and thematic closure to the text's quest for self
and artistic perspective in a vanished past.[4] The parallel Lamming
establishes between one boy's childhood and the community that
constitutes it transforms that childhood into a symbolic embodiment
of Caribbean culture and society in the last stages of colonialism.
Though Lamming leaves future possibilities implicit and unstated,
childhood and community are established as "a creative legacy, the
soil of some other movement in life" (Kent 88).

Lamming's choice of genre signals reservations about autobiography as the appropriate vehicle for reconstructing the vanished world
of his childhood and adolescence from a position in exilic space.
The autobiographical novel as opposed to autobiography suggests a
conflict between the cultivated subjectivity of straight autobiography
and "the world of a whole Caribbean reality," between the author
as subject of the narrative and the author as creator of that narrative. The contradictory impulses of this self-conscious and self-
celebrating text are sustained by a complex rhetorical design.
Lamming's strategy is to split the narrative into contrastive but
complementary first and third person modes of narration that blur
the boundaries between author and authorial persona, and between
the constitutive parts of the authorial persona. The first person
narrative is primarily the autobiographical account of a uniquely
experienced childhood filtered through memory and imagination: a
portrait of the artist as a young man. The third person narrative is
concerned with the problems of the community as they are experienced by others, adults and children, whether or not they could
have been perceived or understood by the child or adolescent.

Lamming identifies himself with the first person narrator by giving the protagonist-narrator a designation that is related specifically

to his own name. The use of G. as a symbolic designation also makes it clear that the protagonist is "other than" the author and serves an allegorical as well as autobiographical function within the narrative. Author and persona merge tentatively to acknowledge a coincidence in person between the two and also to establish the limits of self-equivalence. G. is clearly not the author at the time of writing, but their separate worlds coincide; G. is shaped and formed by the values Lamming invests in the recreated world of his childhood and adolescence. Lamming's fluid position at center and periphery of the text, as author and protagonist of an autobiographical fiction, is sustained and validated by the parallel and overlap between first and third person narratives. The narratives share a common axiological center in the elaboration of a narrative of childhood and adolescence that fuses author and protagonist to a specific Caribbean reality.

Though each narrator is given distinct functions, Lamming does not sustain clear-cut boundaries between them. Abrupt and unsignposted shifts blur distinctions between the first person narrator's dramatic rendering of a conversation overheard, or depersonalized analysis and interpretation of the world of his vanished childhood, and the third person narrator's rendering of the same functions. The overlap of voice and function is evident very early in the text. In the first chapter, the first person narrative moves casually between the alternative dimensions of childhood recreated, adult reflection, and ironic self-assessment. In the second chapter, the focus of G.'s narrative shifts abruptly from the intimate details of a child interacting with his mother and neighbors to a sweeping characterization of the village community and the child's place in it.

> Miss Foster. My mother. Bob's mother.
> It seemed they were three pieces in a pattern which remained constant. The flow of its history was undisturbed by any difference in the pieces, nor was its evenness affected by any likeness. There was a difference and there was no difference. (24)

Immediately following this characterization of G.'s world as typical of a wider order, a depersonalized narrator, using signposts such as "one gathered" and "one could see" (25) to establish collectivity, delivers an authoritative political analysis of the feudal structure of village life as a legacy of the plantation system, using the English landlord, the village overseer, and the villagers to reveal the psychodynamics of British colonial society (25–29).[5] G.'s village is identified as a miniature of Barbados, "the oldest and least adulterated of British colonies" (25). The poetic transformation of G.'s village into symbolic British colony endows G.'s singular childhood with broad social significance. The value Lamming attaches to his narrative of childhood is registered in unequivocal terms. G.'s narrative has a symbolic value beyond its own inner directedness as a lived experience; G. is a colonial child. By the end of the chapter, the narrative returns to the pattern of everyday life in Creighton's Village, to recording the rituals of the public baths, of boys flattening pins and nails into blades on the railtracks, of "Miss Foster, Bob's mother and my mother" conversing under a cherry tree, "not thirteen, not thirty, but three" (33). There is little tonal change in the narrative shift in focus from the feudal structure of Creighton's Village to the Queen's Birthday celebrations at Groddeck's Boy School, where the third person narrator ranges freely from interpretive summary of conversations among different groups of boys to the objective rendering of conversations with little or no interference, and lengthy stream-of-consciousness passages which reveal the inner turmoil of the headmaster.

The intertwining and overlap of distinct narrative modes intensifies the dramatic contrast between the self-referential quality of the first person narrative and the broader social, historical, and cultural contexts of the third person narrative. The charged political consciousness of the third person narrator serves as a constant reminder of the difference between the alternative dimension of G.'s developing sensibilities and intellectual formation and the author as creator of the text. As child and adolescent G. is only partially aware of the constituents and situations of the world that encompasses him. The imperfectly constituted hero and subject of his own narrative, G.'s individual life is validated and extended in the parallel narrative of the third person narrator even as the distinction between the two spheres is neutralized in the metaphysical and artistic whole that is Lamming's autobiographical novel. In the world of childhood recreated, each dimension of consciousness becomes a facet of Lamming's fully empowered imagination imposing form and meaning on a life transformed into a symbol of the sociocultural processes of a specific time and place.

The multifaceted relationship between the contrastive and complementary first and third person narratives illuminates a dynamic relationship between writing and place, and place and childhood. As subject of his own narrative, G.'s relationship to his village as a child and adolescent is passive and essentially filial. He listens, observes, and records. The house which he shares with his mother in the village is one of many. It embodies a common heritage. It provides the window that situates the eye and ear of a ballad memory. In the opening chapters, G. is literally peering through the window (9) or peeping through the jalousies (22). The consonance between the inside and outside of G.'s village home represents the center and circumference of his vision. He is the creation of his colonial village and his sensibility is circumscribed by its boundaries. The entries in his diary in the last months before he leaves home confirm this. The grease-soiled exercise book records the pleasure G. takes in attending the annual Agricultural Exhibition, a conversation overheard at the Miami Club about the sale of the village, and predeparture activities (258–60). Yet G. is weakly assimilated into the collective community that constitutes his lived experience. He sees himself as part of the community but does not see or feel the community as part of himself. His "love for the sprawling dereliction of that life" (224) is in conflict with a cultivated sense of difference. On the eve of his departure he feels no solidarity with his friends. The last entry in his diary reveals a deeply felt alienation from community.

> When I review these relationships they seem so odd. I have always been here on this side and the other person there on that side, and we have both tried to make the sides appear similar in the needs, desires, and ambitions. But it wasn't true. It was never true. When I reach Trinidad where no one knows me I may be able to strike an identity with the other person. But it was never possible here. (261)

He has no sympathy for the prostitute who intercepts him after a farewell party given by friends and, with studied detachment, seeks to appease his mother's emotional outbursts over his impending departure. His ontological fear of self-revelation is linked to the lack of "an intimate, organic axiological participation in the world of others" (Bakhtin, *Art*, 155). The "you that's hidden somewhere in the castle of your skin" (261), paradoxically, lacks the interiority necessary to conceptualize lived experience except as repetitive fragments in a disintegrating diary.

In contrast, the relationship of the third person narrator to the village is affiliative rather than filial. The shifting values of the third person, at times intrusive and at others distant, imposes a symbolic vision on the village landscape that is different though complementary to the one G. receives from it.[6] The depersonalized vision of the third person is also village-based; it replaces G.'s lack of empathy with an overarching ideological identification with the plight of the villagers as opposed to the landlord or overseer. Autobiography is depersonalized and the "solitary" life of a West Indian child gains in coherence and intelligibility from the stories of others, whether it is the story of the boy who is victimized by the headmaster's savagery, or of Mr. Slime, or of the shoemaker, or of Ma and Pa. In the context of *In the Castle of My Skin* as a whole, the alternative consciousness of the third person narrator signals the development of a specific race and class consciousness in the author that is only marginally present in the developing subjectivity of the implied author as a young man. It is a consciousness that effectively transforms G.'s retreat from family, friends, and community as an adolescent hiding somewhere in the castle of his skin (261) into a retrospective that locates native community and territorial history at the axiological center of the autobiographical text.

Lamming's primary concern with a developing male sensibility in the context of an evolving historical conscience calls attention to the gendered space of the text. Girls are rarely mentioned and, except for the prostitute, women are associated with domesticity and socialization. The relationship between village mothers and sons is characterized selectively as a struggle for parental control undermined by absent, irresponsible, or abusive fathers. Nameless schoolboys speculate that mothers are "stupid, that's why most of us without fathers" (46). There is no doubt about the protective instinct of these mothers, but their authority is premised on violence and the threat of violence, and they are associated with a deep conservativism in the society. As culture-bearers they tend to the

colonial hearth. Their creativity is the creativity of sexual reproduc-
tion and nurturers within this cultural context. G.'s mother raises
him to advance within the colonial hierarchy of power, not to
challenge it. Miss Foster is hostile to the overseer and worshipful of
the landlord. Ma cannot accept social change that is not explicitly
sanctioned by God and the landlord. As the symbolic embodiment
of an ancestral colonial landscape that is both nurturing and delim-
iting, G.'s mother emerges as a verifying force within a historically
resonant past, whose scale of influence is radically curtailed by a
natural process of individuation and by her own limited compre-
hension of colonial politics. Edward Baugh observes that the "deep
and intricate relationship of G. and his mother" is "central to the
novel, and is a microcosm of his relationship with the community
or the island as a whole" (24). Lamming achieves a fine balance
between the process of individuation that drives a wedge between
G. and his mother, and the bonds of mutual affection and appreciation that are memorialized in the text as a whole.

In *Reminiscences of Childhood*, Richard N. Coe states the case for
the autobiography of childhood and adolescence as an autonomous
genre with "its own rules and its own inner structural laws, which
are quite distinct from those of standard autobiography; it has its
own archetypal patterns, its uniquely-delineated heroes and hero-
ines, its experiences and motivations" (1). In Lamming's highly
politicized narrative of childhood and adolescence, the contradictions of G.'s consciousness at various stages reveal the text's
overarching concern with the ideas, attitudes, and values behind the
archetypal experiences and encounters of his West Indian boy-
hood—uncelebrated birthdays; school; forbidden adventures at the
beach, at an open-air prayer meeting, within the landlord's compound; the strike and riots; departure from home. Each stage of
consciousness reveals something about the systems of thought and
value in the culture that engendered him. Out of each experience
emerge archetypal figures of childhood and village—mother,
headteacher, fisherman, preacher, overseer, landlord, politician, the
ancestral figures of Ma and Pa. Each is a point of access in identify-
ing the origins of self in a vanished community.

Though the novel begins and ends with domestic scenes involv-
ing G. and his mother, the interim reveals G. interacting with boy-
hood friends and a chorus of nameless village boys who illuminate

the world of other children in the village from which G. emerges.
G.'s individual predicament is always dissolving into the collective
predicament of other village boys, and into the adult world of social
and political relations of which the child has only partial awareness.
This is the technical cunning of Lamming's beginning. The flood
that spoils G.'s hopes for a birthday celebration causes widespread
destruction in the village. The parallel establishes individual difference and shared predicament. The fragility of the village outside
parallels the fragility of G.'s family situation in the absence of an
extended family. The flood invades G.'s house and the roof leaks.
His mother reproaches him for his tears of disappointment and
frustration: "I was wrong, my mother protested: it was irreverent to
disapprove the will of the Lord or reject the consolation that my
birthday had brought showers of blessing" (9). Boredom and mis-
conceived folk wisdom prompt the nine year old to overfeed and
purge his pet parrot. When it dies, G.'s disappointment turns to
guilt and shame and terror. He buries his "blessings in the pillow"
(13) and fights off the devilish phantoms that haunt him that night.
The trivial details of a nine year old's disastrous birthday and his
mother's uncreative attempts at comforting him with conventional
Christian wisdom are given significance as aspects of the text's
ideologizing function. The flood is a direct link to the wider reality
of the feudal structure of life in the village. The repairs to the
village roads are the responsibility of a reluctant landlord who, it is
reported by the overseer's brother, cries "buckets of drops" (97)
when he has to spend money developing and maintaining the
infrastructure of the village. The landlord and his family inspect the
damage, and their privileged position in the village is internalized
in the children's games.

> When the carriage disappeared with the landlord and his
> family, small boys came out to rehearse the scene. Two took
> the part of the horses and trotted along to the fore, while
> another three arranged themselves behind as the landlord and
> his family had done. The boys would trot slowly from road to
> road pretending to make a similar survey, and discussing
> among themselves the plans they had for repairs. (28)

The white landlord is established as a dominant cultural influence
in shaping village values and customs. The children mimic his tea

parties visible to them from the roof of the large brick house on a hill overlooking the village. When the lights are turned off in the great house, it is received as a signal by those below.

> The landlord's light had been put out. The landlord had gone to bed. It was time they did the same. A custom had been established, and later a value which through continual application and a hardened habit of feeling became an absolute standard of feeling. I don't feel the landlord would like this. If the overseer see, the landlord is bound to know. It operated in every activity. The obedient lived in the hope that the Great might not be offended, the uncertain in the fear it might have been. (29)

The child's world is linked to the world of colonial culture and politics and the linkage adds to our understanding of both worlds and the mechanics of cultural production in Creighton's Village.

All the components of Lamming's vision of childhood are endowed with a series of precise significances that illuminate the child's world and the adult world that circumscribes it. The hierarchical and sequential linkage Lamming establishes between school, church, empire, and colonial education parodies the school ethos of such classic texts of English childhood as Thomas Hughes's *Tom Brown's Schooldays* (1858) and Rudyard Kipling's *Stalky and Co* (1899). The occasion is the annual celebration of Queen Victoria's birthday with speeches, parades, and mindless displays of rote learning, followed by the annual distribution of pennies to the children. The English school inspector's speech reveals a fundamental conflict of interest in the school ethos.

> My dear boys and teachers, we are met once again to pay our respects to the memory of a great queen. She was your queen and my queen and yours no less than mine. We're all subjects and partakers in the great design, the British Empire, and your loyalty to the Empire can be seen in the splendid performance which your school decorations and the discipline of these squads represent. . . . The British Empire, you must remember, has always worked for the peace of the world. This was the job assigned it by God, and if the Empire at any time has failed to bring about that peace it was due to events beyond

its control. But, remember, my dear boys, whatever happens
in any part of this world, whatever happens to you here in
this island of Barbados, the pride and treasure of the Empire,
we are always on the side of peace. (38)

The linking of the ideal of the school with the civilizing mission of
the British Empire rings hollow as the narrative unfolds. The archetypal figure of the great headmaster is revealed as a toady who
guards his privilege as "village overseer" with smiles and fawning in
his dealings with the English school inspector, and violence and
sadism in his dealings with the children. The unfolding sequence of
the education narrative intertwines the fixed values of the school
inspector's sense of divine mission with the uncertainty of the boys,
who ask key questions about Queen Victoria, slavery, freedom, and
the minting of pennies and construct their own fanciful answers
from a variety of contradictory sources. The paradox of the school
is that it perpetuates ignorance and confusion among the children.
Lamming's method of intertwining the contrasting preoccupations
and levels of consciousness among the school inspector, the teachers, and the children places as much emphasis on how the village
school culture functions as part of the colonial enterprise as on the
effects of that culture on the socialization of the children.

The components of Lamming's vision of childhood are all charged
with political significance. The day G. spends at the beach with his
friends is framed by their growing awareness of race and class
differences. G.'s imaginative reading of the clouds as social text
reflects this. G.'s mother's ambitions have already marked him as
different from the other boys. He and Bob are surprised into a
recognition of their growing mistrust of each other (110). From their
curiosity about crabs mating to King Canute and an observed conflict between weddings and family life in the village, the boys are
obsessed with language as a mechanism for explaining and understanding their environment. It is the basis for games and metaphysical inquiry. Removed from the constraints of adult watchfulness,
their imaginations roam freely over the fundamentals of village life.
In the King Canute joke the boys play on Bob, language as history
is reduced to sterile incantation: "Sea Come No Further. Sea Come
No Further" (119). In the Jon, Jen, Susie, and Bots, Bambi, Bambina

narratives, language is simultaneously the constructive and de-
constructive framer of the whole etiology of an individual's and a
community's life. The relationship between language and experience is mysterious, an occasion for fun and fear. When Trumper
says that the crabs "looked fishy," Boy Blue prefers "crabby" (133).
Boy Blue's notion of "something going off pop in yuh head" (142)
makes Trumper uncomfortable and calls for clarification on Boy
Blue's part: "I wus makin' joke. Not really makin' joke, but sort of
tryin' to say what I mean without knowin' the right words to say"
(143). The boys are aware that words and experience are different
dimensions and that understanding and negotiating the world is
linked to one's facility with language on multiple levels. A reflective
G. intervenes to put the boys' obsession with language in perspective:

> Perhaps we would do better if we had good big words like
> the educated people. But we didn't. We had to say something
> was like something else, and whatever we said didn't convey
> all we felt. We wouldn't dare tell anybody what we had talked
> about. People who were sure of what they were saying and
> who had the right words to use could do that. They could talk
> to others. And even if they didn't feel what they were saying,
> it didn't matter. They had the right words. (154–55)

The perceived conflict in values between the formal language of the
educated colonial and the intuitive, creative, and secret language of
the boys emphasizes the text's concern with language as cultural
agency and with the foundational values of a rich oral tradition.

The boys' struggle to name and communicate their own reality
occurs in a context quite distinct from the received notions of
school and home. The day at the beach opens up new horizons.

> With the sea simmering, and the sand and the wind in the
> trees, we received so many strange feelings. And in the village
> in the cellar, at the school, in this corner or that corner of the
> house, something was always happening. We didn't notice it
> then, but when something bigger appeared like the sea and
> sand, it brought with it a big, big feeling, and the big feeling

pushed up all the little feelings we had received in other places. (153)

The beach is a site of discovery and magical transformations. The giant of a fisherman becomes a man: "Contact had made him human. Now he was like us. He was only big and strong, as we would say in the village, but he was like us" (153). The awesome otherness of adult maleness as village giant is encountered and assimilated. The fisherman's angry intolerance of their play is linked enduringly to his blackness, his beauty, and his physical strength.

The distinction between myth and reality is difficult to maintain in the reconstruction of a vanished and essentially otherworldly past. In Richard N. Coe's study of autobiography and the experience of childhood, *When the Grass Was Taller*, the elusive borderline between the autobiography of childhood and the novel is a recurring point of reference.

> In the first place, the Childhood, like the traditional novel, is clearly structured with a beginning, a middle, and an end, and, as in the Aristotelian ideal of tragedy, the end is implicit in the beginning. In the second place, the balance between literal and symbolic truth is shifted in the direction of the latter. Incidents are given weight in straight autobiography according to their factual significance; in the Childhood, more often that not, according to their emotional, imaginative, or metaphysical significance. (79)

In Lamming's novelization of childhood, G.'s development to maturity, from childhood through adolescence to young adulthood, parallels the archetypal autobiographical norm. G. is first seen with his mother operating within the confines of the immediate neighborhood. Later, as a boy among boys there are secret excursions in which they scout and test the boundaries of the village on a forbidden beach and within the walls of the landlord's enclave. Finally, he is a young man among men on the eve of a momentous break with the circumscribed existence and understanding of a village youth. The process of individuation is the basic schema of childhood narratives as different as Richard Wright's *Black Boy*, James Joyce's *A Portrait of the Artist as a Young Man*, and Camara Laye's

The Dark Child. Like each of these writers, Lamming alters literal facts in order to clarify the essential truth of his childhood as he understands it as an adult writing in exilic space and time. In *In the Castle of My Skin*, these changes accentuate rather than diminish the experiential archetypes of the autobiography of childhood even as these archetypes are recombined in patterns specific to his experience of childhood in the Caribbean.

Lamming has been forthcoming about some of the liberties he has taken with the factual circumstances of his life in writing *In the Castle of My Skin* (Paquet 13–14). In *The Pleasures of Exile* he explains that Pa's forced departure from the village actually occurred when he was about twelve and not on the eve of his departure from Trinidad as is the case in *In the Castle of My Skin* (226). Moreover, Pa's house is moved to another part of the island; he is not sent to the Alms House as is the case in *In the Castle of My Skin*. Creighton's Village is actually a composite of two villages he knew intimately as a child, Carrington's Village and St. David's (Munro and Sander). In another telling instance, Lamming chooses not to identify the role of his stepfather in his childhood. In these respects, the novelization of childhood in *In the Castle of My Skin* does not represent a radical departure from the autobiographical norm. In each case, the elaboration of a mythology of childhood is served.

G.'s traumatic break with native community at the end of the text is charged with symbolic power as a necessary precondition to achieving perspective, when it is grouped conceptually with the forced relocation and public humiliation of the old man who is archetypal "father" of the village and substitute father of the authorial subject of the narrative. The expulsion of Pa marks the end of G.'s childhood and the completion of the narrative. The creation of Creighton's Village out of Carrington's Village and St. David's affirms and intensifies G.'s symbolic relationship to native space. The poetization of space and time underscores the parallel development of G. and his native world. Creighton's Village is no static recreation of a "typical" village. It celebrates and critiques the underlying unity of human relations in native space and mythologizes Lamming's obsession with defining distinctive features of the community that engendered him and his altered relationship to that community at the time of writing. The erasure of a stepfather underscores the myth of the male child "fathered" by a passionate, ambitious, and articulate mother and emphasizes the ensuing anxieties and tensions of a maturing male subjectivity in the absence of grandparents, siblings, and other relatives.

> My birth began with an almost total absence of family relations. My parents on almost all sides had been deposited in the bad or uncertain accounts of all my future relationships, and loneliness from which had subsequently grown the consolation of freedom was the legacy with which my first year opened. (12)

A child's blank memory engenders loneliness and inquiry. The adult quest for self and community begins in the curiosity of a lonely child and continues in the broader theme of cultural orphanage that is the legacy of colonial history throughout the text.

> What did I remember? My father who had only fathered the idea of me had left me the sole liability of my mother who really fathered me. And beyond that my memory was a blank. It sank with its cargo of episodes like a crew preferring to scuttle the consequences of survival. (11)

In the elaboration of a myth of childhood all the elements of childhood are archetypal. What matters here is not the truthfulness of autobiographical detail, but the value Lamming ascribes to his individual childhood as the key to a wider Caribbean reality. Novelization of the author's childhood gives the written text the self-sustaining integrity of a fictional life condensed and controlled by an elaborate symbolism.

Lamming's manipulation of the genre illuminates an ongoing dialogue between emerging artistic consciousness and historical conscience text. In *In the Castle of My Skin*, the authorial subject is organically connected to a specific geographical and historical reality. References to the great flood, the strike and riots of 1937, and World War II locate G.'s mythical village in a real world, in real time. The empowered authorial imagination imposes its vision on a concrete geographical locality. Literal truth is sacrificed to symbolic truth but remains a visible, verifying context within the text itself.

The historical record is conceptualized as the foundation and inspiration of autobiographical myth.

The polyphonic design of *In the Castle of My Skin* underscores the transformational nature of Lamming's novelization of childhood and autobiography. The contrastive juxtaposition of first and third person narrative modes dominates the structure of the novel, but their authority over the narrative as a whole is muted by a host of village voices that complement and compete with the dominant discourses of the first and third person. Both the self-discursive G. and the collective third person narrator repeatedly defer to a chorus of village voices that name their own reality in a language that is ostensibly of their own choosing.[7] The oral traditions of the village are given great authority in the narrative from the child's fantastical reconstruction of social reality to Pa's dream vision (Lamming, Introduction, xxxvi). G. is a listener as well as an observer. "Sight says too many things at one time. Being does not see itself. Perhaps it listens to itself," writes Gaston Bachelard (215). Whatever G.'s motivation in keeping silence, it is his mother's words that dominate their last supper together. The sections of his diary that he is reading as she prepares the meal are interrupted and finally silenced by her voiced anxieties and frustrations over the impending departure of her son. On the day G. spends at the beach with Trumper, Boy Blue, and Bob, the other boys have a lot to say. They tell long stories and analyze their thoughts and feelings in their own words. G.'s narrative voice is reflective and descriptive, but he defers to the voices of the other boys, who narrate their own anxieties and speculations within the text, often with the minimum of intrusive commentary. The undiluted egotism of the child who expects his mother to produce a birthday cake while a flood is raging outside dissolves into the selves of others.

The same is true of the third person narrative. The anonymous narrator is at times intrusive and domineering, as in the description of the headteacher and the school inspector on the occasion of the Queen's Birthday (chap. 3), or in the description of the hierarchical structure of village life in which the overseer is given mythical monster value as an agent of colonial power (chap. 2). On other occasions, this authoritative voice surrenders to a villager's voice, most notably Pa's or Ma's, or the shoemaker's, or the schoolboys'. These characters are named allegorically according to their function in the village and in the text. Ma and Pa are the oldest inhabitants in the village and are barometers of different attitudes to fundamental changes occurring there. The boys are named simply First Boy, Second Boy, Third Boy, and the victim. After one boy is beaten sadistically by the headteacher, other boys take him to the standpipe in the school yard to wash him clean and talk. As with the conversations between Ma and Pa regarding Mr. Slime and the alleged molestation of the landlord's daughter, their dialogue is represented on the page in the manner of a script, and each voice is given linguistic authority over a wide range of thought responses. Though depersonalized by their symbolic designation, the voices communicate directly and powerfully the individually and collectively felt cultural core of village life. In the process, the village projects an autonomous life of its own "independent" of the values generated by the contrastive juxtaposition of the first and third person narratives. G. and the third person narrator name and interpret the villagers and their world; they also provide an occasion for them to express their own humanity. As facets of the written self, the villagers are given authority and interpretive power over the unfolding historical and political events that dominate their lives. The paradox of these village voices—natives of the split authorial persona—is that they lack the artist's perspective needed to give their experiences the overarching significance the author inculcates into the whole narrative.

> The three were shuffling episodes and exchanging the confidences which informed their life with meaning. The meaning was not clear to them. It was not their concern, and it would never be. Their consciousness had never been quickened by the fact of life to which these confidences might have been a sure testimony. (25)

The carefully constructed dialogue of characters like Ma and Pa, the shoemaker, the boys, and their mothers not only communicates an immediate sense of community with a vibrant moral and philosophical base, but calls attention to the rich range of oral traditions that shape and sustain the community's questing spirit. The poetic tradition begins here in "the regular pattern of talk that filled the villager's life" (92). Lamming invests heavily in G.'s characteristic posture as listener and recorder and in the third person narrator's function as facilitator of village voices. This is not dissimilar to Derek Walcott's model in "The Muse of History":

> Epic was compressed in the folk legend. The act of the imagination was the creative effort of the tribe. Later such legends may be written by individual poets, but their beginnings are oral, familial, the poetry of firelight which illuminates the faces of a tight, primal hierarchy. But even oral literature forces itself toward hieroglyph and alphabet. (13)

The oral traditions of the village are privileged in this written text as foundation and inspiration of the artistic enterprise. They range broadly from Miss Foster's account of her meeting with the landlord to the shoemaker's speculations about history and empire, Ma's creative retelling of Biblical parable, Brother Dickson's exhortations at the crossroads, Pa's dream vision, and the boys' stories and endless speculation about social and political issues they only partially understand. The allegorical subtexts of Bots, Bambi, and Bambina, and Jon, Jen, and Susie, narrated individually by Trumper and Boy Blue as a strategy of self-clarification, reinforce orality as a structural and thematic value in *In the Castle of My Skin*.

The individualized voices of the village introduce a folkloric content that humanizes and intensifies native space and affirms its underlying unity in a national-historical context.[8] Pa and Ma introduce a generational time that is epochal and cyclic. Pa's dream vision of the enslavement and forced resettlement of Africans in the New World is a memory he struggles to retrieve in a self-induced hallucinatory state; it is not an operative part of village consciousness. At the other end of the time-continuum, the children signal a changing village consciousness. They shock their mothers with their mockery of the "white gentl'man":

> Look, look what fowlcock do,
> Look what fowlcock do to you. (21)

Many years later Trumper returns from "America" with a new idiom of race consciousness and political activism that is somewhat different from the values that Pa inculcates during a comparable stint of migrant labor in Panama many years previously. Where Pa dream-speaks the fragmented psyche of the New World African whole, Trumper articulates it in casual conversation.

The village voices are different but they share common preoccupations about their changing world. Apart from Brother Dickson, they use a common language, what Edward Kamau Brathwaite calls the "nation language" of a "submerged/emerging culture" (*History*, 42).[9] This emphasizes the personal-historical gap between the split authorial persona and the villagers. However, the centrality of a wide range of village voices speaking in their own language also emphasizes the underlying bond of sympathy and appreciation that links the split authorial persona in exilic space and time to native space; a native space that is explicitly based in race and class. The two planes of narrating consciousness have the same axiological center in reconstructing a vanished childhood; that center links the split authorial persona in the text to the author.[10]

The line of demarcation between the split authorial persona and the author in *In the Castle of My Skin* is like the collapsing fence between G.'s yard and Bob's (16–17). In his collection of essays, *The Pleasures of Exile* (1960), Lamming provides an interpretive model for the West Indian novel that is similarly based in class and race.

> The West Indian novel, by which I mean the novel written by the West Indian about the West Indian reality is hardly twenty years old. . . . The education of all these writers is more or less middle-class Western culture, and particularly English culture. But the substance of their books, the general motives and directions, are peasant. . . . It is the West Indian novel that has restored the West Indian peasant to his true and original status of personality. (38–39)

The West Indian novel is treated as a cultural icon, the self-conscious representation of a specific class consciousness and practice. These values dominate the last essay in the collection, "Journey to an Expectation." In this essay Lamming invades the self-regulating aspect of *In the Castle of My Skin* with an autobiographical tribute to Papa Grandison, who died shortly after *In the Castle of My Skin* was published. He gives a short interpretive account of what

Papa Grandison meant to him as a child and explains that the expulsion of Papa Grandison from their village was the compelling motivation behind the writing of *In the Castle of My Skin* (228). He quotes the last page and a half of the novel and interprets it as a colonial manifestation of race and class consciousness.

Independent of the retrospective intervention of "Journey to an Expectation," the last pages of *In the Castle of My Skin* provide several clues that Pa/Papa is a privileged ancestral Other in this autobiographical narrative of a fatherless child. Not only does Pa's "last look at the place" (302) coincide with G.'s departure from the village, at their last meeting it is Pa who names the situation:

> "We both settin' forth tomorrow," he said. "I to my last restin'-place before the grave, an' you into the wide wide world." (302)

Pa names the structure of *In the Castle of My Skin* "before" it is written. Speaking in folkloric time of major upheavals—of floods, riots, and landlessness—the old man observes that the sale of the village lands and the forced relocation of many of the villagers was implicit in the devastating floods that spoiled G.'s birthday.

> "You wus small then," he said, "too small to care much 'bout the calamity that happen. But it wus the beginnin' o' so much in this place. 'Twas strike an' then 'twas riot an' what with one rumour an' a next, now 'tis the land. We see Penny Bank an' Society an' now 'tis the end." (303)

The ideological value of G.'s sympathetic identification with Pa as "a colonial symbol of traditional man" (*Pleasures*, 229) is implicit in the form of the text. However, Lamming's retrospective intervention reiterates autobiographical discourse as an aspect of the text's ideologizing function. The denial of authorial ego implicit in the elaborate architecture of *In the Castle of My Skin* is "a natural-naive isolation, a relative isolation, and not an isolation in principle, not an aesthetic isolation" (Bakhtin, *Art*, 165). In its rhetorical design, *In the Castle of My Skin* represses autobiography, but Lamming's retrospective commentary emphasizes the author's wish to root the text in personal-historical experience. It provides interpretive cues for a

reading of the form and the content of the text that calls attention
to its autobiographical center.

The relationship between autobiography and fiction is as fluid as
the relationship between the first and third person narrators in the
text. In his 1983 introduction to the novel, Lamming reverses his
emphasis on autobiography as expressed in "Journey to an Expectation." Collectivity is represented as both the form and the substance
of the text as autobiographical novel.

> The book is crowded with names and people, and although
> each character is afforded a most vivid presence and force of
> personality, we are rarely concerned with the prolonged ex-
> ploration of an individual consciousness. It is the collective
> human substance of the village that commands our attention.
> The Village, you might say, is the central character. (xxxvi)

Lamming changes his emphasis from the rhetoric of autobiography
to the rhetoric of collectivity, from a personal gesture to a medita-
tion on the process of meaning production and his own changing
values. The discourse shifts from the authorial subject as survivor
and living witness to the typicality of the narrative, from the "me" in
the text to the "me" writing and reading the text. Thus the fact that
G.'s mother remains nameless in the text is treated as an example of
the richness and power of the symbolizing process at the heart of
In the Castle of My Skin.

> The mother of the novel is given no name. She is simply G.'s
> mother, a woman of little or no importance in her neighbor-
> hood until the tropical season rains a calamity on every house-
> hold; and she emerges, without warning, as a voice of nature
> itself. (xxxvi)

Authorial ego is sacrificed in a self-celebrating creativity; G.'s mother
is transformed into a symbol of community when she initiates the
pattern of call and response; when her particular voice prompts a
chorus of other voices in recognition of their shared plight.

Lamming characterizes the book published thirty years previously
and offers the reader guidance about the right way to read it. He

uses *In the Castle of My Skin* as the occasion to restate a theory of the Caribbean novel he had conceptualized previously in *The Pleasures of Exile*.

> The Novel has a particular function in the Caribbean. The writer's preoccupation has been mainly with the poor; and has served as a way of restoring these lives—this world of men and women from down below—to a proper order of attention; to make their reality the supreme concern of the total society. But along with this desire, there was also the writer's recognition that this world, in spite of its long history of deprivation, represented the womb from which he himself had sprung, and the richest collective reservoir of experience on which the creative imagination could draw. (xxxvii)

Lamming's emphasis on the specific ideology of his art as generic Caribbean writing is a conscious attempt to mythologize his artistic intent, just as he had done in *The Pleasures of Exile*. He calls attention to the conditions of writing in the Caribbean, in terms of the writer's relationship both to his native space as threshold to community and creativity and to his changing values and his changing audience.

Lamming's shift in emphasis from one retrospective commentary to another appears relative to the material circumstances of publication. *The Pleasures of Exile* was published first in England in 1960, while the introduction printed here was published first in the United States in 1983. In the latter, Lamming adds a new catalogue of concerns about the ideological underpinnings of the text. He reflects "on the role which America was to play in shaping the essential features of the novel" (xl). He clarifies Trumper's sojourn as a migrant laborer in the United States as a salutary one, to the extent that he returns with a new understanding of the political and cultural significance of race, and "with a political experience which the subtle force of British imperialism had never allowed to flourish in the islands" (xli). These themes are explicit in *In the Castle of My Skin*, but Lamming places new emphasis on them in the 1983 interpretive retrospective.

Lamming's anxieties about how the text is read reveal an interesting autobiographical twist. Having made a case for *In the Castle of My Skin* as a generic Caribbean text, Lamming subverts the privilege he claims for the text-context relationship by questioning the method and ideology that shaped the text. He enters into a dialogue with himself about the artistic integrity of his portrayal of the 1937 riots in Barbados. It is both defense and critique.[11]

> The novelist does not only explore what had happened. At a deeper level of intention than literal accuracy, he seeks to construct a world that might have been; to show the possible as a felt and living reality. So for a long time I remained haunted by the feeling that the white landlord should have been killed; even if it were presented as the symbolic end of a social order that deserved to be destroyed. (xl)

In *In the Castle of My Skin*, the dialectics of fiction and autobiography do not exist as simple reciprocity. Like Bachelard's dialectics of inside and outside, "they are always ready to be revised, to exchange their hostility" (218).

In the Castle of My Skin is a modern Caribbean classic.[12] Not only does it contain valuable insights about childhood and society in the colonial Caribbean at mid-century, the elaborate and unconventional structure of the narrative provides an interpretive framework for investigating its own historical moment and ours as well.[13] Lamming's choice of genre reveals an author who is skeptical about unmediated autobiography. The splitting or doubling of the authorial persona into lyrical voice and collective chorus makes autobiographical discourse the subject matter and content of the text. The limitations of G. as a maturing sensibility suggest the limitations of the lyrical hero as narrating consciousness. However, *In the Castle of My Skin* is fundamentally celebratory of self and community in the link it establishes between origins and artistic vision. G.'s departure is prelude to reconnection and return. The autobiographical novel is a narrative space that fuses artistic consciousness to the symbolic native space as imaginative home and enabling ground that "in the castle of my skin" suggests.

Sandra Pouchet Paquet
University of Pennsylvania

NOTES

1. "Exile is an impetus, a positioning, and a perspective. . . . one gets outside a space to look in and see wholly; on the other hand, the space created from outside is, willy-nilly, a projection, subject to the laws generated and inspired by the imagining mind" (Seidel 87).

2. "We are more and more aware of writing as a place in itself, a destination in art arrived at by way of art. And yet an urge persists to enquire into the inspiration and foundation which place affords in the creative process" (Heaney 19).

3. Coe links the origins of the genre to major social upheavals: "But if this motif is most clearly discernible in recent writings, the fact is that the origins of the Childhood as a genre coincided from the outset with a major period of upheaval, with the French Revolution and the Industrial Revolution . . ." (*Grass*, 65).

4. "The formal literary structure is complete exactly at the point at which the immature self of childhood is conscious of its transformation into the mature self of the adult who is the narrator of the earlier experiences" (Coe, *Grass*, 9).

5. Patrick Taylor analyzes some of the remarkable parallels between *In the Castle of My Skin* and Fanon's *The Wretched of the Earth* in *The Narrative of Liberation* (189–92).

6. In *The Place of Writing*, Seamus Heaney makes two important points that are worth noting here: "that the poetic imagination in its strongest manifestation imposes its vision upon a place rather than accepts a vision from it; and that this visionary imposition is never exempt from the imagination's antithetical ability to subvert its own creation" (20).

7. "Unless it is highly fictionalized the autobiography of childhood is of necessity largely descriptive. There is, by and large, comparative little scope for narrative, still less for dialogue, while reflective or analytical passages must be seen strictly as the contribution of the adult" (Coe, *Grass*, 117).

8. Writing about the contribution of folklore to the development of the historical novel in the eighteenth century, Bakhtin observes: "The folksong, the folktale, the heroic and historical legend, and the saga were above all a new and powerful means of humanizing and intensifying one's native space" (*Speech Genres*, 52).

9. An important theoretical companion piece to E. K. Brathwaite's *The History of the Voice* (1984), quoted here, is his earlier essay on nation language, "English in the Caribbean," in Houston A. Baker, Jr.'s *Reading Black* (1976).

10. Writing on autobiography, Bakhtin concludes that "the boundary between horizon and surrounding world or environment is unstable in

biography and has no significance in principle; empathy has maximal significance" (*Art*, 166).

11. It may be that the dialogue with self is also a dialogue with Fanon about the death of the colonizer (Taylor 74, 195–96).

12. Writing about *The Education of Henry Adams*, Hayden White observes that "the classic text reveals, indeed actively draws attention to, its own processes of meaning production and makes of these processes its own subject matter, its own 'context'" (211).

13. Because of its deep resonance and complex structure, *In the Castle of My Skin* illuminates the sociocultural processes at work in subsequent Caribbean narratives of childhood and adolescence. "The consummate text of growing up male in the Caribbean" (Cooke 29) provides a useful apperceptive background for investigating texts as different as V. S. Naipaul's *Miguel Street* (1959), Michael Anthony's *The Year in San Fernando* (1965), Merle Hodge's *Crick Crack, Monkey* (1970), Erna Brodber's *Jane and Louisa Will Soon Come Home* (1980), and Jamaica Kincaid's *Annie John* (1985). Michael Cooke's "The Strains of Apocalypse" demonstrates some of the many ways in which Brodber's text repeats and revises key tropes and rhetorical strategies from *In the Castle of My Skin*. The same case can be made for all of these texts even where they explore the different historical reality of growing up female in the Caribbean, or place an entirely different value on their Caribbean childhoods.

WORKS CITED

Anthony, Michael. *The Year in San Fernando*. 1965. Reprint, London: Heinemann, 1970.

Bachelard, Gaston. *The Poetics of Space*. Translated by Maria Jolas. 1958. Reprint, Boston: Beacon, 1969.

Bakhtin, M. M. *Speech Genres and Other Late Essays*. Edited by Caryl Emerson and Michael Holquist. Translated by Vern W. McGee. Austin: University of Texas Press, 1986.

———. *Art and Answerability*. Edited by Michael Holquist and Vadim Liapunov. Translated by Vadim Liapunov and Kenneth Brostrom. Austin: University of Texas Press, 1990.

Baugh, Edward. "Cuckoo and Culture: In the Castle of My Skin." *Ariel* 8, no. 3 (July 1977): 23–33.

Brathwaite, Edward Kamau. "English in the Caribbean." In *Reading Black: Essays in the Criticism of African, Caribbean and Black American Literature*, edited by Houston A. Baker, Jr., 15–53. Ithaca: Cornell University Press, 1976.

——. *The History of the Voice: The Development of Nation Language in Anglophone Caribbean Poetry*. London: New Beacon, 1984.

Coe, Richard N. *Reminiscences of Childhood: An Approach to a Comparative Mythology*. Leeds: Leeds Philosophical and Literary Society, 1984.

——. *When the Grass Was Taller: Autobiography and the Experience of Childhood*. New Haven: Yale University Press, 1984.

Cooke, Michael G. "The Strains of Apocalypse: Lamming's Castle and Brodber's Jane and Louisa." *Journal of West Indian Literature* 4, no. 1 (January 1990): 28–40.

Fanon, Frantz. *Black Skin, White Masks* (1952). Translated by Charles Lam Markmann. New York: Grove, 1967.

——. *The Wretched of the Earth* (1961). Translated by Constance Farrington. New York: Grove, 1968.

Heaney, Seamus. *The Place of Writing*. Atlanta: Scholars, 1989.

Hodge, Merle. *Crick Crack, Monkey*. 1970. Reprint, London: Heinemann, 1981.

Joyce, James. *A Portrait of the Artist as a Young Man*. 1916. Reprint, New York: Viking, 1963.

Kent, George E. "A Conversation with George Lamming." *Black World* 22, no. 5 (1973): 4–14, 88–97.

Kincaid, Jamaica. *Annie John*. New York: Farrar, Straus and Giroux, 1985.

Lamming, George. Introduction to *In the Castle of My Skin*. 1983. Reprint, Ann Arbor: University of Michigan Press, 1991.

——. *The Pleasures of Exile*. 1960. Reprint, London: Allison & Busby, 1984.

Laye, Camara. *The Dark Child*. Translated by James Kirkup and Ernest Jones. New York: Farrar, Straus and Giroux, 1975.

Munro, Ian, and Sander, Reinhard. "Interview with George Lamming." *Kas-Kas*. Austin: Afro-American Research Institute, University of Texas, 1972, 5–22.

Naipaul, V. S. *Miguel Street*. 1959. Reprint, London: Heinemann, 1974.

Paquet, Sandra Pouchet. *The Novels of George Lamming*. London: Heinemann, 1982.

Seidel, Michael. *Exile and the Narrative Imagination*. New Haven: Yale University Press, 1986.

Taylor, Patrick. *The Narrative of Liberation*. Ithaca: Cornell University Press, 1989.

Walcott, Derek. "The Muse of History." In *Is Mass Day Dead?*, edited by Orde Coombs, 1–27. New York: Anchor Books, 1974.

White, Hayden. *Content of the Form: Narrative Discourse and Historical Representation*. Baltimore: Johns Hopkins University Press, 1987.

Wright, Richard. *Black Boy*. 1945. Reprint, New York: Harper & Row, 1966.

Introduction

THE reading of fiction involves a certain conspiracy of feeling between the writer and his reader. They have both agreed to accord every act of the imagination the status of an absolute truth. And the world of fiction must work toward this end. It may be helpful, therefore, to alert readers to the kind of device which this writer has employed in the creation of that world; and especially since his methods denote a break from conventional practice.

In the Castle of My Skin introduces us to a world of poor and simple villagers; and the village functions both as place and symbol of an entire way of life.

> The village was a marvel of small, heaped houses raised jauntily on groundsels of limestone, and arranged in rows on either side of the multiplying marl roads. Sometimes the roads disintegrated, the limestone slid back and the houses advanced across their boundaries to meet those on the opposite side in an embrace of board and shingle and cactus fence. . . . There were days when the village was quiet: the shoemaker plied lazily at his trade and the washerwomen bent over the tubs droned away their complacency. At other times there were scenes of terror, and once there was a scene of murder.

> But the season of flood could change everything. The floods could level the stature and even conceal the identity of the village. With the turn of my ninth year it had happened again. From the window I looked at the uniform wreckage of a village at night in water. . . . I went away from the window over the dripping sacks and into a corner which the weather had forgotten. And what did I remember? My father who had only fathered the idea of me had left me the sole liability of my mother who really fathered me.

This world is not really the creation of individual wills. There is no privacy since the secret of each household can never escape communal scrutiny. I know your business and you know mine. The mother of the novel is given no name. She is simply G's mother, a woman of little or no importance in her neighborhood until the tropical season rains a calamity on every household; and she emerges, without warning, as a voice of nature itself.

> Then she broke into a soft repetitive tone which rose with every fresh surge of feeling until it became a scattering peal of solicitude that soared across the night and into the neighbour's house. And the answer came back louder, better organized and more communicative, so that another neighbour responded and yet another until the voices seemed to be gathered up by a single effort and the whole village shook with song on its foundation of water.

I cite that passage in order to introduce readers to a characteristic of this type of fiction which has caused some difficulty for the conventional critic of the novel. And what I say now of *In the Castle of My Skin* is also true of other Caribbean writers. The book is crowded with names and people, and although each character is accorded a most vivid presence and force of personality, we are rarely concerned with the prolonged exploration of an individual consciousness. It is the collective human substance of the Village itself which commands our attention. The Village, you might say, is the central character. When we see the Village as collective character, we perceive another dimension to the individual wretchedness of daily living. It is the dimension of energy, force, a quickening capacity for survival. The Village sings, the Village dances; and since the word is their only rescue, all the resources of a vital oral folk tradition are summoned to bear witness to the essential humanity which rebukes the wretchedness of their predicament.

In this method of narration, where community, and not person, is the central character, things are never so tidy as critics would like. There is often no discernible plot, no coherent line of events with a clear, causal connection. Nor is there a central individual consciousness where we focus attention, and through which we can be guided reliably by a logical succession of events.

Instead, there are several centers of attention which work simultaneously and acquire their coherence from the collective character of the Village.

The Novel has had a peculiar function in the Caribbean. The writer's preoccupation has been mainly with the poor; and fiction has served as a way of restoring these lives—this world of men and women from down below—to a proper order of attention; to make their reality the supreme concern of the total society. But along with this desire, there was also the writer's recognition that this world, in spite of its long history of deprivation, represented the womb from which he himself had sprung, and the richest collective reservoir of experience on which the creative imagination could draw.

This world of men and women from down below is not simply poor. This world is black, and it has a long history at once vital and complex. It is vital because it constitutes the base of labor on which the entire Caribbean society has rested; and it is complex because Plantation Slave Society (the point at which the modern Caribbean began) conspired to smash its ancestral African culture, and to bring about a total alienation of man the source of labor from man the human person.

The result was a fractured consciousness, a deep split in its sensibility which now raised difficult problems of language and values; the whole issue of cultural allegiance between the imposed norms of White Power, represented by a small numerical minority, and the fragmented memory of the African masses: between White instruction and Black imagination. The totalitarian demands of White supremacy, in a British colony, the psychological injury inflicted by the sacred rule that all forms of social status would be determined by the degrees of skin complexion; the ambiguities among Blacks themselves about the credibility of their own spiritual history.

All this would have to be incorporated into any imaginative record of the total society. Could the outlines of a national consciousness be charted and affirmed out of all this disparateness? And if that conciousness could be affirmed, what were its true ancestral roots, its most authentic cultural base? The numerical superiority of the black mass could forge a political authority of their own making, and provide an alternative direction for the society. This was certainly possible. But this possibility was also the measure of its temporary failures.

I was among those writers who took flight from that failure. In the desolate, frozen heart of London, at the age of twenty-three, I tried to reconstruct the world of my childhood and early adolescence. It was also the world of a whole Caribbean reality.

Migration was not a word I would have used to describe what I was doing when I sailed with other West Indians to England in 1950. We simply thought that we were going to an England which had been planted in our childhood consciousness as a heritage and a place of welcome. It is the measure of our innocence that neither the claim of heritage nor the expectation of welcome would have been seriously doubted. England was not for us a country with classes and conflicts of interest like the islands we had left. It was the name of a responsibility whose origin may have coincided with the beginning of time.

Today I shudder to think how a country, so foreign to our own instincts, could have achieved the miracle of being called Mother. It had made us pupils to its language and its institutions, baptized us in the same religion; schooled boys in the same game of cricket with its elaborate and meticulous etiquette of rivalry. Empire was not a very dirty word, and seemed to bear little relation to those forms of domination we now call imperialist.

The English themselves were not aware of the role they had played in the formation of these black strangers. The ruling class were serenely confident that any role of theirs must have been an act of supreme generosity. Like Prospero, they had given us language and a way of naming our own reality. The English working class were not aware they had played any role at all, and deeply resented our arrival. It had come about without any warning. No one had consulted them. Occasionally I was asked: "Do you belong to us or the French?" I had been dissolved in the common view of worker and aristocrat. English workers could also see themselves as architects of Empire.

Much of the substance of *In the Castle of My Skin* is an evocation of this tragic innocence. Nor was there, at the time of writing, any conscious effort, on my part, to emphasize the dimension of cruelty which had seduced, or driven by the force of need, an otherwise honorable black people into such lasting bonds of illusion. It was not a physical cruelty. Indeed, the colonial experience of my generation was almost wholly without violence. No torture, no concentration camp, no mysterious disappearance of hostile natives, no army encamped with orders to kill. The Caribbean endured a different kind of subjugation. It was a terror of the mind; a daily exercise in self-mutilation. Black versus black in a battle for self-improvement:

> Each represented for the other an image of the enemy. And the enemy was My People. My people are low-down nigger people. My people don't like to see their people get on. The language of the overseer. The language of the civil servant. . . . Not taking chances with you people, my people. They always let you down. Make others say we're not responsible, we've no sense of duty. Like children under the threat of hellfire they accepted instinctively that the others, meaning the white, were superior, yet there was always the fear of realizing that it might be true. This world of the others' imagined perfection hung like a dead weight over their energy. If the low-down nigger people weren't what they are, the others couldn't say anything about us. Suspicion, distrust, hostility. These operated in every decision. You never can tell with my people. It was the language of the overseer, the language of the Government servant, and later the language of lawyers and doctors who had returned stamped like an envelope with what they called the culture of the Mother Country.

This was the breeding ground for every uncertainty of self. In the riot scene of the novel, a group of men armed with knives, and ready with stones, have ambushed the white landlord on his way home. There is a clear intention to kill him, but the act of political revenge is delayed by argument about its timing. Should we strike now or a little later? Their deliberations go on and on, and betray a latent ambivalence which is finally resolved by the arrival of their labor leader who pleads with them to withdraw. The landlord escapes, unharmed.

When I read this scene some twenty years after its publication, I was surprised by the mildness of its resolution. From the distant and more critical vantage point of London, the past now seemed more brutal. I wondered why I had allowed the landlord to go free. Was it the need to make the story conform to the most accurate portrayal of events as I had known them? No white man had been killed by rioters in Barbados in 1937. But I had taken greater liberty with other facts and done so in the interest of a more essential truth. Now I had begun to think that the most authentic response to the long history of shame and humiliation which had produced the riots demanded that the white landlord should have been killed.

The novelist does not only explore what had happened. At a deeper level of intention than literal accuracy, he seeks to construct a world that might have been; to show the possible as a felt and living reality. So for a long time I remained haunted by the feeling that the white landlord should have been killed; even if it were presented as the symbolic end of a social order that deserved to be destroyed.

The novel was completed within two years of my arrival in London. I still shared in that previous innocence which had socialized us into seeing our relations to empire as a commonwealth of mutual interests. The truth is there was never any such reciprocity of interests, and the various constitutional settlements which would gradually lead to the recent status of independence had a decisive influence in preserving much of the social legacy of the colonial period. Today the region is witnessing with alarm what is, in fact, an upheaval too long delayed. But the tactical withdrawal which the British now so proudly call decolonization simply made way for a new colonial orchestration. The Caribbean returns to its old role of an imperial frontier, now perceived as essential to the security interests of the United States.

It is interesting for me to reflect on the role which America was to play in shaping essential features of the novel. If England dominated our minds as the original idea of ultimate human achievement, the United States existed for us as a dream, a kingdom of material possibilities accessible to all. I had never visited the United States before writing *In the Castle of My Skin;* but America had often touched our lives with gifts that seemed spectacular at the time, and reminded us that this dream of unique luxury beyond our shores was true. This image of America has not changed. Almost everyone had some distant relation there who had done well. I had never heard of anyone being a failure in the United States. And Christmas was evidence of this when postal orders arrived with money and gifts of exotic clothes.

But the United States had also provided the character, Trumper, with a political experience which the subtle force of British imperialism had never allowed to flourish in the islands. After his sojourn in the United States as a migrant laborer, Trumper returned home with a new ideology, and the startling discovery that his black presence had a very special meaning in the world. He had learned the cultural and political significance of race.

Europe had trained black men to wear those white masks which Franz Fanon wrote so bitterly about, and which the racist culture of the United States would tear asunder. America was really the extreme example of Europe, stripped naked of all pretense about having a civilizing mission in the dark corners of the earth: a vast, energetic extension of that demonic Europe which the novelist Joseph Conrad had so maliciously identified as a Heart of Darkness in Africa.

> They were conquerors, and for that you want only brute force—nothing to boast of, when you have it, since your strength is just an accident arising from the weakness of others. They grabbed what they could get for the sake of what was to be got. It was just robbery with violence, aggravated murder on a great scale, and men going at it blind—as is very proper for those who tackle a darkness. The conquest of the earth, which mostly means the taking it away from those who have a different complexion or slightly flatter noses than ourselves, is not a pretty thing when you look into it too much.

Conrad, a child of Europe, understood the cultural racism of his own ancestry. Africa, a human continent to its own people, existed in Conrad's consciousness as a proper symbol of the demonic force which had driven his own white race to raid and vandalize every corner of the globe.

And so, in the United States, the black man was forced to recognize himself as a different kind of creature. Trumper embraced this new status, and on his return home offered it to the astonished villagers as the only foundation for a free human dignity among black people.

> You'll hear 'bout the Englishman, an' the Frenchman, and the American which mean man of America. An' each is call that 'cause he born in that particular place. But you'll become a Negro like me an' all the rest in the States an' all over the world, 'cause it ain't have nothin' to do with where you born. 'Tis what you is, a different kind o' creature. An' when you see what I tellin' you an' you become a Negro, act as you should, an' don't ask Hist'ry why you is what you then see yourself to be, 'cause Hist'ry ain't got no answers. You ain't a thing till you know it.

This stark and bitter message of Trumper, pan-African in character, is supported in argument by the recorded music of black people: " Let My People Go." The voice of Paul Robeson becomes his weapon.

It is difficult to write soberly about the persistent influence of race in the formation of human thought. It holds a unique place in the conciousness of black people wherever they may be; and this is unlikely to change until Africa becomes a black continent whose sovereignty is the product of her own institutions and is protected by an economic and military strength that can defy any intruder. The cordiality which exists between African countries and their former French imperialist masters, and the harrassment of Angola by apartheid South Africa are an odd and cruel sequel to the various declarations of African independence. It is as though nothing had changed except the flags and the expanding scale of western robbery.

There is a sense in which the Afro-American has acquired a critical awareness of this racial drama. He sees through the language of negotiation and diplomacy imposed upon African and West Indian leaders, and is often appalled by the terms of our accommodation to white privilege. But he doesn't often see with the same clarity how the process of colonization may have divided black majorities into conflicting social strata, pruning away from the main body or trunk of our human tree those elitist branches that are trained like termites to work corrosively on its roots. The overwhelming torment of race has made it difficult for Afro-Americans to perceive how central is the conflict of class in the ultimate liberation of black countries. On the other hand a false preoccupation with social status seduces the black West Indian into wishing the racial component away.

Africa broods over the faces, the canefields, the broken huts, and sugar fortunes of *In the Castle of My Skin*. But it is not recognized until the land is asleep, and the ocean threatens the island with the memories of that fatal crossing. An ancestral voice breaks through the dream of the village elder, Pa:

> And strange was the time that change my neighbour and me, the tribes with gods and the one tribe without. The silver of exchange sail cross the sea and my people scatter like clouds in the sky when the waters come. There was similar buying and selling 'mongst tribe and tribe, but this was the biggest of the bargains for tribes. Each sell his own. . . . A man walked out in the market square and one buyer watch his tooth and another his toe and the parts that was private for the coming of a creature in the intimate night. The silver sail from hand to hand and the purchase was shipped like a box of good fruit. The sale was the best of Africa's produce, and me and my neighbour made the same bargain. I make my peace with the Middle Passage to settle on that side of the sea and the white man call a world that was west of another world. . . . We were for a price that had no value; we were a value beyond any price. . . .
>
> I see the purchase of tribes on the silver sailing vessels, some to Jamaica, Antigua, Grenada, some to Barbados and the island of oil and the mountain tops. And then as 'tis now, though the season change, some was trying to live and some trying to die, and some was too tired to worry about either. The families fall to pieces, and many a brother never see his sister nor father the son.

The ancestral spirit, speaking through the voice of an old man on the eve of his death, provides the kind of history which the village could not have learned from its official school. A different myth was planted there, interrupting and, in the view of some students, actually eliminating beyond recall the continuities of feeling and perception which linked Africa to her transplanted sons and daughters in the New World. It is this area of twilight which has attracted and teased the imagination of many Caribbean poets and novelists; and in more recent times has offered a promise of redemption for the cultural nationalist and the political activist.

In 1950 I could not have foreseen the drama that would launch Africa like a hurricane across the ocean and into the hearts of islands and cities of the black Americas. Many who were once afraid of Africa had now become afraid for Africa. The murder of Lumumba reminded us of an old conspiracy within our ranks. "There was a similar buying and selling 'mongst tribe and tribe." But these contradictions were not wholly negative. When the Kenyan novelist, Ngugi wa Thiongo told me that *In the Castle of My Skin* was the signal which alerted him to what he had to do as a Kikuyu and a pan-Africanist writer, I too was assured that the continuities which united Africa and the Black Americas were at work.

This theme has been the main thrust of Edward Brathwaite's work as a poet and historian. But it is a difficult terrain. The demands of labor introduced a more complex world than either Europe or Africa could have bargained for.

> Now there's been new combinations and those that come after made quite a different collection.... Now not only black nor white, but all colours that give credit to the skin in these islands of the west.

Neither China nor India had then left any mark on Barbados. We had lived as a black majority under the fearful domination of a minority of white sugar planters and merchants. There was evidence of considerable miscegenation, but there was always a rigid code of separate development. Blacks divided along lines of complexion, and all were kept severely at a social distance from the white world. The island has never really overcome this barrier; and a concordat of silence descends on any crisis which appears to have its origins in race and color.

Africa existed in Barbados and throughout the Caribbean, and refuses to be buried by the institutions which sought to render it impotent and void of any spiritual force. School, church, the language and ritual of English courts of law, the mysteries of parliament: all these had to be learned in the interests of black survival and social advancement.

But Africa has remained a source of embarrassment here, although the actual nature of the embarrassment may have changed. Once we were truly nervous at any suggestion that we were part of a world that had not graduated to the status of human. We held this truth on the authority of the institutions which mediated our daily lives. We lived the purest racism without acknowledging that any such calamity had really touched our lives.

Today the embarrassment is more likely to be felt if there is a charge that we seek to deny Africa any part in our spiritual formation. The other response is a rhapsodic and uncritical embrace of Africa as a mother once stolen and now miraculously restored to our embrace. It was perhaps this fear the ancestral spirit tentatively warned against.

> So if you hear some young fool fretting about back to Africa, keep far from the invalid and don't force a passage to where you won't yet belong.

Sometimes the twilight startles with signs of recognition: an old woman who places bits of food under a tree and for no one in particular: the spontaneous libation of the rum shop drinker, the hallucinatory form of worship that may suddenly strike a simple believer who can't explain what world she had been transported to. And always a reluctant faith in the supernatural force that heals, or intervenes in moments of domestic crisis. The politician is frequently in search of an obeah man.

Africa invades us like an invisible force we dare not acknowledge, fearing the journey may take us beyond the boundaries of our approved instruction. And all this subliminal life goes on in spite of the determined resistance of the official institutions. The white myths, firmly planted by conquest and enslavement, have been internalized, and continue to work like litmus on the black rock whose history we have not yet summoned to our rescue.

Sometimes the twilight darkens and threatens to obliterate all memory in the tidal wave of capitalist consumerism. America spreads itself like a plague everywhere, capturing the simplest appetite with the fastest foods and nameless fripperies the advertising industry instructs us are essential needs. It is this obstacle the world of the ancestral spirit may not survive. A new class of black housewife now flies from these islands to Los Angeles for some novel brand of underwear. This barbarism has become the style of a new ruling group: a new breed of professional nationalist who may be heard in international councils arguing the case for a new economic order. They are the adolescent offspring of that slave culture which has persisted through school and college, university and people's parliament.

In his introduction to the first American edition of the novel, Richard Wright made this observation:

> Notwithstanding the fact that Lamming's story, as such, is his own, it is, at the same time, a symbolic repetition of the story of millions of simple folk who, sprawled over half the world's surface and involving more than half of the human race, are today being catapulted out of their peaceful, indigenously earthy lives and into the turbulence and anxiety of the twentieth century. . . .

Turbulence is at work everywhere, but anxiety does not adequately describe what has been happening with that half of mankind since Richard Wright wrote his introduction. The catapulted ones have become the subject of their own history, engaged in a global war to liberate their villages, rural and urban, from the old encirclement of poverty, ignorance, and fear.

This is the most fundamental battle of our time, and I am joyfully lucky to have been made, by my work, a soldier in their ranks.

1983

IN THE CASTLE

OF MY SKIN

I

RAIN, rain, rain . . . my mother put her head through the window to let the neighbour know that I was nine, and they flattered me with the consolation that my birthday had brought showers of blessing. The morning laden with cloud soon passed into noon, and the noon neutral and silent into the sodden grimness of an evening that waded through water. That evening I kept an eye on the crevices of our wasted roof where the colour of the shingles had turned to mourning black, and waited for the weather to rehearse my wishes. But the evening settled on the slush of the roads that dissolved in parts into pools of clay, and I wept for the watery waste of my ninth important day. Yet I was wrong, my mother protested: it was irreverent to disapprove the will of the Lord or reject the consolation that my birthday had brought showers of blessing.

It was my ninth celebration of the gift of life, my ninth celebration of the consistent lack of an occasion for celebration. From a window where the spray had given the sill a little wet life I watched the water ride through the lanes and alleys that multiplied behind the barracks that neighboured our house. The white stalks of the lily lay flat under the hammering rain, then coaxed their roots from the earth and drifted across the upturned clay, into the canals and on to the deep black river where by agreement the floods converged. The water rose higher and higher until the fern and flowers on our verandah were flooded. It came through the creases of the door, and expanded across the uncarpeted borders of the floor. My mother brought sacks that absorbed it quickly, but overhead the crevices of the roof were weeping rain, and surfacing the carpet and the epergne of flowers and fern were liquid, glittering curves which the mourning black of the shingles had bequeathed. No one seemed to notice how the noon had passed to evening, the evening to night; nor to worry that the weather had played me false. Nothing mattered but the showers of blessing and the eternal will of the water's source. And I might have accepted the consolation if it weren't that the floods had chosen to follow me in the celebration of all my years, evoking the image of those legendary waters which had once arisen to set a curse on the course of man.

As if in serious imitation of the waters that raced outside, our lives— meaning our fears and their corresponding ideals—seemed to escape down an imaginary drain that was our future. Our capacity for feeling had grown as large as the flood, but the prayers of a simple village seemed as precariously adequate as the houses hoisted on water. Of course, it was difficult to see what was happening outside, but there were paddling splashes of boys' feet and the choke of an engine stuck in mud.

The village was a marvel of small, heaped houses raised jauntily on groundsels of limestone, and arranged in rows on either side of the multiplying marl roads. Sometimes the roads disintegrated, the lime- stone slid back and the houses advanced across their boundaries to meet those on the opposite side in an embrace of board and shingle and cactus fence. The white marl roads made four at each crossing except where the road narrowed to a lane or alley that led into a tenant's backyard. There were shops at each crossing: one, two, sometimes three, and so positioned that the respective owners could note each other's customers. And wherever there were shops there was a street lamp ringed to a post, and always much activity, and often the stench of raw living. The lamps were fuelled with gas and lit at six every evening. When the lights went on, little boys like a bevy of flies assembled around the lamp-post for gossip and stories. Elsewhere in a similar manner men gathered to throw dice or cut cards or simply to talk. The spectacle repeated itself at each crossing where there was a street lamp ringed to a post. The roads bore names—Murrell, Alkins, Hunt—and a curious one-way affection grew between the villager and the road he lived in; just as a mutual antipathy sometimes passed from dwellers in one road to those in another. Now and again those who lived at Alkins would contrive a secret conspiracy against those at Murrell, and the verdict was always the same. The people in Hunt's road, those in Alkins would declare, were a lot of so-and-so's.

There was a public bath for men and women with a perpetual stench of disinfectant pervading the air, and everywhere limestone constructions like roof-less ovens for the disposal of garbage. But most notable was the wood of mahogany trees through which the trains passed from the city on their excursions to the country. There were days when the village was quiet: the shoemaker plied lazily at his trade and the washerwomen bent over the tubs droned away their complacency. At other times there were scenes of terror, and once there was a scene of murder.

But the season of flood could change everything. The floods could level the stature and even conceal the identity of the village. With the turn of my ninth year it had happened again. From the window I looked at the uniform wreckage of a village at night in water. My mother said it was a shame, as was everything that displeased her. And even after many years I would try to fix her label. What precisely was a shame? Was it the weather or the village or the human condition in which and in spite of which the poor had sworn their loyalty to life? But so she said: and having said that, she would suspend her judgment and in an attitude of prayer remind me of blessings that may have missed my memory.

I went away from the window over the dripping sacks and into a corner which the weather had forgotten. And what did I remember? My father who had only fathered the idea of me had left me the sole liability of my mother who really fathered me. And beyond that my memory was a blank. It sank with its cargo of episodes like a crew preferring scuttle to the consequences of survival. Moreover, my mother began to sing, which always happened when I tried to remember. Her voice was clear and colourless. It could indicate but not control a tune which I recognized only through the words.

'I can't get it right tonight,' she said.

No answer.

'You know, we haven't had rain like this for a long, long time.'

No answer.

'You listening?'

'Yes.'

Then she broke into a soft repetitive tone which rose with every fresh surge of feeling until it became a scattering peal of solicitude that soared across the night and into the neighbour's house. And the answer came back louder, better organized and more communicative, so that another neighbour responded and yet another until the voices seemed to be gathered up by a single effort and the whole village shook with song on its foundation of water. My mother was pleased with her unacclaimed but generally accepted supervision. She lit the big brass lamp that hung from a beam bridging the slopes of the ceiling. The space of the ceiling directly over the lamp wore a surface of soot. The lamp swayed in its cradle of wire, a bowl of polished brass, as the flames sputtered along the blue burnt edge of the wick. Standing beneath the flowered brass bowl that contained the fuel, my mother regulated the pitch of the blaze. The smoke circled the flames within the chimney and later settled on the wet ceiling. The light pushed its way about the corners of the house and the partitions in their dying response looked a dismal wreck in reflection. It was the uncertain light one feels on the passage from sleep to conscious waking. The clock shelved in one corner kept up its ticking. My mother retreated to another part of the house where the silk and taffeta designs of her needling were being revised and reversed. I soon followed like a lean trail of smoke tracing a radius round its red origin. And for memory I had substituted inquiry.

'Where you say my grandmother went?'

'To Panama,' my mother answered. 'It was the opening of the canal. She is now in Canal Zone. It's time you wrote her a letter.'

'And my grandfather who was your father?' I went on.

'Oh, he died, my child; he died before I was born.'

'And my uncle who was your brother?'

'My brother went to America,' my mother said. 'It's years now. The last we heard he was on a boat and then take sick, and is probably dead for all we know.' Her feelings were neutral.

'And when my uncle who was your brother and my grandmother who was your mother, when they went away, how old you wus?'

'Two.'

'Two years?'

'Yes, two,' my mother said.

My birth began with an almost total absence of family relations. My parents on almost all sides had been deposited in the bad or uncertain accounts of all my future relationships, and loneliness from which had subsequently grown the consolation of freedom was the legacy with which my first year opened.

My mother seated beside me and in front of the sewing-machine must have sensed the change progressing within me. Memory was again pursuing the line of discovery which inquiry had left off. Late as it was, my birthday was still alive. The morning had opened in clouds which had dissolved the noon into a wet and sudden night.

I had had tea and a bun in the backhouse, and the promise of a cake with nine candles. But the candles had been blown out before the cake arrived, and the showers blessing the day had presumably dissolved the promise like the noon. I wore a long face and a murderous scowl.

'But you can't ask me to make bread out of stone,' my mother said.

On recollection I admitted there wasn't even stone. The neighbour had put her head through the window to speak with my mother. It was then noon.

'All you hear what happen to Foster? Why the house wash away clean clean clean, groundsel, everything gone clean. They put Miss Foster and the children in the Guard House, and you know how many children Miss Foster got?'

'And Mr. Foster?' my mother inquired.

'I was coming to that. Foster swear he won't leave the old house, and went sailing down the river on the roof. They had to fish him from the Deanery wall with a rope.'

The neighbour closed her window and stuffed the crevices with brown paper.

Since it made no difference whether it was noon or night, I went to the backhouse to play with my pigeon. It was asleep on the rod that served every condition of a bird's accommodation. I took it down and patted the head and neck. Its claws ringed the index finger of my left hand as I fought open the beak with the other. Then I fed it till the craw expanded to a pleated curve of feathered flesh, and the shoulders drooped and the eyes closed over a film of water. Immediately I emptied a phial of castor oil down the throat, remembering the villagers always said there was nothing better than to eat well and purge clean. I returned the pigeon to the rod and looked round through the gaping roof at the sky which could not distinguish between night and noon. That night the pigeon died and I with a burning shame in my head buried my blessings in the pillow.

My mother lay beside me recounting the incidents of the previous day and rehearsing rough-and-ready plans for the next. In the dark the crevices of the roof were concealed, but occasional raindrops fell against the bedposts in a scatter of specks that dissolved on my nose. I opened my eyes and saw enormous phantoms with eyes of fire and crowned with bulls' horns stalking through the dark. I closed my eyes and the phantoms went. I opened them again, and one came forward hovering over my head in a jeering silence. I struck a blow that sliced the unfeeling figure of the demon, and my knuckles crashed against the bedposts. My mother groaned.

'The kitchen in a state,' she said, 'and maybe rainwater get into the barrel.'

The barrel was the iron drum in which we kept our drinking water. Once a week a sanitary inspector poked his nose into it and scraped the side with his long enamel spoon in search of larvae.

'Take yer head out my water,' my mother once snapped. 'You can put it in the W.C. if you like but not my water.'

The inspector was offended and made a note in his little blue book.

'Good day,' he said and fled.

I laughed as I recalled the incident. It was an odd little giggle that leapt in my throat, and my mother groaned again.

'The kitchen in a state,' she repeated. 'And the last time you had rainwater you got belly ache. And the inspector comin' tomorrow.' My mother sometimes talked mechanically.

'I wonder what happened to Pa and Ma,' my mother said.

Pa and Ma, I thought. I wondered what did happen to Pa and Ma. They weren't related to us by blood, but they were Pa and Ma nevertheless. Everyone called them Pa and Ma. They were the oldest couple in the village, so old no one could tell their age, and few knew what names they had besides those we had given them, Ma and Pa.

My eyes opened and the phantoms were still there. They were steady under my gaze, but when I closed my eyes they paraded the room from corner to corner. Every night these phantoms that populated my brain came out to frighten me with the freedom which the night had brought them. They danced and jeered through the thick black space of this narrow room. My eyes opened and closed, opened/closed opened/closed opened/closed, but they would not go. I crossed the pillows across my head and clutched the stitched edges of the sheet to my ears.

And my birthday drifted outside in a fog of blackness that covered the land. The·lanes and alleys crossed and multiplied below the tides that towed limestone and clay, shingle and brick through the canals and pipes and to the river that ran far and wide into the sea. At street corners the gas lamps winked within their netted cages, and the light leaking past the frosty domes, fell dully on the water. The moon must have struck somewhere beyond the cluster of mahogany, remote and ineffectual. But the hardy poor like their stalled beloved in the distant cemetery slept peacefully beneath the flying spray. All the voices were hushed, the puddles deserted, the gurgle of the wrestling flood submerged. My birthday making its black departure from the land had been blessed with showers whose consolation was my blessing.

2

THE skillet was caught up and canted and the water crashed against my head and down my body in a swishing cataract.

'Google google, no more,' I said, 'google google, no more.' The pebbles loosened by moisture from the earth slipped beneath my feet. My arms were thrown out, withdrawn, clasped in a shivering lock, opened again, folded once more. The pebbles shifted under my heels. My body tottered from the rapid, convulsive gasps for breath. Now quiet, erect. Balance perfect. The pebbles reassorted. The basement firm. I was ready. The hand was hoisted and the skillet poised.

'Yes,' I said, 'I like it so. Slow. Not fast. Just like that.'

The body was firm, hard, erect, a paved brown track down which the water contoured in, out, around, off.

'I want to see,' a voiced raised over the neighbouring fence. 'G. mother bathing him.'

'Get down,' the elder voice snapped, 'you too fast and malicious. Come inside, you red scamp.'

'She's right,' my mother said in a low, approving tone. 'He's too fast, wanting to see everything except what concerns him. The children today. My God!' The skillet sallied about and over my head and the water poured down slowly, steadily.

'Get up quick,' another voice raised from the opposite fence, 'they going to finish soon.' The heads groped testily over the fence and the eyes peering down on the spectacle widened with delight.

'Look,' I said, pointing at the boys, 'they looking.' My mother wheeled round, swinging the skillet by its wire handle. The heads darted below the sagging fence.

'Vagabonds,' my mother said, 'what you peeping at? You all don't bathe?"

The fence swayed from the pressure it had borne as the boys leapt to the ground. The pumpkin vine snapped and fell.

'Look what they do,' my mother said, letting the skillet fall and moving towards the fence. She held the vine with intimate concern, tracing its ragged zigzag along the fence to where the roots might have been. Now her voice was cracked, tremulous, hardly audible.

'Look what they do,' she said, letting the snapped vine slip between her fingers. 'They kill it, and it was just going to bear.'

Suddenly the whole aspect of the morning had changed. Something, it seemed, had emerged to call a halt in preparation for a new beginning.

'What they do?' the neighbour asked keeping her balance above the fence.

'Kill the pumpkin vine,' my mother said, turning away from the fence with hardened indifference. 'Why the hell anybody worry to plant anything round here only God knows.'

Now the voice spoke as if from an inner void beyond which deeper and deeper within herself were incalculable layers of feeling. The neighbour looked deeply hurt.

'Bob,' she said, 'look what you do to the neighbour pumpkin vine.'

Bob climbed on to the fence. It swayed to and fro. He looked down self-pityingly at the vine, and then across to where I stood naked on the pool of pebbles, waiting. His lips parted involuntarily, and the broad, cream teeth shone in the sun.

'And you laughing,' his mother said. 'You kill the neighbour pumpkin vine, and on the back of it you laugh?' Her eyes reddened and the black skin stretched tight across the bone.

Bob's glance fell obediently to the vine. He winked his eyes as if he wanted to cry.

'Well, what you going to tell her?' his mother shouted. Bob plugged his thumb into his mouth keeping his eyes on the vine.

'Don't look like a jackass,' his mother said. 'What you going to tell her?'

'I going tell her sorry,' Bob groaned, passing the dripping wet thumb between his nose and eyes. He felt the damp on his face and looked up at my mother.

'I sorry,' he said. Then his glance caught me where I stood, naked, waiting. He let his eyes fall to the ground, and against his will laughed. No word was spoken, but the clenched fist boxed mightily into his ear. His head dropped forward, and the body fell over the fence into our yard. It struck out over the fallen vine in convulsive shrieks.

'You shouldn't hit him like that,' my mother said, raising the body.

The woman's fury lanced her like an ache. She threw her hands out to grab Bob's shoulder, and the fence swayed . . . forward, then back, forward again and back, and in its final approach dropped to the ground with a resounding crash. My mother dragging Bob away narrowly escaped, but the woman was thrown forward into the yard where she lay half-conscious. The two yards merged. The barricade which had once protected our private secrecies had surrendered.

'What trouble is this this morning,' my mother said. She lay Bob on the ground, and looked around feeling for some power within or outside her to dictate the next step. My mother on such occasions looked pitiful beyond words. I had often seen her angry or frustrated and in tears, but there were other states of emotion she experienced for which tears were simply inadequate. Seized by the thought of being left alone, she would become filled with an overwhelming ambition for her child, and an even greater defiance of the odds against her. Then she would be silent as she was now, or she would talk in a way that was mechanical while her meaning seemed to go beyond the words. She would talk about pulling through; whatever happened she would come through, and 'she' meant her child. She stood there in the yard looking now a little sheepish as the people like a routed squad of bees appeared, wondering what had happened.

Bob's mother was trying to recover her balance.

'Take Bob inside, quick,' I said; 'take him before she see.'

'Yes,' my mother said, 'yes, quick.' We knew what height his mother's fury could reach.

My mother beckoned two of the spectators and they carried Bob over the fence and hoisted him through the window. My mother received him on the inside and perched him in the corner behind a sack.

'Stay there,' she said, 'and don't move till I tell you.'

Whose side my mother took, the parents' or the children's, I could never tell.

My mother had come back in the yard, and Bob's mother, it seemed, had fully regained her senses.

'Where is you?' she said.

'I here,' my mother said.

'I sorry,' Bob's mother said with much feeling, 'I really sorry.'

My mother didn't answer.

'But if I put my hand on him this morning,' Bob's mother cried, 'he don't live another second.'

On all sides the fences had been weighed down with people, boys and girls and grown-ups. The girls were laughing and looking across to where I stood on the pool of pebbles, naked, waiting. They looked at Bob's mother and the broken fence and me. The sun had dried me thoroughly, and now it seemed that I had not been bathed, but brought out in open condemnation and placed in the middle of the yard waiting like one crucified to be jeered at.

'Look,' one girl said pointing me out to her friend.

'Yes, I see,' the other said, grinning between her teeth.

I pretended not to hear.

'What you doing there naked as you born?' my mother said.

It seemed she had forgotten me, and had suddenly become aware of a situation in which I appeared unpardonable.

'Waiting,' I said. 'I didn't know you were finish.'

'You little fool,' she said, 'you don't want a little boy like yourself to see you, and you can stand there in the middle of the yard and let the whole world look down at you!"

She came towards me with a broken branch. I tiptoed over the pebbles, keeping a keen eye on the branch.

'Don't move,' she said, 'if you move I lash you.'

'But I didn't know you finish,' I said.

She came closer, strengthening her hold on the branch, but concealing any threat.

'Don't move,' she said, 'if you move I lash you.' She clutched the broken branch and came closer. She had hardly stated her case before the arm was raised above her head and the blow struck. I shifted under the upraised arm, circled her twice, keeping a loose hold on her waist, then slipped through her legs and ran off to a corner. On all sides there was laughter, and the fences swayed.

'Don't move,' she said. 'If you move I lash you.' She came closer, and we played a game of cat and mouse in the corner, she darting to one side, I to the other. The fences rocked with laughter. Then she leapt forward, missed her balance and fell lightly against the fence. I tripped over the pebbles and ran into the house. The fences swayed as the laughter peal by peal pelted through the trees.

'It ain't nothin' to laugh at,' Bob's mother protested. 'The children bring too much botheration to parents nowadays. Look what that other one make me do this morning, but let him hide. Night run till day catch him.'

My mother was silent, and I wondered whose side she was taking now, Bob's or his mother's. She looked up a little dazed, but her attention was soon arrested by another woman coming across the fallen fence.

'Is true,' the woman said, 'the children not worth bothering with. You all hear what happen this morning to that other one down the road?' The newcomer had brought bad tidings.

Someone said from the fence, 'Poor Miss Foster, she must have a story to tell.'

'Who you talking about?' my mother asked.

'Gordon,' Miss Foster said.

'Who Gordon?' my mother asked.

'Gordon, Bess gran'child,' Miss Foster said; 'the one with the chigoes.'

'What happen?' Bob's mother asked.

'Well, I tell you,' Miss Foster began. 'He going down the road this morning with a fowlcock. It seem Bess was hard up and decide to sell the fowlcock, the big black one she use to lend me for my bareneck pullet. Well, Gordon with his mannishness say he will try to sell the fowlcock; mind you, he's only eight years and already he want to mix up with money and all that. Well, he see a white gentleman standing at Bellville corner waiting for the bus, and he go up to the gentleman to ask if he would buy the fowlcock. Mind you, the white gentl'man dress for work, white suit, hat, shirt and shoe to match. Nat'rally, the gentl'man get vex, put his head in the air and say to Gordon, "Does you expect me to take a rooster to work?" Gordon ain't pay him no attention, he just hold up the fowlcock, saying look, what a pretty comb. Then he turn the fowlcock round and round in the air till the bird backside was staring in the white man face.'

The girls tittered along the fence, and Miss Foster waited, indignant.

'Believe it or not, my child,' she went on, 'there was the fowlcock backside in the white man face, and before you say the word, before you say the word the fowlcock had mess in the gentl'man face. It went on the helmet, and splatter over the suit.'

Bob's mother and my mother waited, horrified.

'But that ain't all,' Miss Foster said. 'Then a whole gang of them boys, you know the ones from Hunt's Road, the whole lot, Trumper,

Boy Blue, Big Bam, Botsie, Knucker hand, Po King, Puss in Boots and Suck Me Toe, the whole gang come up and start to sing,

> Look, look what fowlcock do,
> Look what fowlcock do to you.

The white gentl'man didn't know what to do and pick up his heels and run like a ball of fire all the way home. The police hear the noise and they come, and when they ask what happen, you know what those vagabonds say, those disrespectful varmints say the gentl'man mess his pants and had to run home for shame.'

The girls and boys jumped from the fence and went in search of Gordon who would relate the episode in greater detail. Soon the fences were deserted, and the women were left regarding each other as women sharing a common misfortune are wont to do.

Bob crouched behind the sack, a stump of a boy dressed in white flour-bag pants and shirt. The shirt was fastened to the pants with pins and occasionally he unfastened the pins to pull the pants above his waist. He was no longer afraid of what had happened. When his mother fell from the fence his skin had changed colour. I had never seen him so frightened. But now he heard the voices outside and assumed that all was well. At any rate for the time being.

'What you going to do?' I asked him.

'I don't know,' he said. He dropped his head and stared at the frayed edges of the sack.

'She says she'll beat the life out of you when she catch you,' I said.

'It ain't the first time she say that,' he said.

'But she will do it this time,' I said. 'Look the blow she give you in the ear.'

'I ain't got feelings any more,' he said. 'I get sort of hardened to it.' He looked up and smiled. His face was wet and heavy and remote.

'But I won't ever hit her back,' he said, 'whatever she do me I won't ever hit her back.'

'You ain't to do that,' I said. 'They say you'll be cursed if you hit a mother.'

'And she don't hit me for purpose,' Bob said. 'She don't do it for purpose. She does it 'cause she's God-fearing. She always say the Bible say "Spare not the rod and spoil the child." And 'tis only that she don't want to spoil me.'

'That's what mine says too,' I said. 'She's always talking 'bout roasting my tail, but she does more talking than roasting.'

'Your mother is different,' he said. 'She don't like to see you cry, that's what all say. She talk and talk but she seldom hit you.'

He peered through the crease of the door to see whether he could be seen from the yard. It was very dark in the corner where he sat, and the light through the crease was like a chalk line drawn against a blackboard. He couldn't see them.

'You'd better go and see what they doing,' he said. 'I want to get out from here.'

I went in the bedroom and peeped through the jalousies. They were still standing in the yard. Miss Foster, who had told the story about Gordon and the cock, was filling in the details. It seemed they had forgotten us.

'They still there,' I said. 'It's going to be hard to get out.'

'Can't you think of a way?' he asked.

'I don't think so,' I said. 'The front door locked and you can't go through the window. Not for anybody outside to see.'

'What about passing by the other side of the house?' he asked.

'They bound to see you,' I said.

'Not if you do what I ask you,' Bob said.

'What?' I asked.

'Ask yuh mother if you can play bear,' he said.

I was frightened. I looked over the half-door to see what was happening outside. My mother was laughing as Miss Foster talked. Miss Foster made gestures as she spoke, and they all laughed quietly together. Bob's mother passed her hand over the rump where the skin must have been bruised. My mother and Miss Foster smiled and Bob's mother smiled too.

I pushed my head farther out over the door and they saw me. They were very quiet now as though they expected me to say the wrong thing.

'Can I play bear?' I asked my mother.

She didn't answer, and the others watched with half-smiles breaking past the lips.

'You dry yuh head?' my mother snapped. Her snap was frightening.

'Yes,' I said. 'I dry it dry dry.'

The others laughed and my mother laughed too.

'But who would think children nowadays could be so brazen?' Miss Foster said.

''Tis true,' Bob's mother said. 'They give you grey hairs in yuh young days.'

Miss Foster said something about grey hairs and they laughed quietly again. They looked more favourable now.

'Can I play bear?' I asked again, and I was wondering all the while what Bob would do.

My mother turned her back and laughed and the others laughed too. Her silence was her approval. I was sure.

'What you going to do?' I asked Bob.

He had already taken down the sack. I was frightened.

'You mustn't talk,' he said. 'You is a bear now.'

'Bring the other sack over yonder.'

He jumped into one sack and asked me to put the other over his head. He gave the instructions and I carried them out. He had taken out the pins from his pants and used them to fasten the sacks. He was completely hidden under the coarse brown sack.

'What you going to do?' I asked him again. I was so anxious and frightened.

'You mustn't talk,' he said. 'Behave like a bear.'

I couldn't see him under the sack. His voice came out like a sound from nowhere. He crawled out from the corner through the half-door and across the yard. I was terrified. He put his hands out, drew his legs up and heaved forward time and again. I wondered what would happen next.

They laughed as they saw him slouching forward moving at times in their direction. Miss Foster looked at my mother and smiled.

'I have a mind to roast his tail now,' my mother said. I shuddered. She took a step forward with the broken branch, and I felt my skin burn with the sting Bob would receive.

'Leave him,' Miss Foster said, 'he amusing himself.'

My mother was reconsidering her decision.

'Let him lone,' Bob's mother said. 'They all bad but you can't bother.'

''Tis true,' Miss Foster said. 'When all's said and done they is ours and we love them. Whatever we mothers say or do, nobody love them like we.'

'I got a mind to roast his tail now,' my mother said.

'Leave him,' Bob's mother said. 'The poor bear ain't do you anything. 'Tis my Bob, he's the one who tail you should roast.'

The bear crouched on all fours past the pebbles and within a yard of the women. They watched him like children at a circus till he had passed the cherry tree, moved behind the fallen fence and was out of sight.

'The things these children nowadays can think of doing,' Bob's mother said.

''Tis true,' Miss Foster said. 'They head ain't make for hat only.'

They smiled, then looked at the fence and were serious again.

'I so sorry about the fence,' Bob's mother said. 'Every time I look at it I can't say how I feel.'

'Don't worry,' my mother said, 'it could have come down in the flood like so many others.'

'Talking 'bout the flood, Miss Foster,' Bob's mother said, 'how you fare, chil'?'

''Tis a long story,' Miss Foster said. 'Let's go over yonder in the shade.'

They sat in the shade under the cherry tree that spread out over the fences in all directions. The roots were in one yard, but its body bulged forth into another, and its branches struck out over three or four more. The fallen fence had receded from their minds. Each smoothed out the dress behind her, letting the lower part of the skirt contract into a bundle of pleats which were drawn up between their legs. They sat in a circle composed and relaxed, rehearsing, each in turn, the tale of dereliction told a thousand times during the past week.

Miss Foster. My mother. Bob's mother.

It seemed they were three pieces in a pattern which remained constant. The flow of its history was undisturbed by any difference in the pieces, nor was its evenness affected by any likeness. There was a difference and there was no difference. Miss Foster had six children, three by a butcher, two by a baker and one whose father had never been mentioned. Bob's mother had two, and my mother one. The difference between six and two and one did not belong to the piece itself. In the corner where one fence merged into another, and the sunlight filtering through the leaves made a limitless suffusion over the land, the pattern had arranged itself with absolute unawareness. Outside at the street corner where villagers poked wreckage from the blocked canal, it had absorbed another three, four, fourteen. But there was no change in the increase. Here where the fences penetrated each other and in silent collaboration produced a corner there were three. Outside where the roads crossed there were more: thirteen, thirty. The three were shuffling episodes and exchanging the confidences which informed their life with meaning. The meaning was not clear to them. It was not their concern, and it would never be. Their consciousness had never been quickened by the fact of life to which these confidences might have been a sure testimony. Outside the others were shovelling earth. They too exchanged confidences while life flowed through them. In the broad savannah where the grass lowcropped sang in the singeing heat the pattern had widened. Not three, nor thirteen, but thirty. Perhaps three hundred. Men. Women. Children. The men at cricket. The children at hide and seek. The women laying out their starched clothes to dry. The sun let its light flow down on them as life let itself flow through them. Three. Thirteen. Thirty. Three hundred.

An estate where fields of sugar cane had once crept like an open secret across the land had been converted into a village that absorbed some three thousand people. An English landowner, Mr. Creighton, had died, and the estate fell to his son through whom it passed to another son who in his turn died, surrendering it to yet another. Generations had lived and died in this remote corner of a small British colony, the oldest and least adulterated of British colonies: Barbados or Little England as it was called in the local school texts. To the east where the land rose gently to a hill, there was a large brick building surrounded by a wood and a high stone wall that bore bits of bottle along the top. The landlords lived there amidst the trees within the wall. Below and around it the land spread out into a flat unbroken monotony of small houses and white marl roads. From any point of the land one could see on a clear day the large brick house hoisted on the hill. When the weather wasn't too warm, tea was served on the wide, flat roof, and villagers catching sight through the trees of the shifting figures crept behind their fences, or stole through the wood away from the wall to see how it was done. Pacing the roof, the landlord, accompanied by his friends, indicated in all directions the limits of the land. The friends were mainly planters whose estates in the country had remained agricultural; or otherwise there were English visitors who were absentee owners of estates which they had come to see. The landlord, one gathered, explained the layout of land, the customs of the villagers and the duties which he performed as caretaker of this estate. The villagers enthralled by the thought of tea in the open air looked on, unseen, open-mouthed.

The wood was thick and wild with tangled weed racing over and along the swollen black roots of the mahogany trees. Patrolling the land at all hours of the day were the village overseers. They were themselves villagers who were granted special favours like attending on the landlady, or owning after twenty years' tenure the spot of land on which their house was built. They were fierce, aggressive and strict. Theft was not unusual, and the landlords depended entirely on the overseers to scare away the more dangerous villagers. The overseers carried bunches of keys strung on wire which they chimed continually, partly to warn the villagers of their approach, and partly to satisfy themselves with the feel of authority. This seemed necessary since the average villager showed little respect for the overseer unless threatened or actually bullied. Many a day poverty, adventure or the threat of boredom would drive them into the woods where the land-lady's hens lay and the rabbits nibbled the green weed. They would collect the eggs and set snares for the birds and animals. The landlord made a perennial complaint, and the overseers were given a full-time job. Occasionally the landlord would accuse the overseers of conniving, of slackening on the job, and the overseers who never risked defending themselves gave vent to their feelings on the villagers who they thought were envious and jealous and mean. Low-down nigger people was a special phrase the overseers had coined. The villagers were low-down nigger people since they couldn't bear to see one of their kind get along without feeling envy and hate. This had created a tense relationship between the overseer and the ordinary villager. Each represented for the other an image of the enemy. And the enemy was to be destroyed or placated. The overseer was either authoritarian or shrewd. The villager hostile or obsequious. The landlord's complaint heightened the image, gave it an edge that cut sharp and deep through every layer of the land. And this image by continual assertion had become a myth which like a rumour drifted far beyond the village. Even the better educated who had one way or another gone to the island's best schools and later held responsible posts in the Government service, even these were affected by this image of the enemy which had had its origin in a layer from which many had sprung and through accidents of time and experience forgotten. The image of the enemy, and the enemy was My

People. My people are low-down nigger people. My people don't like to see their people get on. The language of the overseer. The language of the civil servant. The myth had eaten through their consciousness like moths through the pages of ageing documents. Not taking chances with you people, my people. They always let you down. Make others say we're not responsible, we've no sense of duty. That's what the low-down nigger people do to us, their people. Then the others say we've no sense of duty. Like children under the threat of hell fire they accepted instinctively that the others, meaning the white, were superior, yet there was always the fear of realizing that it might be true. This world of the others' imagined perfection hung like a dead weight over their energy. If the low-down nigger people weren't what they are, the others couldn't say anything about us. Suspicion, distrust, hostility. These operated in every decision. You never can tell with my people. It was the language of the overseer, the language of the Government servant, and later the language of the lawyers and doctors who had returned stamped like an envelope with what they called the culture of the Mother Country.

The landlord was safe. The village was safe. That tension soaring at times to mutual bitterness had produced this image of the enemy, and later there emerged an attitude which the overseer wore like a uniform and which became his substitute for duty. Take no chances. Be on the look-out always, everywhere. Be fierce. Be strict. Be aggressive. That was duty. And the overseer was a shadow of the police constable who patrolled the village at night. He always arrived alert, ready, prepared. He did not come to explain, inform, interpret or share experience like other men in the ordinary run of social intercourse. He came to arrest. Something had to be wrong. The village might have been asleep, but floating somewhere about, around, perhaps within himself was the large, invisible threatening phantom, the image of the enemy. My people. Whenever the constable appeared there was apprehension. People who all the while were relaxed and composed became fidgety, began to suspect themselves. Sometimes they slipped along the alley and over to the neighbouring road to warn the villagers there. The constable was around. Nothing seemed wrong, but something must have been. Something had to be wrong. Children hid behind fences or peeped through the jalousies, frightened, waiting.

Once a quarter or after some calamity like the flood, the landlord with his family drove from road to road through the village. He inspected the damage, looking from one side of the road to the other. Those who were untidy scampered into hiding, much to his amusement, while the small boys who were caught unawares came to attention and saluted briskly. The landlord smiled, and his wife beside him smiled too. The daughter seated in the back of the carriage looked down haughty and contemptuous.

Two horses in an outfit of brilliant polished leather dragged the carriage from road to road through the village, stopping here and there as the fancy took the landlord. The survey lasted all morning, during which he had seen most of the extreme damage and made a rough estimate of the necessary repairs. In the case of floods the repairs were simple. The canals would be re-marked and the wreckage shovelled from the roads. This finished, cartloads of stone and pebbles would be strewn on as a new surface. These would be left for several weeks in their raw upturned state, until vehicles and pedestrians treading upon them from day to day would flatten them out into an even white stretch. The road was new again.

When the carriage disappeared with the landlord and his family, small boys came out to rehearse the scene. Two took the part of the horses and trotted along to the fore, while another three arranged themselves behind as the landlord and his family had done. The boys would trot slowly from road to road pretending to make a similar survey, and discussing among themselves the plans they had for repairs. Earlier, when they had watched the landlord and his friends on the roof of the brick house, they reproduced the scene behind the fence in the open air. They made saucers and cups with a mixture of dirt and water and saliva, leaving them in the sun to bake dry. Then they served tea from the tap of a standing pipe nearby. The make-believe was impressive. The landlord. The overseer. The villager. The image of the enemy. The limb of the law, strict, fierce, aggressive. These had combined to produce an idea of the Great.

The world of authority existed somewhere along the fringe of the villagers' consciousness. Direct contact with the landlord might have helped towards some understanding of what the others, meaning the white, were like, but the overseer who nominally was a mediator had functioned like a bridge which might be used, but not for crossing from one end to the other. The world ended somewhere along the bridge, and beyond was another plane of reality; beyond was the Great, which the landlord and the large brick house on the hill represented. At night the light poured down through the wood, and the house looking down from the hill seemed to hold a quality of benevolent protection. It was a castle around which the land like a shabby back garden stretched. When the lights went out, and the wood was dark, the villagers took note. The landlord's light had been put out. The landlord had gone to bed. It was time they did the same. A custom had been established, and later a value which through continual application and a hardened habit of feeling became an absolute standard of feeling. I don't feel the landlord would like this. If the overseer see, the landlord is bound to know. It operated in every activity. The obedient lived in the hope that the Great might not be offended, the uncertain in the fear it might have been.

*   *   *

Seated on the flat pavement that led to the entrance of the public bath, men talked desultorily about yesterday, today, tomorrow. The disinfectant hummed its keen stench through the air. In the bath the water spurted down from single-holed taps on the raw, naked bodies. Two to a tap for those over fifteen. For the others not under twelve, three. There was no public baths for the under twelves. The supervisor sat behind the narrow table, looking strict, important and aggressive.

Johnson, time. Hayward, time. His voice echoed and the water sang against the stiffened flesh.

Johnson, time. Hayward, time. Two men left the pavement to take the places of Johnson and Hayward. Occasionally the supervisor walked down the timber plank that served as a foot-rest in the middle. He inspected the compartments, unspeaking, harsh, uncommunicative.

Spooner, time. Jones, time.

The places of Spooner and Jones would soon be taken. The supervisor had gone back to his seat behind the table and the voices spoke through the water. On one side three boys were crowded under a tap. The water drowned their whispers.

'You don't know what I can do? Look and see what I can do.'

One boy held his penis up like a main spring.

'Look what I can do.' The boys laughed and their laughter drowned the splash of the water.

The supervisor tiptoed down the timber plank slowly, secretively. The boys, preoccupied, went on with the operation.

'I can do it too.'

'An' me, too.'

'I bet you can't.'

'What you bet I can?'

The whispers slipped through the water.

'Look. Look.' 'No, no.' 'Wait.' 'All together.'

Simultaneously they performed the feat, and the supervisor unbidden saw. Now the tap dripped slowly, sadly. In a minute the boys were clothed. They walked in single file, tense, silent, humiliated.

In the neighbouring compartments the bathers wondered what had happened, but the supervisor with appropriate discreetness made no disclosure.

'Get your clothes on and go. And don't come back.' That was all he said. Back at the table he wrote in his notebook hurriedly, indignantly. His head like the scrawling pen seemed to totter. That's what they've come here for. To get me into trouble. That's what they're like. You can never take chances, never, never, never.

The image of the enemy. My people.

'Haynes, time. Thompson, time.'

Another couple left the pavement. The men dried and dressed. The supervisor sat at the table fierce, strict, aggressive. He was on duty as he watched the men traipse out, and behind them the water thick with their refuse moving slowly, sadly down the drain.

Outside the bath the birds trafficked from tree to tree. The mahogany and fustic trees with the wild weed weeping round their roots held conference over this morning. The sun forced a way through the leaves, past the branches and down to the wild green weed that shone dully. Veering in, out, around, off, the train lines hurried through and past the wood, under the train-gates, over the hill and on, on, on. . . . The small boys waited in the wood listening cautiously for the rhythm of the wheels along the lines, and peering through the trees and away in the distance for a whiff of steam shot from the carcass of the engine. They crouched at intervals of five, three, four yards. On the lines the metal pins beamed. The flames caught and crashed in the wind. The boys slouching at a safe distance from the railtracks watched where the metal seemed to set the lines aflame. On this bright morning so much depended on the pins. Here the boys had set the adventure of the day, and soon in a collision of lines and metal and wheels the life of a knife or several knives would be formed. The pins lay on the lines. The engine hooted and the steam flew wild. The boys like watchmen waited.

The train sped along the tracks, seeming not to move, but drawing nearer and nearer. It tore its way like a fat bully, its face beaming with brass, and its bowels belching the thick, black smoke through the wood. The boys put their fingers to their ears and closed their eyes. The train had shot past. For a moment nothing seemed to have happened. The train out of sight, a strange silence fell over their lips. Then they opened their eyes and saw the metal flattened against the lines, and shaped to their heart's desire. The gleam had narrowed. They scrambled wildly, flashing the fine, narrow blades, comparing their results, and flying their joy winged with shouts through the wood.

Three. Thirteen, Thirty. Boys.

Three. Thirteen. Thirty. Knives.

The pins oval at first with a curved head and fine point were now flat from head to point. The boys dashed about the wood looking for substance soft and tender enough for the exercise of their blades.

The bigger boys came down the railtracks, moving indolently, comparing their blades which were larger and stiffer. They had put nails on the lines. Iron had met iron in a collision on the line. They sharpened their blades on pebbles and threatened the unpicked pears and apples and the small boys' heads as well. The big boys laughed. The small boys looked on enviously at their colleagues in the morning trade. They were afraid to use nails, because it was said they could derail the train. The small boys were obedient, apprehensive, jealous. It would be a long time before their pins would become nails, a long time before they could brandish big blades.

The bath is closed. The train will not return before tomorrow when small boys with pins and big boys with nails will watch their blades take shape. Now it is night with the moon sprinkling its light on everything. The wood is a thick shroud of leaves asleep, and the sleep like fog conceals those who within the wood must keep awake. The frogs whisper and wait. At the crossing where the roads make four a vendor ladles out a village delicacy, black pudding and souse. The cooked intestines of the pig crammed with a potato stuffing makes thick, heavy black coils in the bowl. In another bowl the pig's ears, heels, eyes, tongue and tail swim or float in a pickle of brine. The villagers are assembled around the woman and tray which is hidden to anyone outside the circle.

'A penny pudding, please.'

'Bread and souse, please.'

The voices ring through the night. The woman understands the orders and she can recognize some of the voices. A vehicle draws up abruptly and the crowd make way for the intruder.

'Let the white gentl'man pass,' someone says.

The villagers move back, and the young man, urbane, smiling, makes his way through the passage and gives the order. He makes no demand, but accepts a privilege which they offer. There may be a silent protest, but no one is really angry. Acceptance is all. The young man returns to the car, and the villagers try to recognize the dark girl seated behind the wheel. There is a titter, but no recognition. Her face is in harmony with the night. The car is motored away, and glides along the track somewhere within the wood. The car lights are dimmed, then extinguished, and the frogs whisper and wait. Some of the villagers do not take the food away. They make the order, guzzle the pigs' parts and make another order. Another penny piece, please. Pudding and souse, please, half o' one and half o' the other.

Three, Thirteen, Thirty. It does not matter. They come and go to perpetuate the custom of this corner. Once a week, black pudding and souse. The pattern has absorbed them, and in the wood where the night is thickest it has embraced another two in intimate intercourse. All the lights go out, leaving the moon leaking a little on the leaves. An old woman trips along the roadside drunk. Once a week. Only once a week is she really dead drunk. She takes a turn to the left that leads through the wood. The wind fills her old ears with a noise she doesn't hear. Ahead the light falls more harshly on the flat mound. She trips over the mound and into two dogs bound by their hind parts. She crosses the mound and circles the trees, the same trees several times. In front the bath stands like a sentinel at the edge of the wood. She has retraced her steps, and feeling the familiar stench of that part she closes her eyes and trips along. Objects shift about in the distance. On the pavement of the bath a man and woman are locked in arms, and in their closeness they seem one person. The woman makes circles with her mouth over his mouth. The man wriggles as her tongue circling the air licks the partitions of his ears. He wriggles like a child in cold water, and the woman laughs. The old woman has circled the trees again. Another couple is one with the wall. The air groans, not with pain or delight, but the exhaustion that escapes in an explosion of appetites fed by fire. The old woman has heard this. She totters along, and suddenly as if compelled by a force outside herself she stoops against a tree letting her urine ooze down to the roots. Her underclothes drip, and the moon sprinkles its light on everything. The dogs shaggy and obscene in their excitement, the human couples gross and warm in frenzied intercourse. The old woman walks along, her head awhirl with the intoxication of nothingness. The clouds move back, the light leans down, and life oozes, a thick weight, through her congested carcass.

*   *   *

In the corner the sunlight had narrowed to a ray that struck down like a finger over the three faces. Miss Foster, Bob's mother and my mother. Not thirteen, not thirty, but three.

'And what happen after the thunder?' Bob's mother asked.

'Well, we see a roof fly up in the air like a kite,' Miss Foster said, 'and I turn to Foster and say, "Jimmie, we better get the children out of the way, and pick up the weself and a few piece of clothes and go somewhere." He look round as if to curse me, and then he say, "I not leaving my house." He didn't say the word when I feel a shake and it seem we moving. I jump through the window with two of the children, one under each arm, and somebody grabble up the rest. Jimmie didn't move. The water pour in through the floor boards till it reach his knee, and then he decide to go up on the roof. He climb up and he and the house went sailing down the river while the people shout out, "Look, Noah on the Ark!" Some thought it was a revelation, a sort of first step to the second coming, and they just went on shouting, "Look, Noah on the Ark!" The others laughed quietly.

'And what the landlord say?' Bob's mother asked.

'Well, I went up to see him next morning,' Miss Foster went on, 'but the overseer say he didn't see much point my coming. He say I know the landlord couldn't do nothing 'bout the weather, and that I only go to get him into trouble. I know as well as the world, he say, that the landlord ain't go do nothing. But it so happen, my dear, the landlord must have heard me mouth from outside, and hearin' that Foster and me wus the worst in the flood he sent word to the overseer to say let me come in to see 'im.'

There was a pause. Miss Foster's face beamed.

'I couldn't talk,' she said. 'He sit me down in a rocking chair, an' ask me 'bout the flood. Says he was so sorry to hear what had happen, but we must all pray. I couldn't believe my ears, for I never in all my born days associated white people with God. But he was the essence of niceness. Then to my surprise he call the servant and say to give me a cup of tea.'

Miss Foster stammered as she recalled this incident.

'Teacup and saucer, my child, as you never see in your life. And on the back of it he give me half a crown, sixty cents, believe it or not. I went down on me knees, and I say, "May the Almighty God bless you always, Mr. Creighton. Forgive me saying it, but I know you before you born, and that's what I ask for you. God's blessing." And he couldn't talk, Mr. Creighton couldn't talk for the water in his eyes. I walk down the yard that mornin' with me head high in the air, an' not King George on the throne of England was greater than me. When I come out and see the bad-minded black son-of-a-bitch we call the overseer, I shake my backside (God forgive me) at him, just to let 'im know that I was people too.'

She dropped her head and stared at the ground with an expression of immense satisfaction.

'You never know what coming to you in this world,' she said, 'you never know, my child, you down today, you up tomorrow.' The wind leapt lightly through the leaves. The sun went under the cloud and the shadow in the corner deepened. The sun peered out again, and the light flashed down.

You never know what comin' to you, in this worl'. You down today, you up tomorrow.

The words seem to sally forth from her lips, circle the others and join the indolent breeze through the fence and over the trees.

The landlord. The overseer. The flood. Miss Foster. Bob's mother, my mother. Not thirteen, but three. They were silent now. You down today, you up tomorrow. And in that brief silence they seemed to wonder what would happen tomorrow.

3

IN one corner where the walls met there was a palm-tree laden with nuts, and in front on all sides an area of pebbles, marl and stone. That area wide and pebbled in every part was called the school yard. The school was in another corner, a wooden building of two storeys with windows all around that opened like a yawning mouth. Except when it rained, the windows supported from the sills by broomsticks were kept open. In another corner was the church, a stone building which extended across the yard to within a few yards of the school. The church seemed three times the size of the school, with dark stained hooded windows that never opened. Inside the air was dark and heavy and strange. The mystery of the church frightened the boys, and they never entered it except in their attempt to peeve the sexton by ringing the bell.

The church was not the church school as some churches were called, and the boys never really understood why these two buildings were erected within the same enclosure. The school inspector was an Englishman, and the school was supposed to be of anglican persuasion. The supervising minister of the church was also English, but he was Presbyterian. Twice a term the inspector visited the schools to record the attendance and give intelligence tests. On such occasions the teachers and boys all seemed frightened, and the head teacher who seldom laughed would smile for the length of the inspector's visit. Occasionally the supervising minister came in to give pep talks on the work of the church, and then no one seemed frightened. But the inspector and the minister never met in the school. The head teacher never arranged for them to meet except on special occasions like Empire Day. After the celebrations and parades, the head teacher took them to his house which occupied the fourth corner of the school yard. In one corner a palm-tree, and in the others three shrines of enlightenment that looked over the wall and across a benighted wooden tenantry.

*   *   *

The children were arranged in thick squads over the school yard. One squad represented the primary school, and the remaining eight the classes that ranged from standard Lower First to Standard Seven. Standard Lower First comprised the boys between the age of five and six who were too old for the primary school and not clever enough for the upper school. On special occasions they were called Lower First, otherwise everyone referred to them as

| a | b | ab | catch a crab |
| g | o | go | let it go |

There were nine squads comprising about a thousand boys. The squads were packed close, and seen from the school porch the spectacle was that of an enormous ship whose cargo had been packed in boxes and set on the deck. The squads were all at ease. The boys stood leisurely, their hands met in a fist of knuckles somewhere between their buttocks. Some boys stole a chance to scratch with the index finger. The teachers stepped with great dignity between the rows, inspecting the discipline of the lines, and when they stopped and shouted with military urgency "Tion!' the boys raised their left legs and brought them down heavily on the ground beside the right heels. Their heads were slightly tilted back, and the small hands pressed earnestly against their sides. Some failed to distinguish quickly between right and left and lifted the wrong leg. The naked ankles of the neighbouring colleagues collided and hurt. But no one winced. It was the twenty-fourth of May, the Queen's birthday.

The sun was big in the sky, and it shone, bright and steady, over the pebbles. The green coconuts shone, and the church windows and the galvanized sheets of iron that roofed the school. Everything seemed a heaving tussle of light. The wind came in sharp spasms and the flags flew. The school wore a uniform of flags: doors, windows and partitions on all sides carried the colours of the school's king. There were small flags and big flags, round flags and square flags, flags with sticks and flags without sticks, and flags that wore the faces of kings and princes, ships, thrones and empires. Everywhere the red and the white and the blue. In every corner of the school the tricolour Union Jack flew its message. The colours though three in number had by constant repetition produced something vast and terrible, a kind of pressure or presence of which everyone was a part. The children in the lower school looked with wonder. They seemed to see a mystery that was its own revelation, and there was, therefore, no need to ask questions. The boys in the upper school looked with triumph. They saw a fact that was its own explanation. The red and the white and the blue. How strong and deep the colours were!

On all sides the walls were crowded with people. There were relatives of the children who were in the squads, or children who did not go to that school. The older people saw the flags and talked of the old days. Such a long time ago, but nothing had really changed. There were more flags now, the school was bigger and the children more clever. They could take and give orders, and parade for the inspector. And they understood the meaning of big words, but nothing had really changed. The flags were the same colour. It was a queen in their time. Now it was a king. But the throne was the same. Good old England and old Little England! They had never parted company since they met way back in the reign of James or was it Charles? They weren't sure, but it was a James or a Charles, God bless his name. Three hundred years, more than the memory could hold, Big England had met and held Little England and Little England like a sensible child accepted. Three hundred years, and never in all that time did any other nation dare interfere with these two. Barbados or Little England was the oldest and purest of England's children, and may it always be so. The other islands had changed hands. Now they were French, now they were Spanish. But Little England remained steadfast and constant to Big England. Even to this day. Indeed, it was God's doing. The hand of the Lord played a great part in that union. And who knows? You could never tell. One day before time changed for eternity, Little England and Big England, God's anointed on earth, might hand-in-hand rule this earth. In the '14 war they went side by side together, and they would go again any time. Big England had only to say the word and Little England followed. Big England had the strongest navy, and Little England the best fishermen in this God's world. Together they were mistresses of the sea, and whenever, wherever, the two met on the same side, war or peace, there was bound to be victory.

*　　　*　　　*

A car drove slowly through the school yard flying a flag on its bonnet and then there was only the sound of the wind in the trees. The inspector stepped from the car, and before he had found his feet one of the teachers had bellowed the order. With incredible precision every squad saluted, and there was silence but for the sound of the wind in the trees, and the silence moving gradually from squad to squad broke forth into an earnest, pleading resonance:

> God save our gracious King,
> Long live our noble King,
> God save the King.

At the order of the teachers the boys dropped the salute. They stood at attention, and when the second order was given relaxed. The head teacher led the inspector to a raised platform in the middle of the school yard. The inspector wore a white suit with a red, white and blue badge on the lapel of the jacket. He smiled all the time, while the head teacher grinned jovially as if he and the inspector were part of a secret the others were to guess. The inspector stood at the centre of the platform and all eyes were fastened on him. He looked round in all directions and then spoke. 'My dear boys and teachers, we are met once again to pay our respects to the memory of a great queen. She was your queen and my queen and yours no less than mine. We're all subjects and partakers in the great design, the British Empire, and your loyalty to the Empire can be seen in the splendid performance which your school decorations and the discipline of these squads represent. We are living, my dear boys, in difficult times. We wait with the greatest anxiety the news of what is happening on the other side of the world. Those of you who read the papers may have read of the war in Abyssinia. You may have seen pictures of the King of Ethiopia, and the bigger boys may have wondered what it's all about. The British Empire, you must remember, has always worked for the peace of the world. This was the job assigned it by God, and if the Empire at any time has failed to bring about that peace it was due to events and causes beyond its control. But, remember, my dear boys, whatever happens in any part of this world, whatever happens to you here in this island of Barbados, the pride and treasure of the Empire, we are always on the side of peace. You are with us, and we with you. And together we shall always walk in the will of God. Let me say how impressed I am with the decorations. I hope I shall start no jealousy among the schools in the island under my control if I say that such a display as I see here could not have been bettered by the lads at home.'

The boys and teachers applauded and his voice was lost in the noise. The inspector waited till the shouting died down and concluded: 'Barbados is truly Little England!' He stepped from the platform and the applause was renewed with greater energy. The head teacher came forward and shook the inspector's hand gratefully, then he stepped on to the platform beaming with delight and yelled: 'Three cheers for the school. Hip pip pip .. Hurararahhahrah Hippiippip ... Hurrahhhaararararah ... Hip pip pip ... Hurrrrrrraaaahh. Hippiippip ... Hurrahhhaararararah....

The boys came to attention, and the teachers' voices were raised in a confusion of orders to the squads. They spoke at the same time, but the orders were different, and the movements of the squads taken on the whole were contradictory. When Class 6 was receiving the order to stand at ease, Class 5 was receiving the order to march. The inspector and the head teacher looked on from the platform and smiled at the innocent rivalry. After the orders were given and the lines were dressed to the teachers' satisfaction, the boys marched squad after squad after squad in circles round the platform. In the final circle they marched at the salute, and the inspector returned the salute and watched them march in single file into the school. The parade had come to an end.

*   *   *

Four boys from the upper school returned for the platform. They lifted it into the school where it belonged, and the head teacher and the inspector were left in the school yard. They stood where the platform had been taken away, and talked quietly. The head teacher's hands were locked behind his back, and his teeth showed under the heavy lips. The inspector stood with a slight hump, his hands falling down in a straight, level stretch from the shoulders. His face was smooth and smiling. They looked very comfortable and at home in that easy and formal arrangement of appearances. They made a striking contrast in appearance, but they seemed in a way to belong to the same thing. The inspector was white and smooth and cool like a pebble. The head teacher's face richer and stronger burnt black in the sun. It was pleasing to watch them talk in that way the villagers called man to man, although it didn't seem altogether a case of man to man. They watched each other at times as a cat would watch a mouse, playfully but seriously. The inspector smiled and the head teacher smiled back, and the cat in each smiled too. It was not a reassuring smile. It was not inconceivable that the cat would spring and suck the blood of the other. And there was a terrifying suggestion of sucking about them. The inspector was smoother than anything you had ever seen, except perhaps a sore. Sometimes a villager caught a chigoe flea in his toe. He was careless in his attention, and the flea hatched in the flesh. Under the skin of the toe there would soon be a small bag fertile with fleas. The toe swelled up into a white and shining smoothness. It was an indescribable smoothness of skin under which the fleas lodged. When the toe was pricked with a pin, the skin cracked and the pus spilled out. The smoothness had slid away, but you couldn't forget it. You couldn't forget it when you saw the inspector smile. Smooth like the surface of pus. It gathered and secreted so much so quietly and so stealthily. The head teacher was smooth too, but his surface was coarse and bright and black like the leech the villagers had seen on Mr. Foster's arm. When Mr. Foster was suffering from blood poisoning, the doctor ordered that a leech be placed on the arm. The leech crouched over the arm, bright and black, and the neighbours watched it grow fat with the intake of blood. Walking beside the inspector towards the school the head teacher had that bright-black slouching carriage of the leech, and when he smiled back at the inspector the flesh of his face rose as though the new intake of feeling was fattening.

*   *   *

The second half of the celebrations began with the inspection of the classes. Three classes gave a special performance, and later it was announced which had won the inspector's shield.

The boys were all seated. The inspector sat in a chair on the platform. The head teacher alone stood. He indicated in turn the class which had to perform. The supervising teacher who was torn between fear and anxiety awaited the head teacher's signal, and when it was given he gave the class a quiet prompter and hoped for the best. Nearest the platform was the lower first which got up and recited the lesson they had been learning for the last three months. Their teacher gave them the signal and they intoned all together.

a	b	ab	catch a crab
g	o	go	let it go
a	b	ab	catch a crab
go	o	go	let it go.

They recited it faultlessly and the inspector applauded. The supervising teacher laughed and snapped his finger at the boys. They elbowed each other and grinned quietly. The scene shifted and a class from the upper school performed. Their teacher stood at the side and when he thought they had settled themselves he whispered, ready, steady, go; and the boys recited the lesson they had been learning for the last three months:

> Thirty days hath September,
> April, June and November;
> All the rest have thirty-one
> Except February which hath but twenty-eight and
> twenty-nine in a Leap Year.

The inspector was pleased and applauded, and the scene shifted once more.

The next performance was a test of voice control, and standard 7 in the upper school was the class which performed. There were two teachers to standard 7, but on such occasions only one was allowed to make his appearance. The other stood as one of the boys. The teacher of standard 7 was also the teacher of music. He stood before the class with the ruler raised in his right hand, and the left hand poised. The arms extended making a half circle over his head, and when they met level and pointed direct at the class the voices rose. The first eight rows were trebles, the last three bass, and the one on the side alto. They sang the hymn which the school had sung every morning for the last three months.

> O God, our help in ages past,
> Our hope for years to come,
> Our shelter from the stormy blast,
> And our eternal home.

The performances had come to an end, and all were seated but the head teacher who made a speech. He was pleased with the attendance, which he said was the best the school had had in many years. He announced that standard 5 had won the inspector's shield. The monitor of standard 5 came forward amid applause and took the shield. He gave it to the teacher who hung it on a nail against the partition directly behind standard 5. Then the headmaster announced that three boys would be leaving this term to enter High School.

They had won exhibition scholarships, and he was proud. He spoke with great feeling about their achievement.

'They will pursue what we call the higher studies,' he said. 'Mathematics and Science and such things. Here as you all know we do arithmetic up to and sometimes beyond compound interest. The boys in standard 7 can tell you everything about Stocks and Shares. Algebra and Geometry we leave to the higher school. But without that firm foundation which we give in arithmetic, these boys could not understand those subjects. We are proud of them. The future is theirs, and they will always remember with gratitude the school which taught them the first things they ever learnt.'

The school applauded, and the three boys walked forward and shook the inspector's hand.

'As you know,' the head teacher went on, 'every Empire Day we give pennies to the children. It's the gift of the Queen, and a great old Queen she was. And it is our custom here as in all the schools, to give a penny to the boys in the lower school and those in the upper school up to standard 4. The others get two pennies. Our three exhibitioners will get three pennies each. You must all when you go to spend your penny think before you throw it away. Queen Victoria was a wise queen, and she would have you spend it wisely. Some of those boys in standard 7 think they know what it is to be a king. Victoria was a real queen.'

There was a loud giggle from one corner of the school. The head teacher stiffened, and everyone felt the terror of the change that had come over him.

'And now for the pennies,' he said abruptly, and stepped from the platform.

The pennies were brought in, and the inspector who never waited to witness the distribution got up and made ready to leave. The head teacher blew his whistle and the whole school stood and saluted as the inspector walked out. The head teacher blew the whistle again, and everyone sat. He went back to the platform and surveyed the school. His face was coarse and savage and sad. It was difficult to understand when he spoke. His voice was low and choked with a kind of terror. 'I've never wanted it said that my boys are hooligans,' he said, 'grinning like jackasses when respectable people are around. I've always wanted it said that the boys at Groddeck's Boy School were gentlemen. But gentlemen don't grin and giggle like buffoons, and in the presence of respectable people, people of power and authority.' The school was silent, and everybody seemed to shiver under the threat of his tone. 'Who was it laughed when I said what I said about the queen?' he asked. No one moved.

'Who was it, I ask?' he shouted, taking the thick leather from his desk. It was the cured hide of the cow which had been soaked in resin, and which he used to punish. He took a step forward.

'Who was it, I ask again?' he shouted. 'Speak up or I'll beat every blasted one of you from top to bottom.' The terror mounted. The silence was heavy and terrible, like the certainty of death.

A boy got up from standard 7 and started to speak.

'Come out,' the head teacher snapped, cutting him short. The boy stood where he was, trying to make some explanation. No one knew whether he was the offender or whether he was informing on someone. The boy stepped forward, trying to speak. The head teacher stood trembling as if he feared the full responsibility of what he was going to do. He took the leather from his neck where he had strung it and waited for the boy to approach. The boy refused to walk further forward and the head teacher glowered. 'Come up,' he said again, and stared at the boy as if he were a human symbol of the blackest sin. Suddenly the boy in terror leapt over the desks and benches, tripping over the other boys' heads, and fled toward the door. The teachers caught him as he tried to leap over the banister and brought him forward. He could not speak. Four boys were summoned, and they bound him hands and feet and stretched him flat over a bench. The head teacher removed his jacket and gripped the leather. The first blow rent the pants and left the black buttocks exposed. The boy made a brief howl like an animal that had had its throat cut. No one could say how long he was beaten or how many strokes he received. But when he stood supported by the four boys who had held him down he was weak. The knees tottered and the filth slithered down his legs. The boys lifted him out of the school and carried him under the pipe in the school yard.

*   *   *

'Why you run, you fool?'

'Yes, if it wasn't you, why you run?'

'I could see it din't make no diffcrence,' the boy said. 'He had to beat somebody, and he made sure with me.'

'But who it was?'

'It wusn't me,' he said. 'It was Boy Blue. When the Head say 'bout the queen was a great queen and not like the kings in 7th, Boy Blue ask . . .'

'What he ask?' the boys urged.

'He ask if the queen's bloomers was red, white and blue.'

The boys put his legs under the pipe again and washed him clean.

First Boy: I never ever see him beat anybody like that. Never ever.

Second Boy: Nor me as far as my memory can remember has I seen him take off his jacket in that sort of fashion to fix up a fellow. I didn't do it, but I nearly did dirty myself, when I see him bring that belt down on yuh bambam.

Third Boy: Seems as though he sort of had it waiting for you and you only. 'Twustn't what you could call a nat'ral beating.

Fourth Boy: That's as much as I says to myself. 'Twusn't nat'ral the way he went 'bout it. He sort of had you in his mind and he see there and then his chance to let you out. That's as much as I thought as I wus holding you down.

Second Boy: You mustn't think that 'cause we hold you down, we sort of encourage him to go on when he would 'ave stop.

First Boy: For God sake don' think so. I wus saying to myself all the time what and what I would do with him afterwards if 'twus me.

Fourth Boy: I would tell my father. That's what I would do, tell my father. 'Tis only a father who could sort of deal with him.

Third Boy: Would you tell yuh father how he beat you?

'I don't know,' the victim said, 'I don't know.'

Fourth Boy: How you mean you don't know. You ain't satisfy with what happen, is you or is you? You going to leave it at that?

First Boy: You ain't going to leave it at that, I bet my life you ain't.

Fourth Boy: I'd tell my father. Takes a father to deal with that sort of thing. With me it couldn't end at that. My father would bound to know.

Second Boy: Is you going to tell yuh father how he beat you, or is you not?

First Boy: Ain't you going to tell yuh father? What you got a father for? Ain't a father for that sort of thing when it happen?

'I don't know,' the victim said. 'I don't know.'

Second Boy: What you think make him beat you so? What could it be?

First Boy: What you think? 'Twus more than happen this morning. I'd bet my life 'twus more than the queen an' all that.

Third Boy: What you think it wus? You ought to sort of know.

Fourth Boy: What wus it? Say what's in yuh mind, man, what wus it?

'I don't know,' the victim said, 'I don't know.'

Fourth Boy: If 'twus me I'd tell my father, as there's a God in heaven I'd tell my father.

Second Boy: Me too. If 'twus the first thing I ever tell my father, 'twould be that. I'd tell him.

First Boy: Who won't. Sure I would. That's what you got a father for. Yuh father is a sort of watchman for the house.

Fourth Boy: If 'twus me I'd tell my father.

Third Boy: I not so sure I'd tell my father. I not so sure at all.

Fourth Boy: How you mean? What you mean to mean by saying what you say?

First Boy: Yuh brains has walked out of yuh head. That's what I say.

Fourth Boy: Or yuh head off yuh neck. How you mean you won't tell yuh father? What you got a father for, if you got a father?

Third Boy: If there's one thing you ain't to do is tell yuh father a teacher lash you. It ain't wise to do it. By my dead grangran it ain't.

Fourth Boy: Why ain't it wise or right or whatever you say it ain't?

Third Boy: 'Cause yuh father'll say that the teacher had a cause. That's what yuh father'll say. An' when you tell him you don't know the reason why the teacher do what he do, then yuh father'll tell you why. An' he won't only tell you why, but he'll tell you the teacher didn't lash you properly an' he'll do it all over again. He'll show you how the teacher ought to lash you, next time. It ain't wise to tell yuh father that sort of thing. I know what I saying. I know it ain't wise.

First Boy: It ain't fair. It ain't fair for yuh father to do that. I'd tell my mother.

Second Boy: 'Tis different with a mother. She sort of has better feelings. A mother's sort of very soft. Her feelings is soft.

First Boy: Yes, But she might tell yuh father. You know what these women give. They can't keep anything inside, not that they want to get you into trouble, they don't, but they can't keep in anything, from water back down, no matter what. They got to let it out; an' when you hear the shout, yuh mother'll tell yuh father, an' 'twould be as if you had tell him yuhself. No difference at all. I don't know now who I'd tell.

Fourth Boy: 'Tis alright with me. My father don't live in the same house.

First Boy: But yuh mother'll tell him when she see him. That's what a mother's like. She want bad bad bad to say something an' even if she ain't on speakin' terms with yuh father, just for something to say to let out 'cause she can't keep in, just for that she'll tell him.

Fourth Boy: My father couldn't hit me 'cause he don't support me. An' that's why I alright. My mother won't let him hit me 'cause he don't support me. An' the courthouse won't let him either. The law says a father can't flog if he don't feed. Thank God for the law.

First Boy: Mine don't support me, but if he beat me my mother would say it shows he wus still taking an interest.

Second Boy: Mine won't.

Fourth Boy: Nor mine.

First Boy: Mothers stupid, that's why most of us without fathers. P'raps it's because mothers stupid that fathers don't turn up sometimes to see what's happening. 'Tis a bad thing to be stupid.

Fourth Boy: I rather not have a father around. Believe me, I'd give anything to have a father out of the house at all times of the day. A father in the house is like a bear or a tiger or a lion. You can't talk an' laugh as you like, an' sometimes if you stay in the W.C. too long he come for you. Some fathers don't even want you to do what's nat'ral. They don't.

Third Boy: Rat's father who's the tailor is like that. He support all of them good good good, an' they don't want for anything in this God's world. But they ain't got no freedom. When he ain't there the house is like a concert, 'cause the mother is a sweet woman who gives plenty jokes, but as soon as he put in his appearance, everybody stop talking. 'Tis funny the way it happens. You hear the talking talking talking, an' suddenly somebody say easy easy, daddy comin', an' suddenly everything is like a black-out for the ears. You don't hear anything at all. Not a sound but their father foot coming through the yard. An' it stay silent so till he go out again.

Fourth Boy: We can do without fathers if that's what they like. I do without mine alright. An' then too, if there ain't no father in the house, you get the feeling you is the man in the place. It's a good feeling. When anybody like the sanitary inspector or the police come in an' ask who is the man round here, an' you can say, well there's only one man round here, an' 'tis me.

First Boy: I don't see much of my father, but my second brother father is good. He don't make no difference between us, me and my brother, 'cause he says we is both our mother children. How many fathers you got in yuh family?

First Boy: Look look look, the head teacher looking through the window. Put his foot under the pipe again. Quick quick quick.

They carried the boy to a spot where he could not be seen by anyone from the school, and left the pipe flowing the water through the canal.

Fourth Boy: Turn it off.

First Boy: No. Let him think we cleaning the gutter.

Third Boy: Yes, but all the time 'tis time we think what we should do.

Second Boy: 'Tis true. He shouldn't get away with that. It ain't fair in the sight of God or the devil. Not even Satan would say it wus fair.

Fourth Boy: I'd stone him. He does pass Hunt's Road very late at night.

First Boy: By Christ, stone him. Stone him. I say stone him, an' don't think what you do or don't do afterwards.

Fourth Boy: Wait by Foster fence. Ease yuhself inside the opening space an' just wait there till he pass, an' when he sort of a good way in front of you, let him have it in the back of his head.

First Boy: You going do that. Ain't you going to do it?

Fourth Boy: 'Course he going to do it. It easy easy easy to do.

Second Boy: There ain't nothing in it. We can help you. We'll choose the stones for you. All you got to do is fire them. You going do it?

'I don't know,' the victim said. 'I don't know.'

Fourth Boy: How you mean you don't know? Is not a question of know. 'Tis a question of do. He din't know why he beat you so. Or p'raps he did, but it makes no difference. Know an' don't know is much the same thing. It is a question of do.

Second Boy: Why should a man beat a boy like that? He's an advantage-taker, that's what I say. A man who beat a boy like that is an advantage-taker. He takes high advantage of another.

Fourth Boy: An' there's a way to deal with those. There's a way to deal with advantage-takers. Whenever you meet them, here or in heaven, there's a way to deal with them.

Second Boy: We stone them, that's what we do, stone them.

Fourth Boy: It won't cost you a penny to do it. Not a penny to stone him.

First Boy: 'Tis true. Stones is free. Free free free. Not a cent it cost.

Third Boy: 'Tis a big thing to do. 'Tis a very big big thing you doing.

Fourth Boy: What is a big thing? Why is it a big thing as you say?

First Boy: What make it so big as all that? What make you say it big?

Third Boy: 'Cause of who the head teacher is. Remember who he is here. He's a big school master. Nobody in all this Creighton's village would think of stoning him. He got power and authority here. Everybody respect him here, an whatever he do or not do, people will be on his side. In a matter like this we won't have no supporters at all. We'd be making hist'ry if we stone him.

Fourth Boy: We going to make hist'ry. I always want to make some hist'ry.

Second Boy: Me too. I read 'bout all those who been making hist'ry, William the Conqueror an' Richard an' all these. I read how they make hist'ry, an' I say to myself 'tis time I make some too.

First Boy: We going to make hist'ry by Foster Fence. Let's make hist'ry.

Third Boy: If you going to make hist'ry you got to think how you doing it. Remember who the head teacher is. He could do anything here an' get away.

Fourth Boy: Not anything. He can't get a girl in trouble. That's one thing he can't get away with.

Second Boy: 'Tis true he can do anything else. Not that. He does drink an' all that, but nobody say anything. But he can't get a girl in trouble. 'Tis funny why they should make that law.

First Boy: It ain't so at the high school. A teacher at the high school can get a girl in trouble, an' nobody can ask him anything, 'cause 'tis his private business. But not at the elementary school. If a teacher get a girl in trouble he lost his job.

Third Boy: He can't be seen too close with a girl. An' if they have evidence that he been playing round with one they could ask him questions.

First Boy: Why that so in these schools?

Second Boy: You see, the high school ain't got no supervising minister. We have. An' we have inspector of school too. The high school ain't got that. They sort of on their own. They do as they like.

Third Boy: 'Tis also 'cause the inspector is English. In England they don't have that sort of thing of a man playing round a girl. He sort of write a letter straight away to her father an' say his intentions is so an' so, an' that's that. But no playin' round.

Fourth Boy: 'Tis alright for the English. They white which mean they ain't got much blood in their veins, an' if a man ain't got much blood he don't know how to play round with a girl. Or p'raps he can with one, but not two or three. It takes plenty blood.

Third Boy: I only say you got to remember who the head teacher is. You could make him look like a baby if you did know that he had a girl in trouble, an' you let him know that you would tell the inspector. Everybody in the village would be on your side. 'Cause they won't put up with that bad behaviour. But to stone him when he wus going home after drinking a little liquor, they won't forgive you.

Fourth Boy: We ain't got no evidence that he does do that so we going stone him. What they say after is they business. If they don't like it they can lump it. An' if he die they can get another head. There's plenty would like the job. We going stone him.

First Boy: We going do it. It ain't going to cost us nothing, nothing.

Second Boy: Stones is free. They don't cost you nothing. Not a penny.

Fourth Boy: Not a cent. Not a cent to split his skull in two. In two.

'I don't know,' the victim said. 'I don't know. Maybe 'tis a penny an' a cent that cost me what I get. Maybe 'tis. I don't know.'

First Boy: How you mean?

Second Boy: What it is you mean?

Third Boy: Say what you mean.

Fourth Boy: What you mean by penny an' cent? Say what you mean.

The victim leaned against the wall and looked down at the gutter where the water gurgled on its way. He passed his hand against the naked skin where the leather had made a slight rupture. His eyes were tear stained and his face terribly exhausted. But he smiled as he started to speak, and the boys went closer to hear.

'My mother's his servant, you see,' the victim said. 'She cooks an' does for him an' his wife, an' she knows as whatever goes on in his house. It don't matter what it is, 'tis not easy to keep anything out of a servant's ears. They hear everything as what goes on in an' out of the house. An' 'tis so with my mother who's his servant. All servants is the same, the servants of the white people as well as the servants of the black, an' it ain't their fault. They can't prevent themselves from hearing just as they can't prevent themselves from remembering. An' the head teacher as much as gets it in his head that my mother'll tell me what she hears when she come home in the night. Not that she'll tell me to my face, but I must hear when she's telling my brother's father. 'Tis the same everywhere. Tom's mother who work with the white doctor, an' Boy Blue grangran who wus the Governor's cook. They hear what's happening, an' they all get a sort of front seat in the white people business. They know who like who, an' who don't like who. An' sometimes the white people take them in confidence an' tell them things that wasn't made for the ears of any but those who wus concerned. So 'tis with the head teacher. He feels my mother knows 'cause his wife isn't a saint. She's hot stuff, as they say. His wife don't hide anything. She don't keep anything in, an' tis not once or twice, but time an' time again that she say to my mother whatever his shortcomings is. An' p'raps he get into his head that I come back an' tell all you what I hear my mother say. He p'raps don't like the feeling that we sort of in the know.'

'Yes, I thought so,' one boy said. 'But the penny an' the cent. What about the penny an' the cent?'

'Well,' said the victim, 'as I hear my mother tell my second brother father 'twus like this. He an' his wife is a good pair. They each got a kind of weakness. He can't do without a little liquor as we all know, an' she can't do without a pinch of snuff. My mother says that she takes it all the day long, morning, noon an' night. You just see her put her hand under the dress an' take out a little bag, an' before you say Jack Robinson she's sneezing like a cat. She likes a little sneeze. Says it clears the head, an' help you to see everything brighter an' bigger.'

'What 'bout the snuff?' one boy asked. 'What happen to the snuff?'

'It appear as my mother says,' the victim said; 'it appear she din't have no snuff, and 'twus a little late, so she ask him, meaning the head teacher, to go an' get her some. So she give him a penny an' a half-penny.'

'What's a halfpenny?' one boy asked.

'A halfpenny is a cent,' the victim said. 'She give him a penny an' a cent an' tell him to buy that much. He went alright, but before he go to the snuffshop he decide to go round by Kirton to get a pint. As you know he likes his liquor, an' they say that he's alright till sundown, but after the sun sail down behind the sea he gets a kind of terrible thirst. 'Tis as if you put a ball of fire in this throat, an' nothing is any use for the thirst but half a pint of Kirton best. He takes the one with the black cat on the label wearing a bow tie, an' underneath the words, Might is Right. I never know why they put those words on the label 'bout right an' might. Anyway he went an' had it good an' proper. Nobody knows he wus there, 'cause Kirton don't let him sit down in the open bar where everybody is. He got a special little table where he put him, an' maybe one or two friends of his. They drink in private where you can't see them get drunk. 'Twould seem he drink an' drink till he forget all 'bout the snuff, an' when he wus ready to leave Kirton, he could hardly see where he wus going. He take up his heels as if they wusn't his an' make his way for the snuff shop. So my mother says the wife say he say to her afterwards. So one says the other say.'

'What happen at the snuff shop?' one boy asked. 'He fall down?'

'No,' the victim said, 'not he. 'Twus the cent that fall down. When he wus going in the direction of the snuff shop the cent drop an' fall down as you say. 'Twould seem he din't have no more money but what the wife give him, an' he wus frighten as hell. The cent drop out his hand an' roll in the gutter. He thought he see where it went, 'cause the moon wus big, the sort of moon which show you plain through a glass which side the man sitting. 'Twus a big big moon, an' the gutter wus full of light. Seems the cent roll under the stone in the gutter, so he creep down quiet an' push the stone back to take out the cent, but the cent wusn't there. He look an' look an' look, but the cent wusn't there. Wherever he turn his eyes he turn in vain. There wus nothing but the moonlight under the stone. He get frighten, 'cause he had no more money but the penny, an' it din't look proper for him to credit the snuff, an' in his condition. So it come into his head that he shouldn't lose the penny. An' to make sure he won't lose the penny he lift up the stone again an' put the penny safe an' sound underneath. Then he went in search of the cent, an' when he get back he couldn't find the penny either. He look here an' he look there, but there was neither penny nor cent in sight. Maybe the penny roll away when he roll back the stone. But there it wus, all two both lost. An' how? He put down one to look for the other.'

'What happen after?' one boy asked. 'What happen?'

'That's what happen,' the victim said. 'He had to go home without penny or cent, an' to make it worse blind blind blind drunk. He tell the wife what happen, an' my mother says she never see a woman who wus a head teacher wife get on like that. The wife take off his pants, an' cut his tail. He wus so drunk he couldn't stand up proper, an' she wus in full command. She beat him like a school boy. An' all the time she beating him, she says she never heard it in all her born days, that a big man, an' a head teacher at that, should put down a penny to look for a cent. She couldn't believe her ears, she said. 'Twus never heard of before. She beat him till he turn sober, an' my mother say that when he couldn't stan' it no more, he run out to the verandah an' shout out to the neighbour, "Woolah, woolah, she put them pon me! Woolah, woolah she put them pon me." The neighbour ask him where he left his grammar, but he couldn't hear nothing but his own voice saying, "Woolah, woolah, she put them pon me!" '

The water flowed, carrying the boys' laughter down the canal and beyond the school yard.

In the school the pennies had been distributed and the head teacher who had returned to the platform was sitting behind his desk turning the pages of an attendance register. His short fat fingers trembled as they held the raised leaf suspended between one page and another. He had put the leather back into his desk and everyone seemed happier except the lower school, which sat nearest the platform. They were less than a yard from the platform, and the nearness gave them a feeling of guilt. There was a pause in the proceedings between the distribution of the pennies and the final dismissal of the school. The pause seemed almost a part of the proceedings. The lower school sat quiet and steady. In that pause it was customary for the head teacher to look through the register, and make one or two notes in his little black book. When he blew the whistle to dismiss the school, he would make a few remarks based on the notes he had made in the book. Meanwhile the teachers who sat at the back row of each class occupied themselves with some kind of fiddling. Some sharpened their nails, and others made sketches on loose bits of paper. Most of the boys were busy examining the pennies. They were bright copper. The boys speculated whether it was possible to reproduce them, and made various attempts to represent them in pencil drawings. They would put the penny on the desk, place a sheet of clean paper over it, and shade thickly with

pencil the part of the sheet that covered the penny. They tore away
the circle which the penny had made with its imprint on one side
sharply reproduced. They examined the paper with the imprint and
thought long and hard on ways of making pennies. Some argued
quietly about the size of the king's face, and the way the face had been
stamped on the copper. It was very clever, they thought. It was a
real face, and the face they had seen in other pictures. Some said it was
really a photograph of the king stuck on to some kind of background
and then coloured with copper. This face on the penny was very
fascinating. Could you have a penny without a face? They looked at
it closely and critically, and made notes of their observations. How
did the face get there? The question puzzled them. Some said it was
a drawing of the king made with a pin while the copper was soft.
They had seen lead melt. The hard, colourless slab was put in the pot
and when you looked again it was a shining crystal liquid that gradually grew solid again. The same thing was done with copper. You had
to melt it down, and when it reached a certain solidity the drawing
with the pin was done. It was a long and patient undertaking. But it
had to be done if there was going to be any money at all, and everyone
knew how important money was. It was difficult but necessary. That
was not feasible, some thought. In fact it was very silly to argue that
such a job would be done by sensible people. And the English who
were the only people in the world to deal with pennies were very
sensible. You couldn't involve a king in all that nonsense of melting
down copper and making a drawing. And how would he find the time
to sit till all those million pennies were done? It was very silly. Another
said it would be impossible to use liquid copper for such purposes, and
moreover one man had done all the pennies. It was too much for one
man. Someone agreed that one man had done all the pennies. The
face of the king was the same on every penny and in every detail.
It was not possible for several people working on the same face to
get the same likeness. The nose, perhaps, or an eye and an ear, but not
the whole face, and it was clear to everyone that the face was the exact
face. In every single detail. Nothing differed. Someone said it was the
same penny all the time. One penny, that is the first penny ever made,
was the real penny, and all the others were made by a kind of stamp.
You simply had to get the first penny and the necessary materials and
thousands followed. That meant, someone asked, that you couldn't
spend the first penny. Someone wanted to know how that first penny

was made. Granted there was first a penny from which all the others were made there had to be a first penny made at some time. That wasn't difficult, the boy explained. The penny was made as you saw it without the face of the king. It was heated by a special fire so that it would receive and keep the mark made on it. It was shaped and washed properly, and finally sent to the king who pressed it on one side of his face. The picture came out as we saw it. That was why we saw one side only of the face. Sometimes he pressed it against his nose. More difficulties were raised. If some were pressed against the face and some against the nose there had to be more than one penny. There had to be two pennies at least. Some argued that the king couldn't find time to press all the pennies in the world. He couldn't put all those pennies against his face, because it would make him sore. He would be sick with the feel of copper. He couldn't do it. The boy reminded them that he had to do one only and the others followed by the stamp method.

But all the arguments for the stamp and the drawing were thrown overboard since one boy had it from good authority that the king was never seen.

Maybe as a baby and later as a boy. But when he became a king no one ever saw him. No one could see him. That's why people often asked you if you thought you were a king. And not long ago the head teacher had said something about certain boys feeling they were kings. It was a big thing to be a king. It meant that you were getting the feeling that you lived in a big room all by yourself where no one could see you and you were your own man. Free and alone. Someone wanted to know how the king's face appeared in the papers. They had seen him time and again in the newspapers, and some who had gone to the cinema had seen pictures of the king taking the salute and inspecting the ranks. The papers didn't know what they were doing or saying, the boy argued. The newspaper was always behind the news, not in front. You shouldn't ever go to the papers for information. They usually printed what they thought people liked to see, and they had no explanation to give. It wasn't the king they saw. That wasn't the king at all. It was the king's shadow. Some of the boys laughed. They thought he had meant that the king's shadow followed him wherever he went and the photographs were taken of the shadow and not the king. He explained it at length. There was a shadow king who did whatever a king should do. It was the shadow king who went to parades, took the salute and did those things with which we associated the king. The shadow king was a part of the English tradition. The English, the boy said, were fond of shadows. They never did anything in the open. Everything was done in shadow, and even the king, the greatest of them, worked through his shadow. Somebody asked if you were ever talking to a real man or a shadow when you talked to an Englishman, and the boy said yes. Some of them were the man and the shadow at the same time, but more shadow than man. But you had to be careful when you had anything to do with English people. It was always difficult to distinguish between the man and the shadow, and sometimes it was all shadow. The man got lost somehow and nothing remained but the shadow. Most of the boys couldn't understand this talk about the shadow. Someone said that it wasn't true to say that the king wasn't seen because he had a wife and children. He wasn't really alone and in a world by himself because his family was always there. They were human like anybody else. The children were the princesses whom many had seen in the pictures with their father and mother. The boy objected. He said there was more ignorance around than he had believed possible. It was all a part of the tradition for the king to have daughters and sons who were called princesses and princes. Those words were part of the tradition too. But they were making a big mistake if they thought the king had anything to do with all that. There was a real king, but he wasn't actually involved in all the things we saw. It was the shadow king all the time. The king was alone. He dressed himself and did all that was necessary for himself. He was not seen. That was the tradition. What we saw was the shadow. That's why the children referred to him in the company of others as His Majesty. They couldn't call him daddy like you and me. It wasn't the right thing to say. He was no daddy because he was alone. But they were his children? one boy asked. Yes and no, the boy said. They were and they were not. You mean to say, one boy was asking, you mean to say that it is also the shadow king? . . .

The head teacher blew the whistle and there was silence. He closed the notes. He remained seated and everyone understood that he was not ready to dismiss the school. When he was ready to do that, he would stand and look serious and sad. The habit had grown among them. Each knew the gestures. Each followed the instructions that were not spoken. When the whistle made its little screeching noise, everyone understood something by it. If he blew it once that meant something, and if he blew it twice that meant something quite different. The habit had formed and settled. He was not ready to dismiss the school. They knew that. This whistle was blown to restore silence. The buzzing had grown too loud, and he blew the whistle to remind them that he was still there. Everyone understood. Silence made its presence like a man who had come into a room for a brief look around and would soon disappear. The boys looked at each other and smiled or made faces. The buzzing was coming back slowly. It came up like a head peeping from behind a wall. Very slowly. It wasn't quite there in the peep and push towards an appearance. It was there when it was there, that is, when its presence had been made complete. And it would remain till something smothered it. The buzzing came up. It was present and would remain till the whistle was blown again. Then it would take itself away like a snail slouching smoothly and neatly and with a strange respect and fear into its shell. Everyone understood.

In another class the boys were buzzing about the queen. The queen the head teacher had mentioned. Queen Victoria. It would appear that those who stood nearest the wall had overheard the older people talking about the queen. She was a great and good queen, the head teacher had said, and the old people had said something similar. They did not quite understand it. They understood the flags. They understood them because they did not need to question them. The flags explained their presence, and the parade and the inspector. All these things were simple. They simply were. But the old people on the wall had talked about the queen in another way. They had talked about her as a good queen because she freed them. That's what they said, a little boy was repeating. They said she made us free, you and me and him and you. I heard them say that. How it was the queen that made them free. I heard it too, another boy said. I thought it was so strange, but I didn't worry because it didn't refer to me. The queen had made them free. They must have been locked up once in a kind of gaol. That's what it was, one boy said quietly. Most of them were locked up in a gaol at some time in the past. And it would appear that when this good and great queen came to the throne she ordered that those who weren't free should now become free. It was beginning to make sense. Now they could understand what this talk about freedom meant. One boy said he had asked the teacher, but the teacher said he didn't know what the old people were talking about. They might have been getting dotish. Nobody ever had to make him free. That's what the teacher had said. Nobody ever had to make him free. The boys understood. The old people must have been convicts, and on the queen's accession they were freed. It had nothing to do with them. It was disturbing. The thought of not being free. How could you bear it? If you were told that you couldn't do this or that, and you couldn't go here or go there. Cruel! Another boy spoke quietly. He was not satisfied with the others' explanation. It was a case of the pennies and the king all over again. He said he heard someone say something about slave. An old woman said that once they were slaves, but now they were free. And she said that's what the good and great queen had done. She had made them free. The small boy was puzzled. He understood the meaning of jail and prisoner. He had seen the prisoners several times. They passed in chain gangs early in the morning on their way to work. And he knew what that meant. They were being punished. After they had served sentence they would be free again. But the old woman on the wall wasn't talking about that. She was talking about something different. Something bigger. That's how it seemed to him. He asked the teacher what was the meaning of slave, and the teacher explained. But it didn't make sense. He didn't understand how anyone could be bought by another. He knew horses and dogs could be bought and worked. But he couldn't understand how one man could buy another man. He told the teacher what the old woman had said. She was a slave. And the teacher said she was getting dotish. It was a long, long, long time ago. People talked of slaves a long time ago. It had nothing to do with the old lady. She wouldn't be old enough. And moreover it had nothing to do with people in Barbados. No one there was ever a slave, the teacher said. It was in another part of the world that those things happened. Not in Little England. The little boy didn't like the sound of it. He had dismissed the talk about slaves, but he was very anxious for the old woman. Who put it into her head that she was a slave, she or her mother or her father before her? He was sure the old woman couldn't read. She couldn't have read it in a book. Someone told her. Moreover she said she was one. One of these things. Slave. The little boy had heard the word for the first time and when the teacher explained the meaning, he had a strange feeling. The feeling you get when someone relates a murder. Thank God, he wasn't ever a slave. He or his father or his father's father. Thank God nobody in Barbados was ever a slave. It didn't sound cruel. It was simply unreal.

The idea of ownership. One man owned another. They laughed quietly. Imagine any man in any part of the world owning a man or a woman from Barbados. They would forget all about it since it happened too long ago. Moreover, they weren't told anything about that. They had read about the Battle of Hastings and William the Conqueror. That happened so many hundred years ago. And slavery was thousands of years before that. It was too far back for anyone to worry about teaching it as history. That's really why it wasn't taught. It was too far back. History had to begin somewhere, but not so far back. And nobody knew where this slavery business took place. The teacher had simply said, not here, somewhere else. Probably it never happened at all. The old woman, poor fool! You could forgive her. She must have had a dream. A bad dream! They laughed quietly The whistle was blown. Silence, silence! It came up like a ghost and soon faded again.

*   *   *

The sun was making a new slant. It came through the window in a straight strong shaft and shot hard on the headmaster's head. The skull where the hair was thinnest shone bright. He read in the small black book. His face was heavy and austere. He read and made notes as he read. It wasn't usual for him to stay so long over the notes, but no one seemed to notice. The boys had found several things to occupy their minds. The pennies and later the old woman who had talked about freedom. The teachers were similarly engaged. Some sharpened pencils as a pastime, and others read. At the back of class 4 the teacher had been fidgeting with an envelope. It was for his colleague in class 5. He took it from his pocket, looked at it with a kind of delight and then wrote on one side: Mr. Slime.

The class 5 teacher polished his nails while the boys went on with their buzzing. He was a very smart young man. He was the best dressed of them all, and wore brilliant ties. The head teacher wasn't sure that he liked him, but he did his work well. There was something a little flamboyant, almost vulgar, about his dress. He sat in the back row with his fingers crossed, talking quietly to the boy beside him. The head teacher scribbled in the small black book. A fly alighted on his nose. He was steady. The fly remained making his skin itch where its legs made a thin wink-like rub. He passed his hand over his face and the fly disappeared. The buzzing was steady and subdued. It was interesting to follow the degrees of buzzing. Sometimes it was in the nature of a low general prayer. All the voices spoke in that murmuring monotony which you heard in the church. At other times it was chaotic. You heard them at intervals, and if you had a sharp ear you could distinguish which class it was. They spoke now in the manner of a prayer, quiet, steady and serious. Their heads were pointing towards the desks. What were they worried about? The pennies and the king? Or was it the old woman and her talk about the slave? They were all serious in different ways and about different matters, but they were quiet. The buzz was quiet.

The teacher of class 5 stood up, trying to make a signal to one of his colleagues. When a teacher wanted to relieve himself, he could arrange for someone to take over the class till he returned. He walked alongside the class winking his eye. There was no response, and he walked back towards the back row. He walked up again repeating the wink of the eye, and this time the colleague saw him. It was the teacher of class 4. They understood each other very well. The teacher of class 5 sat down on the bench beside the boys and waited. It was not safe for the teachers to buzz among themselves. When the head teacher blew the whistle, silence would mean their silence as well, and the boys would be amused. They talked quietly with the boys. If the whistle were blown, and the teacher stopped talking, the boy might receive the impression that it was for him and not the teacher. But if two teachers were talking, and they both stopped, that was a different matter. The boys would get ideas.

As the other teacher made his way towards him, the teacher of class 5 got up again and walked to the door. He seemed uncomfortable in his movements. The class 4 teacher walked towards the door trying to attract the other's attention to the envelope in his pocket. They were together when the class 4 teacher raised a hand cagily from his pocket and the teacher of class 5, against his will, ran through the door towards the lavatory. The envelope fell between them. No one saw when it happened; nor indeed what had happened.

The boy stooped slowly and took up the envelope. He was sitting at the end of the bench which the class 5 teacher had vacated. He had not seen when the letter fell, but when he eased round to make room for those higher along the bench, the envelope caught his eye. He looked at it quietly under the desk, and thought what he should do. He was certainly going to read it. But there were other things to be

done. He was thrilled with this new possession. He had some knowledge to which he wasn't entitled. What would he do after he had
read it? Would he return it to the person who had written it? He
didn't know. It could easily have been written by one of the boys.
They did write letters. Sometimes as an exercise, but more often to
girls whose affection they were trying to win. He held the envelope
and looked at it steadily under the desk. His neighbour saw and made
a sign.

He was no longer alone in this knowledge. The neighbour saw the
letter and whispered quietly. It isn't yours, the neighbour whispered.
The boy was indignant. He held the envelope more tightly. I'll bet
my life it isn't yours, the neighbour insisted. The boy was more angry.
What would you bet? he whispered back. What would you bet?
Let me see the address, the neighbour whispered. Bet first, the boy
said. If you're so sure it isn't mine, then bet. Make a bet. Why couldn't
he bet if he was so sure it wasn't his? Who wrote it? the neighbour
asked. I mean, who must receive it? Did he write it to a girl, or was
he receiving it from a girl?

The neighbour was very curious about that. It was important. The
neighbour had never received a letter from a girl, and he feared this
boy might have been able to boast of greater success. And suppose it was
the same girl. If it turned out to be the same girl they were after, what
could he do? They took these things very seriously. It was their early
training in the jealous response. The neighbour looked on schemingly,
and the boy held the letter, smiling. He didn't turn up the side where
the address would have been written. The neighbour insisted. The
boy would not turn it on the other side. The neighbour was con-
vinced. It isn't yours, he whispered. Somebody had given it to him to
deliver. He knew that. It might have been the teacher. Sometimes the
teachers did that. They gave the boys letters to deliver, some addressed
to girls, and some to the head teacher. It was a common thing. The
neighbour smiled. Now he knew what it was all about. He had had
to do a similar thing before. The teachers sometimes asked a loan
from the head teacher, but they didn't know how to go straight to
him, and make the request. They wrote a note and sent it by the
boy. The boy knew the contents without reading, because the head
teacher had nothing to hide. He would reply in cash. He would give
the bearer a shilling or two, telling him to deliver it to the teacher.
It was often done. Such was this note. The neighbour laughed. The

boy was angry. He dangled the letter at the neighbour. You'd like to know who it's from. How he would have liked to know! He would know if he wanted to. If he wanted very badly to know then he could know. You would have to say, sir. If you said sir, then you could know. The neighbour looked on angrily. He wasn't sure. Suppose it wasn't a note to the head teacher. Suppose it did come from a girl. It didn't matter. Sometimes boys did that. They wrote letters to themselves. That was it. Now he knew. That was it. He had written it to himself. That's why he couldn't turn the other side. He was afraid the handwriting might be detected. What a silly trick! The neighbour was enthusiastic. You wrote it to yourself. That's it. You wrote it to yourself. The boy was angry. He didn't like that kind of insult. He grew very angry. He hadn't written it to himself. That was a lie. He knew it. He didn't mind the lie, but he was hurt that anyone should think that of him. He had never done such a thing in all his life, and he never would. His neighbour got excited. He saw the boy was angry. That's what it is, he insisted. You've written it to yourself. The boy had to retaliate. He had to find a reply that would sting. I'll show you who it's from, if you want to see. What should he do? He had to do something in the extreme. Who? The neighbour insisted. Your sister, the boy whispered. It's from your sister, and if you want to see what she's got to say you can. It's all in the family, I and all. I'm in the family too. The neighbour was quiet. He boiled with insult. His sister! He knew she hadn't written it. He didn't know for certain whether his sister knew this boy, but he didn't think she would write him a letter. Or would she? You never could tell with a sister. Sisters had their own life, and they might be as anxious for something in one direction which similarly excited your desire in another. You couldn't tell. But he didn't like the idea of his sister's name being dragged into this. The boy insisted. I can show you if you really want to see. He dangled the letter under the desk. The neighbour's blood boiled. He hadn't spoken since the boy had mentioned his sister. He sat quiet and stern looking down at the letter. The boy played with it under the desk. Look. Look. Have a peep. Your sister has a fairly good handwriting. And when everything is said and done she isn't a bad piece. He couldn't stand it any longer. He would report the matter, or box the boy in his ear. The teacher of class 5 had not returned, and the other teacher was too far away. He didn't want to get up and walk over to the other side. The head teacher might see, and that would mean a lot of explanation.

He looked down angrily at the letter. The boy was in full command. He knew no one could reply to such a charge. It was a charge. When you told a fellow you knew his sister in a certain way things always went badly afterwards. Boys didn't like the idea of their sisters being talked about. They would talk about other boys' sisters. But you mustn't ever say a word about theirs. It hurt. It hurt terribly. The boy knew he had hurt, and he couldn't stop hurting. I'm not so bad for a brother-in-law. After all, what have you got that I haven't got? I've got brains and beauty. What more could your sister want? I can give her everything. Everything. She'll want for nothing with me. He whispered softly. The neighbour was enraged. He watched the letter under the desk. The boys buzzed. No one seemed to notice what was happening between them. The others in class 5 were busy discovering who the shadow king was. The talk got around. And what was all this talk about slave? He watched the letter closely. The boy's thoughts seemed to stray. Now was his chance. He would snatch it. Now he would know whose it was. Was it from his sister? He doubted it. It was from one teacher to another. He was sure. Probably the teacher of class 5 had asked him to deliver it to the head teacher. The suggestions flew wild in his head. Now he would know. The words knocked about. Sister. Teacher. From teacher to teacher. Sister. From teacher to teacher. He was overcome with anger and curiosity. From teacher to teacher. He snatched at it. There was a noisy tumble on the bench.

The head teacher had seen. He looked up from his little black book searching in the corners of the school for the teacher of class 5. The boy walked up slowly with the letter. He delivered it, and the head teacher motioned him to his seat. The letter lay on the desk. No one seemed to notice. They saw the boy deliver the letter and return. Perhaps it was just another of its kind. From one of the teachers to the head teacher. The buzzing simmered like a prayer said quietly by all in the church.

The head teacher closed the small black book and opened the envelope. Two photographs fell from it. His lips curled back as lips do after one has had a dose of castor oil. You wait with an expression of bewildering disgust for the purge of that unspeakably unwanted thing. He could not understand what had happened. He looked closely, looked away and looked again. Castor oil. You did not want to take it. But they said it was good. You were forced to take it. Now you were sick in the stomach, and would remain sick until the purge was complete. He looked at the two photographs. The first was a photograph of his wife sitting beside a man whom he could not recognize. The man's face was buried in her lap while she smothered the back of his head and neck with a kiss. He dropped the photograph quickly and turned to the other which showed a white couple. He was sure that was not taken in the island. It was impossible. They were naked and the position was obscene. Castor oil! Castor oil! On the back of the photograph with his wife a note read: 'I hope the boss doesn't see this, Barbara.' The other was as brief but printed in pencil so that the characters revealed no identity: 'As we were last evening, Stephen.' The lips kept their curl of disgust. It seemed that curl would be permanent. Castor oil! When would the purge come? The horror of its failure to come! The head teacher sat with his head in his hands querying the name Stephen. Which Stephen could it be? The teachers of class 4 and 5 carried the same first name; and neither the photographs nor the notes were helpful. Only one thing seemed clear and that was the name the class 4 teacher had written on one side of the envelope: Mr. Slime. The head teacher read the name again, and as he read, it seemed some other part of him was forming the judgment. Then he looked in the direction of class 5 and noticed that Mr. Slime was absent. The judgment was complete.

The boys buzzed. The shadow king. The pennies. The slave. They were unaware of what had happened. The head teacher was sitting with his head in his hands as he had so often done. He must have been thinking of the boy he had beaten that morning. He didn't seem sure of himself after he had beaten that boy. They buzzed. Everything would be alright. They would work on the pennies when they got home. There was no need to worry about the old woman who talked about the slave. She was doting, poor soul. The boys who had quarrelled about the letter were quiet. The boy confessed it wasn't from the other's sister, but he didn't say what it was about. He didn't know, and he kept his ignorance secret. The other was more at ease. It was for the head teacher. That was clear. No fuss was made. When the teacher of class 5 returned, the head teacher would deal with him. He would give him the money he had requested. There was nothing strange about that. The shadow king. The pennies. The slave. The letter. Everything was quiet. The buzzing was quiet. The head teacher sat quiet. No one knew what was taking place in his head. The teacher of class 5 had not returned. He raised his head slyly from the palm of his hands and surveyed the school. He was sure no one knew what had happened. The letter was sealed, and he assumed rightly that the boys had not seen the contents. He wondered for a moment how they had come by it, then his thoughts strayed to something else, and in a moment came back to the question of the others' knowledge. He wasn't sure what he felt. He was immediately glad to think that no one knew what had happened and he was at the same time overcome by the shock and strangeness of his knowledge. He hadn't given his wife a real thought. He would get round to that some time. For the time being, these seconds that seemed to move and yet stay steady, he was concerned about the others' knowledge. He consoled himself with the thought that no one knew, and yet it was uncertain consolation, for the knowledge was unbearable. It ran like a wild rabbit through and across his mind. The boys were buzzing and they seemed comfortable in their buzzing. The teacher of class 5 had not returned but the others were fiddling in one way or another. In these surroundings he was alone with this knowledge of what had happened. He wished that the teacher would return. He would have somebody to share the knowledge. And suddenly he wished that the teacher would not return since he was afraid of what he would do. What would he do?

For the first time the question presented itself. He treated it rather shabbily. His mind had flitted again to the question of the others' knowledge. He knew no one had seen what the letter contained, no one in the school. He knew they didn't know, and he was afraid of that double knowledge. He didn't know what to do with it. It was like a sore burning the flesh of the neck where the collar rubbed. This knowledge that the others didn't know what was going on. If they knew, if he knew that they knew, he could dismiss the school quickly and be left alone to think his way out. But they didn't know and he was waiting to see what would happen to himself. He felt a strange impotence of action. He wanted the teacher to return, and in the same train of thought he wished he wouldn't. He held his head in his hands. He wanted to think of his wife, but that thought was too big for the occasion. If someone had told him that this strange impotence of thought and action seized a man in such a predicament he would have laughed. He would have thought to go straight for his wife or the teacher or both. He would have dealt with the matter like a strict and sensible school master. Now he couldn't. He sat quietly with his head held down hearing the buzz of the boys. It grew quietly, sank quietly and started to grow again. It might have been a captivity of flies arranging their consolation. The boys were examining the pennies. He looked at them for a second through the space of the fingers. They didn't know. He knew they didn't know, but he was uncertain of the meaning of his knowledge. The boys were grinning quietly, but he knew they weren't grinning at him. They couldn't do that because they didn't know what was happening. He thought he might call the boy who had brought the letter. Perhaps he would say how he had come by it. He raised his head and dropped it again. He would not call the boy. He had seen what was inside and that was all that mattered. The boy might become curious. He felt for his actions. He didn't know what to do next, but he knew something had to be done. He wished the teacher would come back. Obviously the teacher didn't know what had happened. He couldn't have known that the letter was delivered to him. If he came back he would call him. He would ask him questions which might help him to understand what was going on between his wife and this man. He raised his head and quickly dropped it again. There was nothing to understand. It was clear that something had been going on between them. 'Don't let the boss know.' He repeated the words, lingering on boss. There was nothing more to know. He had to do something. For a moment his anger boiled, simmered and almost as sudden sank deep into him. He couldn't even be angry for as long as he would like. What would he say to his wife? That was too big to be dealt with now. He had to deal with the teacher first. Between himself and his wife it was a private affair. The teacher made it wider. The teacher extended the limits to include the school, the boys, the village itself. What was he going to do? He rubbed his knuckles into his eyes and looked up slyly through the spaces of the fingers. It was a rotten day. That boy he had beaten, and now this envelope. He felt afraid of what would happen next. He had never known the feeling before. Something was going to happen. Something you were sure of, but could not foresee. He tried to recall what he was thinking when the boy snatched at the envelope and he saw. He couldn't. That part of him, it seemed, had come to an end. He didn't know what he would do now, or what would happen in a minute or two, but he was sure something was brewing.

Something was undermining him. Until a minute ago he was strong and solid. Now he was being undermined. He couldn't act, because

he didn't know what to do. He tried to think of what he might do.
It wasn't always like that. Formerly he had the ready response, the
manufactured word or phrase, and the cultivated face. He had always
had these for any occasion. He had set them against the teachers, the
ministers, the inspector. These were the things they had to deal with.
Now these had retreated. They had all become inoperative. It was
almost like being a boy again. He was like one who had had a lucid
interval and thought he saw for the first time everything that had
missed him through the pile of years. Everything was smooth, steady
and clean till he saw the photographs. Now the world had turned
upside down. He was like a little boy trying to ask for time to prepare
his answer. He had beaten that boy this morning as a school master
should beat a boy. He had met the inspector as a school master should
meet an inspector. He had spoken and worked as a school master
should on Empire Day. He had done it today as he had done it for
years. It was like passing your hand over your collar. It was thought
and done in the same breath. Now that fluency of action was lost.
Something had undermined him. He was like an idiot who argued
passionately that he had remained the same age throughout his life.
He didn't know what to do. It was unbearable. He looked in the
direction of class 5, but the teacher had not returned. He dropped his
head and tried to think. Of course it would have been easy to drop
the matter. No one knew about the envelope. No one except the teacher
and himself. He could have got out of it easily if he and the teacher
were involved, and not his wife. It was very difficult to leave her out
of his considerations. She was too big a thought for the occasion. If
he didn't think about her yet, it was simply because she was too big.
She had to be left last. He would talk with the teacher. He would try
to get rid of that first. He would ask him for an explanation, and warn
him that nothing of the kind should ever happen again.

His thoughts strayed.

That was not possible. He couldn't commit himself to a teacher in
that way. He knew what teachers were like. You couldn't trust a
subordinate. He didn't know whether this teacher might not have
made a joke of the affair. He might relate the whole story to the others.
The head teacher was in a pickle. He didn't know what to do about
the old girl, his wife, so he asked to hush it up. He couldn't risk it.
He knew teachers. He was one himself. He had abandoned that course
of action. Whatever he did, he had to remember too what his duty

was. He was not only a teacher in that school. He was the village teacher. He couldn't encourage the kind of immorality which this teacher represented. In the village they trusted him. The simple villagers sought his advice on everything. Marriage, religion, sin, work. . . . He told them what to do and invariably they did what he advised. They made allowances for his shortcomings such as drinking. They accepted that as something one in his position might do, but it did not interfere with his work. It did not interfere with their respect for him. They respected him as one who knew their ways. He had grown up in the village. A poor boy who had done well. He was liked as an assistant teacher. He satisfied the authorities, and he had won the villagers' admiration. He read the lesson at the big church, and on occasions he buried the dead. The supervising minister was fond of him. He was a public man in that simple sense. The villagers had no power. They were weak in everything except their trust. And he couldn't undermine that trust. If they knew that he had taken this teacher's immorality with leniency their attitude to him would have been different. It was strange. They respected in the highest degree everything that they violated. Many of them were immoral in the sense this teacher had been, but they seemed to treat their own immorality as a bad habit. It was something peculiar to themselves. When someone like a teacher proved immoral in the same way, they were unforgiving. The village head teacher represented the unattainable ideal. He had to live in a way which they admired and respected but did not greatly care to follow. He had to think of them in any decision he made. He had accepted the responsibility that went with their implicit trust, and he could not now deny it. If he did so he would have to admit that he was a coward or a hypocrite. He gave them the impression that he was what they expected him to be. If he failed to live up to their expectations he would immediately become one of them.

Everything was simple till he saw the photographs. Teaching, eating, loving, hating. He did them all by a kind of habit. Now he had to decide. He had to do something, and he didn't know what it was. He shook his head in his hands and wondered. Was it so with other people? Did these things happen to others? They had gone on living, smooth and clean like a train on the line. And suddenly there was a hitch. Something went wrong that caused a kind of explosion in the head and made tremendous difficulties out of what had hitherto seemed a commonplace. What was he going to do?

He shook his head again. He hoped a similar thing wouldn't ever happen to one of these simple villagers. If he, a school master, a big school master, as they regarded him, couldn't meet this emergency, how would they? How could a villager be expected to get a ready response, a new tactic for a problem which had never appeared before? Something big, something that undermined the roots of life as this difficulty seemed to undermine his self-assurance. His mind focused the problem again. What was he going to do? He had decided once more. He would report the matter to the inspector. He reached that decision in sheer desperation. He was sorry, but there was nothing he could do. He knew what the inspector would say. There was no doubt about that. The teacher of class 5 had had the last of his prosperity. A violation of this kind was corrected by one kind of punishment. He thought for a moment of the teacher's reaction. He couldn't help himself, he couldn't prevent the stray of his thought. He thought of others in a way he hadn't done before. Perhaps it was the terror of his knowledge that made him bring others within the limits of his decisions. He thought of the teacher. He looked in the direction of class 5, but the teacher had not returned. What would he say to the inspector? It was difficult to decide. The teacher would not be alone in his punishment. He was married. He had a wife and three children. They would have to share that punishment. He knew that much about the teacher's private life, and that knowledge carried with it a kind of condemnation. What right had this young man to think of carrying on with any other woman? He deserved whatever judgment the inspector would pass. And he knew what that judgment would be. Dismissal. Nothing short of dismissal. He was sure. And he was sure he deserved it. He thought of the photographs and he tried for a moment to think of his wife. But always she seemed a little too big for the occasion. She had to be left last. He would tell the inspector.

He had made up his mind. His thoughts strayed again. He had made up his mind till he remembered the teacher's wife and children. His discharge involved his wife and children, and they were in no way responsible for the teacher's blunder. They had nothing to do with his guilt. Yet they would have to share his misfortune. He couldn't go through with that decision. He couldn't. The teacher's punishment would be their punishment as well. He couldn't bear to think of it. Perhaps he had better drop the matter. He would drop it. His thought strayed again. He couldn't. He would report it to the inspector, but

he would put it leniently. He would ask the inspector to deal leniently
with the matter. He would make an example of the teacher which
would have been a kind of punishment that excluded his wife and
children. Perhaps it would have affected his promotion. That too
might affect his wife and children, but less drastically. He thought
again. He couldn't take the inspector for granted. You never could
tell. He distrusted the inspector. He distrusted the smooth, clean smile.
He didn't know what the inspector would do. He had no influence
in such matters. The inspector might applaud. He might let escape
what seemed a confidence, but you couldn't trust him. In a matter
which related to his work he was aloof. He wouldn't consult or be
influenced by the wishes of a school teacher. They were all like that.
All English officials were like that. He knew them. They knew how
to get along. They knew how to get their work done. They smiled.
They were civilized. They behaved decently towards the people with
whom they had to work. But they would never admit confidence in
a matter that related to their work. These English officials had an
almost inhuman sense of the right distance to keep in human relations.
It was noticeable the way they listened. You could never say you had
their confidence. Never. They were listening and as they listened they
learnt. In such a matter he was on the side of the teacher. If he attempted
to safeguard the teacher's interest, he would certainly find the inspector
against them both. You could never tell. This inspector hadn't shown
himself different from those he had known in the past. He thought of
the teacher's family, and he shook his head again. He would drop the
matter. For their sake he would drop it.

His mind focused the problem more sharply now. He was beginning
to see more clearly. Could he really trust the teacher? Could he really
hope that the matter would end there? Was it safe to trust one who
was so emotionally unstable. It might happen again. A similar difficulty
might occur with another teacher. What would he do then? He would
have to act in the light of his present decision. What was good for one
must be good for all. And he had to think of himself above everything
else. His power in the village. His authority in the school. What would
he do? His mind had become more undisciplined now. He was farther
away from a decision than he was when he started to think of one. He
peeped through the spaces of his fingers and saw the boys. They
buzzed happily. They hadn't a clue what was going on. Was it like that
with other people? Life went on flowing happily or stupidly like a sea,

while here in one spot something tremendous was happening. The buzzing grew steadily. Here is the king, one boy was explaining. The king lives here. The queen lives here. The buzzing soared. In this room the shadow king . . .

He blew his whistle and silence was present like a man taking an authoritative look round the room. As quickly it was gone.

*　　　*　　　*

I know what it is, one boy was saying, I know what it is. He spoke very well. The old woman isn't an old fool. She knew what she was saying. She was a slave. We're all slaves. The queen freed some of us, but most of us are still slaves.

The boys listened intently as the buzzing soared in another corner. The head teacher sat quiet, his hands stuck against his forehead.

She wasn't a fool, that old woman. She has a good memory. When Lucifer, that is the devil, when the devil was sent from his garden, he carried with him a lot of angels. The angels who were on his side said they would go with him, and they left heaven for the earth. That is where we are living now. It was a terrible sight the way they walked out of that garden. But they said they didn't care. They would get along all right without God. The boys listened. It was like a Sunday School lesson. They came down to earth, the boy went on, and they made a home here on the earth. But it didn't last long. They had got so used to the garden that they couldn't tear themselves away. They thought they could, but they were wrong. The garden was like something in the blood. When something is in the blood you can't get it out unless you take out the blood. They couldn't manage very well on the earth because they couldn't get rid of the garden. The garden was in the back of their minds all the time. They tried to turn their backs against it, but they couldn't turn their memory. It was deep, deep in them. And then they got very sad. They couldn't stand one another. The sight of one another on the earth made them sick. And it wasn't long before they started to fight. That was the beginning of war. The angels of the devil who were the first men couldn't stand the sight of one another on the earth. They couldn't help themselves. It wasn't that they wanted to kill one another. It wasn't that at all. It was simply that they couldn't help themselves. And from that day war never stopped. They passed it on to us from generation to generation. And the older the earth became the more

we got to hate the sight of one another. And the worse the fighting
became. Some of the angels said they would go back to the garden.
Others were ashamed. The devil said he would die first. He would die
before he submitted to returning. But God wouldn't have them back.
He said he wouldn't have them back until they had all repented. They
had to say they were sorry. They had to become slaves in a sort of way.
It was all right for those who didn't want to stay on the earth. They
could do it so easily, but the others found it very difficult. They couldn't
do it so easily. They were slaves. Soon they all became slaves. You see,
they had it deep in them to get out of the garden. They did want to
see something new, something different. But when they saw the something they couldn't stand that. It gave them a kind of delight to know
that there was something else. If ever God drove them out again they
would have somewhere to go. But they were afraid. They couldn't
stand being alone on the earth. They wanted something to hold on to.
And they all agreed to go back. They say they would repent and go
back. And they were terribly ashamed. They were ashamed because
in a way they didn't want to repent. They feel they could manage. But
it was the garden. They couldn't get the garden out of their minds.
And the more they thought of the garden, the more ashamed they
became. And the more they repented. They were all slaves. And they
made us slaves too. The queen freed some of us because she made us
feel that the empire was bigger than the garden. That's what the old
woman meant. The queen did free some of us in a kind of way. We
started to think about the empire more than we thought of the garden,
and then nothing mattered but the empire. But they have put the two
of them together now. The empire and the garden. We are to speak
of them the same way. They belong to the same person. They both
belong to God. The garden is God's own garden and the empire is
God's only empire. They work together for us. God save the king
who will help us to see the garden again. That's all we have to think
of now, the empire and the garden. But the old woman wasn't wrong.
We are slaves. We are still slaves to these two. The empire and the
garden. And we are happy to be slaves. It isn't the same as being a
prisoner. Nobody wants to be a prisoner. You aren't free when you're
a prisoner. But it is different when you are a slave. When you are a
slave of the empire and the garden at the same time, you can be free
to belong to both. And you can be free to be ashamed of not thinking
enough about them. The more you think of them, the more you are

ashamed, and also the less you think of them the more you are
ashamed. My mother who is a Sunday School teacher has explained
it well. There is nothing for us to do, she tells me, but rejoice in our
bondage. That is what she calls it. She doesn't say slave. She says
bondage. When the time comes we shall be taken out of the bondage
by what she calls grace. That's not a girl she's talking about. It's
something else. It's a sort of salvation. That's what she says sometimes. Salvation through grace. We're all going to the garden again,
free again, and especially those who here on earth belonged to the
empire. We'll be free again. The others will perish. Those who refuse
to go back to the garden because they are stubborn, they will perish.
And not only through fire. My mother says it's loneliness. They will
be lonely in a way they can't stand. The loneliness will make them
giddy. Giddy and sick. Because they were stubborn. You can't live
without God, my mother says, you can't unless you're prepared to be
lonely and sick. And that's more than an ordinary man can stand.
Those who choose the garden will find things different. They'll be
slaves all right, as the old woman says. They will be slaves, but everything will be better and easier. Very much easier.

The boys had listened patiently. They knew the other's mother
was a Sunday School teacher, and they felt she spoke with some
authority. They were a little afraid. They agreed that if things were
as the boy said, it would be better to belong to the empire and in the
end get back to the garden. After all there was nothing to lose by
belonging to the empire. They were all very poor. And moreover the
empire made them put on things like parades. They enjoyed the
parades and the flags and the speeches. It made them feel a little more
important than they were. Listening to a speech from the inspector!
It gave you a feeling of being grown-up, and when you marched and
saluted you felt like a soldier. A real soldier. They would choose the
empire and the garden. There was nothing wrong with them. And
they had everything in their favour. Flowers. Flags. Pennies.

*   *   *

The head teacher dropped his hands and stood. He stood alone on
the platform with the whistle held between his lips. Everyone knew
he would soon be ready to dismiss the school. It was one o'clock. It was
very hot in the school, but the boys had grown used to the heat.
They wiped the shirt sleeves across the brow, and scooped the sweat
from their necks without effort. They sat quiet, trying to escape the

head teacher's glance. He was standing with his back turned to the school. He looked out across the village. When he shifted as though he were going to turn they dropped their eyes. They didn't want their eyes to meet his. They couldn't bear to look him straight in the face. There must have been something defiant or too intimate in a look that went straight and strong from eye to eye. That was true of the boys as well as the teachers. They seldom looked one another straight in the face. When they spoke their heads met level, but not the eyes. Perhaps it was so with everyone. Sometimes a teacher might have been staring blankly down the corridor where a boy with his back turned slouched over exercise books. The boy was engrossed. He watched the exercise books or marked them with concentrated purpose. The teacher didn't notice. Something was happening in his head, and he stared blankly waiting for it to pass out. But suddenly the boy might look up, and catching the teacher's eye would feel captured. He had done nothing wrong, and it was not his intention to do anything wrong. He had simply been seen by the teacher. He must have felt in his engrossment that he was alone. There couldn't have been anyone there to take notice of him. But suddenly his concentration collapsed, and he saw that he was seen. He did nothing wrong, but that didn't matter. He was seen by the teacher. It didn't happen between the boy and the teacher only, because it had nothing to do with authority. It also happened between teacher and teacher. One teacher would go up smilingly to another and remark that he noticed he was seen. Doing what? Nothing. He simply noticed that the other had seen him. He asked what was wrong. He was sure nothing was wrong, but he thought it strange that the other was watching him. What was he thinking about him? The other would be puzzled. He had seen him but he hadn't noticed him. He did see him standing there, but there was nothing wrong. They smiled and parted, but the teacher who thought he was seen wasn't at ease. Deep down he felt uneasy. He had been seen by another. He had become a part of the other's world, and therefore no longer in complete control of his own. The eye of another was a kind of cage. When it saw you the lid came down, and you were trapped. It was always happening. Sometimes when you stood alone in the public square where the buses parked, and the people went to and fro buying nuts, looking around, you got the feeling sometimes that they were looking at you, and if you were too sensitive you wanted to hide. Or in the cinema before the lights were dimmed. You walked down the carpeted path with all those people sitting above and around you, sitting snugly and critically between their ears and their neighbours. It seemed the whole cinema like the public square had turned into one enormous eye that saw you. A big cage whose lid came down and caught you. Often you would wait in the foyer till all the lights were put out. You would wait till it was too dark for anyone to see, and you stalked down the carpeted path, a black shape among black shapes. The feeling was good. There was something absolutely wonderful about not being seen. You could thrust your arms out or scratch without delicacy. It was the same in the school lavatory when you closed the door. The little cubicle became a black patch, and you made faces at the wall, or recited quietly the poems you had learnt by heart. You rearranged the lines in your head, so that each couplet would have a neat end rhyme. No one could see or hear you, and you mumbled your freedom away. The things you would say and do. The things you could say and do! The darkness brought a strange kind of release, and you wished secretly in your heart that darkness would descend on the whole earth so that you could get a chance to see how much energy there was stored in your little self. You could get a chance to leave the cage. You would be free.

The head teacher's back was still turned to the school, and he stared up at the church steeple. Silence was there in the school, but it seemed uncertain now. The boys shifted a little. The buzzing was very quiet, almost inaudible. The head teacher's body seemed to fill the space of the window where he stood with the whistle held between his lips. He looked very tired. For a moment it seemed that he had escaped from the cage of the eye. Anyone could look at him, and it didn't matter. His back suggested an inhuman bigness. In this school the other's eye was not a cage for him. The school seemed so little. It was very difficult to tell what he was thinking now. Perhaps the question had simply stuck there in his mind. What shall I do? The teacher of class 5 had not returned. What would he tell him? With his back turned as powerfully against the school, he looked like a bully. Perhaps he was a bully. You couldn't look at him even when his back was turned. He wasn't something you respected. He was a big bully. You feared him. You couldn't look at his back because you were afraid. He looked very tired. What should he do? What should he do?

He blew the whistle and there was complete silence. He blew it again and the boys stood. He had turned to face them. He blew it again, and they all sat. They knew the orders. They were trained. Each pipe of the whistle meant something, and they knew that something. They were well trained. There were times when he would blow it again and again until they had understood what he wanted them to do. They stood and sat till he dismissed them. They couldn't leave till they had interpreted the instructions of the whistle faultlessly.

He blew it again, and they all stood. It seemed the proceedings had come to an end. It was usual for him to make a speech. But he looked too tired. He walked to the edge of the platform and spoke a few words. He asked them not to shout along the streets, not to cross before looking left and right, and not to be rude to anyone older than themselves. Then he asked them in a very tired voice to remember what the inspector had said. He was pleased with the parade. Barbados would always be Little England. He asked them to remember that, and let it be a feather in their caps. Everyone was puzzled by his look. He looked so tired and sad. And when he spoke he seemed to do so with difficulty. Something was wrong, but no one knew. They were greatly relieved when he took the whistle from his lips and said quietly 'Let's sing the school song.'

The teacher of music took up his position on the platform. He signalled the school, and the voices soared gradually. They marched as they sang, keeping time with their feet and awaiting the signal to depart. The voices rang louder as the march gathered momentum. They turned left and right in the direction of the doors and marched in single file towards the school yard. The teacher of class 5 stood at the door as the last ranks of his class filed past. He had just returned. He looked in the direction of class 4 wondering what secret his colleague, the other Stephen, was inviting him to share. He had seen the contents of the other's pocket, but the dead weight within him that urged an evacuation had forced him to leave before securing the evidence. He seemed as calm as ever. Nothing had happened to him. The head teacher's back was turned. He looked out into the school yard as he always did when the boys marched out. The teacher of class 5 walked towards the platform. He was going to say why he had stayed away so long. It was a little longer than usual. But nothing was wrong with him. He had neither missed nor discovered anything. He waited patiently for the head teacher to turn his back.

They were alone in the school.

In the school yard the boys were examining the pennies. They straightened their caps and the shirts in their pants. The flags flew wild. The palm tree swayed left and right, and the church steeple seemed to listen as the wind carried their chorus across the village and into the sea.

4

Old Man: Ma.

Old Woman: Yes, Pa.

Old Man: 'Tis a good round year come an' gone since we feel those floods, an' I says to myself sittin' here how the children will have something to tell they children the way these houses walk all 'cross the water. 'Twus a sight as never ever want to leave you whether you want it or not, the way the water went rolling down the gutter with tots an' tins singin' a song o' halleluja on top.

Old Woman: Pa.

Old Man: Yes, Ma.

Old Woman: Does you do it deliberate when you says things to vex my spirit? 'Cause when you talk as you talk just now you make me to remember the song the children sing, One two three, the devil's after me, four five six, he got a lot of tricks, halleluja, halleluja. Before cock-crow this big bright Monday mornin' you wus sayin' something 'bout the landlord how he wus gettin' old, an' praps he may soon make up his bed an' die, though it ain't in my power or your own to say, an' then you go on to say how we don't know what sort o' person the new landlord will be 'cause there ain't no more sons in the Creightons. 'Twus before the cock crow that you says that, an' now out of a clear sky you remember the way you remember to tell me 'bout what come an' gone ever since a whole full year. Tell me to me face, Pa, does you do it for purpose? Does you do it for purpose, Pa?

Old Man: You know full well I ain't that sort o' man, Ma. I ain't that sort o' man or ever wus, but I sees sometimes how a thing change, an' when you least expectin' to besides; you see how that thing change there in front of yuh eyes, an' I wonder to myself if 'tis a change for the better or worse. Ever since we get the news 'bout the schoolmaster Mr. Slime I feel a sort o' change happen, an' though I ain't got the words to repeat what's in my mouth I feel it all the same. They says he wus the best teacher in the whole school from top to bottom, an' my heart hurt me to think what might happen to the children. It ain't everyone as got the gift to give a little learnin' an they says all of them that he had it. Now look what he go an' do. He open a Friendly Society an' a Penny Bank, an' in the twinklin' of an eye, Ma, before you says Jack Robinson, he has them all two both flyin'. A year before we never ever hear' bout such things, an' now there ain't a single soul in all Creighton's village who ain't in Society an' Penny Bank all two at the same said time. Everybody puttin' they pennies one by one week after week, an' only God knows what that sort o' thing'll lead to. An' on the back of it, look what he says he goin' to do next. Look what he say he goin' to do.

Old Woman: Pa.

Old Man: Yes, Ma.

Old Woman: Let 'im do what he says he'll do, an' may the Lord God Almighty go with him. You an' me, we's both member of Society an' Penny Bank, an' 'tis as much as to give thanks for, 'cause we reap the benefits more than once. So far so good, but I'll say this much an' no more, I'm a old woman with little or no sense, but sometimes it seem a sort of understandin' walk straight into my head. I look out over yonder in front o' me an' I see how the pigeon put out his wing an' fly better than any airplane in the big blue sky. An' that poor pigeon ain't got no engine, no oil nor no pilot to put him from here to there, yet he move wondrous in the air, too wondrous for my words or yours, or any of these who study big big books, an' I says to myself the works o' the Lord is really wondrous. 'Tis beyond the wisdom o' the wise, an' if the Almighty God can put His hand out to help a poor pigeon who ain't mean more to Him than your soul an' mine, I says to myself there ain't no reason why He won't deliver us in His own good time. I pray the grace of God go with Mr. Slime in all what he do or don't do, but bank or no bank, the riches o' this life is as naught in the sight of my Saviour. 'Cause this world's evil, Pa, 'tis very evil. That's all I got to say.

Old Man: P'raps what you says is so, p'raps not, but you always use to tell me a story, 'bout the man Moses, Ma, an' how he rise up when nobody wus least expectin' to take his people out the land of Egypt. I never ever forget to remember that story 'cause when you says how the frogs come from wherever they come from to plague King Pharaoh, I remember the way those crabs come out in the flood an' crawl all 'bout across the road an' if they'd get at us we'd all 'ave sing we praises. I remember it good, good, good, an' I says to myself sittin' here, p'raps Mr. Slime is another Moses come to save his people, 'cause I know him before he born an' after, runnin' 'bout here in his shirt tail. I follow him grow up. When I hear the way the men an' women welcome him the night he speak his speech 'bout the future an' what an' what the future got in store for us how we'd be much better off when he wus finish doin' what he say he would, I says to myself 'twus Moses all over again.

Old Woman: I don't understan' full well what it mean by politics an' so on, but I know good an' proper what Mr. Slime mean when he say what he say 'bout better house an' so on. You can't look up over yuh head but you see the old roof with a hole here an' a hole there, an' there be some, believe it or not, who ain't know where to step for the weakness o' the floor boards, all that I understan' perfect well, an' it don't take much tellin' me to make me understan'. What an' what he say 'bout better house is true, but it ain't in my right, Pa, it ain't in my right to put him side by side with Moses, 'cause Moses wus God elect. God call out Moses from wherever He call him to make him do what He make him do, an' that's as big a callin' any man can expect. But we ain't know 'tis the same with Mr. Slime though I wish him from the bottom o' my heart God's blessin'. You got to be careful, Pa, when you quote the holy scriptures, for the Lord Himself says there be some who will get up to prophesy in His name an' the name o' His chosen flock, but beware, beware how they come. The devil got more tricks than what John read 'bout, so you have a care how you call the name o' the Lord's anointed.

Old Man: 'Tis all the same, I says to myself, except that I didn't know Moses. I din't know him pers'nally 'cause I din't ever see him face to face, an' we all knows Mr. Slime in a sort o' way. We see him. You know as I do how he use to run 'bout here in his shirt tail an' you watch him grow up into a big big schoolmaster with everybody having the right respect for him. It ain't anything I got to tell you 'cause you know. We hear how the children talk 'bout him, an now we got the Penny Bank an' the Friendly Society. What more you want to know 'bout a man who grow up an' live from day to day under yuh eyes? What you think put it in his head to leave his post as a big schoolmaster—an' you know as I do what that mean—what put it in his head to give up all that an' start on this new thing? What could put it in his head to do it; an' look, look the way how the people take to him. There ain't one as not pay him the right an' proper respect for what he go an' do for them. They all got they bank book, no matter how little it is, an' they got they Society card, an' they know for certain if they in compliance they will get a decent an' proper funeral when 'tis time for them to go 'bout they business. An' that ain't all, 'cause he say in the speech he speak the other night how he goin' to make us owners o' this land. I couldn't sort o' catch my breath when I hear it, but 'tis a big thing to expect, an' they all tell him in turn, an' 'twus only fair o' them to tell him, that he wus they chief an' they'll follow him till they die. He wus they chief now an' for always, an' when the time come for them to put a man like themself to rule, 'twill be he, an' no one else.

Old Woman: Pa.

Old Man: Yes, Ma.

Old Woman: I ain't pay no min' to what you say 'cause I know deep in my heart of hearts that 'twill be emnity if that's his intention. He goin' to make you an' me owners o' this lan' an' he ain't say yet what he goin' do 'bout Mr. Creighton. 'Twill be emnity 'twixt them both, 'cause it ain't the nature o' earthborn to sit back an' give up all possessions an' not make a big to-do 'bout it. On my word, ol' as you think Mr. Creighton is, he won't have it; he ain't goin' to sit back an' let Mr. Slime chase him off the village like a lappy dog. He too great for that, an' if he see the worse comin' to the worse he'll sell it. I'll bet my life Pa, as I sittin' here, he'll sell it. An' it won't be Slime he sell it to, not 'cause he can't buy it but 'cause o' the emnity. He'll sell the village, Pa, an' 'twill be fightin' an' quarrelin' from them till Thy Kingdom Come, take it from me. It ain't the nature o' earthborn to sit back an' give up all like Christ would have do if he wus landlord an' he see trouble comin'. I says let's have a good roof an' make my heart happy. Why he don't help we to repair the house, nor buy the land. What we goin' do with it? Give me good shelter, but when it come to takin' from here to give there, much as I might like to own the spot o' land myself, I says be careful, an' I'd tell any man, Mr. Slime or else, who think 'bout doin' such a thing, to watch his steps.

Old Man: Who you think would be right in the sight o' God, which of them, Mr. Slime or Mr. Creighton?

Old Woman: It ain't in me to hurt my head 'bout such things. I not goin' to fly in God's face 'cause He knows best, an' what He think right ain't in my power to know. That's why I always says to you, pray, you just pray an' let the will o' the Lord have its way.

The old man sat at the window looking out at the shops and the people passing across the crossroads. The old woman lay deep in a long chair with a cane back and leather bound arms looking out through the half-door and on to the sky. They both smoked clay pipes, and when the smoke went up in thin puffs their eyes watered within the wrinkled skin of the lids. The old man's head was bare but for a fringe of white hair along the temples and down the back of the skull. It was of a beautiful brown colour, clean and smooth. His eyebrows were long and wiry, and the bones of his face showed hard and high under the skin. The old woman's head was almost naked too, but she kept it covered with a white cloth that fell smoothly from the top into a flare gathered up and fastened with a safety-pin at the back. They had been sitting together ever since the meal which they took at midday and which was called breakfast. The old man had fed the pigeons and made a mixture of oatmeal and water for the white goat. Then they sat down in their chairs and talked. The old woman reclined deep in the chair with her legs stretched out over a bench while the old man at the window let his chair lean back against the partition so that the fore legs were hoisted from the floor. They sat and talked for the rest of the day, breaking their talk with pauses that might last sometimes for an hour. The old woman dozed while the old man sat silent thinking. The day had changed colour sharply and the twilight falling over the houses suddenly turned to night. Sometimes someone rapped at the window to ask whether they wanted anything, but they had usually bought their food earlier in the day. The old woman went out in the morning to shop while the old man worked in the yard sweeping the goat pen and feeding the pigeons. Once a week, on Saturdays, the old man went to town to collect their pensions which amounted to a few shillings a week. But the goat gave milk part of which they sold, and the pigeons were always breeding. They seemed quite healthy and always looked quite happy except when there was some calamity like the flood.

Under the window and beside the narrow flight of steps that led to the door there was a small palm tree that bore small hard nuts the size of beads. The young branches came up in the centre like a closed umbrella, and the leaves in foliage opened like a fan. Neither leaves nor branches could now be seen in the night. In a corner on a mahogany table the oil lamp burned low. The window remained open as they talked and the wind coming through from both sides made the flame flick up and down in the chimney. The light fell dimly on the panes in the front door. On each pane there was painted on the inside a bird perched on a twig, and when they fell quiet they shifted their positions to take a look at birds on the glass. Outside the gas lamps at the corner burnt dully, and the men were sitting leisurely round the post talking about the new Friendly Society and the Penny Bank. The shops were still open, but they were empty. The shopkeepers sat behind the counters adding figures and arranging tins on the shelves. The old man brought the chair down level on the floor, and the old woman who hadn't spoken for some time jerked her body as if in surprise. The sudden noise of the chair legs on the floor gave her a shock, and she looked up at the old man as though she might rebuke him. Her eyes were weary and her expression tired. She took her legs from the bench and tried to sit upright in the chair. The old man stood, closed the top window and sat down again. He played with the stick he had taken from the window. He tapped it on the chair rungs and whistled a tune. Occasionally the old woman looked up at him as though she were disturbed by the noise. He stopped, waited till she had settled again in the chair, and went on mechanically with his tapping on the rung. He leaned the chair back again, and felt with the stick for his clogs. He pushed the stick under the canvas top and pulled the thick wooden soles along the floor in front of him. The old woman sat up erect and sucked her teeth. The wind came harder and the light went out. The old woman sucked her teeth again, and the old man felt for the matches in his pocket and lit it again. She seldom rebuked him, but when he did something that displeased her she made a face, or shot a glance which he understood, and he was obedient. He would stop whatever he was doing, or wait till he thought she wasn't paying attention.

Old Man: I wonder what time it would be now?

Old Woman: Look see if light on the hill.

The old man closed the bottom half of the window and walked with the stick he had taken from it across to the back door. In the distance he could see vaguely through the trees the lights from the brick building on the hill. The old woman shuffled towards the door and when she reached it the light in the landlord's yard went out. She walked back to the table by the old man's chair and took up the lamp. She brought the small mahogany table nearer the bed and placed the lamp on it. The old man remained at the door looking out through the night that hung thick and heavy over the wood. The shops were closed and the streets deserted. It was very quiet but for the whistle of the wind in the trees. The old woman dimmed the light and started to undress. The old man kept his position at the door with his back turned, feeling with his ears for the stir of the birds in the corner of the yard. The pigeons were tripping about in the coop, and he pushed his head farther out to sense the interruption. He often went out at all hours of the night to see whether rats had got into the coops, and whenever he heard the kind of shuffle they were making he felt for his stick. He stood quiet, listening. The old woman went on with her undressing. She heard the pigeons shuffling about, and she mentioned something about a dog. One of the boys had a new dog which strayed about at night. The old man put his head farther out and listened again. Something was forcing its way through the fence. A stone hit the fence and the animal barked. They were both relieved. It was a dog. The old man looked in the direction of the goat pens and listened for the animal's stir. Nothing happened, and he pulled his head farther within the house and went on looking out at the sky.

After removing the dress the old woman put on the night shirt and removed the other clothes from underneath. She held her hands under the night shirt fighting with the large safety-pins. She took them out slowly and lay them on the small table. Then the underwear fell to the floor. She put the underclothes under the pillow and removed her head tie. From fence to fence the other houses looked like empty black shapes in the night. The old man remained at the door, trying to put the objects together. Sometimes when he stood at the door at that hour his memory swelled up and the words came tumbling from his lips. There were so many things for him to remember. And in his later years he acquired a strange kind of anxiety. He seemed so frightened when he talked sometimes that the old woman would have to put her hand on his head to remind him he was not alone. She sat on the bed watching him at the door. She never liked him to stay there so long, but she had a feeling he liked to look out at the night, and she didn't want to deprive him that. Yet whenever she got a chance she would try to turn his attention from the darkness and the houses outside. Often in the morning he would tell her strange dreams he had, and she told him it was his fault. He had no right to spend the night looking out at the dark. He dreamt of silver and pork and sometimes of weddings all of which she said were bad. Weddings and pork in the dreams always meant death, and she warned him continually that silver was disappointment. But he always dreamt of these things, and particularly of silver. It seemed to her sometimes that he was using the same raw materials to produce different dreams. She sat nearer the bottom of the bed trying to attract his attention without disturbing him. She passed her hand over the white sheet and along the dry sacks that were spread under the sheet. She stood up again to raise the night shirt higher along her chest. The old man remained at the door. He was tapping the stick on the floor while the old woman fidgeted with the night shirt. She wanted to call him, because the wind was coming now and again and disturbing the light from the oil lamp. She walked across to the front door and tested the lock. It was safe. She unlatched the window and latched it again. He heard her but he didn't move. It was strange how she urged his obedience in the day. She would make a face or glance at him, and he understood. But in the night she gave him a kind of freedom. She persuaded and coaxed him and sometimes when he related things that seemed to frighten him, she held his hand and listened quietly. Moving toward the bed she knocked the table and one of the pins fell. She put it back, and shook the pillow. She held the underwear in her hands for a moment and whispered something. She put the underwear back and went on in a whisper. The old man glanced back and asked her to speak louder. She looked at the pins again, and started to talk with her face turned to the partition. The old man was listening.

Old Woman: 'Tis the same story, old yet ever new the way life go on, whatever they says. Time wus I had my arms with strength, but now fumble I must like rats in the ledge, an' 'twill be so with the young ones what come after. Day in day out I unbutton these said same underwear in the said same manner, an' my heart ain't hurt me when I hear how the young ones say what an' what they got, fastener an' zip an' V piece come so high up they can slip in an' out before you says Jack Robinson. In the olden days we ain't know 'bout those things, yet God's name be praise all the same, 'cause 'tisn't many as linger on so long after the 'lotted span. My eyes still open to see the light an' my heart to receive His goodness.

Old Man: Yet 'tis change all the same, Ma. I mean the fastener an' zip you talk 'bout. 'Tis change an' in the self-same manner I say to myself without tryin' to vex yuh spirit, in the self-same manner I say 'tis change with Mr. Slime.

Old Woman: Pa.

Old Man: Yes, Ma.

Old Woman: Would please me body an' soul if you'd give me a little rub just alongside the rib by the heart. The pains comin' an' goin' again an' again as they always does.

Old Man: I hope they ain't too bad, Ma.

Old Woman: I won't say so, not worse than any other time.

Old Man: 'Cause there ain't no more rub, Ma. Last night finish the Candian Healin' oil every drainin' drop.

Old Woman: Then let it stay till tomorrow, but shut the back door an' come in yuh corner soon, 'cause I want to put out the light.

The old woman had felt her way over to the side of the bed which she called her corner. She put a sack over her feet and lay quietly waiting till the old man had changed his clothes. He stood at the door shaking slightly as he rested against the stick. He turned his head in the direction of the landlord's house and looked out over the trees for a while. There was still a flicker of light coming from the windows of the house, but the light in the yard had gone out. The light in the house burned low on the mahogany table beside the bed, and the old woman lay with her face turned to the partition and away from the rest of the house. She was hoping the old man would soon undress and get into bed. When the pain twitched her she elbowed the spot on the left side of her body. The old man was still shaking as though he had seen something in the dark. He held his glance in the direction of the landlord's house. He was shaking as though he remembered something. He wasn't afraid to die, nor was he ever worried about pains, but in recent years he was caged by a kind of curiosity that made him shake and grow cold. The old woman couldn't understand it. When he trembled in bed at night as he related these experiences she would hold his hand and listen quietly. There was nothing to worry about, she would say, since the Lord knew best. She stroked his naked skull and soon they both would fall asleep. He closed the back door and limped across to the bed keeping the stick to support his weight. The old woman cleared her throat and eased her way further into her corner. The lamplight was brighter now, and he turned the wick down a little. There was a splutter along the wick and the light went out. It would seem he had turned the wick down too low. The old woman cleared her throat and said something about the matches, but he didn't pay attention. He put the stick on the floor and started to undress. He felt for his night shirt and removed the other clothes in the dark. The old woman cleared her throat again and lay on her back. It was black in the house. He laid the pants flat on the floor alongside the bed, and bundled his shirt and vest on top. Then he crouched under the sheet. His hands were cold and the old woman understood what was happening. He was thinking again about Mr. Slime and the land, or perhaps he had remembered something that happened when he was abroad. He shook quietly beside her and she waited till he said something. When he grew frightened he would speak, and she would hold his hand and listen. He eased himself round and she felt his body against hers shaking quietly under the sheet. She turned to face him. She put her hand on his head, and he cleared his throat and eased himself round again. The words had toppled from his lips.

Old Man: Would you say it matter after all, Ma, the strugglin' an' strivin' for this an' the next. 'Course you won't say so, but seems a time come when you want to feel different from what you feel, an' you begin to bother a bit 'bout what others says an' do, an' 'bout what they is. I look up over yonder there at the house on the hill, an' I wonder what it feel like to be big an' great.

Old Woman: You wus great once, Pa, wusn't you? As great as any man jack that jockey the face o' the earth. You'd riches an' all the rest the world has to offer, an' you ain't have a single God blessed thing to complain 'bout. Not one single thing in this God's world. You only got to think back a bit on yuh past, Pa, an' ask yourself in yuh heart of hearts if it ain't true. You wus well off once, Pa.

Old Man: 'Tis what I says sometimes to myself. Sitting here or there it come to me how things make a change. Time wus when money flow like the flood through these here hands, money as we never ever know it before. We use to sing in those times gone by 'twus money on the apple trees in Panama. 'Tis Panama my memory take me back to every now an' again where with these said hands I help to build the canal, the biggest an' best canal in the wide wide world. Me an' me sister dead an' gone, God rest her in her grave, an' as many as me memory can't hold. An' once I come as near as any man to winnin' the Duckey, an' the Duckey money is bigger than any Sweepstake money, an' you know what that mean. But they always say that if you come so near to winnin' the Duckey an' you ain't win, there be bad times for you 'head. But we wus great in them days as you says.

We know what it means to drive in coach an' buggie, an' whatever the Great do in the open air. We wus great as you says. We wus great alright.

Old Woman: 'Tis a next Panama we need now for the young ones. I sit there sometimes an' I wonder what's goin' to become o' them, the young that comin' up so fast to take the place o' the old. 'Tis a next Panama we want, Pa, or there goin' to be bad times comin' this way.

Old Man: 'Tis what Mr. Slime says. Two nights ago gone by he put it to them that he'd a plan in his head, an' if everything work out as he say it would work, there goin' to be big times comin' this way. He use a word call em'gration as what an' what he would do here an' now for this present generation. An' he give a full an' proper explanation of it all, what will happen an' what an' what they got to do. Says 'twus more people in this island than the lan' could hold or the law allow. 'Twus a high burnin' shame to put on a piece o' land no more than a hundred an' something square miles, that's as he call it, square mile, 'twus a shame as he say to keep two hundred thousand people on it. Then he give them all the facts an' figures as he understan' them, and they head start to swim with facts an' figures. You an' me an' all o' we he says when you put us together from top to bottom wus that amount of people, something hundred thousand, an' he says wus a record population for the size o' the piece of land anywhere in this God's world. An' he go on to say the only manner of way to deal with that sort o' thing wus to get rid o' some; an' since it ain't in your power or mine or his own nor right in the sight o' God to shoot them down, he says 'twus best to send them where there wus too much square mile for the handful o' people living there. An' 'tis as he say he will do.

Old Woman: 'Twill be a next Panama all over again. You'll go an' you'll come back an' they'll sit under the lamp-post an' say night after night what an' what they use to do. 'Twill be Panama again, Pa.

Old Man: Not this time, he says. This time, he says, 'twill be America, a lan' where he say there be milk an' honey flowin' as it use to flow in the ancient time. An' there an' then he give them a sort o' inside history of America. But he ain't call it by that name all the time. He christened it by a next name which he call the United States where they say money flow faster than the flood. 'Tis like Panama multiply seven times seven, an' that'll produce only God in Heaven knows what.

Old Woman: 'Twill be the same all over again, Pa. Money come an' money go, an' 'tis a thing that move through yuh finger as the said same water you talk 'bout. You take it from me, 'twill be the same.

Old Man: You makin' the mistake of your life, Ma. 'Twill be different. The States money goin' to be different 'cause of what Mr. Slime say. Says there ain't nothing to prevent you or me or any man Jack once he got the money, there ain't nothin' to stop him ownin' this lan'. An' the time is fast comin' when every man Jack will have belongin' to him the spot o' land his house on. That's as what he says an' he figures himself that 'tis time now to start the ball rolling.

Old Woman: Pa.

Old Man: Yes, Ma.

Old Woman: Seems to me you see yuh salvation in Mr. Slime. He's get a chance to go to yuh head like rum to a next man's, an' now you hear the shout you can't think or say nothing that ain't bound up with him. But I tell you already, an' I'll tell you again, I won't store no riches here on the earth, Pa. I won't store no riches here where we see when we least expectin' flood, famine an' all the pest'lence that God 'flict the earth with. It ain't no place to store riches, Pa. I won't worry my head 'bout the land 'cause 'tis always more trouble than profit, an' in yuh ol' age as you is an' me there be other things we got to think 'bout. Think 'bout the other land, Pa. You may think me stupid an' dotish when I tell you these things, but I ain't. An' tell me to besides, Pa, tell me from yuh heart straight to my face why you want to buy this land. What it is at the bottom of yuh heart or Mr. Slime heart or any of them that make you want to own it. Tell me that, Pa. Tell me the truth.

Old Man: I ain't know exact, Ma, an' Mr. Slime never so much as say except that he feel that you an' all the rest who been here for donkey years, 'tis time that we own it. If Mr. Creighton an' all the Creightons from time past can own it, there ain't no reason why we mustn't. That's as what Mr. Slime say. It ain't fair for you an' me to go on year in year out for more years than anybody can remember paying rent week after week. An' though 'tis a small rent, an' 'tis when all's said an' done a small rent, he say it ain't fair. 'Tis only right he say that every man should own his own piece o' land at some time or other. 'Tis the ambition o' every man to do that same said thing, an' he say it ain't only poor simple people like you an' me, but 'tis the way the big folk think too. They think it safe to own too, an' then he give a sort o' inside history o' some o' the nations, how they all make it they business before anything else to own the land they live on or the land nearest to them. 'Tis a lucky thing when you got a man at the head who know what he talkin' 'bout that's why I sort o' put some trust in him. 'Cause 'tis education that's his steering-wheel takin' him here an' there, an' those who ain't got it must show the right an' proper respect for those as has it in plenty, an' Mr. Slime is one o' those.

Old Woman: What I says to myself, Pa, an' what I tell you repeatedly time an' time again, is that you can't carry these things with you. I ain't had the privilege of poking my nose in the big big books which tell you everything you want to know, but I understan' in my own way that a man can't carry all these things with him. When you an' me make up our bed and get ready to go 'bout our business we goin' to leave all those things we own right here behind. An' others who we ain't know nothin' 'bout an' can't know 'cause we dead, those others goin' to come an' take an' keep it till they time come to do as we do. That's what I know without the help o' the big books. You an' the rest make yuh big big preparation for today an' you never ever give a single thought 'bout what goin' happen tomorrow. An' you don't care, but it seem to me that what goin' happen tomorrow though it's in front, it got somethin' to do with what happen-in' today. An' that's how I as look at it. An' I don't care who want land or who take land, the nations or anybody else, I'd only like to ask all o' them put together what they goin' do with it. When the time come for them to leave this here spot if they can take that said land they buy up, if they can take it in that six foot deep. You can't carry it with you, Pa, can you?

Old Man: 'Tis as what I says to myself sometimes but not for a single soul to know. You can't carry it with you, an' 'tis that that frighten me. It frighten the life out of me sometimes. When I sit there at that window or stan' in the half-door at night it come to me sometimes like the devil in hell self an' I want to run. Sometimes I talk an' talk to fill up the time an' in a kind o' way to turn my 'tention from what I see, but it come at me again all the time that same said thing you say. You can't take anything with you, an' I ask myself why. Why can't you take it with you, an' if it ain't matter what you do or not do since it all got to go in the six-foot hole. You r'ally think it ain't matter, Ma?

Old Woman: It ain't matter, Pa, 'cause 'twill all pass away in God's good time. You got to keep that at the bottom o' yuh min' an' don't forget it. You got to think o' tomorrow, 'cause it is a part o' today, an' before you do what you say you goin' to do today you got to ask yuhself what goin' to happen tomorrow. 'Tis tomorrow I think 'bout, Pa, tomorrow, when the clouds pass away an' the roll is call up yonder an' I'll be there in the said same company as my Lord an' Saviour Jesus Christ.

Old Man: Then it ain't matter, Ma, it r'ally ain't matter.

Old Woman: Nothin' ain't matter, Pa, but the blood of the lamb shed for your sins an' mine. 'Tis the only thing that matter. Seek your salvation in Christ.

Old Man: I not givin' in to anything you say, Ma, but sometimes to tell the truth I wonder what it feel like to die. That feelin' sometimes take hol' o' me an' shake me like a man. Some says 'tis like the old to want to die 'cause they live till they tired, an' there be some like you, Ma, who say it ain't matter 'cause they sort o' know what's in store for them on the other side. When yuh think 'bout it like that I confess you can lay yuh bones down an' rest an' don't give a thought to what happenin' or goin' to happen; but it ain't so with me, Ma, it ain't so at all. I get so frighten sometimes when I ask myself what next, an' I ain't see no answer comin' to help. Sometimes the feelin' want to stay with you like 'tis a sickness, an' you get away by pretending you doin' something else. You try to talk 'bout this that an' the next, an' if you young you go out an' drink an' live as the rest live 'cause 'tis the only way to get away, but when you ain't young you find after a time there ain't nowhere to go. An' I get so frighten sometimes, Ma. 'Tis as if you'd put a chil' in the wood alone an' ask the poor infant to fin' the way out. It ain't that I 'fraid to die, 'cause I see plenty die, but 'tis the thought what happen next, an' if nothin' goin' to happen then 'tis even worse the thought o' how you had to worry yourself 'bout what you ain't know. You don't worry an' yet you can't stop worry.

Old Woman: There ain't nothing to worry, Pa, there ain't nothin' to make you shake as you shaking. What you frighten 'bout except that you harden yuh heart an' turn yuh back. What you frighten at yuh age 'bout? What 'tis that frighten you so?

Old Man: I never ever before tell you this, Ma, an' I don't call to mind ever ever tellin' anybody else. But once 'twus a way back in

Panama I touch a dead man. He wus a frien' who we all know well, an' I don't know what get into me, but when he wus there in the box an' when no body wus looking, I move back the glass an' I touch him. An' when I touch 'im I feel as if 'twus a different person. He wus dead 'tis true, an' 'twus the same body I use to see day after day that shake my hand morning, noon an' night, but I had the feelin' I can't quite explain that 'twus a next person I touch. Not the man I did know so well. An' I wus frighten, Ma, I wus frighten in a way I wus never frighten before. That said same dead body in the box seem it wus a different person. I wus never frighten of myself like thinkin' I goin' off my head or anything like that, never ever; but when I touch that body an' I feel the other person I turn cold. An' it haunt me to know what sort o' person I would feel like if somebody did touch me when I dead. 'Twusn't the dead body, Ma, 'twus the other person that frighten me. An' it come into my head that if the person I feel wus there in the dead body, that person is always somewhere in the livin', an' it frighten me. It frighten me when I wonder now I'm alive an' got my senses what that other person is.' Tis a hell of a thing, Ma, to have to live with something inside you that you don't know. You never feel it, Ma. You never think you'll be afraid to die, Ma?

Old Woman: Pa.

Old Man: Yes, Ma.

Old Woman: Stop shakin' as you shakin' an' say to yuhself just for a little moment, say to yuhself you is a chil' again.

Old Man: Yes, Ma.

Old Woman: Close yuh eyes an' come close to me, Pa.

Old Man: Yes, Ma.

Old Woman: An' say after me:

> Gentle Jesus, meek and mild,
> Look upon a little child;
> In my little bed I lie,
> Heavenly Father, hear my cry,
> Should I die before I wake
> I pray the Lord my soul to take.

5

AT the same hour every morning the whistle screel shot up like an alarm through the rumbling of cart wheels. The whistle was a small metal instrument with a curved mouthpiece that fitted evenly under the lips, and a sunken throat carved open on one side. It contained a pea-shaped ball which, breath-driven, flew frantically from side to side and seemed to throttle the screel of the whistle. The echo cut across the air so that those who were loitering about made way for the cart. The volume increased, the rumbling greater than the whistle, as the cart came towards those for whom it would make the next stop. Someone shouted, 'Savory!' and soon it dashed sharply round the corner. Savory, a short dapper man who gripped the handles was partly hidden behind the body of the cart. His head stopped in line with the roof, but his legs through the space between the wheels were visible from the knees down. The villagers ran up to the stop and made a circle round the cart. Savory raised a side of the roof which remained up till the business was over. The mingled odours seeped out: hot salt loaves, cocoanut cakes, jam-puffs, fish cooked in oil, turnovers, drops: all local names which they had given this mixture of flour, water, lard, butter, salt, and various extracts of oil.

They buzzed round the cart sniffing and coughing and shouting in excitement. As the crowd thickened the voices rang louder and louder until no single order was clearly audible to Savory. Those who were farthest away from the cart couldn't see him at all and screeled loudest. Small boys slouching on all fours crept their way through the legs of the tall men and women, and emerged often unnoticed in the front row nearest the cart. Others tried to raise themselves to the men's shoulders and tripped over from shoulder to shoulder to the cart. The shouting lasted till the voices grew hoarse or the crowds lessened. Then it gave way to a joke or a comment which could be heard by anyone nearby. Savory dashed from side to side, a short, stout man drenched in sweat.

Someone said, 'Why the loaves so hard, Savory?'

And another, 'You fry the fish too brown, Savory.'

Then an old woman feeling her way through the crowd observed, 'Nothin' please you people.'

And Savory rejoined, 'You never speak a truer word.'

He hardly spoke except to confirm or advise, and only on matters directly relating to himself. Comments followed and jokes too: and often comment and joke were indistinguishable. Movement was freer now the crowd was smaller and the voices were more restful. Joke followed comment, comment joke, and soon both merged into the regular pattern of talk that filled the villager's life. Talk was humorous, censorious and often filled with gossip. Sometimes someone had read or heard about something published in the paper and would break the news to the others. It was usually unpleasant. Things were going from bad to worse, they would agree, and suddenly their talk was filled with a kind of manufactured indignation. They were seriously anxious about the times. They had the unlettered man's respect for the written word. There was something formidable, even sacred about a book. Only truth, it seemed, could be put in print. Comment followed joke merging into the pattern of talk which later petered out, giving way to the usual public brawl which was louder and more arresting. Savory was still busy, and the crowd, it seemed, was thickening again.

'You know,' a woman said, bringing her head close to the neighbour's ear, 'Cutsie makin' child for Boysie.'

'Not true,' the other snapped really wanting to believe.

'But I tellun' you,' the woman insisted. She slipped her hand under the dress to fix the brassière on her shoulder. 'She three months gone.'

'And what Brother Bannister say?' the woman asked.

'They try to hush it up,' the other said, 'but God can see the blackest ant on the blackest piece of coal on the blackest night.'

'We can see too,' the woman said angrily, 'They been tryin' to make the church o' God an excuse for they bad livin' ever since.'

This whispered dialogue crept under and into the chime of coins and the shuffle of the paper Savory used for wrapping. The paper was cut in thin transparent sheets large enough to cover the loaves. These were clearly visible through the paper, which was quickly softened with oil oozing from the cakes. But that didn't matter since everyone earned much the same thing and bought much the same amount of food. The crowd had thickened again, and the surge of voices was gradually rising. Savory shuffled round briskly, solemn and silent and active and conscientious. He calculated change, wrapped the loaves and occasionally dashed behind the cart to chase small boys off the wheel and examine the axle. He hardly spoke. Encased in his blue dungarees that showed beneath the white canvas apron he worked with passionate ardour, coughing and whistling and scooping the sweat from his brow with an arched thumb. He wore a blue cap with a short peak and a white feather stuck at the top. It was the most attractive part of his uniform, the white feather.

The girl Cutsie sat on the grass mound against the lamp-post circling a stick through layers of powdery marl. The wind raised the marl and the circle merged into the wrinkled surface of the canal. She levelled the patch with her hand and tried again, until the circle was clearly and deeply lined, and the encircled patch heaped to an inch or two above the line. Across the road a small boy amused himself in a different way. He rested against the shop step supporting his weight with both arms thrown back, while he plugged his toe into a narrow crab hole. The hole smoothly rounded till he arrived was soon totally blocked with the up-turned earth. He kept plugging into it as the earth fell in and soon it became a hole within a hole. Next to him was Bob. He made music from a comb wrapped in brown paper. The paper covered the comb teeth through which he blew a tune and the music blared forth. He often changed his tone, and with each change the sound was like that of a different instrument.

Cutsie went on mechanically patterning the marl, and the boy with his toe in the earth plugged deeper and deeper, while Bob bellowed his music through and across the neighbourhood. These activities were a regular pastime. These were the weapons with which a villager killed time. They were all three waiting till the crowd thinned out.

Two cross-roads away the shoemaker was sitting behind the work bench in his small shop. He sat with his knees together and his body bent rigid over the cradled boot. There were three other men occupying the corners of the shop. The shoemaker punched a hole with the awl, threaded a brief stitch along the edge of the sole and then waxed the twine. It was all done with an ease that made it seem one action. He looked up and the men smiled.

'Savory busy this morning,' one said. He was an overseer's brother.

''Tis always so,' said Mr. Foster, ' 'Tis the same every morning.'

The shoemaker glanced through the open door on to the crowd

round the cart. He looked again and held his glance long and steady as the people shuffled round the cart. He quickly bent over the boot and made another stitch, unspeaking and with serious concentration. The men sniffed the odour which filled the shop and looked at each other. It seemed as though they wanted to say something. The shoemaker looked up and down again and the men sniffed quietly. It was about nine o'clock and the sun was already pouring its light through the trees and into the shop. Now and again the men crouched farther into the corner to escape the gleam. The old woman Ma came out from the corner house and made towards the cart. A little boy touched the man in front of him, and the man indicated to his neighbour that Ma was in the crowd. They moved back quietly leaving a narrow passage through which she walked towards the cart. Savory saw her and took her basket receiving the change and despatching the item without speaking. He knew what she wanted since her order never changed in all the years. She always took two coconut turnovers, one for herself and one for the old man, and two fish cakes. She retreated to the fringe of the crowd making conversation with someone as the people hustled forward renewing their orders.

'What time is it now?' the shoemaker asked, making another stitch.

The men looked at the small alarm clock on the bench and saw it was half-past nine. They looked at each other as though they wanted to speak. Mr. Foster stood up and stretched himself full length. Someone knocked on the partition that separated the shop from the shoemaker's living quarters and the shoemaker opened the latch door and slipped inside.

'What you r'ally think 'bout Slime?' Mr. Foster asked.

The overseer's brother smiled. It was a confident, happy, reassuring smile. 'What I think 'bout Slime?' the overseer's brother said, 'ask that little fellow what he think 'bout Slime.'

Mr. Foster called the little boy to ask him about Mr. Slime. The boy looked puzzled at first.

'What class he use to teach,' Bob's father asked.

'Class 5,' the boy said. 'He wus a good good teacher.'

'Why he left the teaching?' Mr. Foster asked.

'I don't know,' the boy said. 'None of we know.'

They looked at the boy as though he were under cross-examination. He must have felt for a moment that he had had something to do with Mr. Slime's resignation.

'We don't know,' he said, 'except that it wus he want to start a friendly society.'

'Is you a member of the society,' Mr. Foster asked.

'Me and all me brothers,' the boy said.

'You sure he wus a good teacher,' Bob's father asked. The men smiled.

'Sure, sure, sure,' the boy said, shaking his head.

'Good,' said the overseer's brother; 'thank you.'

The boy leapt across the canal and ran towards the cart.

The men looked at the clock and at each other. It wouldn't be long before they heard whether the strike would be called off. Mr. Slime had seen them the day before and explained the situation. He had spoken as their representative with the shipping authorities and he had made it clear that they should not return till he had thought the conditions satisfactory. They knew the conditions meant wages and so on, but they were vague about the details. Each knew, however, that the strike involved a possible increase in his wage. It was the first time any of them had committed himself to such an action, and they were unsure about everything except that they had a leader whom they could trust. They trusted Mr. Slime. But the experience was very exciting and in a way very dangerous. Bob's father could go back to fishing if the strike failed and he lost the job, and Mr. Foster kept goats and pigs. Moreover he had been able to buy another house. Life was always easier if you had certain shelter. The overseer's brother had neither trade nor resources, but his brother could, as an overseer, help him if he wanted to. He didn't seem to worry much. It wouldn't be long before Mr. Slime turned up, as he had promised, to say what agreement he had reached with the shipping authorities.

'Well, what you going do?' the shoemaker asked, taking his seat behind the work bench. There was a trickle of tea along his chin and the cave of a jaw tooth was filled with bread. The men sat quiet and contemplative, feeling for an answer. The shoemaker held the boot on his knees. The thick skin of his brow was heavily creased, and when he chewed the remnants of bread as he spoke, the bones of his face made a ridiculous seesaw movement under the skin. His manner was always courageous and authoritative, and particularly so this morning. It might have been that he was not really involved in the strike. He had a trade which he knew perfectly and worked at with success. He was really the spectator. If the strike was successful he would know the reasons, and if it failed and the men were thrown out of work he would tell them with a spectator's sympathy why everything had happened. The privilege of the spectator seemed such a great luxury. The men looked at him as though they wanted to say that it was all right for him to talk, but it would be they who had to feel the situation. They looked at the clock.

'I don't know,' Mr. Foster said. 'We got to wait and see.'

'You not going back?' said the shoemaker looking steadily at the Mr. Foster.

'No,' Mr. Foster said quickly, 'I not going back till the chief say go.'

'Nor me,' said Bob's father. 'I not going.'

The shoemaker took the boot from his lap and pitched it in the corner.

'I like you so,' he said, ''tis the only way you'll improve your condition.'

'Stick together is what I say,' said the overseer's brother.

'And now you get educated people behind you,' Bob's father added, 'you can't fail.'

''Tis true,' said Mr. Foster, 'education is the thing. I always say a man is a dog if he ain't got a little education.

'And along with it a handful of common sense,' said the shoemaker.

They were very enthusiastic and very confident.

'I'll see if the three of you ain't a proper pair of men,' said the shoemaker. 'If you ain't there to unload those boats, Christ, they can't unload of themself. And the Great can't do it. They can give orders and all that, but they can't do one honest day's work.'

''Tis true,' said Mr. Foster, 'without we, work come to a stan'still.'

''Twill give the landlord something to think 'bout,' said the overseer's brother. He put his hands in his pocket and scratched. 'Already the flood shake him.'

The men looked at him in bewilderment. They always expected him to say what the average person didn't know. He was the overseer's brother.

'What it got to do with the landlord?' the shoemaker asked.

'He's partner in the firm,' said the overseer's brother. 'Jones an' Creighton Shipping Company Limited. He's the Creighton part of it.'

The men looked at each other quietly.

'Christ, he'll dirty his pants,' said the overseer's brother. 'I tell you when he had to spen' that money on repairing the roads after the flood he cry. My brother say he cry buckets of drops.'

The men sat silent contemplating the new situation.

''Tis a funny thing,' the overseer's brother went on, ''tis r'ally a funny thing. He's a nice sort of man, the landlord; he kind, he will give you if he think you r'ally need, he's r'ally like that, but if he got to spend any r'al sum of money, it give him heart failure. And he got more than he could ever spend in this God's world. What you say to that?'

The men thought.

'If you ask him for a shilling,' the overseer's brother said, 'or two or three shillings, he will give freely freely, but if he know that he got to spend a few hundred dollars, which is no more than three shillings compare with what he got, boys, he will cry buckets of tears.'

'What'll happen if we don't unload the boats?' Bob's father asked.

'They'll stay where they is, that's all,' said the shoemaker. 'When the ship people ready they'll either take them back where they bring them from, or if they rotten they'll dump 'em in the sea.'

'An' what's worse,' said the overseer's brother, 'we got to load the boats with sugar. That's worse. What he'll lose on that ship load of sugar that won't go away will repair these roads seven times seven.'

'He'll want to give us notice,' said Mr. Foster. The men looked sharply at each other. This seemed a new situation altogether different from the failure of the strike and the loss of a job.

'Then he'll have to give everybody notice,' said the shoemaker angrily.

'Don't be foolish,' said Bob's father, 'he can't give everybody notice. There won't be no more village.'

' 'Tis true,' said Mr. Foster, 'you couldn't have the land without the village.'

'And he can't do without the village either,' said the overseer's brother.

'He couldn't feel as happy anywhere else in this God's world than he feel on that said same hill lookin' down at us.'

'What you say is true,' said the shoemaker, 'a place gets in the blood. I couldn't have this old shop anywhere else but right here where it is.'

'That's why if I get notice I won't know what to do,' said Mr. Foster. . . .

'I won't even know what to think.'

'Leave it to the chief,' said the shoemaker, 'that's what you got a chief for.'

They were going to leave it to the chief. The shoemaker took up the boot and set it on his knees while the men stared out of the door at the crowd round the cart. What would happen, they wondered, when Mr. Slime returned. If the strike was a success and they were given more wages, they were still as tenants at the mercy of the landlord. They turned the matter over and over in their minds trying to find as best they could a solution that would fit any emergency. There was no question of leaving the village. It was true that one village was like another, but their habits were formed and it was difficult for any of them to start from scratch among a new set of people. Whatever happened they weren't going to disappoint Mr. Slime. Since his resignation from the school he had worked as hard as any man in the village to improve their condition.

The year after he left the school he won his seat in the general election with a great majority. It had seemed to everyone that he had resigned from the school with the intention of doing bigger and in a way better work in another field. He had been responsible for the education of the children, but he had extended that work to include the education of the workers. They had never meddled in politics and they were never easy prey to promises, but Mr. Slime had won their sympathy completely. No one questioned why he had resigned, since the reason seemed clearly demonstrated in the new role he was playing. He was their chief and the chief of many others who lived beyond the village. The shoemaker was thinking too. Until the overseer's brother told them about the landlord the matter had seemed quite simple. For a moment they wavered, but they were capable of making a decision; and whatever they may have been ignorant of they understood the meaning of trust. And trust in a school master they understand even better.

They couldn't conceive for a moment the land as being other than the village, and on careful reflection the threat of notice to a whole village seemed ridiculous. It would have been a threat to the landlord himself. His happiness seemed to depend on it as much as theirs. It was always the case of the English settler in the island. For reasons which were different the land had got into their blood. They might return to England for a month, six months, a year, but those who had settled for any time always slipped quietly into the position of making the island a home away from home. And particularly in this island. They had made it so much their home that they brought not only their habits but the very name of their original home. They called it Little England with the pride of the villager who thought the name carried with it a certain honourable distinction. They were thinking of what the overseer's brother had said. The landlord couldn't do without the village any more than they could. The shoemaker thought of that too, but he was suspicious of the attachment. While the others thought of Little England the shoemaker thought there was something suspect in the Englishman's attachment. That is what reading had done for him. He always read the papers, and whenever he got a chance he read a book. Sometimes he would invite the boys from the High School to meet at the shop and argue about news they had read, and he made a mental note of the things they said. He would ask them to lend him a particular book one of them had mentioned. And once he had read a book by a man called Priestley. He never forgot it. Pasted on the partition in one corner of the shop was a piece of paper with the name, J. B. Priestley. And whenever you asked him who was Priestley, he elaborated with the greatest excitement what he had read in this book. No one knew about Priestley and often the boys poked fun at him about using false names. Many of the boys from the High School who had often stopped to talk hadn't paid any attention to this passage written by Priestley, but he thought it held the clue to some important secret, and he stuck to Priestley. Priestley had known nothing about landlords, but he had said something in this book about colonial governors, and the shoemaker understood what that phrase meant.

It was the first time that he started to think of Little England as a part of some gigantic thing called colonial. Priestley had said that one of the big problems they would have to face from time to time in England was that of helping colonial governors to readjust themselves. After their term of office in the colonies they returned with strange notions about their relations to servants and the servant class. And Priestley also said that that sort of thing could go very far. These colonial governors who were not always very educated or even very educable could convince themselves that what was merely a temporary privilege should become a permanent right. Not a privilege, the shoemaker often repeated to himself, not a privilege but a right. He had seen in cinemas, at parades and wherever the

Governor had appeared the homage he was paid. The Governor in Little England was not only the representative but the equivalent of the king in Big England. For a while he didn't think of the Governor in Little England, but of him as an ex-Governor living among shoemakers in Big England. He felt a curious sympathy for the shoemakers who might not be able to see Little England's governor as Big England's king. And that is what this writer had said. You had a problem reminding these people that what was merely a privilege was not at different times and in different places their right. The shoemaker looked up from the boot and said something about J. B. P. The men laughed quietly and Mr. Foster said jokingly that it would serve him right if he learnt from the best authority that there wasn't any such man. He could never quote this writer's exact words, and he didn't remember the name of the book. He didn't care to. He had that passage which was a clue to a big secret.

'You din't read the papers today?' the shoemaker said quietly. They were tired of his argumentative, contentious tactics and they didn't answer. They laughed quietly and went on thinking about what Mr. Slime would say. He smiled to himself and thought over what he had read in the paper. The morning paper had carried a long article describing the incidents that had occurred in the civil disturbance which was then taking place in Trinidad. There had been several cane fires and people had marched with stones and sticks to the public buildings. There had been threats to intern the leaders of this riot, and the fear was expressed that a similar uprising might take place in the other islands. The shoemaker thought quietly on the article and the passage from Priestley's book and other books he had read. If he were a politician one might have said that a speech was taking shape in his head. He was ignorant of the details of the civil disturbances in Trinidad, but he knew that they must have been in the nature of the strike which was about to begin on a large scale in Barbados. He knew Trinidad through the annual cricket tournaments which were played in the two islands. One year Barbados invited Trinidad to compete in the game, and the following year Trinidad would invite Barbados to play at Trinidad. There was a tradition of tournaments that had helped more than books, newspaper reports or history lessons at school to remind the people in Barbados that there were people with similar habits and customs living in Trinidad. The tournament sometimes included British Guiana and now and again Jamaica. But Jamaica was

the least known. They were farther away, and for various reasons
their cricket teams came less frequently. Yet Jamaica cricket had captured the Barbadians' imagination. Every boy who felt his worth as
a batsman called himself George Headley. In most cases the only
knowledge most people might have had of Jamaica was the fact that
George Headley was born there. The shoemaker looked up at the partition directly behind him. Pasted in two rows on the boards were the
Press photographs of cricketers he had clipped from the daily paper.
Some wore caps and blazers and the sweaters with the colours that
could only be used by those who had represented the territories combined against England or Australia. The players were of mixed colours.
Slightly above the top row was a picture of one George Challenor
who might have been a white planter in Barbados. Beside him was
George Headley against whose name was printed in pencil the words,
THE BLACK BRADMAN. The shoemaker looked at them and recalled the
stories he often told of each. Learie Constantine, Derek Sealey whom
he called the wonder boy of West Indian cricket, Clifford Roach,
Mannie Martindale, and Bertie Clarke who was going to be the best
spin bowler the world had ever seen. The baggage man who went
by the name of Flannigan had made the prophecy, and Flannigan
was never wrong. The shoemaker made another stitch in the boot and
looked out at the people pushing around the cart. He was thinking
about the strike and the riots in Trinidad and the cricketers, and in
a way he couldn't explain to himself they all seemed to belong to the
same line of events. He rested the shoe on the floor and looked at the
men. They were watching the villagers buy their loaves and they
smiled occasionally at the trick the small boys played between the
men's legs. The old woman, Ma, was still talking to another woman.
Her wrinkled skin had lost its shine even in this bright morning sun.
The shoemaker looked at the cart and the men and the boot on the
floor. He was going to say something, but he was waiting for the right
moment to start. The speech had been forming in his head. He was
thinking on the books he had read, and particularly of the English
writer who seemed to hold the clue to what was happening in Trinidad
and Little England. He wondered whether there would be riots in
Barbados. He couldn't imagine any crowd of villagers marching to the
Governor's house with stones and sticks. The villagers were peaceful.
They asked for nothing but a tolerable existence, more bread, better
shelter, and peace of mind to worship their God. The words had

spilled. His mind could contain them no longer. He looked at the cart quickly and then back at the men. They were anxious. 'There got to be somebody to do something,' he said. He looked at the cart again and shook his head. There was an unbearable resignation in the shake of his head. What he imagined seemed impossible.

'Look at them,' he said, pointing towards the cart, 'that's what they do.' He was indicating the women who were in a majority. 'They shop in the mornin', talk 'bout they children all day long, what they do an' not do an' in the night they cook a tumblin' load of food.' He waited to recollect his thoughts. 'Well, they got to be somebody to do something.'

''Tis true,' said Mr. Foster, 'men for one thing, women for a next.'

'An' 'tis the fathers who got to get up an' get,' the shoemaker said; 'nobody ain't goin' do it for us.' He was very excited as the words spilled. 'You have to think 'bout the children,' Bob's father said. 'They can't grow up in they father shoes. What's sauce for us isn't sauce for them.'

'That's it,' the shoemaker insisted. ' 'Tis your children you got to think 'bout. Don't let them run wild like stray dogs as if they ain't got no owners. They ain't got no chance to go to high school an' get the sort of job decent respectable people gets, but you can give them something as good. A good trade and some facts 'bout the world.'

''Tis what I tell my boy,' the overseer's brother said; 'I tell Trumper day in day out he gotta think 'bout the future. Playin' cricket morning noon an' night, and goin' to the sea in the holidays for the whole God blessed day ain't goin' to make a man of him.'

'The times is changin',' said the shoemaker, 'if nothin' change ever in Creighton's village, times is changin', and all I gotta say to you here an' now is this, if times goes on changin' changin', an' we here don't make a change one way or the next, 'tis simply a matter that times will go along 'bout it business an' leave we all here still waitin'.'

'We'll sit an' wait till Thy Kingdom come,' said Mr. Foster.

'You can't tell the times to stop,' said the shoemaker; 'might as well talk to stone.' He set the boot on his knees again and the men waited quiet and serious. He rested the boot on the floor again.

'I've no education,' he said, 'but I remember what I pick up here an' there. An' from the time the great Marcus Garvey come down an' tell us that the Lord ain't goin' to drop manna in we mouths I start to think.'

'I remember Garvey,' said Mr. Foster: 'God bless his name.'

'Things change an' times too,' said the shoemaker; ''tis all in history.' The men watched him seriously as his small bright eyes danced under the lids.

''Twas once a marvellous empire,' he said, 'a marvellous empire own by people call Greeks an' others, 'twas a man call Alexander the Great.' He pointed to the partition which bore a picture of Alexander the Great. It was one side of a leaf torn from some history book. The shoemaker looked at it for a moment and snapped his fingers.

' 'Twas a man,' he said, 'no monk, an' he do it all by 'imself. He build a great big empire an' rule the whole God blessed worl'. But the times change an' that change too. That come to a end like anything else. An' then 'twas another great big empire, the Roman Empire, they's the ones we read 'bout with England. Every little schoolboy know 55 B.C. and the Battle of Hastings; 55 B.C. was the Roman battle with Caesar an' all of them. They had the whole God blessed world to themself, an' no man Jack could tell them to come back 'cause 'twas theirs. The world wus theirs. But when the times change and things they change too. All that come to a end. An' ther' wus others. The Spanish Empire an' the Portuguese Empire; I've read a story here an' there 'bout the whole lot of them.' He filled his lungs. Then ''Twas the great big Britsh Empire,' he said. 'That's what we here is part of, Barbados or Little England, God bless her soul, is part of that. But times goin' change again an' things too, and that big British Empire goin' change too, 'cause time ain't got nothin' to do with these empires. God don't like ugly, an' whenever these big great empires starts to get ugly with the thing they does the Almighty puts His hands down once an' for all. He tell them without talkin,' fellows, you had your day.'

'What'll happen to we in Little England when the big change come?' Mr. Foster asked.

'P'raps we'll start seein' 'bout getting a empire too,' said Bob's father.

The overseer's brother laughed quietly.

'But 'tis strange the way they give Little England the best education,' said Mr. Foster. 'I don't think there's any part of this God's world barring England sheself where the education is to a such high pitch.'

''Tis true,' said Bob's father; 'I once hear a Englishman say he wus teacher at one of the high schools, that Harrison college was as good a place of education as any same place that teach the same things any part of the world. An' he travel all over the world.'

'But if you look good,' said the shoemaker, 'if you remember good, you'll never remember that they ever tell us 'bout Marcus Garvey. They never even tell us that they wus a place where he live call Africa. An' the night that he speak there in Queen's Park an' tell us that we wus his brothers who for some reason or next went elsewhere, I see a certain teacher in that said high school walk out from the meeting.'

'Why he walk out for?' Bob's father asked.

''Cause he din't like Garvey tellin' him 'bout he's any brother,' the overseer's brother said. They laughed.

''Tain't no joke,' the shoemaker said; 'if you tell half of them that work in those places they have somethin' to do with Africa they'd piss straight in your face.'

'But why you goin' to tell men that for,' said Mr. Foster, 'why tell a man he's somebody brother when he ain't.'

'That's what I mean,' said the shoemaker; 'you say it ain't true too, an' that's what they say only in a different way.'

''Tis true,' said Bob's father, 'no man like to know he black.'

'That's what I mean,' the shoemaker said, 'that's just what I mean.'

He turned his head and looked long and steady at the mirror that hung against the partition.

The dialogue had circulated.

'Some say it's Boysie,' a woman was saying, 'and some say is Sonnie, but the truth is she six months gone.'

'Four,' another corrected.

'I say six,' the woman insisted, 'you always two months behind the times.'

The remark was unluckily timed. The woman didn't like the other's tone and even less the challenge which it implied. But that was the way of villagers. They had no patience with choosing the right moment for anything. An assault like their daily bread or life itself just happened.

'It take a Parker to know everybody business,' the first woman said. She was angered with the other's claim to better knowledge.

'What you know about me,' the other said hotly, 'tell me straight to me face, Sheila, what you know about me.' Her manner was confident. Sheila had to keep it up. The unwritten the laws of the public brawl demanded that. The dialogue had blazed into a petulant outburst. It had become public property.

'The world know you, Baby,' Sheila said. 'You's the last person in this God's world to talk about anybody.'

Baby Parker waited apparently gathering her forces. The crowd wavered between open alliance and a concealed effort to find out what had happened. Savory closed the cart by letting the upraised side of the roof drop down, and rested leisurely on the wheel.

'Baby Parker is known,' Sheila was explaining. 'Everybody know Baby Parker.' She had turned her back on the woman and addressed the crowd in the manner of a public speaker. The occasional repetition gave a fine emphasis to her feelings.

'I could give your story to the worl',' she said, 'but people who is people don't do that sort o' thing. You ain't people, Baby Parker. You foot never touch shoe nor you head hat. You ain't people I say.'

A titter ran through the crowd. Baby Parker had retreated to a dignified silence. She was silent but unafraid. She looked in the early sunlight hard and defiant.

'Give me me cakes, let me go, Mr. Savory.' She had dismissed Sheila. The crowd tittered. Savory opened up the cart and the business went on. Baby Parker collected her cakes and made a way through the crowd.

'People or no people,' she said, sauntering towards the shop, 'I ain't no man killer. I'm clean as a dice, Sheila, clean. And you ain't. You ain't.'

'What you say?' the other woman asked advancing to meet her. 'I didn't hear you.'

The shopkeeper had foreseen what would happen and indicated that neither should enter the shop. Baby turned away and traced her steps back in the road to where Sheila was waiting to meet her. They stood face to face, an arm's length between them. The crowd made a circle round them.

'Tell me what you say,' Sheila challenged again.

'You's a nasty woman. You ain't clean.' The tone was confidential. The circle narrowed as the crowds pressed in on the woman. They stood close, just an arm's length, breathing rapidly and heavily in a mutual exchange of murderous glances.

'Repeat that,' Sheila said.

'You ain't clean.'

The crowds pressed closer. Someone shouted, 'Susie, come quick, t'ings happenin'.'

And in fact they had happened. The women in a murderous embrace had fallen to the ground and were biting fiercely at each other's limbs. They rolled over and over until their faces were completely whitened from the marl, and their eyes reddened and watered from the dust. In their wild movements they crushed and scattered the pebbles which rent their clothes, and as the layers of cloth fell away, the marl stiff and wet with sweat cleaved in cakes to their skin. The circle of spectators widened letting in air and making the way clear for the contestants. They had tumbled over into the canal, and by the force of their bodies had been propelled to the surface of the road again. Each struggled to tighten and secure her grip so that much depended on the strength of their arms. But they snapped their teeth like dogs, and when it was possible sunk their nails deep into each other's skin. The crowd shrieked with hysteria. Their voices joined with the wind in a sweeping blast through the trees and over the housetops. The women, stretched full length in a slackened embrace, wrestled, exhausted, cursing and crying. Small boys sped round the corner, some on skates, others in a race behind their wheel-barrows. Their voices yelled with the thrill of this wonderful occasion. It was like a public ball to which everyone had been invited and where there were no restrictions at all. The wind and the shrieks and the straining voices of the small boys were indistinguishable. On the roof of his cart Savory sat solemn and silent looking down on a village that must have seemed like hell itself.

A constable appeared, and the crowd in their turn disappeared. The women stood up relaxed, almost callous, and evidently waiting for him to speak. Their clothes were badly torn and their bodies showed black and blue beneath the flying strands of cloth. Their teeth and nails had made deep and wide marks on the skin, and in parts there were thin surfaces of blood. Each stood with hands akimbo expressing, presumably, defiance and even triumph. The constable stalked powerfully towards them. His manner was prompt and abrupt, and under his thick black and white uniform he looked very official. The helmet and belt and silver buttons streamlined along his tunic were brilliant in the sunlight. He fetched the black notebook from his breast pocket and slipped a pencil from behind his ears. It was hidden by the rim of his helmet.

'Why all you can't live like the people in Belleville?' he said, turning the pages of the book. 'Every day you fightin' and cursin' and fightin' and give me more work than I care to do. What wrong with you people at all?'

The women did not speak.

'What's yer name?' he asked not looking up from the book.

'Sheila Grimes,' one woman said.

'Spell it,' he said.

Before she had spoken he had started again. 'I been doin' a seven o'clock duty on the other side of the main, and the white people don't even talk, they so quiet.'

'They too great to talk,' a small boy interrupted. He was giggling. The constable wheeled round in an attitude of defiance but the boy had scooted off like a rat.

'Come with me,' the constable said, turning to face the women. He pocketed the book and placed the pencil behind his ear. He seemed very angry. Here and there the remnants of the crowd drifted about, appearing not to loiter. Savory had blown his whistle, and with it the echoing rumble of the cartwheels had given another warning to those who waited at the next stop.

The men had followed everything quietly from the shoemaker's shop. At first they were tempted to go nearer the corner and get a better view of the fight, but the shoemaker objected. He distrusted the constable and he wasn't sure that one of these might not have been arrested for loitering or instigating the fight. He told them to sit quiet and see what happened in a village where there wasn't anyone to lead. They looked on like spectators and shortly before the constable arrived, Mr. Slime drove up. He had parked the car outside the shoe-maker's shop, and he spoke to the men from inside. He had told them to return to work at midday. He gave no detailed explanations, but he assured them that for the time being the situation was satisfactory. The shipping authorities, among whom was Mr. Creighton the land-lord, had met. They were reconsidering the matter, and Mr. Slime was promised that there would be a revision of the wages within a fortnight. The men would be paid the new wage from the day of the strike. The end of their waiting had seemed so unexciting. None knew what precisely he expected, but when they heard what had happened they were a little disappointed. They were all going to return at midday to the waterfront. It was as if nothing had happened.

The air was clean and quiet and fresh again. Over the housetops in the distance thin layers of smoke seemed to drift and expand and dissolve in the air. It crept along the treetops, laced the leaves and was gone. In the houses cooking and washing were going on. Someone was singing. The day in spite of its turbulent dawn was coming to life quietly, correctly. With one woman on either side of the constable, the three sauntered leisurely along the rail tracks towards the high wall that separated one set of tenants from another. The villagers called such a display assault and battery and it was usually a sure occasion for the immediate arrest of the offenders. But this constable had a different way of doing things. His manner was always impressive. The official air never gave way to the familiar even when the familiar was intended.

'He's wicked, worthless man,' someone said. 'He like women too bad.'

'And he ain't going do them a thing,' another added; 'they goin' to fix it up between them.'

Then the old woman fumbling along the roadside observed, 'It is the way we live.'

The men stood outside the door of the shop reconsidering their action. They were still worried about the landlord, but for the time being they made no fuss. It was clear to them that the matter was not over. The landlord might retaliate, but whether or not he did, Mr. Slime had hinted that all wasn't finished. He told them there were other matters of even greater importance than the strike. But they must go back to work. The strike was only the beginning. The roads were clear again. They watched the constable and the women turn the high wall and walk out of sight. The girl, Cutsie, and Bob sauntered away. They looked as if nothing had happened. The girl was still holding the stick with which she had been disturbing the dust in the canal, and Bob carried the comb that made his music. Everything seemed clear and clean and quiet.

'What they fight for?' Bob asked.

'God knows,' said Cutsie, 'I don't.'

The wind came quietly, not caring what had happened. It went its way like Bob and Cutsie, ignorant, unheeding, happy.

'Why your father not working today?' Cutsie asked.

'God knows,' said Bob, 'I don't.'

6

THE parakeets were screaming from the treetops, and below them the dew dripped from the hedges and the high grass which we scaled. Behind us in our path the grass lay slaughtered by footprints with the water shivering over the edge of the blades. The grass rose high before us, and the dew making a sea of dots on the surface of the blades looked like a thousand eyes in the opaqueness of the near morning. It was five o'clock, and the bell from the landlord's yard was ringing as we crossed the village boundary on our way to the sea. Bob's bathing clothes were wrapped round his fist so that they looked neat and compact like a boxer's glove. I wore mine under my pants, carrying a towel strung over one arm. The bell rang and between the intervals we could hear the parrots' scream interrupted by the returning din. The bell stopped, and there was nothing but the parrots' scream rising like a wailing massacre to the sky. Above us was the morning star hard and distant like a diamond. It had a quality of light like the dew, but did not shine. It seemed a solid, four-pointed flame that would crack under the hammer and scatter from the blow in a million splinters, each remaining solid and steady like the star itself. We saw the star but did not speak; and suddenly I knew something was wrong. But it didn't matter, for equally suddenly on the other side of the sky the clouds cracked and through the jagged aperture the light came out in a shifting haze. In the distance it seemed to grope like a blind man through the dimness of the streets. We were now in Belleville where the white people lived, and the streets bordered by palm trees were called avenues.

Here the houses were all bungalows high and wide with open galleries and porticoes. Bottles of milk were grouped on the steps, and occasionally light flickered from the kitchens where the servants were preparing early coffee. We walked down the avenue whacking the hedgerows and kicking pebbles from the pavement to the street. The morning was taking shape, and when I asked Bob to wait while I slipped behind a palm tree to pass water I could see very clearly what was happening. There were the parakeets again, hopping from bark to bark and screaming their cry through the light. We walked the whole length of the avenue which ended at a cross street, narrowing on the other side into a lane that led through a shabby little tenantry. Bob stooped and picked up a pebble which he placed under his tongue. Removing it he faced the east and threw it over his head. That was a good luck token. Then he mumbled to me with his head tossed callously to one side that we should take different routes. He wanted to see which route was shorter, and said he would take the lane that led through the back tenantry. 'No runnin', he said. 'We'll walk as we been walkin' all the time.' I said all right, and he swaggered down the lane. I waited, watching how the rickety lane squeezed its way between the houses. There was a pause in my awareness, then I realized I was standing at the corner turning Bob's idea over and over in my mind. Suddenly I ran down the lane to where Bob had made a turn to the left. I eased my way against the fence, and at the turn thrust my head out and, it seemed, into another head that had made a similar movement from the other side. Our nuts knocked in the half-light. Bob, half-dazed, said he didn't think I would spy on him, and I recovering from the concussion asked him why he had come back to spy on me. We looked at each other; but no one spoke, and I knew something was wrong.

Now the apertures of cloud had widened into valleys through which the light flowed like a broad river over the descent of plains. I had taken the cross road which started where the avenue ended. Here the houses presented much the same spectacle, movement and space. The morning was now a clear indication of day. The parakeets' scream had died down or fused with the other birds' carolling, and these were several. The sparrows chirped a quick, staccato cry that seemed more like an accident than an intention, while the blackbirds clawing the leaves made a strained high-pitched wail as mournful as the colour of their feathers. Only the doves seemed to have found some peace in these surroundings. They were nearly all on the ground fluttering from the pavement to the street and back, tripping along the hedge-rows, leaping to the lower limbs of the trees, and diving back to the road. They paraded in thick squads on the tennis lawn. The brown bodies seemed to slope up all together to meet the blue-ringed necks and the heads that were neither round nor flat. The sun spotted them, and they marched in circles over the lawn. The line was broken, but the movement was regular, as they crossed the green turf from one end to the other, keeping time with their coos and carrying in their eyes all the colours of the rainbow. Neither the sparrows nor the blackbirds making their noise from the trees flew down to join them, and suddenly it occurred to me that in the village the sparrows and blackbirds which were the commonest victims of our snares had seldom been joined by the doves.

I sauntered towards the end of the road watching the clouds all the way. The sun had scatted them in several directions, giving them many shapes. Over a broad patch of sky they had collected into a thick, white wave. It seemed to be driven by some force outside it, but soon the wave burst from inside, and the eruption moved gradually towards the surface. It became thinner and whiter, breaking up into shapes of islands and men and beasts, and the shapes disintegrated into specks that flew like spray in the face of the laughing sky. The sky was like a great big bully choosing the life and death of these tottering shapes. I looked at the other side of the sky where everything was more peaceful and the clouds were enacting a legend. On that side were the men and beasts. Under a lion's neck where the mane fell down in a thick fluff two lambs lay sleeping. The lion's chin pointed down to the basement of sky so that a space was formed that curved over and about the sleeping lambs. Some yards away two men were exchanging words in an altercation that seemed to involve life and death. It was clear on close examination that they were men, but the shapes were not satisfactory. The animals were more accurately constructed. The men looked disfigured. The light was unsteady, and the figures seemed to take on different colours. One grew whiter and whiter as the sunlight sloped away in its favour, while the other became thicker and more cloudy as if it were ready to rain. The shapes suddenly got clearer and the colours more definite. The rain cloud had turned black with a face full and heavy like many a villager's. The figures were still, and they looked across at each other hard and steady as if they were involved in a common chaos which neither could understand but both greatly desired to redeem. They looked and their eyes were no longer there but they seemed to see in some other way, each the other! And as they looked the clouds curving over and about their heads made an arc of words that read: ARE YOU NOT A BROTHER? The shapes sharpened in outline, the white one getting heavier and darker; and finally they burst into broad trickles of rain that ran down the precipice of the sky. The dissolution was complete. It was not clear who had spoken, and the clouds had written no answer. But the men had departed. The incident was as vague as the clouds that gave it meaning, and I simply repeated the question, looking back to get my bearings from the avenue and seeing all the way the beautiful big houses. I forgot the words, becoming aware of Bob, and wondered whether he had reached the beach. It was drizzling as I reached the end of that road. I looked around me, and sniffing the salt air from my nostrils ran to meet the tumble of the sea along the shore.

Bob was breaking sea-eggs on an iron pipe that stretched from the land across the shore and into the sea. He cracked the shells against the pipe, then parted them and dipped the broken halves in the water before scooping the fleshy innards from their layers. Innumerable shells were strewn along the shore, and the light showed the dying movement of their spikes. He broke another egg, and I trotted towards him hoping to share the innards, but he cut short the operation. Without much fuss he scooped the innards from under the green guts of the sea-egg and tossed the shell back into the sea. He ran up the beach pretending to be in search of someone. I ran after him, but he quickly changed direction, and turning behind the bath-house was soon lost amidst the grape trees. I saw clearly that something was wrong. I walked down the beach, and making sure that my clothes were safely bundled on the rocks flung myself into the sea and swam out under and around the yachts. When I came up to the surface I felt the water in my ear. It veered with each movement of the head, and the scrawl and itch it made along the inner flesh was like the feel of a lizard limping over the body. I swam to the shallow and jumped on one leg, jerking my head from side to side. The water broke a way through the ear and leaked out in a trickle over the lobe so that the passage of the ear in its new freedom gave me a feeling of immense relief as when the bladder is eased after urinal congestion. I lay back letting my arms and legs float on the water and wondered what was the matter between me and Bob.

Was it Thursday or Friday? I didn't remember, but Bob was sitting on the shop step making patterns with a piece of charcoal. On my way home from the morning class, which we called private lessons, I stopped at the corner to say hello to him, but my mother saw me from the verandah and shouted me to hurry up. I ran home, and my mother unhooked her belt from a nail and lashed me thoroughly. Bob heard the screeling, and came down to our house listening. Every boy went, when it was possible, to hear the other get a flogging, and Bob came and heard what my mother had to say about the corner. She talked as she flogged so that I could see, presumably, why I deserved to be flogged, and I never talked back because it was not the custom in our house for the accused to talk back. She flogged and talked as she flogged about that corner. She had no use for that corner where the men were always gambling and the women dropped remarks, telling each other about themselves. I saw the belt; and her voice like an unexpected resurrection come through the water.

'An' all I talk to the boy about that corner he won't hear. Mornin', noon and night I pray and I preach to the boy. I tell him what the worl' is like an' what he must expect, an' the boy won't hear, won't hear, won't hear not a single word I say. I don't say you mustn't play, I don't say you mustn't have friends, but that corner is no good for you. I tell you repeatedly, once, twice, three times, I tell you to choose. Either you go with the gang at the corner, obey them, do as they tell you to do and live as they live and don't let me waste my time, or you do what I say. You can't serve two masters. I know what the old people say is true. You carry a horse to the pond but you can't make it drink, an' if you've no mind, then there's no use my tryin'! All my labour will simply go into Maxwell pond. The mind is the man. That's all I have to say, an' I'm tellin' you, I'm tellin' you once, twice, for the third and last time I tell you, if I catch you at that corner again, I'll roast your tail alive.'

Bob had heard enough and he was back at the corner plugging his toe in the earth, thinking perhaps on what he had heard my mother say about the corner and the gang. It was then the fight broke out. My mother heard the shouting and approached me with the belt threatening another beating. 'The same thing I saying to you, an' if I didn't call you only God knows what would have happen to you. But thank God I've got eyes to see and senses to understand. But hard ears you won't hear, hard ears you mus' feel.' And I felt the sting of the belt tight on my leg, and cried again louder than ever. 'Hard ears you won't hear, hard ears you must feel.' She raised the belt again, but I couldn't resist the switch-over that took place in my head. The laughter burst through my tears, for she had called up with those words the image of the class room and the pot-bellied teacher Mr.

Bruce, whom we mocked with the same words: 'Hard ears you won't hear, hard ears you must feel.' I couldn't stop laughing because of pot-bellied Mr. Bruce while I shivered with the tears on my cheek and my mother standing over me with the hand raised, and the belt dangling above my head. The tears streamed and the laughter through them, so that my mother couldn't tell which I wanted to do, or even which I was doing. It was like a bright morning with the sun and the rain pouring down with equal force and the villagers wondering what weather to expect. She moved as if to strike again, and I told her quickly what I was thinking, what had happened, how it was she who made me laugh by saying, hard ears you won't hear, hard ears you must feel, and making me remember pot-bellied Mr. Bruce whom she knew better than I did. Then the switch-over took place in her head, and she started to laugh as if there was something even funnier about Mr. Bruce than I had known. She laughed, and her head went back like a girl's so that the sun coming through the crevices of the roof streamed into her eyes, making them water and leaving her face as wet as mine. There was something so funny about Mr. Bruce that each time I tried to pronounce his name I collapsed with laughter, and she collapsed too, so that we seemed to laugh and cry and laugh and cry all together like children at a circus, and we never seemed to stop laughing that morning, I in the bedroom combing my hair, and she in the kitchen preparing my breakfast before school, both of us laughing and laughing.

On the following Sunday I was on my way to Sunday School while Bob, Po King and Boy Blue were playing hop-scotch at the corner. My mother always came out on the steps to watch me until I turned that corner, and she stood on the steps watching me closely all the way. What preoccupied her more than the corner or the boys were my shoes. I wore my best shoes on Sundays only, and on these occasions my mother's attitude towards me and the pebbles in the street was like that of an overseer. She was fierce, aggressive and strict. She had a feeling, it seemed, that I would enter some secret conspiracy with the pebbles against the shoes, and when I returned home in the later afternoon, she examined the tips and soles and heels with a closeness I had noticed in jewellers testing gold.

When I reached the corner I looked back to see if she was still there, and her voice with the sharpness of a bullet castrated my glance. 'What you looking back for?' she shouted. I kept my head straight

and stepped with meticulous care round the corner, ignoring Bob
and the boys at hop-scotch. I walked ahead, never looking back for
fear she might be there behind me, ready to make a judgment on my
intentions.

I put these incidents together and wondered where Bob fitted in.
And at that my head scraped the sand and I was aware of the sea and
my surroundings. I had drifted shoreward, my body afloat on the
water. I shook myself and walked up and down the beach, letting the
sun dry me. Bob's clothes were bundled on the rocks some yards
from mine, so I knew he hadn't gone. If I could find Bob, I thought,
I would have the whole thing out with him. Whatever was said or
done, I knew what I wanted; and that was to be a boy among the boys.

The beach was lit up with the sun, and the grape vine running
wild over the sand tangled between my feet. The girls were building
castles, one lying with her back to the sea as a blockade against the
water while the others laid the foundations. The little red-back crabs
were peeping out from under the grape vine, and for the first time I
saw two crabs in strange intercourse. It was like a revelation, seeing
the claw-fastened bodies pressed together. Their claws went over and
around each other while their aprons clung together. Their eyes like
little red pellets lay flat in their cavity so that they seemed in their
silent exercise to be asleep. That was a lucky experience, I thought, for
if I saw Bob now I could begin by telling him about the crabs. I
walked along the edge of the grape vine, past the soldiers' cemetery,
and on towards the lighthouse.

The sea made a ragged curve round the land. On that side of the
lighthouse it seemed a rough separation from what I had seen on the
other side. It was difficult to tell where the difference set in, for the
land jutted forth from the shore into a needle point. The lighthouse
was a kind of wooden sentinel marking the separation of the shore
from that part of the land which continued in its needle stretch into
the sea. But it seemed the separation of the sea began where the needle
of the land finished its point. On that side where I had bathed it was
still and clear as crystal with occasional patches of moss colouring the
monotony of the white sand. Sometimes we would drop pins in the
water, let them sink down to the sand and then dive them up. But
before we dived we could see the metal making a dull glimmer against
the darker shade of the sand. Farther out the bigger boys scrambled
for coins. The white men who invariably were tourists tossed the

coins in all directions from the club, and the boys hustled below the water. There the sea was deeper, and the pennies never reached the sand, for the boys could see them all the way sagging down to the sand. If the white men were enjoying themselves they would order the boys not to leap before the coins had settled. The boys dived and the white men watched the sprawling black limbs in their scramble. Some minutes later the boys would surface, disputing the accusations they made against each other. Some complained of being kicked, and others of being scratched in the scramble. The white men laughed, and later decided to settle the dispute by tossing more coins. If the dispute went on after their return the white men would tell them to fight it out, and the boys fought.

A fight in the sea required four boys, two of whom were actual contestants. The other two carried the contestants on their shoulders. The white men couldn't understand how they did it, and they looked curiously as if they were inspecting animals while the boys mounted to the shoulders of their supporters, letting their legs hang down in the water. The supporters did a kind of half swim, barely keeping their heads above water. It took less than a minute for their balance to be disturbed and when that happened they mounted again and again until the fight became a meaningless horseplay, and the white men ordered them to fight without supporters. Without supporters the contestants swam up against each other, making a terrific splash as they swam, and shooting the water at each other's heads by a forceful jerk of the wrist. The splash was their weapon, and the fight went on until one surrendered, unable to bear the stinging salt of the sea in his eyes. Then the white men tossed a coin, and the winner caught it. The water never carried anyone away on that side, and the waves when they came seemed like gifts of sea horses on which the children rode. They rose and fell in a gentle flow like rows upon rows of earth in ploughed fields, and the sea was like a wrinkled field curving and stretching until it reached the point where the land needled the waves.

Few knew what it was like at that edge of the land, but on this side of the lighthouse everything had changed. The air was laden with the odour of the sea, sharp and raw, and the sea tumbled. The waves rose higher and higher till everything beyond them was hidden, and the white foam flew up in a mad sacrifice to the clouds. Sometimes we thought something had gone wrong under the sea and the island would be washed away overnight by the water. Some people said it was the submarines which made the sea erupt. The submarine gave off a certain kind of gas which was bad for the coral formation of the land, and through some inexplicable intercourse of land and sea the waves exploded. Others said it was the works of God manifested in different ways. On one side the calm and the peaceful signified the merciful life-giver, and on the other the tempestuous and destructive meant the tormentor of evil spirits. The sea, many thought, was God's reminder of his power. Everyone guessed why these two faces of the sea were so different, and there were many guesses, but none differed about the danger they saw in the riotous waves. No one entered this side of the sea except the fishermen whose boats had drifted behind the light-house and were capsized. When that happened the catch was lost, and the fishermen went down into the fighting sea with curses on their lips. They drained the bottles of rum that were saved, and told God what He could do for them. They told Him to blind them if He could and their mothers and the whole race of fish-feeding black bastards whom they were going to die for. And in the frenzy of death they sank like jubilant sinners snarling their defiance against the unheeding ocean. Days later they were washed up on the shore blue-black and swollen, and their stench was the stench of rotting fish.

*   *   *

There they were, Bob, Trumper and Boy Blue. They stood on the very spot over which a fisherman's dead body was once washed. Their backs were turned to the land, and they made a V with Bob as the point where the wings of the letter would fuse. It looked like the kind of ritual one saw when men came out to preach at the street corner. Their faces were turned to the sea and Bob's hand was held up with all but two fingers clenched as if he were blessing the unseen fish. Meanwhile Trumper and Boy Blue looked closely at the sand deepening below his weight. I went quietly down the slope of the beach trying to make sense of the affair. They kept their backs turned, and no one saw or heard my approach. I stood directly opposite Bob, so that the V had now been converted into a diamond with Bob and me as the points where the wings would have fused. Far out the sea tumbled. The waves jumped and skipped, crashed and flattened out, dying a foaming white death before they could reach the boys.

'We'll wait for the next,' Trumper said.

The next wave leapt and went the way of the others.

'You'd better go nearer,' Trumper said. Bob took a step forward towards the sea. The waves fell in a foaming monotony along the blue surface. They waited, Bob looking out to sea, while the others looked down where his toes and heels left their line in the sunken sand. The scent of the air was like iodine, and raw fish and grape leaf. It filled the nostrils and the ears and the eyes so that everything smelt and looked and felt like iodine and raw fish and the liquid of the grape leaf.

'Remember,' Trumper said, 'remember not to forget the words!'

'What's the words again?' Boy Blue asked.

'What yuh mother give you ears for?' Bob said.

'I don't remember with my ears,' Boy Blue said.

'What you remember with?' Bob asked.

'With my rememberin',' Boy Blue said.

'Stop argurin',' Trumper said. 'This is too serious a matter.'

'What's the words again?' Bob asked.

'Chris', you worst than Boy Blue,' Trumper said.

'Quick, before the wave comes,' Bob said.

'Open yuh ears and hear,' Trumper said.

'He don't hear with his ears,' Boy Blue said.

'All right, don't start that again,' Trumper said. 'These are the words.'

'Quick,' said Bob. 'Quick.'

'Good,' said Trumper. 'Listen. The words are: Sea Come No Further.'

'When is he to say that?' Boy Blue asked.

'Just when it goin' touch yuh toes,' Trumper explained.

'Good,' said Bob.

'You better repeat it beforehand,' said Trumper.

'Yes,' said Bob. 'Sea Come No Further.'

'You better say it to you'self all the time in case you forget at the last moment,' Trumper said.

'No,' Boy Blue argued, 'you won't believe it after a time. I fin' when I repeat a thing, a word, for example, it sound after a time as if it ain't a word, but just a kind of noise.'

'That's true,' said Bob. 'I'll say for the last time. Sea Come No Further.'

'An' just when it goin' touch your toes,' Trumper said.

'An' suppose it don't touch?' Bob asked.

'Then you'd be better than the King,' Trumper said.

'Who king is this?' Boy Blue asked.

'Canute,' said Trumper. 'King Canute.'

'Where he come from?' asked Boy Blue.

Bob and Trumper laughed.

'He's the king in the hist'ry book,' said Trumper.

'But where he live?' asked Boy Blue.

'He don't live,' said Trumper, getting angry. 'It's hist'ry.'

'You mean a story?' said Boy Blue.

'If you want to call it that,' said Trumper.

'Where did you read it?' said Boy Blue.

'In the Michael John,' said Bob. 'It's really wha' I hear the others say, 'cause I don't read that sort of joke. I prefer the newspaper.'

'I know Michael John,' said Trumper. 'It's the book wid B.C. 55 and the Battle of Hastin's.'

'An' it's in that they give the joke about Canute?' Boy Blue asked.

'It ain't no joke,' said Bob. 'Look! Look! Look!' The wave climbed the air like a mountain heaving itself forward with the spray flying and the body getting more and more hollow. It came forward like a fat fool, not knowing where it was going, or what to do with its fury. I retreated up the beach.

'You better start sayin' the words now,' Boy Blue said.

'Yes,' said Trumper. 'Now!' And he and Boy Blue made ready to run.

Bob arched his back and we heard the syllables stumbling past his lips. 'Sea Come No Further. Sea Come No Further.' His voice went out like the squeak of an insect to meet the roar of the wave.

'Come no further,' said Bob, shivering with fear, 'come no further.' The wave came forward like a thundering cloud, crashed and shot like a line of lightning over the footprints that were the only sign of our fugitive king. We collapsed in the grape vine, sick with laughter.

*   *   *

Bob did not return and we sat under the grape tree looking out across the sea. The sun went under cloud and we noticed how the shade of the sand deepened, and the sea in a level patch turn to dull grey. The sun surfaced the clouds and the light was everywhere once more. We looked at the sand and the sea and it seemed we could see the gradations of light, but one got the feeling the light had climbed from below the sand and the sea. A fisherman walked up the beach in our direction dragging a large fish net after him, and we watched him till he turned behind the lighthouse and was out of sight. The beach seemed empty but for us three sitting in a half-circle on the sand under the grape tree. We were silent.

''Tis always like this,' Trumper said suddenly, and we were startled by the fall of his voice on the air. It was as if someone had dropped a pebble on a pane of glass.

'What's always like what?' Boy Blue asked.

'I mean the way we is here,' Trumper said. ''Tis always like this at home. The way we is here. My mother over yonder in that corner, an' my father down there in that corner, an' me somewhere else. An' you get the feelin', you know, that everything's all right. 'Cause of the way everybody sittin', just sittin' there, an' for the moment you feel nothin' ever change. Everything's all right, 'tis the same yesterday an' today an' tomorrow an' forever as they says in the Bible.'

'I know what you mean,' Boy Blue said. ''Tis always like that at home too. 'Specially when my sister ain't there, an' my grangran don't sneeze. There ain't no noise at all, an' I don't know for you, but I get the feelin' that I always this size, an' all. I try to remember, I can't remember myself bigger or smaller than I is now.'

'As you say so,' Trumper said, 'you make me wonder if we ever was older than we is now.'

'How you mean?' Boy Blue asked.

'Well, they always say you get older,' Trumper said, 'but that's to come. That's something you don't know 'bout. You's fourteen this year, an' next time you'll be fifteen, an' then sixteen, an' so on an' so on; but you ain't ever fourteen an' then thirteen an' then twelve an' so on.'

'No,' Boy Blue said, 'you ain't ever that; although they say that after a certain age you start to get a child again, like Pa and Ma, for instance.'

'Once a man twice a chil',' Trumper said.

'That's what they say,' Boy Blue said, 'though I'd like to be one time a chil' an' two times a man. Is so hard on you when you've got to be a chil'.'

'You can't talk, for instance,' Trumper said.

'Nor you can' say what's in yuh mind,' Boy Blue said. 'An' when you ain't cryin', you quiet.'

''Tis true,' Trumper said. 'Sometimes I get frighten when I see my mother baby starin'. Seems he ain't seeing anything, an' yet he seeing something.'

'My mother baby can't see,' Boy Blue said, 'an' that is worse. He more than frightens me sometimes, 'cause the sort of look he carries on his face makes me feel he still seein', like cross-eye Botsie who when his face turns one way see everybody passin' the other way. Sometimes I put my head right down to his nose an' peep to see if I could spot his eyes under the lid.'

'You mustn't do that,' Trumper said. 'You'll frighten him.'

'But he can't see,' Boy Blue said.

'It don't matter,' Trumper said, 'you'll frighten him all the same.'

The waves had settled for a while and the wind, it seemed, had lodged in the trees. Nothing moved but the tide of the wave drifting gently to the shore. There was no one on the beach but us three sitting in a half-circle on the sand under the grape tree. Behind us was the soldiers' cemetery where the trees were thick, and the sound most arresting when the wind came. The broken wall covered with moss and vine veered in and out through the trees, and in the open spaces were the red signals: KEEP OFF. No one could go beyond the signals. Farther away behind the trees were the oil tanks from which the ships in the harbour drew their supplies of fuel.

On the other side was the lighthouse which climbed so many feet in the air. The top was like a glass-chimney which you brought down over the bedroom lamp that remained burning low all through the night. The bright red and green glass at the top was always burning in the sun. When the sun went down a new light came on from inside, and the panes never lost their brightness. We looked around at everything, and we started to get afraid of our own silence.

'Just like this as you wus sayin',' Boy Blue said. ''Tis always like this at home. Even when my mother an' father fight, it don't take long before it get like this again.'

'True,' Trumper said, 'an' when my mother beat me, she says all the time she hittin' me, let's have a little peace in the house, an' when I finished cryin' it seems the peace come. Just like this.'

''Tis the same with all of us,' Boy Blue said, 'except that p'raps the peace is more with some than with others. The peace is plenty with us, 'specially when my sister ain't at home. An' sometimes sittin' here or there or anywhere for that matter, I feel that where I sittin' now I wus sittin' all the time, an' it seem I wus sittin' since

I can remember myself. 'Tis as if time like the clock itself stop, an' everything you tell yourself is all right.'

'That said thing happen to me,' Trumper said. 'I wus sittin' under the cellar at home. I don't remember why I went under the cellar, p'raps I wus searching for eggs. But anyway, I wus there, under the cellar, an' it seem everything wus dark as everything always is under the cellar, an' it seem I wus all by myself there under the cellar, jus' looking at the dust and dirt an' rubbish under the cellar. It wus quiet, quiet, quiet, an' I wus just there all by myself just lookin' at nothing in particular, when suddenly somebody say something 'bout the weddings, an' I right away rush out from the cellar to hear what's wrong with the weddings, an' I hear the story 'bout the weddings, but all time it seem to me something gone. I had the feelin' that something, I don't exactly know what, but something wus gone. Seems to me sometimes it wus the cellar that disappear, but not the cellar I lookin' at as I listen to the story. 'Twas as if there was another cellar in that cellar, an' 'twas the other cellar which disappear.'

'That's happen to me too,' said Boy Blue, 'an' where you wus sittin' wus a worl' all by itself, an' then the something happen, an' that world come to an end, an' you got to get up an' go to the other world where the new something happen. It sound stupid, but 'tis true the way it happen.'

'Stupid or not it happen to me with the weddings,' Trumper said.

'Who get marry?' Boy Blue asked.

'Nobody get marry,' Trumper said.

'An' how you mean there wus weddings?' Boy Blue asked.

''Twus like this,' Trumper said. 'You know Jon who can pitch marbles so clean? He put down four marbles here, he stay there a mile away an' before you say Jack Robinson he scatter them all. Well, 'twus Jon. For a long time he wus living with Susie who live down the train line, an' Susie had two children for him, Po King an' Puss in Boots, Number one. It seem Jon join the Free for All Brethren an' get save; he says he turn to the Lord an' so on. Brother Bannister take him in an' try to make a hand of him. He wus comin' on good, good, good, an' it seem he start to make much of Brother Bannister daughter, Jen. He was *muching* up Jen plenty, but nobody say anything, cause they consider in the church that all who break bread is of the same family. An' Brother Bannister, for God knows what reason, give Jon all the rope he want. Poor Jon forget he wusn't always what he say he wus, an' he got real entangle with Jen an' before you say Jack Robinson he get her in trouble. Jen wus in the way, an' Brother Bannister call on Jon to marry Jen, an' say if he didn't come like a man an' bear his own burden like a Christian an' a man, what an' what he would do with him. There wus talk 'bout shootin' an' all that. Jon get frighten an' he go straight an' put the matter before Susie. He ask Susie what she think 'bout it. When all wus said an' done, 'twus she, Susie, who he had to think 'bout. Susie come right out an' ask him what she think Brother Bannister would do if he din't marry Jen, an' he say with his tongue between his teeth that Brother Bannister swear by the church he would shoot him. It seem there ain't no man in all Creighton's village more 'fraid to die than Jon, an' he put it to Susie that if Brother Bannister did shoot him as he say he would the children don't have no father. Susie din't like the sound of it. Seems he wus askin' her to let him marry Jen. But she won't hear a word of it, an' she put it to him that if he an' she, meanin' Susie, went an' get marry quiet, then he, Jon, could put it to Brother Bannister that it wus against the law to marry Jen, whatever her condition. An' after all, she Susie it wus, who had a rightful claim to him. But Jon couldn't get out of his mind that Brother Bannister wus goin' to shoot him if he didn't, as Brother Bannister say, bear his burden an' do his duty to Jen as a man an' a Christian, saved through the blood of the lamb. He put it to Susie that once he wus alive, everything would be all right, an' that nothing matter for the children sake, but that he be alive, 'cause if anything happen to him the children won't have no father no more. Susie refuse, an' she swear by her dead grangran that if it wus brought to her notice than Jon marry Jen she would poison his guts out. Poor Jon wus betwix' the devil an' the deep blue sea, as they say. On one hand Brother Bannister with a gun, an' on the other Susie with a bottle of arsenic. He tremble like a chil', an' say to Susie if that wus so, they had better go an' get marry quick an' quiet. But Jon wus like a feather in the wind that go now here and now there, an' he couldn't make up his mind 'cause he din't have a mind to make up. So when Brother Bannister approach him again, he put it to Brother Bannister that if anything wus goin' to happen between himself an' Jen they would have to do it quick an' quiet, 'cause Susie swear she'd poison him. Brother Bannister had to save his face from shame, 'cause of his position in the church, an' he says once Jen get marry, he din't care how it wus done, once there wus a ring before anything happen.

Poor Jon had make the same promise to the two of them, an' with
each he state the same condition, quick an' quiet. He wus like a feather
in the wind, an' all 'cause he frighten to die. 'Tis a hell of a thing when
you got to decide an' you ain't sure what you deciding between,
an' worse when you ain't got nothin' to decide with. That wus Jon.
No an' yes wus the same thing. An' when Jen say do so, he do so, an'
when Susie say do so, he do so, an' the two so's din't add up to one so,
not even up to the day of the weddings. I don't know if to call Jon
a fool or a ass, you never knew what might have been happenin' in
his min', but up to the day of the weddings he din't know which
church to go to, 'cause he had sent Jen to one church an' Susie to
another, an' on the same same day. On all sides everything wus quiet.
Jen wus goin' to marry in her father church, quiet, quiet, an' Susie in
the big church quiet, quiet, an' nobody wus takin' notice, 'cause
when the priest in the big church read out the things you call banns,
an' say there wus goin' to be a weddin' between Miss McCauley an'
Mr. Trevelayn, it didn't make much sense to anybody. The names
din't connect, 'cause in the village everybody know Susie as Susie
an' Jon as Jon, an' to say Mr. McCauley and Miss Trevelayn wus
like sayin' alias Jack an' Jill. It jus' didn't make no sense. An' that's
jus' what happen. Susie went to one church an' Jen to another. An'
the two of them wait for hours, an' Jon never turn up. He wusn't with
Susie an' he wusn't with Jen. Then the talk get around. Somebody
say they see a car in the churchyard for a damn long time an' went
to see what happen. An' the news spread like wildfire, like wild bees
who don't want to see the hive again. An' some went to tell Jen it wus
Susie who wus goin' to marry with Jon, an' others went to tell Susie
it wus Jen who wus goin' to marry with Jon. 'Twus a big, terrible
mix-up. People bawl for murder when they hear, an' they turn out
like if it wus a funeral to see the brides who din't make sure about the
groom. Everybody start to wonder what could have happen. Some
say this, an' some say that, but no matter what some say or not say,
everybody start to refer to Jon as the cock in the yard. An' some say
cocks wus gettin' scarce. What a scandal it wus, an' I hear things
about cocks I never hear in all my born days. 'Twus a hell of a
mix-up, an' I hope never to hear of such a thing again.'

'An' how they fin' Jon?' Boy Blue asked.

'They din't fin' him,' Trumper said. 'The police search, an' Brother
Bannister search, an' lots of others, an' they couldn't fin' him. Some

say they saw him pitchin' jus' 'bout the time the wedding would be, an' some say probably he wus that sort of person, once he had a marble you couldn't get him to do anything else. Some say he went to the sea, an' some say this an' some say that, an' they went to look for him wherever they think he might be. Then there wus nearly a fight between Brother Bannister an' the priest, 'cause the priest tell Brother Bannister he wus a hypocrite, an' wus encouragin' the poor people to sin, an' Brother Bannister tell him back all he heard an' din't hear 'bout him. I never know there wus so much to tell 'bout the clergy, an' only God in heaven knows if it's all true, but we here on this earth can only hope it ain't true, the things I heard about the clergy. An' all that through Jon. They din't fin' him an' they never would have find him, 'cause he wus sittin' at the top of a mahogany tree in the cemetery. He had a good view of the two churches, an' so he says afterwards, he see when Jen go in, an' he see when Susie go in, an' he see when Jen come out an' he see when Susie come out, but he couldn't move 'cause he couldn't make up his mind, an' when everything wus said an' done he had to think 'bout his life. He stay there quiet as a mouse an' he see all the commotion, an' he hear all what they wus sayin' 'bout where he wus, an' he just look an' listen. An' when it turn dark, an' the tree wus steady as a lamp-post, an' you couldn't see nothin' but the light of the stars on the tombstones he climb down. Not before did he dare move. The graveyard wus quiet an' silent like nothin' he ever know before, an' he sit down betwixt two graves with a teeny-weeny bit of light on his shirt sleeve, an' wait. An' 'twus there 'twixt the graves that foreday mornin' catch him, lookin' up at the mahogany tree where he had sit all day the day before, turnin' his mind now this way, now that, like a fowl feather in the wind.'

The sea heaved and our laughter was lost in the wash of the waves. A wave shot forward right up to the line of our footprint in the sand. When the water slid back the sand sloped sharply to the sea, and the foam of the wave making brief bubbles over the sand shaped itself between the spaces of our toes. It formed a pattern that looked like a honeycomb after the bees had deserted the hive. The space between the bubbles was clear and distinct like a hole. We kept our toes still and watched the bubbles burn crystal in the sun till the wind blew them into the sand that slid back to the sea. The foam was very pretty, and quite different from the foam one saw floating over the surface of molasses. The bright brittle look of the sea-foam was soothing with the wind settled in the trees and the sea steadying itself to a tide that rippled along the level of the water. Silence was there again, hanging over the trees and the sea and falling through and over the flow of the wind. It was very quiet and very still. Boy Blue lay back and looked up at the sky. He wanted to see how long he could look at the sun. The rays fell like burning glass and his eyes seemed to turn liquid in the light. His bones were big and strong under the black skin. The skin was solid and smooth, and fitted over the bones with wonderful evenness. There was a toughness about Boy Blue's skin that made it seem impervious to the sun. The light struck it, and seemed to rebound as he gazed through the shimmer and on to the sky. His nose shone beneath a thin layer of sweat. The crease of his mouth where the lips met in a black curve was sharp and distinct like a split in the flesh. He had black lips that seemed all the blacker when his teeth showed. The teeth were broad and white against dark gums. Occasionally he grinned at the sun, and the lips and the flesh of the cheek receded as if the rays of the sun had forced them back gently. He couldn't look at the sun very long, but he held his face at the same angle, letting his lids flick up and down in the light.

Trumper was looking out across the sea. He sat with his arms thrown back. His face was smaller, but his body was larger than Boy Blue's. He was about fourteen and just six months younger than Boy Blue. He had short, matted hair, black and stiff like wire. His face seldom betrayed any emotion. It was thin and plain and smooth with a single scar over the right eye. His ears were the right size for his face, and so was his nose. There was one remarkable feature about that face, and that was the eyebrows. The skin was too smooth and slightly swollen, and the eyebrows were not long and free like hair, but short and curling like weak strands of silk. When the sun struck full on his brows, it was the skin under the hair and not the hair that shone. The flesh of the brows where the hair sprouted up had a sore, worn look. The look of skin that has been shaven for the first time. No one knew how Trumper had come by these short silky eyebrows and the sore, worn skin that held them. But there were several suggestions, and the best known was probably the right one. When he was nine he had been sent to a reformatory school. It was an institution for boys who had been convicted, but were too young to serve sentence in gaol. Trumper had gone there, and, so the story went, he had experienced among other things the shaving of his eyebrows. When a boy was unmanageable his eyebrows were shaved clean, as a reminder, perhaps, that he was different from the others. Trumper never said that was true. He never said whether the boys had their eyebrows shaven, but that was the suggestion. But there was something queer about his eyebrows, and he knew it. The saving grace about his face was the colour of his skin. He was black too, but not as black as Boy Blue. No one was as black as Boy Blue. Trumper was what we called fair skin, or light skin, or, best of all, clear skin. Boy Blue was simply black. His blackness made us laugh. Every child in the village had a stock response for the colour, black. We had taken in like our daily bread a kind of infectious amusement about the colour, black. There was no extreme comparison. No black boy wanted to be white, but it was also true that no black boy liked the idea of being black. Brown skin was a satisfactory compromise, and brown skin meant a mixture of white and black. The best-looking girls in the village and in the whole island were those whose mothers had consorted with white men. They were brown skin, soft, chocolate creamed with long hair that curled and flew in the wind. There was a famous family on the island which could boast of the prettiest daughters. Their father was an old Scotch planter who had lived from time to time with some of the labourers on the sugar estate. The daughters were ravishing, and one was known throughout the island as the crystal sugar cake.

Neither of us could be called crystal. And there weren't many in the village who weren't black. Simply black. But though we were nearly all black, we all used the colour as a weapon against interference. If we lost our temper we would charge the other with being a black fool, or a black ass. Among the better educated, and the Great, the obscenities might not have been used in public, but they were affected in the same way. They often said of the village teacher how very bright he was, but he was so black. . . . The little girls in the lanes met in the evening to play 'pick up' and they would discuss among themselves the future of their shade. They were very blunt about it. The blackest among them would say, I don't mind being that colour, or even a little darker, but I won't like to be that. And the last that meant the colour of pitch. Sometimes we amused ourselves by asking each other why he was so black. And someone would say it wasn't good for the brain. And there was always the danger of the blood getting black. Whenever that happened the accused lost his temper and would reply that the saucepan or the pot had informed the kettle or the frying-pan, and so on. But Boy Blue never lost his temper. When you asked him why he was so black, he would answer with serious conviction: 'Just as I wus goin' to born the light went out.' Nobody could reply to that. The light, we admitted, had gone out for many of us.

Trumper passed one hand over his head and looked down smilingly at Boy Blue. Boy Blue was still looking up at the sky, testing the strength of his eye by the light of the sun. Trumper watched him, and suddenly brought his hand down on his stomach.

'What you thinkin'?' he said, laughing into Boy Blue's face. The blow had brought Boy Blue erect. He was waiting to speak.

'You cut my wind,' Boy Blue said.

'Well, don't stay there an' stare like a you-know-what,' Trumper said. 'They got a place where they put you when you start to sit an' stare all day.'

'I wusn't sittin',' Boy Blue said, 'I wus lyin'.'

'It makes no difference,' Trumper said, 'starin' is starin' whatever the position, just as peepin' is peepin' whatever the hole.'

'I wus thinkin' 'bout the story,' Boy Blue said. 'I think they should put Jon where you say they put those people you mention.'

'P'raps they should,' Trumper said, 'p'raps they should put all of us. 'Cause no man can say what he would have do if he wus in Jon's boots. If a man frighten to die, he frighten to die, an' there's no gettin' away from that. Death is a man in pants 'though he don't carry a stick.'

The waves heaved forward and rushed up the shore. When they sank into the sand and slid back to the sea, we saw three red-back crabs. They were forcing a passage through the sand. The sand made a heap like an ant's nest, then fell away and the backs emerged. The backs were deep red and the claws were pink. The claws raised almost above the backs as they propelled themselves. And they were covered with wiry bits of hair like a man's hand. They crawled along, brushing the sand with their aprons, and when the claws came up from the sand and the whole body groped forward, they left a varied scrawl along the sand. It made the pattern we might have drawn with a finger. They moved forward slowly and uncertainly like old women, crouching and sprawling in turn. We could find no colour for the eyes. They were so pretty. Not red or green, or bright yellow, or deep orange, or anything definite, but a wild, enchanting mixture of all these colours. Crabs' eyes were the most puzzling we could recall. They looked transparent in the light. When the crabs lifted them to half an inch above their backs, we tried to say what they were like. They were like pellets made of glass, and applied to hinges that would soon crack and fall. When the moon was full the boys of the village tried to see the man in the moon. They would fill a pint glass with water and stare through the bottom up at the moon. The colour of the light reflected in the water and over the glass was indescribable. When those who had no glass asked what it was like, no one tried to explain. We simply said, 'Here, take this and look!' The colour of the crabs' eyes was like the colour of the light reflected from the moon through the glass and over the water. And the movement of the crabs' eyes was as wonderful. They were lifted so that they seemed to see all around and in all directions at the same time. In that position they looked like sitting figures, and when they returned to the oblong cavity where they rested, the movement was effortless. It seemed the crabs had nothing to do with it. The eyes moved about at will and the crabs might have been hidden somewhere in the shells waiting to get a wire from the eyes about the surrounding weather. Crabs' eyes seemed so much like a man's hand. A man's hand that moved about like a machine that was left to work following its own instructions. Sometimes when you turn your fingers over and around, letting them go in and out in all possible shapes, you look down at your hand in its movement, and are aware of something outside of you. You watch, and the fingers keep up their enchanting game of cracks and creases, dancing and squirming. You stare, and the hand seems to stare back, an independent object, making a message through its instruments, the fingers. The crabs' eyes had that quality. They had something in common with the crab locked away in the shell, but they moved freely. We watched them crawl up the slope of the sand, and suddenly the waves slithered up and hurried them beneath the slope.

'You don't like crab?' Trumper asked, nudging Boy Blue in the ribs.

'I like crabs all right,' Boy Blue said, 'but I wus thinkin' 'bout Jon. Why he choose the cemetery of all places?'

''Cause 'twus where the tree wus,' Trumper said.

'But there's plenty other trees,' Boy Blue said, and he seemed very worried.

'I don't know,' Trumper said, 'except that I wus sayin' to myself that Jon thought the weddin' had to be, an' he went there to see who would take his place.'

'But nobody could take his place,' Boy Blue said, 'cause in the first place, nobody but a few people know 'bout the weddin'.'

'It din't make no difference,' Trumper said.

'It must make a difference if he wus the man who had to be there,' Boy Blue said.

'Not necessary,' Trumper said, 'not necessary.'

'How you make that?' Boy Blue asked.

'This is what I mean,' Trumper said. 'What I mean is like this. We all get a feelin' inside that certain things got to be, an' it make no difference what is, or what's not, that particular thing gottabe. For instance the sun. When you see the sun you know there gottabe light. An' don' say something wrong with yuh eyes, 'cause the sun ain't got nothin' to do with that. Is simply and purely a question of if there's sun there gottabe light. An' you don' ask any questions 'cause there ain't no questions to ask. An' with the sea, 'tis the same. When you touch the sea with yuh toe you know there gottabe wet. An' you don't ask questions 'cause there ain't no questions to ask. What maybe or maybenot don't matter, 'cause if there be sea there gottabe wet. In the said, same way, if there's weddin', if priest an' preacher, and church an' bride, if all these things is there, then there gottabe weddin' an' it ain't have nothing to do with what maybe, or maybenot, if there's these things, church, priest, preacher, an' so on, then there gottabe man. If there's weddin' there gottabe man. Deep inside you, you know there's gottabe that, if there's those other things, an' you don't worry yuh head, 'cause it ain't have nothin' to do with you. There's no need to worry, so you just sit an' wait to see what'll happen.'

'But if you's the man, an' you ain't go,' Boy Blue asked, 'how you goin' to get out of that?'

'It ain't matter,' Trumper said, ''tis a question of what gottabe, an' it ain't have nothin' to do with you, even if you's the man. 'Tis like the sea all over again. If you put on big big boots, an' you touch it with yuh toes, you don' get wet, but deep down inside you know in yuh heart of hearts there's gottabe wet. 'Cause 'tis a question of what gottabe. It ain't got nothin' to do with yuh toes an' where they maybe. So with a weddin'. If there's weddin', then there's gottabe man, an' it ain't 'ave nothin' to do with you, or where you is. 'Tis a question of what gottabe. That's p'raps the way Jon feel all the time.

An' then the thought of losing his life make him feel that way more still. He say to himself, there's gottabe man, an' it ain't make no difference where I am, there gottabe man, an' he stay where he wus to see what wus goin' to happen. Is a big feelin', this waitin' to see what you don't know, but what all time you feel is pretty sure. An' Jon wait, 'cause that wus the way he feel so he wait for such a long time they leave the church, an' up to then no man had so much as make his appearance. P'raps they should have stay a little longer.'

'But s'ppose,' Boy Blue went on, 'suppose Jon did see a man go in, an' there wus weddin', what would you say to that?'

'I'd say nothing to that,' Trumper said, "cause that's as much as what Jon wus expectin'. He wus simply an' purely sayin' to himself that 'though he be in the tree, if there's weddin' an all that, there's gottabe man, an' deep down he expect a man to go in. Is the sea an' the toes all over again.'

'That would make it that there wus two Jons,' Boy Blue said, 'one in the tree an' one in the church, whichever church he did choose.'

'P'raps three Jons,' Trumper said, "cause there wus as much weddin' preparation in one church as there wus in the other.'

'Three Jons,' Boy Blue repeated, 'one in the tree, an' one in each church. But it don't make sense.'

'P'raps it don't,' Trumper said. 'But that's what it is for all I know. There wus Jon in the tree tellin' one Jon to go to one church, an' the other to go the other church. 'Twus simply an' purely a question of one Jon tellin' the other to go an' do what the other din't want to do, that's all.'

'It don' make sense,' Boy Blue said. 'It ain't what the teacher does call logical.'

'P'raps it ain't,' Trumper said, 'but that don't make it not so. Logical or logistical, or whatever they call it, is logical or logistical an' so on, an' sense is sense, as we all know, but all that ain't got nothin' to do with what is. An' what wus in Jon min'?'

'I don't care what you say, Trumper,' Boy Blue said. 'You can't be in a tree an' two churches at the said, same time.' There was an urgency in his voice.

'I don't know,' Trumper said. 'P'raps you can if you feel you can.'

'But you don't seriously believe that, Trumper,' Boy Blue asked. He was asking the question as if the answer would make a great difference to what he wanted to say next.

'I don't know,' Trumper said. 'I r'ally don't know.'

"Cause sometimes I feel,' Boy Blue said. 'Sometimes I feel that I ain't goin' to die. I sort of gets that feelin' now an' again, that I goin' to live on an' on, no matter what happen to all the rest in the village. My mother says to me everything's got to die, 'cause 'tis the will of the Lord, but it don't make no difference to what I feel, that I ain't goin' to die. No matter what happen to the rest, I ain't goin' to die.'

'Suppose somebody kill you?' Trumper asked.

'It ain't the same thing,' Boy Blue said.

"Tis the same t'ing by a different name,' Trumper said.

'The same thing by a different name ain't the same thing,' Boy Blue said.

'P'raps it ain't,' Trumper said, 'but it sound alike to me.'

'Then why they make distinction betwixt kill an' die?' Boy Blue asked.

"Cause to kill mean when somebody kill you,' Trumper said, 'an' to die mean when you die yourself.'

'An' if somebody die you, what you call that?' Boy Blue said.

'I don't know,' Trumper said, 'I don't know.'

The crabs had forced a passage through the sand. They crept up the slope of the beach in single file. When the waves came up, they crouched waiting till the foam had petered away. The sand turned dark brown in the cloudly light, and we tried to follow the movements of the crabs. The centre crab crouched low on the sand while the other two moved deftly towards the centre, clawing wildly at each other. The claws cut through the air and fell limp to the sand. The centre crab crouched deeper till it was almost sunk in the sand while the end crabs kept up their violent clawing. The hair on the claws glinted in the light, and the points were dotted with grains of sand. It was a slow-drawn-out crab fight with the centre crab sinking deeper and deeper in the sand as the other two came together with the claws clinched and their aprons fastened. There were all three bundled together, and later there were two only. The centre crab had disappeared beneath the sand while the two crabs wrestled. They were stuck like things put together, and they reminded me in that embrace of the crabs I had seen earlier on my way up the beach. I asked Boy Blue to look close and tell me what he thought about the position. They looked so terribly together like the other two I had seen. The difference was in their movement. These wrestled, and the backs shifted with each tussle. The others were steady, and quiet and sacred in their lack of movement. Boy Blue said he thought the movement looked fishy, but they were certainly fighting. Then I told him about the two crabs I had seen together on the sand in the shade of the grape leaf. Trumper listened and looked at the crabs. They were steady now, and Trumper said it looked fishy. Boy Blue said it was better to say crabby. It looked crabby. We watched them in that twist and shift of quiet and suggestive crabbiness. They were so quiet now. Very quiet, and no movement at all, like sleep. There was no sign of the other crab. The sea simmered, and we watched with the wind watering our eyes the absolute togetherness of these objects. Crabby and quiet and clean. So very clean! A wave which had foamed away before reaching the shore drifted up the sand. The slope deepened, and the crabs turned over and over down the shifting sand. We were silent.

'Does it ever happen to you?' Boy Blue asked, and our ears twitched with the suddenness of his voice. Whenever the silence was broken, by the sea under the trees, we received a little shock. It crept quickly down the back and then fled away like a shiver.

'What ever happen?' Trumper asked.

'The way a thing put itself together,' Boy Blue said. 'You hear something, an' it come to you as a kind of surprise, then it connect up with another something you'd hear long time back, an' what with one thing an' another, they all put themselves together into a big something. Suddenly when they all together you see yourself face to face with something that is true or very very strange. Or it make you remember something that you didn't remember all the time.'

'What you thinkin' 'bout?' Trumper asked.

'Jon,' Boy Blue said. 'Jon an' the weddin's, an' the way he went into the cemetery. It all come together as one, an' then seein' the crabs fightin' or doin' whatever they wus doin'. It all link up an' it make me remember what happen to Bots, Bambi an' Bambina.'

'What happen in the end to them?' Trumper asked. 'I only heard a part of the story. 'Twus a high burnin' shame the way they treat Bambi. So my mother used to say. A high burnin' shame. She couldn't find any other words.'

'Well, Bambi is dead,' Boy Blue said. 'But Bots and Bambina still alive.'

'I know Bambi is dead,' Trumper said.

''Tis what happen to Bots an' Bambina that make me wonder,' Boy Blue said. ''Twus nearly like Jon an' Jen an' Susie, except that Bambi did get marry. He not only get marry, but he get marry in royal style. As you know he wus livin' with Bots an' Bambina both all two at the same time, for a long, long time. An' they all had children for him. Bots had Puss in Boots Number Two, an' Suck Me Toe, an' Bambina had three, Sugar Shine, Turtle Dove, an' Stumps. An' Bots an' Bambina wus the best of friends, an' the children who wus half brother an' half sister live like real brother and sister without any talk 'bout half or quarter. They live real splendid together, an' so did they mothers. Everybody says there never know in all the village from top to bottom a set of people who live in love an' harmony like Bots, Bambina an' Bambi, with the children there, not in the same house, but in the same sort of feelin' of you belong to me an' I to you. An' it went on like that for donkeys years. Then like a kind of nightmare 'cause you ain't expect anything so terrific, a white woman, or lady, whatever you choose to call her, come to live in the village. Some say she wus a German who wus comin' to take some notes 'bout the people. Some kind of notes 'bout the way they live, but nobody believe that, 'cause nobody don't take notes 'bout human beings. You may take notes 'bout pigeons an' rabbits an' that kind of creature, but we never hear in all we born days 'bout people comin' to take notes 'bout other people who wus like themselves. So nobody ain't take no notice.

'But there wus another rumour that she wus a funny woman, used to work with spirits an' that sort of thing, an' we start to wake up, that is we who live in Hunt's Road, where Bambi live. But the story change, an' some say it might have been a spirit, but not the sort of spirits we been thinkin'. They start to say she like black men, an' she use to pay so much an' so much for them to show themselves. Some believe that, an' some didn't. Some say white people din't do that sort of thing, an' others that there wusn't anything on this black God's earth that white people won't do, an' particularly those who come out from England. Not that the English white people wus cheap an' bad, but those who come out. Some say they know for sure that white people who come out from England wus a sort of scum who sort of din't know how to live at home. They say all sort of things, an' maybe they wus right, maybe they wus wrong. But this white woman keep comin' to the village time an' time again. Then when we hear the shout, it wusn't for no black men, 'though she might have had a little time if she feel the itch, an' it wusn't no spirits either. She wus encouraging the people who had children to get marry. It wus a hell of a joke, the way she went 'bout it. Some say they had no time for all that bullshit, but others say they had nothin' to lose. An' they went an' get marry. A hell of a joke I tell you, it wus. She got hold of Bambi an' persuade him to get marry, an' he take it into his head to do so. He had to choose, jus' like Jon an' Jen an' Susie. But he din't have no trouble with either. What wus on his min' wus whether he should do it at all. The white missis tell him yes, he should, 'cause it wus better to live in one mortal sin than two, an' then he had to think of the children growin' up. He never know what might happen, an' if they had to go for a job in a high place, any kind of real, big job like the Post Office or the Government Savings Bank it would be much easier if the child had a name. Bambi tell her she make him laugh, 'cause all his children had names. 'Twus the first thing he do when they born, look for a name. But she says that wusn't what she mean, they din't really have a name if they wus livin' as they wus. An' you had to think 'bout the future. People would be askin' lots of questions in the future 'bout who they father wus an' so on, an' not only they father but they father father. Bambi say it didn't make no difference one way or the other, but that he would try it out, an' when he give the next chil' a name, he would wait an' see if any change took place.

'He put the matter to both Bots an' Bambina, 'cause it didn't make no difference either way. He didn't like Bots' children any more than he like Bambina's. He wus supportin' all of them. It just din't make no difference, so he say in order to be fair, he would toss for it. He gives Bots heads on a penny, an' he give Bambina tails, an' he spin the coin. Bots win, an' he marry Bots. The white woman say she couldn't care less who or how he marry, once he marry one of them.

'There wus no trouble at all as with Jen an' Jon an' Susie. Bambina din't turn a hair of her head. She says she din't see anything to make a row 'bout, once Bambi din't stop supportin' the children, an' she wusn't goin' to have any other man if Bambi went to look for her as he did, no more often an' no less. 'Twus no question of one better than the other, just a question of what come into Bambi's head at the time, an' in the particular case, a question of which side the penny falls on. Everythin' wus alright up to the day of the weddin'. Bots an' Bambina meet at the baker shop an' they buy together as usual an' talk 'bout what they would do later. Bambina went out of the way to make Bots' dress an' all of that, all the children wus there, an' they had a hell of a time in Bots' back yard under a tarpaulin. Food! My God, you never see much food in all yuh life, chicken an' rabbit an' goat an' every manner of meat the Almighty put on this God's earth. They eat an' drink like hogs, not makin' nastiness or anything like that, but just loud an' happy. An' when they finish they make speech, the sort of speech that would have put the head teacher to shame. Everybody say they din't know Bambi had such a commandin' of the English language, an' whenever he use a long long word, or a sort of good, big phrase, everybody drain they glass an' bawl for murder. They thought the devil in hell self had get up from sleepin' for the noise they keep, an' Bambi went on talkin' like a politician, only he wusn't tellin' no lies. He believe in his heart of hearts what he wus sayin'. He talk till he had hiccoughs an' his old mother from the back had to come up an' tell him in his ear that he shouldn't talk no more or he would overstep the bound an' make a fool of himself. So he turn to everybody an' says how please the old lady wus with him an' ask him not to go any more in case he spoil the performance. He sit down an' they clap him till he wus sick. An' they lift up the ol' lady an' tell her how she hadn't lost her sense 'though she wus old, she sort of know when the devil had had his due. Then when the speech wus over they sing an' dance, an' Bots kiss Bambina an' Bambina kiss Bots an' Bambi kiss all two of them both. An' they all laugh an' laugh till they cry. People say they never see them so happy. An' God alone knows what happen, but it wasn't six months after that trouble set in.

'People have a way of sayin' that trouble don't set up like rain, an' 'tis true. Nobody sort of really notice how Bambi change, but he wus changin'. He start first of all by not talkin' too much, an' people wus surprise, 'cause when he wus round, his mouth wus like a trumpet. He used to talk like a typewriter, tattattattattattat, an' sometimes you couldn't sort of get the meanin' of what he wus sayin', just tattattat-tattat. But all of a sudden, his tongue wus sort of tie up, an' he turn quiet, he just say yes an' no, an' nothin' more than that. Nobody could understan' what come over him, an' Bots notice an' wus afraid. Bambina notice too, but she din't say nothin'. Then it got so bad Bots went to put the matter to Bambina; she say how Bambi wus a change man an' she din't have an inklin' of what could have come

over him. Bambina says she notice too, an' that Bambi wus not the
Bambi she use to know. He had change in every manner of way, an'
wus a high burnin' shame that a man who wus so nice an' sweet could
have change like that. They din't know what to do or say 'bout it.
They says they just wait an' see what happen. But they really din't
believe that anything wus serious wrong, 'twus just a matter of a
change that come over him. It happens to men at that age. Just when
they lose they wisdom teeth, they sort of make a change, an seem
strange. Some went mad, but Bambi wusn't the sort to go mad, 'cause
he had a very big head an' his brain had plenty room to run 'bout,
an' he still had a lot of hair on his head which show that he wus still
full up with common sense. Hair wus the sign of common sense.
Whenever you see a man with no hair on his head, you had to watch
out, anything could go wrong in his head at any time, 'cause he had
nothing on the naked skull to sort of stop the shock of the sun, an'
the sun wus so damn hot in the village. But Bambi had plenty hair
so there wus no need to worry.

'A fortnight after Bots see Bambina, Bambina went up to see Bots,
an' she say that her left eye wus jumpin' sixty to the secon' an' she din't
like it; she ask Bots if she sure Bambi din't eat something wrong, 'cause
she din't like the way her left eye wus jumpin', it always mean trouble.
Bots says not as far as she know, but she wus beginnin' to feel funny
too. Only the other morning she see a big black bee. The bee fly
through one window, an' then made a circle, an' instead of goin'
through another window which would have mean good luck, it turn
an' turn an' went back through the same window it come through.
That wus bad bad luck. An' Bots say too that she notice Bambi start
to drink, an' he wus a sort of man who would have a drink now an'
again, but not as a practice. But now he wus makin' it a practised habit,
this drinkin', and you couldn't say two words to him, before he say
he wus goin' to buy a pack of cigarettes and when he got back he wus
blind blind drunk.

'It went on an' on an' soon Bambi wus the hardest drinker in the
village; they say they never see a man put away rum like that; he use to
make it look like water, the way he put it to his head, an' snap his lips.
Every Saturday night, he wus blind drunk, an' one Saturday night in
particular he got so drunk he din't know what to do with himself, an'
he went home an' he beat the life out of Bots. He beat Bots till she
couldn't sit on what God give her, an' when he wus finish with Bots,

he went for Bambina, an' what he forgot to give Bots he give her. Bambina bawl for murder, an' the police had to come. But they din't arrest Bambi 'cause everybody say that he wusn't like that at all, he wusn't the sort of man to hit a woman, but somethin' had gone wrong in his head. The whole of Hunt's Road, though they wus sorry for Bots an' Bambina, stand up for Bambi, 'cause they say something wus wrong, 'twusn't the real Bambi doin' what he wus doin'. So they let him go, but that din't help, an' he took to the habit of beatin' them time an' again. Every Saturday night he went for them an' he beat them like you beat a snake, Bots an' Bambina, all two of them both, one after the other. People say he beat them till they piss, poor things. He din't have mercy on them. An' they couldn't stan' it no longer. They just couldn't stand the way Bambi wus carrying on, an' they both swear that somebody had give Bambi somethin' to eat; Bots got blue vex an' went tearin' down to where Bambina live, an' she start to talk like a person who had lost the tongue. It wus as if Bots' tongue wus doin' all the talkin' an' Bots din't have anythin' to do with what her tongue was sayin'. She curse Bambina goin' an' comin', back an' front, 'cause she say it wus Bambina who had put Bambi so. An' Bambina din't forget to tell Bots what she know 'bout her, an', boy, that wus plenty. She tell Bots what she do an' din't do to make Bambi marry her, an' people couldn't understand it. Bots an' Bambina who wus such good friends, you couldn't see one without seein' the other, the way they turn on one another. Trouble don't set up like rain, 'tis true, 'cause if you'd tell anybody in all Creighton's village that this would have happen 'twixt Bots an' Bambina, they would have ask you to see a doctor.

'But there 'twus, enmity 'twixt the two, an' for what, you couldn't say. An' one mornin' Bots an' Bambina fight till they nearly kill one another. The idea, everybody had to say, the idea that the two of them who live so good together should have let the devil come between. An' the fight wus so bad that the next night the open-air preacher who had heard close his meeting with the hymn, "Satan go way, Satan go way, Satan go away an' let Jesus come in." The people sing like it wus the end of the world, 'cause they wus really frighten with what they see happen between Bots an' Bambina an' after the flood which they had some time back that nearly drown so many of us they start to feel that the Lord Almighty had really put His hand down. That's what the preacher said, the good God wus payin' the village a visit, an' He come first in the flood an' next in the fight, an' the way He would come next time the preacher say, only He Himself could say why He did it, 'twould be hell an' damnation. Nobody know if hell an' damnation come after, but 'twus death that come. One night Bambi fall down an' dead, easy so. He had a heart attack, an' before you say Jack Robinson he wus dead. 'Twus at Bambina house, an' all Bambina shake him, it ain't make no difference. He wus dead. The preacher wus right. The good God had come again. People wus so sorry, 'cause they like Bambi very much. 'Twus a good thing, he get save. Nobody know what get in his head, but the night before, he heard the voice callin' him to confess his sins before God an' be saved before time change to eternity. So the preacher say, he died within the fold. His sins wus black, but it didn't matter. God wus such a merciful an' lovin' God that He only wanted to see a desire in you for the light an' He'd do the rest.

'But 'twus a high burnin' shame what happen after. When the undertakers hear that Bambi wus dead, two of them drive up like wild hogs to ask for the body. They come tearing way through Hunt's an' they nearly kill two old women which would have given them two more jobs. They had a big argument, an' Bambina say she would give the funeral to the one who get there first. The other get vex an' he went an' tell Bots that she wus the rightful owner of the body, 'cause he wus marry to her. Bots come down mad as a tiger cat an' tell Bambina she want Bambi dead body. An' they argue it out between them. Bambina say he die in her house, an' it wusn't she, Bambina, who send him to die there, so it must have been the will of the Lord. Bots said that in life he wus hers an' in death he should be also, an' Bambina could not hear her own ears for the way she talk. She ask Bots what she mean by life, what she mean by in life he wusn't hers, meanin' Bots, any more than he wus hers, meanin' Bambina. They quarrel an' they nearly fight, but Bots' undertaker take her away an' say not to worry. Everybody wus please with the way he try to make peace.

'But it din't end there, an' this is the part that send water to my eyes an' make me frighten when I talk; it make me frighten 'cause I begin to think there ain't no difference twixt dead an' living.

'Twus after midnight. They had wash Bambi an' prepare him for the funeral which wus the next day. Bambina undertaker had the job done an' they say Bambi did look sweet an' nice in the box. They dress him in his best suit, the black serge he use to wear on special occasions, an'

at the top they put his white handkerchief an' a red carnation in the
button-hole. He wear his best shoes an' socks an' there wus no difference between him then an' the day he get marry, 'except that now he
wus dead. Bambina friends come in to look at him an' everybody say
how it look as if he wus sleepin', an' he must be sleepin' 'cause nobody
could believe Bambi wus dead. The children look at him an' touch the
tip of his nose with the finger, he look so like if he wus alive. 'Twus a
little after midnight, an' Bambina wus sleepin' in a corner in the same
room with Bambi. People say she shouldn't do that, but she say in
life she wusn't 'fraid of Bambi an' she din't see why in death she
should be. She wus fast asleep, when in come Bots an' her undertaker.
They creep in quiet quiet an' not a word, not a sound pass the lips.
The lamp was burnin' low on the table, 'cause Bambina always sleep
with a light in the room, says she can't sleep in the dark for any sum
of money. The two of them crawl like crabs quiet quiet, not a sound,
an' they size up the coffin. The undertaker put on his torch light an'
there wus Bambi in the coffin. They hadn't put on the lid of the coffin
yet, an' you could see him from head to toe.

'The undertaker tell Bots easy in her ears that 'twus a shame to bury
him in those good boots an' that they would change them when
they get home. They size up the coffin well an' proper, Bots at the
top by Bambi's head an' the undertaker at the bottom by his feet,
an' gradually they lift him out of the coffin, quiet, quiet, not a word.
The undertaker had his car outside waiting with the door wide open,
so they could just throw Bambi in when they reach, an' tidy him
up later. They lift him out quiet, an' they wus both surprise how
light he wus, must have been the rum wearin' down his constitution.
They wus really flabbergasted by his weight, an' they move quiet,
quiet an' easy to the door. Everything went first class an' there poor
Bambina in the corner fast asleep with her eyes shut tight as a drum
an' not knowin' what going on under her nose. They step easy an'
then they had a little trouble gettin' him through the door, and
'cause 'twus a little narrow, so the undertaker motion to Bots to
turn him sideways an' Bots wus equal to anything he tell her to do.
They lean him sideways, an' when they had got him half-way
through, the big camphor balls that stop up his nostrils drop out
an' wake up Bambina. She couldn't believe her eyes. She turn the
lamp wick an' look an' it din't make sense. She see Bambi sort of
half standin' up an' she wus so frighten she bawl for murder. Then

she realize what wus happenin' an' she step under the coffin an' come out the other side. There wus trouble. They fight like hell she and Bots, an' the undertaker put down Bambi an' start to run, but everybody wus awake. People hear Bambina scream an' before you say Jack Robinson they wus there on the spot, an' with them too wus Bambina's undertaker, an' then the undertakers start to fight. They fight till they break the lamp an' nearly burn down the place, an' there wus poor Bambi, can't move 'cause he dead. 'Twus like hell self with the fire on the floor an' the four of them fightin' an' poor Bambi stone cold dead, not able to move. The police come an' take statement an' it turn out that neither Bambina nor Bots din't have the money to bury Bambi, an' they din't have enough on the Society card for the Society to bury him. The undertakers wus hopin' they would sell the house, but the house wusn't belonging to Bambina or Bots. An' so in the end the Government had to take the body. They sen' it to the mortuary an' the next day Bambi had a poor man's funeral. 'Twus a high burnin' shame that that had to be. Why everybody, good, bad an' indifferent should get a good funeral with wreath an' people to walk behind the hearse, an' Bambi all alone should go in a poor man's spot. 'Twus really sad.'

Boy Blue paused to catch breath and we waited.

'To tell the truth,' he went on, 'I never hear the like of it before, never, never, never. I've as much as heard of people fight for money, an' clothes, an' sometimes for big property, an' I've known times p'raps when men fight for women an' the other way round, they say that in the war the soldiers are told they're fightin' for life, but I've never heard before in all my born days that the livin' fight for the dead. The things that happen in that village histr'y ain't begin to start to know yet. An' people go on livin' as if nothin' happen.'

''Tis true,' Trumper said. His face was tense and the short eye-lashes seemed to twinkle in the light. 'Those things never happen in histr'y, an' even if they did, histr'y ain't got eyes to see everything.'

'An' what I don't understand is this,' Boy Blue said, 'things never happen so between a man an' a man, or a woman an' a woman. Is always a man an' a woman. Whenever real trouble, the sort of trouble as with Jen an' Jon or Bots an' Bambina, whenever you get that sort of trouble, is at the bottom of it a woman an' man.'

'An' not so much a man an' a woman,' Trumper said, 'but the thing they call marriage. Like Bambi an' Bots an' Bambina. They live alright for only God knows how long, an' as soon as one get marry to the other, it don't matter who marry who, as soon as they is that marryin' business, everythin' break up, break right up.'

'P'raps it don't belong to some people,' Boy Blue said. 'There is a sayin' marr'age ain't make for everybody, 'tis an old sayin', and seems true.'

'That mean for certain people like you an' him an' me an' so on, Trumper said; 'but it seem it don't belong to certain people, meanin' a lot of people put together, like the village for instance. Except for those who live sort of different, who live in the village but don't really sort of belong, except for those, there's always that said same breakin' up when marriage makes his appearance. I don't know. I only know I ain't ever goin' get marry.'

'You mustn't say so,' Boy Blue said. 'You can never tell, never, never.'

'But I tellin' you I ain't,' Trumper said. He spoke with great confidence. "Cause there's so many other things bad 'bout it,' he said, 'you can't sort of get 'bout as you like, an' the woman always seem to think she's got some special kind of claim on you, as if you're a kind of pigeon or a fowl. You say you goin' here or there, she want to ask you where, an' sometimes you don't really know where you goin', you just takin' a walk to stretch yuh legs, but she says you lyin' as she can't believe a word of what you sayin'. You can't pitch or play bat-an'-ball when you like 'cause there's a chil' to feed, an' this to do an' that to do, an' when you ask what the bloody hell she wus doin' or would 'ave do if you din't come along and put yuhself in all that, she up an' tell you; don't trouble trouble till trouble trouble you. An' you can tell her to fly in hell 'cause there's the police court ready to land you in gaol an' only God knows what.'

The worn flesh that held the eyelashes shone. His temples twitched with a strange kind of excitement, and his expression was very serious. He was more serious than Boy Blue had thought. He looked down at the sand, watching the foam feel a way through the spaces of the toes. Very serious.

'You still can't tell,' Boy Blue said, 'you never know. You never know as you youself say when something go off pop in yuh head an' you ain't the same man you think you wus. You start to do an' say things which you know is true but it seem it ain't you doin' an' sayin' them. Who could have believe what would have happen to

Bambi—Bambi of all people. But something go off pop in yuh head, an' it turn out you ain't the same man you used to think you wus. An' 'twus the same with Jon. Chris', of all places a tree. Who the hell put it in his head to go up in a tree? You never can tell, as you youself know full well.'

'This sort of goin' in you head don't sound safe to me,' Trumper said.

'I wus sort of makin' joke. Not really makin' joke, but sort of tryin' to say what I mean without knowing the right words to say. An' I say goin' on in you head 'cause I ain't 'ave no bigger an' better word, but I don't like it at all, 'cause it could mean all sort of things. A thing go off in yuh head pop pop, an' you's a different man. You ain't the same sort of person you wus, an' the next thing you hear, you ain't the same sort of person everybody is. You start to feel you different from everybody else, an' if that sort of thing go on you'll feel that there's nobody like you. I don't mean that you'll get great, an' don't want to speak to anybody. I don't mean that at all. I mean you'll get the feeling there ain't no other man like yourself, that you is you, so to speak, an' there can't be any other you. An' that everybody else is different from you. You start to believe you see things nobody else see, an' you think things nobody else think, an' that sort of thing can take you far, far, far. When you hear the shout, nobody will want to see you, an' you youself won't want to see anybody, an' 'cause of something goin' off in yuh head pop, pop, an' you can't control it. Boy, you'll get so lonely 'twould be a shame. You'd be a sort of man on a rock with nobody else standin' near you, although there's plenty other people 'round, that's how you'll feel, 'cause it gone to yuh head that you is different from everybody else. If you really want to know what 'twould feel like, imagine youself the last man left in the village, everybody dead, dead, dead, an' you the only one left. That is what could happen if that feelin' of bein' sort of different go to yuh head.'

'It could happen,' Boy Blue said curiously. 'I could imagine all of them dead, an' I the only one there. But this thing of feelin' different ain't the same thing. That could happen too as you say, but it take a big big change to make you so.'

''Though it sort of frighten me,' Trumper said, 'I'd like to see it happen. Just as a kind of big joke, I would like to see something like that happen, but not to me only, to everybody, to the whole village, so that everybody get that big bad feeling that he different from everybody else, an' nobody don't know what to do, 'cause you don't know what the other fellow would do after you, an' you ain't sure of anything at all, 'cause you ain't sure that another pop, pop, pop won't go off in yuh head an' make you somebody different again before you say Jack Robinson. 'Twould be a hell of a business. You couldn't ask anybody anything, 'cause nobody know anything.'

'That won't be a good t'ing,' Boy Blue said, "cause everybody would sort of confuse like when you got a big, big job to do an' it give you bad feelings. 'Twould be a kind of sickness in yuh stomach. Every time you look up you feel you lookin' down, a real kind of bad sickness at the bottom of everything.'

'I don't think it could happen though to the whole village,' Trumper said. 'It couldn't, 'cause we do so many things the same way. Everybody in the village sort of belong. Is like a tree. It can't kind of take up the roots by itself; we all live sort of together, except for those who don't really belong. An' 'tis the same in the other villages, Deans village, Case village, Spooners village, is the same thing; they sort of got the little things like us; they got the village choir, an' they go in for the competition every Christmas mornin' 'gainst us an' the rest; they have the church for everybody an' they school for boys an' girls. I don't ever get the feelin' whatever I say that anythin' could change so. An' I won't like it, 'cause 'tis so much more easy this way, everybody sort of steady an' know what they want to do an' so on. I like that.'

'But it could happen all the same,' Boy Blue said, 'p'raps not to every Tom, Dick an' Harry, but one or two. In a kin' of way it happen to Jon an' Bambi. But when it happen to you an' you got to go on livin' it must be terrible.'

'We'd better stop talkin' 'bout that,' Trumper said, "cause it kind of frighten me. It don't ever happen to a lot of people, village or no village. People who teach an' work in the post office an' the bank, it don't happen to them. They is like we in a way; they go to work an' go back home, an' they go out next day an' go back home again, an' they keep they head on straight. They got better jobs an' so on, but they live sort of the same way, eatin' a little better, but nothin' ever go pop, pop in they heads, an' nothin' ever will, take it from me, 'cause they's sensible, quiet, nice people with they head on straight. That sort of thing don't ever happen to such people, 'cause they know an Ace for an Ace an' a Jack for a Jack. I hear them talkin' sometimes. Only the other day I hear the teacher say how he just want to put in

so much time an' see if he can get out, so that the future would be
bright for his children, just as his father try to make it bright for him.
The father make it bright for him an now he's a big school master, an'
he is goin' to make it bright for his children an' so on till time change
for eternity. An' all 'cause they's sensible people with they head on
straight, an' they know an Ace for an Ace an' a Jack for a Jack. They
ain't know no sort of thing goin' pop, pop, pop, pop, pop, pop, pop
in they head. Nothin'll ever change in the village.'

'P'raps you right,' Boy Blue said.

'Even when the teacher say 'bout a war, an' you think everybody
gone mad 'cause of the way they kill one another, the teacher say they
got a reason. They don't do it before they give one another a good an'
proper reason for what they doin'. An every soldier who sort of push
a knife through another's guts got a good an' proper reason, the
teacher says. It ain't ever 'cause anything go pop, pop in his head.'

'Never,' Trumper said, 'never, p'raps to one here, an' one there, but
in the whole village, never, nothin'll ever happen here to this village
that ain't happen some time before, an' if anythin' happen, it won't
ever be the sort of thing to make people heads go pop, pop, pop.
Never, never, never.'

The crabs had emerged from under the sand. They were quiet and
tranquil making a triangle in their order as they climbed the slope.
The waves were more quiet now and the sand seemed firmer. The
wind had sailed away somewhere and everything was still. There was
no wind at all. On the lighthouse a seabird had perched, its head and
neck stretched direct across to the sea. The feathers didn't make a
wrinkle. It was so still. The crabs crawled farther and farther up the
shore. The silence of the sea and the trees and the sand under the
grape leaf made us feel that their claws were making a sound against
the sand. They buried and lifted them alternately, and with each
movement their bodies were pushed up another inch or two along
the shore. The bird was still on the lighthouse, and we were trying
to guess what it would do next. It seemed the same bird we had seen
some weeks ago on the other side. We called it a seabird, and that
was the only name we knew for it. The beak was long and pointed,
and the end slightly hooked like a shoemaker's awl. The colour of the
feathers was dark grey with here and there a patch of brown on the
back, and the sleekest white along the neck and down the breast to
the tip of the tail on the under side. There was a black patch on the

top of the head. We looked at it for want of something to do, and when the sea and the wind and the trees turned silent we had to find something to do to remind ourselves that we were still there. We were tired talking. And we had got a little afraid of all we had said. There was nothing better or safer than to look at the bird on the lighthouse. And its colour and ease in the stillness of the air deserved a look. The crabs were still moving up the shore, farther and farther away from the sea. The higher they reached the easier and quicker was their movement. The sand was much firmer, and it was with effort that they raised the claws. The eyes were at rest in their cavity, and the body raised in its movement was like a house on stilts.

The fisherman who had passed us some time ago came out from behind the lighthouse and looked up at the sky. We were more at ease when he was there and we weren't talking. He put his big, coarse hands above his eyes and looked round in all directions. He stood there looking up and around like a sailor viewing the sky through binoculars. We wondered what he was going to do. His manner was so assured. It gave us a good feeling, the way he stood with his hands poised and his strong lofty chin pointed skyward, and it made the sea seem to us a little tamer. The waves were hurrying up again, and they reached his toes. You might have brushed his pants with a feather. He didn't notice. The sand was firm where he stood, and the water hurried along, lapping his big, bare feet. He didn't twitch. We looked and laughed. He seemed so confident in his strength, looking up at the sky with his hands over his eyes like a rare kind of binocular.

He returned behind the lighthouse, and some minutes later came out again dragging a large fish net behind him. He stretched it out over the sand, and we watched him disentangle the fine ropes and plug the ends. The water rushed up rapidly and the sands were becoming slacker. A big wave came, flattened out along the shore and in its retreat the sand shifted sharply. The fisherman's foot slid back, and he crouched on all fours to restore his balance. It didn't seem to matter. He didn't look down to see what was happening. We were amused and delighted and a little puzzled by the way he took everything for granted. The waves were like flies playing about a baker's hat. He tolerated them, bore their sting and their buzz till he was ready to brush them off. The fisherman shook his feet in the water with the same ease and the same indifference. The wind came again more strongly, and the net made a lazy wrinkle over the area of sand which it covered. The fisherman held the ends and looked at it as if he wanted to say something about keeping quiet. The sand was shifting, and the net had moved nearer the sea. He didn't smile or laugh or look angry. The expression on his face had nothing to do with the net or the waves that washed up against his feet. It was just an expression, that was all. None of us would have spoken to him for all the money in the world, because he seemed so big in that steady, concentrated purpose of plugging a net in the sand. It was the same when he looked at the sky. You wouldn't have dared disturb him. He was not the sort of man you would say hello at, but you watched him and wished secretly that you could tell what he would do next. You wouldn't have liked him to know that you were paying attention.

We had never seen anyone fish on this side and we were all the more anxious to see what would happen. There were no boats on the sea, and the waves lashing wildly in the distance made us wonder all the more what the fisherman might do. He was kneeling in the sand holding down the ends of the nets. Boy Blue said he didn't think he was going to throw the net in, but it was customary for the fishermen to put their nets on the beach to dry in the sun. It wasn't good for the nets, he said, that they shouldn't touch land when they weren't being used in the sea. We didn't think the fisherman would enter the sea, and if he intended doing so, we were happy not to be in his boots. We might have gone to the brink, but nothing could have moved any of us to enter the sea on this side. It was utterly deserted, and in spite of the colour and splash of the foam the whole aspect was terribly forbidding. The tide dwindled to a clean clear line along the shore, and the fisherman slid back again. It was fascinating to watch the waves foam away far out while the after tide crept up the sand. Whatever happened on the shore they were wild and lashing farther out. No one ever knew how often or how far up the shore they would come. The fisherman's feet were sliding back continually, and we laughed quietly. It always happened to us on the other side. When the waves were exhausted and slithered back to meet the outward moving tide, the sand fell away and we slid with it into the body of the sea. Sometimes we stood at the brink of the slope where the sand was beginning to get firm in its stretch up the shore. The tide slid back and we moved forward, face seaward, trying all the while to see how prehensile were our toes. It was one of the many games we played in the sea.

Something similar was happening to the fisherman, but it wasn't a game for him. He was serious as death, as we say. His back was turned to the sea, and when the waves came up he slid back on his knees. He didn't seem to care what happened behind his back. His balance restored, he crept another inch or two up towards the net. A wave rushed up again, and the same thing happened. He brushed the water from his hands and stood. It seemed very irritating now. He was still trying to get the nets plugged into the sand, and it seemed he had a special way of doing it. He must have known that the sand wasn't going to keep firm for his sake, but he tried, not like a novice who wasn't sure what would have happened. It was someone who had seen it all before. He knew what he was doing. It must have been very irritating now, the way the net slackened when the wave came up. Sometimes he raised himself erect as if everything was finished to his satisfaction, and suddenly the water had trickled up and the sand loosened. He tried and tried again, and each time with a similar result. The sand was no good. It was impossible. He looked down at the net as if he were giving it the reasons for his failure. It was something they understood. He dragged the net up the beach and tumbled it into a wrinkled heap on the grape vine. He was finished. It was useless to try again. We wanted to laugh as he walked back towards the lighthouse. We couldn't. There was something powerful and corrective about his big figure. He walked back slowly looking up at the sky as if it had told him something that wasn't true. His elbows were enormous. We wondered at the breadth and bigness of his back. It seemed to stand up on its own. If you saw his back first, you might get the feeling that there was something terrifying in front of it. You might have liked to have a look at his face, but not for him to know. There would be a kind of impertinence in the attempt. We were aware of it as we looked at him. He wasn't the sort of person you looked at without feeling terribly little. His giant frame urged that sensation. In a way we were glad to see him go. It gave us the chance to talk about him. You couldn't risk that when he was there on the beach. We watched him turn the vine and disappear behind the lighthouse, and we wondered how soon he would return. He had left the net on the grape vine, and that probably meant that he wouldn't go away for a long time. Boy Blue looked at Trumper and Trumper said, no, before Boy Blue spoke. He knew that Boy Blue was going to say something about going to have a look at the net.

It wasn't the sort of thing you would have done easily. We wondered whether he had taken much notice of us. He never really looked in our direction, but when he did so, there wasn't any sign that he had seen us, although we weren't very far. We had a feeling of release and frustration when he went. We were glad to be without him there looking round, and not sure what he might say if he saw us. But we were sorry we hadn't the chance to say something to him. It would have given us a big thrill. We could have related it to Bob with a good, deep feeling of pride. We had talked to a big fisherman, and we would say how very big he was. It was like climbing a mountain before anyone else. On that account we were very sorry he left.

'Let's go,' Trumper said. He had hardly spoken when the little crabs appeared. They were nearer the sea now. When we had seen them last they had crawled up to the grape vine, but they must have cut a way back through the sand while we were watching the fisherman. The eyes were raised, and they limped slowly towards the sea. The sand seemed firmer where they were.

'You like crab?' Boy Blue asked. He smiled as he asked the question.

'I like crab,' Trumper said, 'but these too small.' He too smiled as he spoke.

'What don't kill does fatten,' Boy Blue said.

Boy Blue left us and crept towards the crabs approaching them from the back. Crab-catching was a pastime which we used to test our speed as well as lightness of touch. After heavy rains the village was often invaded by crabs, large blue-back creatures sprawling stupidly here and there to get their bearings. The men and boys came out in droves with sticks and pokers and traps of every description. Children and women screamed when they saw the catch. Sometimes it yielded hundreds of crabs, and the boys and men who had trapped them made a prosperous business. Even those who had condemned crab-catching as a dirty sport bought them. They were delicious if you prepared them well. But these crabs that leaned uncertainly on the slope of the shore were different. They were very small and decorous, like cups and saucers which my mother bought and put away. You couldn't use them for drinking purposes. They were too delicate and decorous. These little crabs had that quality. Small, enchanting bits of furniture with which the shore was decorated. You wouldn't eat them although the meat might have been as delicious as that of the big village crabs, which were ugly and gross in their crawling movements.

Boy Blue didn't really want to eat one of these. He wanted to catch them as a kind of triumph. He could show what he had done after spending so many hours on the other side of the lighthouse. Catching things gave us little boys a great thrill. Sometimes we shot birds and carried them exposed in the palm of the hand. Everyone could see what we had done, meaning what he had achieved. It was like talking to the fisherman, or climbing a mountain which no one had hitherto dared ascend. The thrill of capturing something! It was wonderful! Boy Blue looked like a big crab crawling on all fours, and he made us laugh with the shift and shake of his slouching movements. The crabs dropped their eyes and remained still. It was always very difficult to tell what a crab would do. Sometimes they would scamper wildly if you were a mile away, and at other times they would crouch and bundle themselves together the nearer you approached. They seemed to feel that they were unseen because their eyes were dropped level in the slot that contained them. Boy Blue lay flat on the sand with his hands stretched out full length. The crabs were trying to make a way in the sand. They had seen him but there was no great hurry in escaping. Perhaps the sand was their domain. They could appear and disappear at will while you waited and watched. His hands had them covered but there was no contact. The difficulties had only started. When you were catching a crab with bare hands you required great skill. You had to place your thumb and index finger somewhere between the body and the claws of the crab. That was very tricky, since the crabs' claws were free like revolving chairs. They could spin, it seemed, in all directions, and they raised and dropped them to make any angle. Hundreds of boys were squeezed time and again in their effort to trap the crabs barehanded. If you missed the grip, or gripped a minute too soon the claws had clinched you. And the claws cut like blades. You had to know your job. You had to be a crab catcher, as we would say.

A master at the art, Boy Blue considered he was. He had caught several in his time. The art had become a practised routine. It was simply a matter of catching them. In this art he carried the same assurance and command we had noticed in the fisherman. He lay flat with his hands pressed on the crabs' back. He was trying to gather them up all together. His thumb had found the accustomed spot between the claw and the body of the crab. The crabs were still but buckled tight, so that it was difficult to strengthen the grip. Sometimes they seemed to understand the game. They remained still and stiffly buckled, and when you least expected the claws flashed like edged weapons.

The waves came up and the sand slid back. It seemed they would escape. If the waves came up again the sand would be loosened and they could force a way easily into the sand. Boy Blue had missed his grip. The wave came again and the sand sloped. Boy Blue slid back and the crabs were free from his grip. He propelled his feet in the sand in an attempt to heave himself forward. His weight pressed down. The wave receded and the sand shifted sharply. He came to a kneeling position and the sand slipped deeper. The crabs were safe. He threw his hand up and stood. The sand shifted under his feet and the waves hastening to the shore lashed him face downward. The salt stung his eyes and he groped to his feet. Another wave heaved and he tottered. The crabs! The crabs had disappeared. We could not understand what was happening. Boy Blue was laughing. It made us frighten the way he laughed. A wave wrenched him and now he was actually in the sea. We shivered, dumb. A wave pushed him up, and another completing the somersault plunged him down. He screamed and we screamed too. He was out of sight and we screamed with all the strength of our lungs. And the waves washed our screams up the shore. It was like a conspiracy of waves against the crab catcher. We screamed and the fisherman came out from behind the lighthouse. We motioned him to the spot where we had last seen Boy Blue. There was a faint scream in the air. We could not understand how it had happened. We could not follow the speed of the fisherman's movements. He had gathered up the net and tossed it in the sea over the area we had indicated. He hauled earnestly and the body of the net emerged with the strangest of all catches. Boy Blue was there. He was rolled up like a wet blanket. We were dumb with fright. He looked so impotent in the net. His eyes were bloodshot and his body heaved with a great flood of wind. He gasped and gasped, like a dog that had strained itself with too great speed in the chase. The fisherman hauled him up the beach and emptied the net as if it contained a useless dead thing. He looked at Boy Blue with a kind of disgust. Boy Blue was like a fly which had buzzed too long. You slapped it down and were sorry that you made such a mess of your hands. You might have left it. But you couldn't. It was unbearable. A necessary evil. Slapping it down. That's what it was. A necessary evil. The fisherman looked down at Boy Blue, unspeaking. There was

no trace of what we would call bad temper. Just a kind of quiet disgust.
Boy Blue sat silent, his teeth chattering and his whole body a shiver
of flesh in the wind. We could not speak. We were afraid of the
fisherman. The way he looked at us! He was like someone who had
been sorry for what he did, and yet not sorry since he knew it had to
be done. He looked so terribly repentant and at the same time there
was an expression which we could not define. Under the marble eyes
and the impenetrable stare there must have been something that cried
out for life. He knew the catch was not a fish, but he hauled the net
with the earnestness that could only have meant a desire beyond his
control for the other's survival. Now he looked so terribly penitent.
We were frightened.

'I should have let you drown,' he snarled, and his voice held
terror.

'Thank you, sir,' Boy Blue said, catching his breath. It was the first
time Boy Blue had spoken.

'By Christ, you should have drown,' the fisherman snarled again.

'You mustn't say that,' Boy Blue said. We were stunned by the
impertinence of the words. But there couldn't have been impertinence.
Boy Blue was shivering like a kitten that had had a bath.

'Why the hell shouldn't I have let you drown?' the fisherman
shouted. It was the first thing he had said that made us think he was
really human like us. The way he said it! He now looked angry.

'Tell me,' he snapped. 'Tell me to my face why the hell I shouldn't
have let you drown?'

''Cause if I'd drown I wouldn't have been able to tell you thanks,'
Boy Blue said. He was serious and the fisherman walked back towards
the lighthouse.

He walked up the shore with his big, broad back turned against us.
He looked the same giant we had seen earlier, but a little more human.
There was a kind of contact in what he had said a few minutes ago.
We realized he could be angry. It didn't seem so at first, but now we
felt it. He was only big and strong, as we would say in the village, he
was only big and strong but he was like one of us. His anger was
human. His absolute command and assurance as the waves washed up
against his feet and the net spread before him were not. That was not
human at all. We watched him walk up the beach towards the lighthouse, and we didn't speak. Some hours ago we had discovered a
giant. Now we had discovered a man. The giant was the man, but
being a man he could no longer be a giant. The man had undermined

the giant. We did not say that because we had no words with which
to say it. We felt it. Contact had made him human. Now he was like
us. He was only big and strong, as we would say in the village, but
he was like us. He could kill another man if he wanted to do so, and
he could save a man from death if he wanted to do so. He had the
strength. He was stronger than all of us put together. Perhaps he was
stronger than all the village. It made no difference. He was only big
and strong, as we would say in the village, but he was like one of us,
just like one of us. A man.

As he approached the lighthouse he turned and faced us. We waited
and watched, dumb. No one had spoken since Boy Blue.

'Get yuh arse from out this side of the sea,' he shouted.

'Yes, sir,' we said in unison.

He turned and moved towards the lighthouse, his hands pointing
down to the sea and his back, big and broad like something that had
a life of its own. He was out of sight. We looked at each other,
unspeaking, and each seemed to see what the other was feeling. He
was only big and strong as we would say in the village, but he was like
one of us, just like one of us. A man.

The little crabs had appeared again. Boy Blue looked at them and
as quickly looked away.

'Don't look that way,' he said, and led us by the arms towards the
other side of the lighthouse.

We walked through the grape vine disentangling our feet from the
leaves. We uprooted the patches of moss and fern that covered the
narrow dirt swamps. And we didn't look back. It was hours since we
had left home. We had talked and talked and talked. We had talked
a lot of nonsense, perhaps. But anyone would forgive us. With the
sea simmering, and the sand and the wind in the trees, we received
so many strange feelings. And in the village in the cellar, at the school,
in this corner or that corner of the house, something was always
happening. We didn't notice it then, but when something bigger
appeared like the sea and the sand, it brought with it a big, big feeling,
and the big feeling pushed up all the little feelings we had received in
other places. We weren't ashamed. Perhaps we would do better if we
had good big words like the educated people. But we didn't. We had
to say something was like something else, and whatever we said didn't
convey all that we felt. We wouldn't dare tell anybody what we had
talked about. People who were sure of what they were saying and
who had the right words to use could do that. They could talk to

others. And even if they didn't feel what they were saying, it didn't matter. They had the right words. Language was a kind of passport. You could go where you like if you had a clean record. You could say what you like if you know how to say it. It didn't matter whether you felt everything you said. You had language, good, big words to make up for what you didn't feel. And if you were really educated, and you could command the language like a captain on a ship, if you could make the language do what you wanted it to do, say what you wanted it to say, then you didn't have to feel at all. You could do away with feeling. That's why everybody wanted to be educated. You didn't have to feel. You learnt this and you learnt that, and you knew a Jack for a Jack and Ace for an Ace. You were alright. Nothing would ever go pop, pop, pop in your head. You had language to safeguard you. And if you were beginning to feel too strongly, you could kill the feeling, you could get it out of the way by fetching the words that couldn't understand what the feeling was all about. It was like a knife. If you wanted to slaughter the pig, you got your knife. The knife hadn't a clue what was going on in the pig's head, but when you wielded it, the job was done. It was so with language. When the feelings came up like so many little pigs that grunted and irritated with their grunts, you could slaughter them. You could slaughter your feelings as you slaughtered a pig. Language was all you needed. It was like a knife. It knifed your feelings clean and proper, and put an end to any pop, pop, pop in your head. Perhaps we would do better if we were educated. For the time being we weren't going to say a word to anybody. Not a word.

'You mustn't tell Bob,' Boy Blue said, looking at me. 'An' you in particular.'

'Tell him what?' I asked.

'You mustn't tell him about the crabs and the fisherman,' Boy Blue said. 'He would laugh. He would want something to laugh at because of the big wave.'

'I won't,' I said.

'You mustn't tell 'im,' Boy Blue said, ''cause he didn't want you to come round here an' see what he wus goin' to do. He didn't want you to know about Canute an' all that. He told us he never said a word to you this mornin', and he wus tryin' to get away from you all the time.'

'I won't tell,' I said, 'I won't tell him.'

*   *   *

We walked down the beach to where our clothes were bundled on the rocks. Bob was dressed and seated on the rocks, waiting.

'What happen?' Trumper asked, keeping an unsmiling face.

'I wus frighten,' said Bob.

'It was the same with Canute,' said Trumper.

'Yes, but that was a joke,' said Boy Blue, 'this wus real.'

'A king shoul' not have run,' said Trumper.

'Is alright for you to talk,' said Bob, 'an' a joke in a book is a joke in a book, but if Canute or anybody else wus there in my place, I would have like to see him stand up.'

'Canute ain't no joke,' I said.

Bob glowered. 'I wus expectin' you to say that,' he shouted, 'that's why I didn't want you to know what wus in my mind this morning, but you's a blasted liar and a shamefaced liar too if you can stand there an' tell me that any man could have stand up there on Graves End where I wus this mornin'. Stan' up an' face that wave.'

'That's true,' said Trumper. 'It ain't his'ry. It's common sense.'

'An' 'tis all right for those who ain't got no sea,' said Bob.

'Is true,' said Trumper.

'Or even if they had,' Bob went on, 'for it ain't the same thing. 'Cause I goin' tell you somethin', smooth sea or rough sea, there ain't no sea like the sea in Barbados.'

'What 'bout the English sea?' Trumper asked.

'There ain't no English sea,' said Bob. 'The sea you see there in front of you is the only sea in this God's world an' if any of you doubt me you can ask my father.'

'But where the boats come from then?' Boy Blue asked.

'Don't ask a question like that,' said Bob. He knew he had no knowledge of history, but in matters relating to the sea Bob knew he could speak without contradiction.

'You should know more geography,' he said, taking a seat on the rocks. 'If a boat start to sail from here by the club, an' keep straight, straight without turnin', you know where it will end up? Anyone of you know where it'll end up?'

'I don't know,' said Boy Blue.

'Well, I'll tell you,' said Bob, 'it'll end up round there by the lighthouse.'

There was something mysterious about what Bob was saying, and no one spoke.

'An' you'll notice somethin',' Bob went on, 'if you look good at the funnel at those big ships, you'll see they all paint in the same colour, an' they carry the same flag, red, white and blue. You know what that means, 'tis the same ships all the time. 'Cause from a logistical point of view, if a ship leave here by the club an' keep straight, straight without turnin', it bound to end up round there by the lighthouse.'

We waited, impressed with the certainty of Bob's knowledge.

'It's exactly,' he went on, 'exactly what Christopher Columbus mean to say when he say that too far east is west.'

He paused. 'An' if you doubt me,' he said, 'if any one of you don't believe me you can ask my father.'

'I not goin' to argue,' said Trumper, 'but I think there should be land somewhere else.'

'Well, if you doubt me,' said Bob, 'you can ask my father.'

'Is true your father is a fisherman,' said Boy Blue, 'an' he been a fisherman from the time he wus our age, but . . .'

'Is no but,' said Bob angrily, 'he been farther out there in the ocean than any of us here, an' he never see any other lan'.'

Bob was aggressive. We listened contemplatively.

'But what about America?' Trumper asked.

'America?' Bob got up from the rocks.

'You talking about the olden times,' he said. 'You talkin' about a way back in 1492. But Barbados wus discovered by the English in 16 something or the other, an' that is modern times.'

'An' who discover America?' Trumper asked.

'The English too,' Bob said quickly.

'An' where the English come from?' Boy Blue asked.

'From England,' Bob said, making the question seem ridiculously simple.

And now we knew we had him cornered.

'An' where's England?' Boy Blue asked.

Bob smiled and to our utter astonishment spoke with a kind of religious conviction: 'Barbados or Little England, an island of coral formation set like a jewel in the Caribbean Sea.'

We heard the words, and we knew they weren't Bob's.

'That ain't in no Michael John hist'ry book,' Trumper said.

'Cause 'tis no joke,' Bob answered. ''Tis facts. Facts.'

We walked away from the sea in silence through the hot afternoon. The surface of the street was soft where the asphalt had cracked and swollen in the sun. We crossed our heads with paper and grape leaves. Everything was quiet and hot, but the wet and ooze of the sea. The tide turned gently till it ruined itself against the rocks. In the distance beyond the harbouring ships the water was level and still. On one side of the street the school garden blazed with roses in the sun. Fire spilled from the petals along the green leaves and down the thorny barks of the black branches. The grass was a strong brown, low-cropped like a moustache in stubble. On the side by the sea the shade was deep and soothing over the esplanade. It was an open square with beaches and a grass plot trimmed into a circle around the small stone fountain. The area was gravelled with a surface of asphalt. A large grape tree sprawled its branches over the benches. At the other end the black-branched evergreens bunched together to make a deeper shade. The leaves were close and thick. In the centre between the shades and in front of the fountain was the small bandstand. It had a brief flight of five steps curving into the flat arena where the police band played once a week in the afternoon and once a month at night. It was like a picture in a book. People sat leisurely on the benches as the tide came up calmly against the rocks, broke and receded towards the harbouring ships.

' 'Tis like that sometimes in the village,' Bob said.

We hesitated for an answer since nothing should be said about Boy Blue and the crabs.

'Those people goin' to sit there till the fish boats come in,' Bob said, 'just as they sit under the fustic trees waitin' for the fishwomen to come round.'

'What you goin' tell yuh mother?' Boy Blue said, evading the issue.

'I don't know,' Trumper said, 'p'raps I'll say we been trying to catch a fish, a big, big one for breakfast.'

'Not breakfast,' Boy Blue said, ' 'tis two o'clock.'

'We been up here nearly ten hours,' Bob said.

'What you goin' tell yours?' Trumper said, looking at me.

'P'raps I'll say I went to see Smitty,' I said.

'Who's Smitty?' Bob asked.

'She does the scrubbing,' I said. 'I'll say I went to see her 'bout nine o'clock, an' she make me stay 'cause she was 'fraid that a little boy who wus out since five without food would faint in the road. Then I'll say that after I eat 'twustn't good manners to leave, an' the longer I stay the better manners it seem, so I stay an' talk with Smitty.'

'You goin' to be a lawyer,' Boy Blue said.

'Or a politician,' Trumper said.

' 'Tis the same thing by a different name,' Bob said, ''tis the same thing since they both equal to blasted liar.'

We trotted in rows of two through the avenues and across the boundary of Belleville towards the village.

There were no parakeets in the trees. It was quiet like the esplanade beside the sea, and the morning star had resigned its place to the sun, burning bright in the sky.

7

WHEN night fell it was as though the darkness had dropped from the sky. At four o'clock the sun appearing to move towards the sea shone from the west with a scarlet brilliance and the white marl roads gleamed. The wind had gone away and the trees were steady. At this hour the village had seemed unreally still. Sky, trees, wind, clouds: all these things which earlier had seemed immediate were now remote and inactive. There were no clouds at all and the sky deeply curved looked hard and solid. The sun bleeding its light over the land seemed to hang on to the sky as though it were a foreign and unwanted body. The trees resembled the lamp-posts in their carriage, upright, steady and stupid, and the houses scotched on the groundsels of limestone, neutral and resigned. At one corner in the shade of the mahogany trees an old woman sat behind a tray of oranges, plums and nuts. The tray was placed on a bench the shape and size of the one she sat on. She wore a white head tie and a blue apron. She was asleep, her head drooping forward, the chin lazily closeted in the sink of the neck, and her lips hanging loose and slack. A small boy nestled near her, stole a plum from the tray and stuffed his mouth before dropping his head in a nod to the ground. The old woman half-opened her eyes, scratched her ears and mumbled something to the boy. He didn't answer. She passed her hand along his head and closed her eyes again. The boy waited, then looked up and lifted a banana from the stem. Then he stuffed his pockets with more plums and nuts, not more on the whole than a penny's worth. He quickly rearranged the bananas, shuffled the plums and nuts into a new heap and sat down quietly. Another glance at the old woman and soon he had circled the trees and was out of sight. No one noticed. The old woman slept, and in her sleep on the wooden bench she was like the houses, old and weary and remote.

But out of these bodies which seemed lifeless there had grown others that at other times turned the air into a battle front of flashing light. The high wall which ran through a great part of the village, separating one set of tenants from another, bore bits of bottle along the top, and the light from the green edges seemed to cut through the air. Also many of the houses were roofed with galvanized sheets of iron, and the reflected light seemed to rebound from these into the light that leapt from the broken bottles along the high wall. In the distance the trees seemed steady as before, but nearer one noticed that the branches wavered slightly, and occasionally the leaves were disturbed. At four o'clock the air was a blinding shimmer, the village an unbounded arena where the light contended. At five o'clock there was only shade. The galvanized sheets of iron and the broken bottles looked a dull un-reflecting grey over the houses and the high wall. Gradually the leaves seemed to take on the colour of the light, and between the branches the open spaces seemed to be filled up with grey. The twilight was deepening and the street lamps at the corner went on. Lamps were lit in some of the houses, but one knew rather than felt the presence of this light. From now on there was this gradual collision of light, the receding light of day and the light of the gas lamps and the house lamps coming to life. The old woman had steadied the tray on her head, balanced the benches over one arm and walked away. The twilight was deepening into a thicker darkness. And suddenly as if at a signal for action the gas lamps seemed to shine with an aggressive steadiness and the house lamps blazed. The take-over was in the nature of a new beginning. The lamps in the shops went on, and there was movement about the lamp-posts at the corner. The light came out from all the windows and the shops and the ringed posts at the corner. It heightened the darkness of the land and the sky which now seemed overcrowded with stars. It was six o'clock. It was night.

But there was another light less assertive than the gas lamps. At the crossing where the roads made four a small gathering of worshippers stood in a circle round a table. There was a white table cloth over the table and on the cloth a green bottle that held a candle in its neck. The candle gave a flame that leapt up and down in the wind. At the centre beside the table the leader sat giving instructions for worship. There were two or three spectators among whom were Trumper, Boy Blue and myself with another boy who stood very near the circle of wor-shippers. We were quiet and curious as the leader talked to the others about the proceedings. We had come early in the hope of getting away before the crowd came. The preacher paid us no attention, but the boy whom we didn't know was engrossed in conversation with one of the

women. The women were in the majority and they called each other
sister. Sister Jones and Sister Bell. There were two men who were
referred to as Brother. Brother Franklin and Brother Low. The
preacher was Brother Dickson, tall, big boned and aggressive, with
a black face and large hands. Trumper said we should move farther
away from the worshippers since they had a way of getting into the
spirit. When they got into the spirit they danced and shouted in
strange language. It was the act of speaking in tongues. And when
the spirit was more than they could control they insisted by force
that those who stood nearby should help to bear the burden of this
new energy. We walked a pace or two farther away and waited. At
a signal from the leader the worshippers knelt and prayed in silence.
As if by silent agreement and long practice their prayers were of equal
length, and they got up together intoning a low amen. Then the women
sat, some on benches, others on chairs, while the men stood washing
their hands in the air and moving their lips in broad benevolent smiles.
Suddenly a woman stepped forward brandishing a tambourine and
screamed a hymn. She shook the tambourine and her hips with
passionate glee, and Trumper whispered to me that she would soon
get the spirit. We couldn't follow the words of the hymn, but the
worshippers whose ears were trained recognized the hymn and joined
her. Another woman stepped forward in a similar way with her tambourine. Then another and another. The instruments flashed in the
candle-light as the sound rocketed to the sky. The open-air meeting had
begun. The spectators had increased. When the noise was heard they
came from all parts to join in the singing. The crowd came in a steady
flow as the voices and the tambourines pealed through the night.

The hymn finished, the leader walked over to the small boy and said
something about his soul. The boy seemed willing but frightened. All
eyes were turned in his direction. This was what the spectators had
come for. They liked to see how others got saved, and sometimes
they heard their testimonies which were often embarrassingly intimate.
Their candour was a sign of their purge, and they confessed without
question the sins they had committed in thought, word and particularly the deeds that related to the flesh. The small boy was resisting.
The preacher said something again about the soul and the boy dropped
his head. His resistance was weakening. The preacher made mention
of the wrath of God, and the worshippers expressed their sorrow in
a low drawn-out groan. The boy seemed terribly frightened and

penitent. The preacher held his hand and the women knelt intoning a hymn of initiation.

'Will you stay tonight?' the preacher asked, and the crowd was quiet.

'I can't,' the boy said quickly, but it wasn't a direct refusal. He was frightened. The preacher seemed very hopeful and repeated the question. The boy shook his head and the preacher let go of his hand.

'But you must, my son, you must.' His manner was tender and solicitous. His voice unsteady and almost broken with concern. It was amazing how he seemed to melt into a single emotion: this concern for the other's salvation.

'Don't harden your heart,' he said. 'It's better when you're young, your sins are fewer, and if you're cut off without warning forgiveness is easier.'

The preacher had taken a step back and he seemed to address his words to everybody. Trumper nudged Boy Blue and said it was time for us to leave. 'Seven is the age your eyes are opened,' the preacher said. 'You become responsible. You're past seven now, and if you were called home tonight, you would have to answer that call yourself. You have crossed beyond the boundary of innocence, no father, no mother, God father or God mother. You are alone, naked in sin, and you must accept and be saved before it's too late. Salvation through Christ is the key to heaven.'

'Yes,' the boy said, 'but the candle frightens me so.' The boy shivered. The preacher looked round at the light that lengthened out over the faces of the worshippers. He seemed puzzled by what the boy had said, for there was nothing about the candle to frighten anyone. The women waited anxious. 'You see,' the boy said, 'the candle makes me remember Elvirah and what she does do. She does burn candle to keep away the spirits 'cause she's Roman Catholic, as they say they got to burn away the spirits.' There were tears in his eyes and the preacher seemed deeply moved.

'Good Lord be merciful,' he said. 'Spare the innocent from the guiles of Lucifer, and show them the way.' He was remarkably eloquent and he kept a special language to meet every new situation. The boy was going to cry. The preacher's hands were clasped to his neck and his head thrown back so that his chin pointed skyward and the white of his eyes showed dull. He brought his head down sharply and fixed his eyes on the boy in an expression of deep distress.

'The candle won't help her,' he said, 'for it's not the candle that matters. It's the light, the light of the Annointed shed through grace upon the blackness of man's heart. When you see the light, you'll forget the candle and the evil of those who worship images. They are false gods. We have no false gods, only one God, the god who sent His son and Saviour Jesus Christ to the world to die for our sins. Those who carry candles have never seen the light. They are the disciples of the evil one. And it's this you can be spared from if you stay tonight, see the light and be born again, a living soul and a new man in Christ!'

The preacher knelt in the dust and held the boy's hands tightly in his. Their hands shook, but the boy seemed more deeply shaken by the other's supplication, and his knees responding mechanically to the prayer knelt too. They knelt together on the marl road within the circle which the worshippers had made round the table. We were engrossed and Trumper who had been urging us to leave understood and remained. They had drawn nearer to the table, and the preacher's face shone without reflection, black and wet like bronze in a fine drizzle. His skin was coarse, his fingers thick and tough. I seemed to feel the clutch that kept the boy transfixed to the ground, a prisoner in the light, condemned to be saved, to be free from the evil one, free from the flesh and the whole world of profane longing. The preacher spoke as they knelt. Three or four of the gathering had knelt making a small circle round the boy and the preacher. Kneeling there they seemed in a way to have lined up against him. It was a conspiracy of prayer in the cause of his salvation. The clasp of the man's hand gave the feeling of a closed door through which there would never be escape, and the man's face in its attitude of prayer seemed other than nose, eyes, ears, bone and flesh. I closed my eyes against it, and when I couldn't hear the voices or failed to make sense of the prayers I saw the face solitary and wet and black like bronze in a fine drizzle. The preacher paused, and suddenly spoke again, hardly parting his lips.

'Will you stay tonight?'

The boy bowed his head low to the ground and remained there resigned and submissive. The women sang the hymn of initiation and the preacher stood exhausted but satisfied.

'We better go now,' said Trumper, "cause 'tis 'bout this time the lights go on when anythin' happenin'.' He brought his head close to mine so that his words might not be overheard. The boy was still kneeling beside the preacher incapable of further resistance. They had become the spectacle for everybody's gaze. Those who were there

when the boy knelt with the preacher were anxious to see what was
going to happen, and those who came late pushed forward through
the crowd to see who it was. There was a quiet buzzing as they looked
trying to recognize the convert, and the buzzing grew louder with the
low murmur of the worshippers. Then it died down and everyone
was quiet, waiting to see what would happen next.

Trumper put his head close to Boy Blue's and whispered what he
had said to me. Boy Blue smiled and went on looking at the preacher
and the boy. Trumper elbowed him again, and Boy Blue made a noise.
The man who stood beside him made a sign with his finger, and Boy
Blue turned serious. Trumper spoke again. 'You gettin' frighten,' Boy
Blue said, not turning his head to speak. 'It ain't that I 'fraid,' said
Trumper, 'but we gotta go now 'cause it gettin' late. It ain't no sense
goin' when everythin' at a big pitch 'cause you don't know what gone
before.' He held his head down as he spoke. 'We gotta go.'

One of the women who sat in the circle near the table looked up
and frowned. Trumper was silent. The woman kept her head down
for a while, but we knew from the look on her face that she would
soon look up again. She seemed to bite her lips as she stared down
and across at the preacher and the boy. We wanted to go, but we also
wanted to see what would happen to the boy, and it probably wouldn't
have been long before the preacher turn to us to put questions about
our salvation. Behind us the crowds had grown thicker and it was
always difficult on such occasions to force a way out. Moreover we
were secretly ashamed to let the others see us leaving. This always
happened at the open-air meeting and in the big church. If you got
up to leave before the service was finished people stared at you till
you were out of sight. It made you feel shamefully rebellious as
though you were turning in disrespect against what you had seen.
At the open-air meeting it was likely that the preacher would stand
and say what he thought about such behaviour. The priest wouldn't
have interrupted the service to make a comment on anything, but the
preacher took no chances with the unsaved. If he could persuade them
by first making them a public example of cowards, then he would do
so. And often it worked, and he thought it good for them. There
was nothing to be ashamed of in salvation, and salvation was more
urgent than anything else. Trumper elbowed me in the ribs and made
a sign with his head. He seemed irritated now by our delay. 'We
gotta go now,' he said. 'Why you make me find out for you what

I find out, an' now you don't want to come? Tell me straight if you comin' or if you ain't, 'cause I can go long by myself.'

The woman looked up and frowned again. She held her glance this time as though she wanted us to be aware of her annoyance. She couldn't stand this disrespectful babbling in the presence of God, and God was present; for they had always said that wherever the two or three are gathered together in his name there He was also. She was still looking at us. Suddenly she turned her head and whispered something about respect for the word of God. The neighbour turned to another and whispered what the woman had said. The complaint was passed on to another three or four. They looked up and stared altogether as the first woman had done. The man who stood beside Boy Blue realized what was happening and so did those who stood nearest to me and Trumper. The woman seemed to want others, the saved and unsaved alike, to understand how she felt, and quite often the unsaved shared this kind of annoyance. We were gradually becoming as much a spectacle as the small boy and the preacher. We looked at each other and decided that we would go. And we didn't want anyone to understand why we were going. The women had dropped their heads.

'One by one,' Boy Blue said, 'an' I goin' first. Then you come a few minutes after an' then Trumper or the other way round, but all together.' We pretended not to hear or notice that Boy Blue had forced his way through. Trumper and I went on watching the preacher and the boy kneeling beside the table. They were praying in silence, and now the boy in the light looked terribly scared. The preacher was moved by his submission. The women looked up and seemed a little more at ease when they noticed that Boy Blue had gone. They had a feeling that he was what they would call the ring-leader. It was he who was prompting us in this disrespect. Trumper elbowed me again and made a sign with his head. The man beside him moved back and Trumper walked away. The man had understood what was happening and he seemed to keep the space clear expecting that I would leave at any moment. The women looked up, and it was clear that only one of us was left. They were sure that the first boy was the devil's one. It was Boy Blue who had brought us to mock the word of God and when this proved more than we could do he decided to take us away. They whispered among themselves in a kind of quiet indignation. Soon everything was quiet. The preacher had got up and was standing over the boy. I didn't know what would happen, but I had always

heard them talk about sacrifice. I didn't know the meaning of sacrifice
and I told myself that it was sacrifice which would follow. I was sure
they were going to sacrifice him, and I wanted to see how it was done.
The women looked across at me and the preacher saw them. He didn't
seem to understand why they looked at me as they did. They dropped
their heads and suddenly looked across again. The preacher turned
away from the boy and made towards me. His face held the same stark
uncalculating purpose I had noticed when he persuaded the boy to be
saved. My thinking had become confused and for a moment I thought
only of escaping that face and joining Trumper and Boy Blue. He
made towards me with his hands clasped and his head held up. I took
a step back, saw him approach, turned and fought a way through the
crowd. There was a flutter of giggles from the spectators. I heard the
laughter. It became more and more distinct like the noise in a concert
hall. I looked around for Trumper and Boy Blue hoping in the mean-
time to hear what the preacher would say. I heard a man say that if
he wasn't careful he would lose the soul which he had fought so hard to
win, and the laughter increased. Then there was a noise which seemed
to be the preacher's voice, and soon the voices of the worshippers rose
above the laughter and everything was under control. I walked away
to join Trumper and Boy Blue as the voices carolled their testimony
to my heart:

> A ruler once came to Jesus by night
> To ask him the way of salvation and light.
> The Master replied in words clear and plain
> You must be born again.
>
> You must be born again,
> You must be born again,
> Verily, verily I say unto you,
> You must be born again.

But for the street lamps where the roads crossed there was no
light. The glimmer of the candle had got lost within the thick circle
of worshippers and spectators, yet I thought I could see the preacher's
face standing out like a rock in the darkness and we could still hear
the hymn about the Master who went to Jesus by night. We hadn't
spoken much since we met. Trumper seemed a bit angry that I
should have stayed so long. He thought I shouldn't have cared

about the women whispering among themselves or the way they looked at us. We walked very quietly between the trees over the weed, and I had a feeling we were thinking about the same thing. This wasn't the first time we had met together at an open-air meeting, although it was the first time we were going to do what Trumper had suggested. The words of the hymn seemed to fall like a fine drizzle through the trees and into our ears. You must be born again. You must be born again. There was something very frightening about them, and particularly the context in which they were placed. The hymn had been started in order to control the tittering of the spectators, and also perhaps because I had fled. It was as though one were reminded of an outstanding debt. The preacher was a kind of spiritual bailiff who offered salvation as a generous exchange for the other's suffering. You must be born again. You must be born again. They seemed to pursue us, and it wasn't clear whether we were still hearing the voices, but the words were there. You must be born again. Trumper spoke and brought an end to our long silence. It was obvious from the tone of his voice that he was playing brave. The voice was raised and he spoke quickly as though what he was saying should not be considered too long or too seriously. He mumbled an oath about the preacher and then spoke aloud. Boy Blue and I were uneasy.

"Tis what Mr. Slime say,' he said, 'they turn us dotish with all these nancy stories 'bout born again, an' we never ever give ourself a chance to get up an' get. Nothin' ain't goin' change here till we sort o' stop payin' notice to that sort o' joke 'bout a old man goin' born again. It ain't only stupid but it sound kind o' nasty, an that's what Mr. Slime want to put a end to. He mention that said same thing last night in the speech. An' he call it tomfoolery. 'Tis what got us as we is, he say.'

'Seems to me there be only two great men round here,' said Boy Blue, 'Mr. Slime an' the landlord. An' if you don't watch out there goin' soon be one, Mr. Slime only. The landlord will sort o' stay where he is in the big house, but Mr. Slime will be sort o' captain o' this ship. 'Cause a day don't pass here when somebody ain't got something to say 'bout him an' the Penny Bank an' the Friendly Society. He get in a short space o' time a kind o' black Jesus.'

'We didn't say nothin' 'bout him the other day at the sea,' Boy Blue continued. 'An' we talk 'bout only God knows what, an' we never ever remember to say nothin' 'bout Bank an' Society an' all that.'

''Twus different,' said Trumper, 'what we wus talkin' 'bout is kind o' different.'

''Tis true,' said Boy Blue, ''tis certain things you can talk 'bout without bringin' in Mr. Slime, 'cause the Bank an' the Society an' that they call the politics don't belong there.'

''Tis as you say,' said Trumper, ''tis so 'cause those things ain't sort o' day to day. They ain't real for people, or they ain't what they call practical. The sort o' things we talk at the sea is only for you an' me when we kind o' dreamin'. They don't belong to anybody else except they want to start their own kind o' dreamin'. But the politics an' all that concern everybody put together at the same said time.'

''Tis good to dream,' said Boy Blue, 'but it ain't good to dream all the time. Although what we say at sea wusn't no dreamin'. I for one wusn't always dreamin', or if I wus then there is something real in this kind o' dreamin'.'

'It ain't good,' said Trumper, ''cause sometimes you get a kind o' nightmare like the way we did feel now an' again when we talk 'bout the loneliness.'

'An' it won't be good for Mr. Slime,' said Boy Blue, ''cause if everybody start this business o' dreamin', makin' a special little kind o' world of dreams for themself there won't be no need for what they call the politics. They won't have much time to think 'bout anything that concern a lot o' people put together at the same said time. An' when everybody get that feelin' for himself then there won't be no more the people. 'Twill be only me an' you an' he an' she.'

'What you think 'bout what Mr. Slime say 'bout buyin' the land?' Trumper asked. 'He say he goin' to make us owners o' this land.'

'That is dreamin' too,' said Boy Blue, 'although a different kind o' dream.'

'To tell the truth, I ain't want no land,' said Trumper. 'I want to go away.'

'Where you want to go to?' Boy Blue asked. 'You always talkin' 'bout you want to go away.'

'I don't know,' said Trumper, 'p'raps to America. They say things good there.'

'Mr. Slime call it the promise land an' some who been an' come back says 'tis the bread basket o' the world.'

'What they mean by that?' Trumper asked.

'Seems it mean you can get all you want to eat,' Boy Blue said.

'Food in galore, an' so they says you don' have to cook it yuhself. 'Tis all new.'

'Who goin' cook it for you if you don' cook it yuhself?' Trumper asked.

''Tis only what I hear them say,' said Boy Blue. 'You push in what they call a dime through a little hole, and the plate o' food come out at you through another hole. An' some say you can put in a next dime in a next hole an' you hear the music whatever you want to hear while you eatin'.'

'I ain't like the sound o' that much,' said Trumper. ''Tis true this business of cooking with wood give you a lot o' trouble, 'cause you got to keep blowing the blasted fire an' the smoke get in yuh eyes all the time, but when all said an' done I like the look o' a pot on the fire, an' I like to hear a pot boiling 'cause it make you feel something happenin'; an' if there's one thing I like, too, 'tis to see the way my mother turn food out from the pot to the plate. It give you a kind a good big feelin' in the bottom o' yuh stomach an' yuh mouth start to water an' move without yuh permission. Seems to me all these little things make food what it is. Something to make a big fuss 'bout, an' that's what my mother always say. Eat, Trumper. Eat an' give God praise for what you see before you.'

'What I don't like 'bout the American way,' said Boy Blue, 'what I don't like is that you got to eat in the open air. An' everybody can see you, how you hold a bone or put yuh finger nail between yuh teeth, an' I ain't know the rules for this game 'bout table manners. 'Cause as you know we all here when we goin' to eat we close the back door.'

'An' I don't like, too, this business 'bout food comin' at you through a hole,' said Trumper, ''cause only God knows where it come from.'

We had found the track that led through the wood to the house on the hill. Trumper beat the bush and the hedges with a stick he had cut from the mahogany tree. As he and Boy Blue spoke about America and what Mr. Slime had promised it seemed that they were trying to put off what was going to happen. They didn't talk easily about America, and I wasn't sure whether Trumper was losing heart for the adventure or whether they were trying to forget the words of the hymn. You must be born again. I was torn by both considerations. The words kept coming back to me with a kind of shock, and I was also apprehensive about what Trumper was taking us to do. The voices of the worshippers had stopped singing, and it was very quiet in the wood. Ahead of us we could see a light in the landlord's house. There wasn't any sign that much was going on, but Trumper was sure of what he was doing.

'I always get a funny feelin' when I gettin' near it,' he said. ''Tis as if you treadin' on holy ground.' He seemed less confident when he spoke.

'I want to know if you think it safe to go inside,' Boy Blue said, ''cause they got dogs, an' I don't like the look o' the big black Alsatian I see lying 'bout the yard in the morning. They say he does drink blood.'

'They won't have the dogs loose,' Trumper said, ''cause they have to take care o' the visitors. The dogs ain't know the sailors, so they would have to chain them up.'

'You better tell us what goin' to happen,' Boy Blue said, ''cause I got a feelin' we ain't goin' to get inside that wall without something bad happen.'

Trumper didn't reply and Boy Blue seemed too frightened to press for an answer. We walked along in silence. We were circling the wall that went round the landlord's house, and it was very still but for the noise of the frogs in the bush and the occasional scamper of the cats. It would seem the cats always assembled in the wood near the wall where they fought and screamed and copulated. Trumper knew that, and he and others had gone at night on several occasions to watch the cats. They mated with a kind of ferocity which fascinated and terrified the boys. Trumper held the stick against the wall as though he were a blind man feeling his way. We could hear the knock and scrape it made along the bricks. The cats screamed and Trumper halted.

''Tis those blasted cats again,' he said. 'Only God knows why they come here to do they business.'

The cats were screaming in the dark, and we were getting frightened. I didn't like the scream of the cats, and Boy Blue kept quiet which meant that he was afraid to talk. Trumper stooped to pick up a stone. He held his hand on the object which seemed too large for his grip. He took it away quickly and put it back again. Then he squeezed and raised his arm. The object dropped and Trumper fell back against Boy Blue trembling. Boy Blue struck a match and we saw a kind of jelly-like ooze on Trumper's hand. He wiped it on his pants while Boy

Blue held out the match in search of the stone. And then we saw
what Trumper had held and squeezed. It was a couple of frogs, black
and bulbous. They had fallen to the ground with a thud, and yet they
weren't dislodged. They remained in their hideous posture like a child
making its clumsy scale over the bench. Trumper said 'Jesus Christ!'
and we continued walking towards the house on the hill.

'What time they goin' to start?' Boy Blue asked.

We were all getting impatient, and Trumper seemed a little shaken
after his contact with the frogs. I hated the sight of the frogs although
I could remember poking at them from the rear with sticks. Trumper
was getting easy again.

'I think they start already,' he said, 'but they don't dance this side
o' the house,'tis why we ain't see no more light. 'Tis like a palace this
place.'

The stick jammed into the crease of the wall and the other end
nearly punched him in the ribs. He wrenched it out and put his hand
to feel the wall. He was quiet for a while as though something had
happened.

'This is it,' he said. ''Tis here we got to go through. This is it.'

We drew nearer to feel whether Trumper had really found a way.

''Tis this,' he said, dismissing us with one hand. ''Tis the little
wicket gate we got to go through.' He turned to us and started to give
orders. His confidence had been completely restored and we, too,
were more comfortable. I would have liked to see his face, but it
was dark.

'We goin' to go in now,' Trumper said, 'then we goin' to creep
right cross the bush, you followin' me an' takin' the time from me.
We got to get over yonder by the trees an' right there we can take
a front seat on the grass. Take the time from me an' don't talk till you's
talked to.'

Trumper took a key from his pocket and opened the small gate in
the wall. I was sure Boy Blue turned to look at me, but we didn't speak.

'You got to keep as quiet as you can now,' Trumper said, 'or you'll
get what you don't like; an' crawl on yuh guts like a crab.'

We were standing within the wall a few yards away from the landlord's house. It gave me a tremendous feeling like house-breaking or
in another extreme passing an examination. The house looked so much
bigger than I had thought. It was like some of the castles we had
seen in pictures. There wasn't much light on our side, but we could

see from the reflection in the distance that the other side was fully lit.
We bent low and crept through the bush and between the trees to
the other side. No one spoke except Trumper who kept reminding
us not to talk and gave occasionally the orders we should follow. He
kept in the centre a little ahead of us.

'We got to get round the other side quick,' he said, ''cause the
overseer goin' be about here soon.'

'How you know that?' Boy Blue asked. We had turned uneasy
again.

'I goin' tell you later,' Trumper said, and we were silent.

As we crept towards the other side we could feel the change in
the weed under our knees. It was getting more and more unlike the
ragged cluster near the wall. On the left we could see the garden and
on the right ahead of us a large trash heap. The heap was made from
the dry blades of the sugar cane. It went up and over like an enormous
curve of ice-cream lifting itself from the cone. We knew those heaps.
You could lie at ease on the top, and sometimes holes were made in
them which were helpful in games like hide and seek. Two or three
could enter the hole in the heap and remain hidden. In the day it
looked like a cave. We circled the heap and settled on the weed
between the trees and out of the light. On another occasion we might
have been scared as we were earlier when we were coming through
the wood. But the novelty of this place admitted no other emotion
but curiosity and excitement. We were well hidden and we sat easy
and quiet taking in the spectacle before us. The music had started
again and the sailors were dancing. Most of them looked tidier and
more civilized than the sailors we saw in the streets. Some of the
women wore evening frocks decorated with big bright buttons and
jewels and necklaces that went around the throat like a decorous dog's
collar. They all seemed very merry, and particularly the sailors who
were drinking all the time. We didn't speak. It was so different from
the open-air meeting or the school concert or anything we had seen.
It was like what we called the other world. The music stopped and
the sailors pretending to be angry shouted 'More!' Soon it started
again and they danced. Two sailors started to dance together, but a
third came up and whispered something to them. They parted quickly
and joined the girls who were sitting nearby. We sat easy and quiet
on the weed, watching: Trumper, Boy Blue and me in a kind of half-
circle safe behind the trees. When the music stopped the women came

out with the sailors and they walked arm-in-arm up and down the grass plots in the garden. My ears burnt and I felt an unusual stiffening of the limbs. I had never walked with a girl arm-in-arm and I wasn't sure that Boy Blue or Trumper had done so. Another couple came out and the sailor's arm went round her waist till his fingers reached his uniform. Trumper said quietly 'Jesus Christ!' and I knew he was feeling the strange emergency of passion. I was beginning to think what I would do if I had a girl nearby, and since there wasn't one I started to speculate who she might be when we left the wood and went back into the village. As there was a God in heaven I was going to do something with a girl.

The couples scattered in different directions while those who had remained in the house went on drinking. It seemed so rich and satisfying and in a way quite astonishing to us.

'You never been so close,' Trumper whispered, and his teeth seemed to chatter.

'Never ever,' said Boy Blue. ''Tis like a next world, the music an' the drink an' all that, an' particular the way they hold on to one another.'

''Tis like a Christmas,' Trumper said. 'Except that this does happen more than once a year. What we seein' there is sort o' regular for them.'

'What you mean by that?' Boy Blue asked. 'The sailors ain't always here.'

'They have this often,' said Trumper, 'sailors or no sailors. When they ain't no sailors 'tis friends o' the landlord an' the daughter an' so on. But they always give the sailors a big time, bigger than the rest.'

'When those sailors come in?' Boy Blue asked. He was getting very curious.

'They come in this mornin',' Trumper said. ''Tis the H.M.S. *Goliath*. Seem the landlord an' those who know had word 'bout they comin'. An' they only stayin' for a day an' a night, they say, so that's why they put on this.'

'Some o' those sailors ain't look like real sailors,' said Boy Blue.

'What you mean by real sailor?' Trumper asked. 'A sailor is a sailor.'

'They look so good behave,' Boy Blue said. 'Sailors ain't usually decent so.'

'I don't know,' said Trumper. "P'raps these is the good decent ones.'

'Must be so,' said Boy Blue, "cause it ain't like sailors, that is the ones we see in the street, it ain't like them to go close to a woman without doin' something to she there an' then. They ain't got no kind o' shame, 'cause we does see them in the street and the motor car an' even the bus the way they kiss up the women and feel them on the bubbies.'

Boy Blue swallowed heavily as though there was something in his throat. 'I see them do all sort o' stupid things,' he said, 'like put the woman bubby in they mouth and suck suck as if they was a little baby tryin' to get milk. An' the police fraid to tell them anythin'. You never see a police talk too hard to a sailor no matter what bad behaviour he behave.'

'The big shot ones ain't like that,' said Trumper. 'They got what they call class in the navy, an' every man you see in that uniform ain't just another Billy Sailor. They have different pedigrees.'

The music started and the couples walked back into the hall. Trumper said something about taking a seat on the trash heap, and Boy Blue asked him if he was mad. If we were permitted to be where we were it might have been possible to sit on the trash heap which would have given a better view. But Trumper wasn't serious. He was pleased not only by what he was seeing but by what he had done. It was he who brought us. The light in the hall changed from bright white to a very deep blue. The music seemed to drag, it was so slow, and in the half-dark they seemed to swagger like drunk people. We couldn't see the faces and we shifted to improve our position. Then the lights changed to light pink, and we could see the faces. It changed back to bright white and the sailors shouted their dissatisfaction. It changed to pink and there was a rumble of voices as though pink were not satisfactory. The deep blue came on again and they shouted hurrah. That was better. They seemed to prefer the half-dark and so did we since it was safer for us. The lights didn't come bright again, and we sat and talked quietly, listening to the music in the foreground.

'I don't understan' how you find out 'bout all this,' Boy Blue said. 'You only tell us to come come, but you ain't say yet what is what.'

'You ain't satisfy with what you see?' Trumper asked. He was smiling.

'I satisfy alright,' Boy Blue said, 'but I like to know what is what.'

'I fin' out this mornin',' Trumper said. 'The overseer been down home to see my father who's his brother as you know. But my father wusn't home, an' the overseer start to talk to the girl Cutsie who wus there waitin' for my father too. An' I hear him say 'bout what wus goin' to happen.'

'What he tell her for?' Boy Blue asked. He was unsparing in his questions.

'Why you want to know everything for?' Trumper asked. 'He tell her 'cause he wus tryin' to fix something with her. She wus to meet him in the wood by the little gate, an' he give her a little key an' tell her that if he wusn't ready by the time she get there she must open the gate and sit quiet on the grass till he come, 'cause it wusn't safe to stay outside the wall alone, an' if she lock back the little gate everything would be alright.'

'The man she ain't gone with God ain't make yet,' Boy Blue said angrily.

'But she ain't go,' said Trumper. 'She left the key home an' I take hold of it 'cause I say by hook or crook I wusn't missin' this. She ain't like the overseer at all although he in a position to do things for people. An' I always hear the men say that. She is a good girl. She don't get on as a proper girl should, but they say she make so an' if you make a certain way you can't change. But they say 'tis one thing 'bout her, although she knock 'bout herself here, there an' everywhere she won't give the governor a piece if she ain't like him. She got to like you before anything can happen.'

'An' what the overseer goin' to do?' Boy Blue asked. He was getting uneasy.

'He ain't goin' to see her, that's all,' said Trumper.

The music had stopped and started again. The light remained deep blue.

'When you up here,' said Trumper, 'on a night like tonight you see how it is nothin' could change in the village. Everything's sort of in order. Big life one side an' small life a next side, an' you get a kin' o' feelin' of you in your small corner an' I in mine. Everything's kind of correct.'

'That's what Mr. Slime say he goin' to change,' said Boy Blue. 'He say time an' again there ain't no reason why everybody shouldn't have the big life.'

'He won't change what is,' said Trumper. ''Tis a question of what is.'

The music had stopped and the light changed to bright white, but the sailors made a noise and it turned to deep blue again. We went on talking quietly. Boy Blue wasn't sure whether Mr. Slime could change these things but he had a feeling that it would be nice if some of the people in the village got a bit of the big life. Trumper thought so too, but he was sure nothing could be done about it. Things had to be as they were, that was all.

'The way a thing happen,' said Trumper. ''Tis like . . .'

'Trumper,' Boy Blue interrupted. He was shaking with fright. 'I see somebody.'

'Where?' asked Trumper, 'where?' The whispers were like brief gusts of wind.

'By the trash heap,' Boy Blue whispered. He could hardly get the words out of his mouth. 'The person come out from behind, an' I don't know if it is they hear us but they just ease back quiet.'

'Lay low,' said Trumper, 'an' don't talk. We got to get out o' here.'

We lay flat on our stomachs looking towards the trash heap. All our visions had collapsed. We didn't want any girls any longer and the big life had vanished. The music went on, but we hardly heard. Trumper felt in his pocket for the key, and thought for a while how we might escape. I wondered what would happen if we were caught, and Boy Blue lay flat in a steady tremble. Trumper was thinking. He seemed more assured of escape than anyone else, and occasionally he touched us on the shoulder to indicate quiet.

'Creep round easy see if you see anybody,' Trumper said. He was breathing heavily. The words came out in a gust of breath.

'Who, me?' Boy Blue asked.

'No,' said Trumper.

'Why me?' I said. I had got more frightened.

''Cause you's the smallest,' said Trumper. 'It won't be so easy to see you in between the trees.'

I didn't know what to reply. The others were quiet. I eased my way clumsily over the weed and towards the trash heap. The music had stopped and it was very quiet. I hoped the music would start again so that my breathing might be smothered. I didn't expect that this would happen or I would not have gone, and I was afraid when they left me alone. Trumper and Boy Blue might have managed to cut a way round the other side, and what I would do alone within the wall was inconceivable. Moreover, I didn't know what punishment I would receive for entering the yard at night. The music had started again and I was glad. I crouched further, and then the music stopped and the sailors were hearing some explanation about the next dance. They spoke so loud you could hear faintly what was being said. The explanations were given and the music started soft and slow. I moved nearer the trash heap, and then a voice spoke and I started. Boy Blue was right. There was someone somewhere. The voice spoke again like a girl's and another voice grunted. It made a noise as though the person was dissatisfied. I lay low, holding my breath, and the voices spoke.

'It's the first time for me, you know, the very first time.'

'Come close, let me kiss your ear,' the male voice said.

'The end piece of the ear, darling; it's the softest flesh anywhere.'

I was sure it wasn't Cutsie and the overseer. The girl's voice was speaking again, more audible now.

'Is that what they do?'

'That isn't much, baby,' the male voice said. 'I can do things that'll make your head spin round and round.'

'I couldn't afford to let anything happen,' the girl said. 'Not here of all places. And Mama isn't well.'

'Nothing'll happen,' the male voice said. 'Come closer so that we don't seem two people but just one. And don't speak a word, nor make a noise; and in the closeness and the silence I promise we'll be one and we'll be safe.'

'How do you know nothing will happen?' the girl said. She was anxious.

'England expects every man to know his duty,' the male voice said. 'Come close.'

They were silent now. Boy Blue and Trumper had crept closer towards me, but no one risked speaking. We lay flat waiting to hear the voices. And then the worst happened. It seemed he couldn't have suppressed the noise.

'Jesus Christ,' Trumper shouted, and my heart leapt. 'Ants, we in a ants' nest!' The voice was lower when he said ants, but we were overheard.

'Who's that?' the male voice shouted. The girl walked out on the other side of the trash heap.

'Run,' said Trumper, 'run for your life, boys.'

We had panicked. The man came pelting after us and his voice rose higher and higher as we gained ground. He didn't know the yard, and he stumbled from tree to tree. The music had stopped, and the crowd, it seemed, had poured into the yard. We heard the voice shouting after us, there, there. It was difficult to think. We made our way towards the small gate, but we remembered that the overseer might still be there waiting for the girl. Then at Trumper's suggestion we scattered in different directions. It was like a criminal's escape. We crouched behind the bush and nothing was heard but the man's voice and the occasional quiver of the bush. We ran again and stooped behind trees, and then the torchlight flashed from the little gate. It was the overseer. I was well hidden behind the tree. The man couldn't see where we had disappeared but he came pelting towards us and rushed like a fool into the overseer's torch. He must have been a little drunk.

'What goin' on here?' the overseer said. Other sailors had run to find out what was happening.

'There, there,' said the man, 'the native boys.' He pulled the overseer in a mad search through the bush, and then Trumper shouted again.

'The gate, boys,' said Trumper, and we had burst altogether through the hole in the wall. Nothing was clear but the man's voice calling out, 'There, there, the native boys.' The overseer called after us. The strange man had given up the chase and the overseer took over. We slipped from hedge to hedge between the trees scaling the grass, stumbling and colliding in the dark. And the wonder was we didn't fall. We shot down the track and towards the bath.

'Here,' said Trumper, 'lay low.'

We crouched under the hedge, quiet and breathless and soon the overseer ran past like a vehicle left on its own.

'Now,' said Trumper, 'we got to get into that crowd.'

'Back to the open-air meetin'?' Boy Blue asked.

'Yes,' said Trumper. 'Walk straight with your head in front all the time and look as if you get there for the first time. One by one.'

The crowd which had grown thick and shifting had formed a circle within a circle. The worshippers made the first circle with the preacher standing at the centre beside the table. The boy whom we had left had taken a seat on a bench among the worshippers. One of the women was talking to him while he shook his head as though he understood and accepted what she was saying. Almost merging into the first circle was the second which the spectators made. They were very quiet and serious. It would seem there was a break in the proceedings. Some souls had been saved, and the preacher was resting before making a last attempt to save the remaining sinners. Boy Blue and Trumper had met in the crowd, and soon we were standing together. Two or three women who stood near us seemed to think something was wrong. They whispered something and on occasions gave us a glance. There was a rumbling outside the spectators' circle and we heard one man rebuke another for disturbing. Trumper thought it was the overseer. The man made another rebuke and the crowd laughed. There was an exchange of threats and the crowd began to grow fidgety. The worshippers stood and started to sing. The men went on in their exchange, and soon their voices were lost in the singing.

The voices of the worshippers soared, and the attention of the spectators was taken back to the meeting. The preacher knelt and prayed in silence. The candle had burnt down to a short white stub an inch or two above the bottle. The flame leapt more wildly in the wind, and down the neck and over the shoulders of the bottle, the used portion had melted into twisted white stains. Some of the worshippers seemed worried about the future of the candle. It wouldn't have been a good sign if it had burnt out before the open-air meeting had come to an end. The flame consumed it rapidly and the rim of the bottle looked bruised from the heat. The crowd outside the worshippers were conscientiously quiet. The voices had stopped singing and the preacher stood again. He made the plea for the others' salvation while the worshippers like a supporting cast reinforced it. They understood perfectly when they should intone the amen, or break into singing. And they knew what hymn suited the particular incident. The preacher had mopped his brow and was speaking. Trumper and Boy Blue nestled closer to me, and we held our heads down listening.

'Now or never,' the preacher said, increasing his volume, 'now or never is not our cry. But now rather than never. Don't put off for tomorrow what you can do today.' The worshippers intoned their support and the preacher took breath. He mopped his brow again and pocketed the handkerchief. The crowd of spectators were still.

'Tomorrow, my Lord, tomorrow, is the cry you console yourselves with. Because you think the moment is not now for you to turn away from the world. You are not ready to receive the blessing of God made manifest through the death of His only son our saviour, Jesus Christ. But I tell you, my dear brothers and sisters in Christ, as well as you who stand outside the paling of grace, I put it to you that you may not be given another chance. Tonight you say to yourselves, those of you who have not as yet received the message, you say to yourselves, tonight you must dine and dance and wine in the sin of the flesh, spend your youth and strength, the apple and peach of your days following the ways of the world and the evil thereof. But I put it to you, my dear friends, many are called but few are chosen, and there be some of you here tonight who have come not of your own free will but directed and guided by the spirit of God who chose you out and made this the night on which you should hear and answer His call. You must make your choice now, for I say that for such of you, and there are many here, I put it to you there will be no tomorrow. For you there will be no tomorrow.' The words seemed to fall from his lips after an appointed pause. He spoke them slowly and with great seriousness, and the worshippers murmured their sorrow for those who would not see the next day. One woman shook with terror at the thought of her death that night. The man beside her egged her on to go forward and kneel, but she was terrified. The preacher had repeated the words again. For you there will be no tomorrow. The woman made a grunt and the preacher went on.

'Remember, remember what Christ did to the fig tree. It is a lesson for you and me.'

The woman turned and asked what Christ did to the fig tree. The preacher had caught the question. He was sharp and ruthless.

'He smote it,' the preacher said. 'He cut it down. He made it barren, and that's what he can do to you this very night. He can cut you off in the twinkling of an eye.' His voice was almost prophetic with threat.

The woman started to cry, and the man egged her on. The shrieks reached the preacher and he became more excited. He repeated the story of the fig tree, and suddenly the woman burst into tears and threw herself forward in a confused outpouring of confession. The worshippers started to sing. The preacher went on trying to keep his voice above the others. The woman held her head down waiting for someone to ask her questions, but the preacher went on addressing the crowd. They were quiet and serious and at times very sad. Boy

Blue and Trumper kept their heads down. We were still shuddering
under the threat of the overseer. It was dangerous to leave now, since
the overseer might have been prowling round the circle of spectators.
We had a fear he might have recognized Trumper's voice, and we
remained with our heads held down. The worshippers had got up
and were making small attempts to persuade some of the spectators.
The preacher hadn't stopped. This was the final round of pleas. It was
late and the candle burnt down rapidly.

'You who stand outside the palings of grace scoffing and jeering,
you who feel too proud to humble yourself before what is Great and
Good, remember it will be noted against you in that Book of books
that on this night you heard the call and rejected Christ. You said to
him, away with you, I have chosen the enemy. You who hide because
you're ashamed, you'll be found out, and you who run because you're
afraid, you'll be caught.'

Trumper looked up and his face shivered in the light. He elbowed
me in the ribs but I couldn't understand what had happened. There
was a rumble on the outskirts of the crowd, and Trumper elbowed
me again. He whispered quietly, but the whisper didn't reach me.
Then Boy Blue came closer and tried to drop his head lower. I looked
up and saw what had happened. The overseer had forced a way
through the crowd. He looked around in all directions, and then he
fixed his gaze on me. I returned it militantly as though there was
nothing to be afraid of. He made towards us, easing his way clumsily
through the crowd. The man on the outskirts went on rebuking. It
seemed the remarks were directed at the overseer. The latter came
across, and then Boy Blue eased his way forward and walked towards
the table. He knelt beside the table, and the worshippers began to sing.
The preacher was deeply moved.

'Suffer the little ones to come to me and forbid them not,' he said.

The women stopped singing and watched. The overseer came
closer. I didn't know whether he suspected us. He was nearer now, and
Trumper saw. Another man moved back and the overseer took a step
forward. Trumper held his head up and forced a way through the
crowd. He knelt beside Boy Blue. The overseer looked suspicious. He
made towards the table and the preacher turned to receive him, but he
wasn't responsive. The man on the outskirts of the crowd was still
rebuking. The overseer touched Trumper, and the spectators didn't
understand what was happening. The overseer hadn't come to be

saved, that was clear. The preacher grew furious. He threw his hand out and shouted louder than ever: 'Touch not the Lord's annointed.' There was a titter from the crowd and the man on the outskirts spoke louder. The preacher spoke with great passion and the overseer retreated. Trumper and Boy Blue kept their heads down. Another boy went forward and I stepped quickly and joined him. We knelt together, our eyes closed. It was difficult to think, and this seemed the safest escape. The overseer was still there. The man on the outskirts kept up his rebuke. 'For you there will be no tomorrow.' The preacher played with the words. The air had turned heavy and solemn. Another boy came forward and then a woman. I opened my eyes and saw Trumper. He was shivering. The overseer stood where he was. Another boy came forward and the overseer made towards him. The preacher became more indignant and the crowd was angry. The overseer seemed to be set on interrupting. The man who rebuked him on the outskirts came forward and said he would pitch his arse out the circle. The preacher patted the man on the back and told him not to sin in the sight of God. The crowd was against the overseer. The preacher was indignant. And the tide it seemed had turned in our favour. Trumper kept his eyes closed while the overseer stood where he was in the first row of spectators, angry but more subdued. The crowd had subdued him. A boy came forward and knelt beside me, and then a woman and another. And I saw no more. But I heard them coming, the sinners who were making sure, the souls for whom there would be no tomorrow. The candle had gone out. The night turned to pitch, and for those who knelt there was only the fervour of prayer, and winding through the passages of the ear the rich and solemn intonation of the worshippers.

> Into my heart,
> Into my heart,
> Come into my heart, Lord Jesus;
> Come in today,
> Come in to stay,
> Come into my heart, Lord Jesus.

8

THE silence was longer than any they had known. The old man had finished another pipe and spat through the window on to the roots of the palm tree. He poked his head over the sill to see where the saliva had settled. The earth between the roots was moist, and a nut small and rounded like a bead was black under the coat of slime. He spat again and shook the saliva from the stem of the pipe. The back door was open and the windows on all sides let the smoke out into the yard. The old woman lay back in her chair with her legs stretched out over the bench. Her face was twisted with a sour expression. Her hands fell forward clasped on her lap, and occasionally she looked at the clay pipe on the table. In different circumstances she would have lit it and smoked. But she was shaken by what she had heard, and there was nothing she could do but sit and wait for her shame to pass away. She didn't know how to tell the old man what had happened. It wasn't only improper to repeat the details of the story, but she had a feeling the old man would have been more disturbed than she. She kept her head down looking at her feet stretched over the bench. The old man levelled the ash and drew at the pipe. The smoke rose high and thick and the cloud passed between them.

She had seen the landlord earlier when she went to pay the rent. He was riding on horseback down the stretch that extended from the garden to the wall. He wore his riding boots and a white helmet, and the horse trotted in a circle along the wall towards the garden and down the stretch again. She had watched them before entering the office where the overseer received the money. When she left the office and crossed the stretch the landlord pulled up alongside and asked her how she was getting on. She was very pleased. She gave him her blessing and commented on the strength and size of the horse. He dismounted, tied the animal to a tree and strolled with her towards the large trash heap in the sun. She wished Pa had been present. It was a great delight to have the landlord in intimate heart to heart talk. He wanted to know whether she could explain why things had changed so greatly in the village. He had been living in the village for more than thirty years, but the changes that had taken place in the last eight or nine years were beyond anything he could have imagined. Disrespect, strife and the threats silent but sensed on all sides. They talked at length and she told him she would discuss the matter with Pa. Pa usually knew who did what in the village, and it was likely they could find out and even correct what was wrong. She had noticed the changes too, and she had often talked with Pa. But she had never foreseen disrespect, and she hated violence. In a way she had thought some of the changes were good, and the landlord agreed. There were certain things that had pleased him greatly, but these weren't an excuse for the disrespect which he had had to suffer in recent times. He could bear anything except disrespect. It knocked at the roots of his world. It made him feel that nothing would be too big, too wicked to be attempted against him. He was afraid and the old woman was ashamed. She didn't know how she could tell the old man what the landlord had told her. Her shame increased with every concession the landlord had made. He had addressed her as an equal. They sat together in the chairs trying to unravel the changes. The landlord had spoken his feelings towards the village, and finally as though it were an uncontrollable burst of confession he said what he would do if things got worse. He couldn't stand it much longer, and he had given the matter much thought.

The old woman didn't know why the landlord had chosen to speak to her as he did. At first it seemed a great privilege. Later it seemed more like an opportunity. But she was glad nevertheless, since he could have chosen to speak with someone else. Perhaps he respected her age. She and Pa were the oldest villagers. They could do nothing to alter his decision, but he must have felt that he owed it to them to say now and again how he felt about what was happening. Then he told her the story which had made his wife sick and which she wouldn't have believed were not the source of information beyond suspicion. Had she been told by anyone else her reactions would have been different. Her shame grew and spread through her like a sickness. She wouldn't have thought it possible. It was as though she bore responsibility for the other's actions. She looked at the old man without appearing to notice what he did. He was looking towards the shop where a few boys were grouped on the steps. Occasionally he made a kind of music with the bowl of the pipe on the sill. She hadn't spoken since she said how worried the landlord had been. The old man didn't seem too concerned because he thought he understood why the landlord would be worried. The changes had meant a threat to his power. The old man hated violence too, but the changes that were taking place didn't involve violence. Nobody assaulted. Things simply happened and people seemed to understand more. The old woman was still waiting to speak. The silence had made itself felt and the old man asked what had happened. She replied. 'The vagabonds.' She had come near to using the word earlier, but this was the first time she had actually used it. The old man didn't understand. He asked who the vagabonds were, and she didn't answer.

Old Man: If there be ought on you min' 'tis better you speak it out. You make me to feel the dead take possession o' the place the way you sit as if your tongue tie with a kind o' string.

Old Woman: I shame too bad, Pa. It ain't everything as you ought to talk, but the way he look when he say what he say it make my heart hurt me. It make me shame when I hear what I hear. It ain't in me, Pa, it ain't in me to judge the livin' or the dead, but it ain't seem right what taking place in this land. It ain't seem right in the sight o' God or man. 'Tis a high burnin' shame.

Old Man: I says to myself, the landlord gettin' old, an' there comes a time when a man can't keep up with the pace o' the world. You know it. An' I says to myself the landlord ain't got nothin' to lose by lettin' the load go. There ain't no reason under the sun he should cling to the land so. I don't want it for myself 'cause it ain't long before I go to rest these ol' bones in the grave, but I say let a thing go for what it worth. He's too old, Ma. Too old for such botheration.

Old Woman: The landlord ain't old, Pa. Maybe he look ol' an' no wonder too, but he ain't got as much age as you or me; an' look how you hold on to this life. 'Tis the same said thing. 'Tis the weight o' what he got to go through make him look ol'. He says to me sittin' in the sun beside the heap o' hay, he says we won't ever understan' the kind o' responsibility he feel for you an' me an' the whole village. He say it wus a real responsibility. There ain't much he can do whatever anybody may say, but he'd always feel that responsibility. We ain't his children he say, but the feelin' wus something like that. He had to sort o' take care o' those who belong to the village. Things wus never as they should be, he say. He know that full well. But nothin' take 'way that feelin' o' responsibility he feel for you an' me an' all o' we here in this corner o' God's earth. An' he say we wus lucky 'cause there be some in this islan' who never knew anybody to feel that kind of responsibility for them. He ask whether I'd ever know any Poor Whites, 'cause their own be a hard hard lot, he says. They get separate somehow from the other whites an' nobody notice them, black or white. To me 'twus always a wonder to see one o' them here or there but I didn't know their lot till he tell me. An' he says he didn't think there wus any people like them any other part o' the world. They get cut off from their own somehow, an' they had to go on livin' in the same land but as if their skin ain't make no difference. 'Tis why they call them Poor Whites. 'Tis the only place in these parts he say you see white people doin' all kind o' nasty low-down work, an' the Poor Whites as a class he say is worse off than the poor blacks.

Old Man: I think they wus all o' them from a place call Scotland, but I never ever see them live in the village. They keep most together in the country working on the land.

Old Woman: When they come to town 'tis usually to do servant work for the bigshot coloured.

Old Man: But why the white people don't ever take in some o' them to work as gardener or something o' the kind.

Old Woman: Only God knows except p'raps that they don't like to employ their own in that kind o' work. People got a way o' helpin' you if you need some help, but they never ever worry to help if your condition be such that you need all the help you can get. The worse off you be the more you frighten them, so the safest way out is to leave you to yourself. An' that's what happen to them. But it ain't so with we here in the village. Thank God, as Mr. Creighton say, we here always know that we had somebody to sort o' take care o' things. We had somebody in charge, but things changin'. They almost turn upside down with Penny Bank an' Friendly Society. An' though these things is good alright they bring others that ain't the same. The landlord say he believe what Mr. Slime do wus good, but he wusn't sure what he had in min'. Then he tell me what a terrible thing greed is. It grow like a sickness on you till you can't catch yourself. He say he din't know if Mr. Slime wus greedy, but he din't like what wus happenin'. There wus nothin' he could do 'bout the flood way back 'cause 'twus God's work, but when the men refuse to go to work in the shippin' company where he got business he say he see trouble comin'. He din't like it at all. 'Twus the first time anything o' the kind ever happen and from then on he wusn't himself. Anything could happen. But when what he say happen I couldn't believe my ears, Pa. Whatever happen with Mr. Slime an' so on he say he couldn't believe this other thing wus possible, the way those three little vagabonds come from wherever they come from to disrespect him as they do. He couldn't bear it, Pa, an' I nearly cry there in front his face. I nearly cry for the shame I feel.

The old woman stopped abruptly, and the old man who had been looking through the window as he listened turned and looked at her. He hadn't heard the last of what the landlord had said, but he was startled by the old woman's mention of the vagabonds. Then she said she could have cried, and he wondered what she meant. He knew how she felt about the land and Mr. Slime, and he thought she might have been referring to those who had been competing for the kind of power which the landlord had. He recalled the strike and the Penny Bank, and he felt a deep sympathy with Mr. Slime. In a sense he was on Mr. Slime's side. He wouldn't have liked to think that the landlord was disrespected, and his dislike of violence was no less than the old woman's. He saw the changes which had taken place in the village, and he felt they were part of a bigger change with which he associated Mr. Slime. The old woman was less sympathetic. She welcomed the Penny Bank and the Society. These were good. She didn't like the strike. Now she regretted everything. Nothing could make up for the kind of disrespect which the landlord had suffered. She was on the landlord's side. She was sure the old man would understand, and he would probably agree that the landlord deserved their sympathy to the exclusion of the Bank, the Society, Mr. Slime. She wondered how she might begin to tell him. The landlord's story was incredible.

Old Man: There be more in the mortar than the pestle. What make him tell you all this?

Old Woman: P'raps he want somebody to talk to, or p'raps he believe we might know who those little vagabonds wus.

Old Man: What the vagabonds do to make him call them that?

Old Woman: I couldn't believe my ears to tell the God's truth, Pa, an' I feel such a great shame when he say what he say, I couldn't stand it.

Old Man: Somebody dead? Somebody kill somebody?

Old Woman: Worse than that, Pa, seems a thousand times worse than that. The vagabonds try to force rudeness on the landlord's daughter. 'Twus the night he entertain the sailors, an' nobody know how they get through the wall, but it would seem they had been planning it a long time, an' they get in however they get in, the three o' them. Who they be only God knows. But they nearly outlaw the landlord's daughter. 'Twus a good thing, Pa, 'twus a good thing one o' the sailors wus there on the spot to save her business. The poor chil' they say wus takin' little fresh air. She ain't thinkin' no more 'bout what goin' to happen than the man in the moon, an' then out come those three wicked brutes to tear her to pieces, and 'twus only the grace o' the Almighty God who let the sailor be where he wus, or they would have make a mess o' the child.

The old man didn't speak. He was obviously outraged by the story of the vagabonds who had assaulted the landlord's daughter. He would never have thought it possible. This, too, was a change. All the other changes seemed a little soiled by this. He didn't know what he wanted for the village, but he felt the other changes suggested what the village could be, and he was pleased. This change had soiled everything. He didn't speak.

Old Woman: Now 'twill happen what I always expect. Mr. Creighton swear in my presence, Pa, he swear by the dead an' the livin' that if the slightest thing happen to unsettle him, he'll get rid o' this land. He can't stand it no more. So he says first 'twus the flood an' what an' what with repairs to all the roads. Then the strike an' the confusion on the wharf gettin' the men to go back to work, an' most o' them belongin' to the village. An' what with one little thing an' a next it wear his constitution down. Now this evil above everything else. That those vagabonds should think to do what they do. It need no more than a drop, Pa, to flow over the cup. An' so he says he got friends who will be willing an' ready to buy it, an' then we'll see the difference. He say he know for certain it won't be the same again. That's why he wish to God nothing will happen to make him get rid o' the land.

Old Man: It don't sound good, Ma. It don't sound good at all.

Old Woman: There ain't much we can do but pray, Pa. Pray.

9

THE morning broke foul through the trees and over the house on the hill. The earth was damp from the showers that had fallen lightly the night before, but the canals weren't flooded and the houses were unaffected, The streets were almost deserted and all shops but one at the corner were closed. Earlier a few people had met at the corner waiting for Savory. They sat on the shop steps and talked as usual, and after an hour or more they dispersed. Savory hadn't come. Neither Bob's father not Mr. Foster had gone to work, but the children asked no questions. The shoemaker was working in his shop, but one of the doors was closed. You could only see him through the window working the leather below his waist. At about nine o'clock the school was crammed with children, but an hour later several had left. Some of the parents stood outside in the school yard talking quietly. The head teacher and the assistants had met all together in the common room, and sometime later the head teacher blew the whistle and told the boys that work would be stopped for the day. Many more parents went to the school to confirm the head teacher's decision.

The clouds were thick under the grey sky, and the sun forcing a way through the clouds heaved a little light here and there over the fences and on the door steps. The girls from the girls' school met the boys returning home. Their head teacher had made the same decision. The sun went under cloud and the day turned dark. It was dismal.

The parents couldn't understand what was happening, but one of the girls said that her head teacher said there was fighting in town, and it was possible the fighting would soon spread to the village. The head teacher at the boys' school had made no explanation, but one boy said the teacher of class 4 had warned them not to loiter in the streets. No one knew what had happened in the city, but there was no doubt something was wrong. The women were perturbed. Bob's mother went to ask Mr. Foster if he knew what would happen. She was afraid that Bob might get involved in the fighting if it spread to the village. Mr. Foster was vague. He said something might have been happening, but he wasn't in the city and therefore he couldn't say. Some people met at the corner to ask one another what would happen, but it was useless. No one knew what was happening. There was fighting in town and the fighting would soon spread to the village. They returned to their houses and waited. The sun came out and there was light over everything. It was difficult to predict the weather since the sun was shining through the rain clouds. But they wished it would rain. If the rain came and the streets were flooded the fighting might come to an end. Others were hoping the sun would come out and brighten up the land.

It was difficult to act since everything depended on the fighting in the city which no one had seen. Those who were loitering at the corner went back into the houses. It was certain Savory would not come. Mr. Foster dressed and went to the guard-house where the local police were stationed. He promised he would return with some news of what was going to happen. A few people took seats on Mr. Foster's steps and waited. They had hardly settled into their talk when Mr. Foster returned. He told them very abruptly to go home. They refused and insisted that he should say what the police had told him. He walked up the steps through the passage they had made and entered the house. The people waited outside and he came out to the window and asked them to leave. They refused again, and a little later he spoke. He hadn't seen the police. The guard-house was closed. A woman shouted, O God! when she heard. Mr. Foster said it would appear all the local police were recruited for the fighting in town. Some might have been sent to Government House, but it seemed the village was without the protection of the police. The fighting was spreading. The people returned home and waited. From one end of the street to the other the houses were closed. The doors were locked or bolted, and the occupants peeped out through the jalousies or under the windows which are prised open now and again. There was a kind of terror in the air. The villagers were quiet and frightened within. The sun came out and dispersed the rain clouds, and soon it was bright all over the land. All the shops were closed. The school was closed. In the houses they tried to imagine what the fighting was like. They had never heard of anything like it before. They had known a village fight, and they were used to fights between boys and girls. Sometimes after the cricket competition one village team for various reasons might threaten to fight with the opponent. These fights made sense, but the incidents in the city were simply beyond them. There was fighting in the city. That was all they were told, and they repeated the words and tried to guess who were fighting whom. But they couldn't follow it clearly. It wasn't Mr. Foster or Bob's father or the overseer's brother who was fighting. It was simply the fighting. They were fighting in the city. And the fighting would soon spread to the village. That was all that was clear. And they couldn't say they understood that.

Bob's mother pushed open her window wide and looked over the trees to see what was happening on the hill. It was midday but the bell in the landlord's yard wasn't rung. The landlord's house was closed on the side Bob's mother could see. For three hours they had waited for news of what had happened in the city, but no one had come from that way. It was unbearable. She closed the window and sat on the chair with her head resting on the sill. Bob's father went over to speak with Mr. Foster and he had remained there ever since. Bob and Trumper sat in a corner of the house wondering what they would do. It was three hours since the fighting was supposed to spread to the village, but it hadn't reached. They thought for a while that they would steal away and go into the city. But what would they do? If it was clear who were fighting they might be able to take sides, but it was impossible for them to engage in a danger which was simply called the fighting. They were fighting in the city, and they asked themselves who were they. If Bob were sure that his father had something to do with the fighting he could have gone ahead, find out which was his father's supporters, and his allegiance would be automatic. It would have been the same with Trumper. If Bob were in the fight he would understand which side he was on. But the situation was perplexing. There was fighting in the city. They spoke quietly in the corner, and it seemed they had reached a decision. Bob looked at his mother, but she paid no attention. She had got up from the chair, peeped under the window and sat down quickly. The streets were empty. They left the house and went into the yard. Bob's mother didn't stir. They stood outside talking quietly. They were going to climb two or three fences, cut a way through a neighbour's backyard, and take the road down the train lines and towards the city. They would see what had happened.

Bob's mother sat at the window waiting for the sound of steps outside. His father hadn't returned from Mr. Foster's house. Trumper clenched his hands behind his back and Bob put his feet in the palms and pulled himself up to the fence. He scaled it, and Trumper using a different tactic followed. They scaled another and another and walked out of sight towards the train lines.

Bob's mother sat at the window. The old man, Pa, opened the front door and came out into the street in his clogs. He wore an old panama hat and carried a stick. The old woman opened the window and poked her head through. Pa walked down the road towards Mr. Foster's house while Ma remained at the window. He rapped at the window with the stick, but no one opened. He rapped again and shouted Mr. Foster's name, and Bob's father looked out. Bob's mother opened the window and saw them. Bob's father was terrified. He shouted at the old man to return to the house, but Pa went on trying to get his words over the noise. They were quiet and Pa spoke. Another three or four windows opened and all eyes stared at Pa alone in the street. He told the men that he had seen Mr. Slime pass up the road while he was feeding the pigeons, and he wanted them to know. He urged them to get in touch with Mr. Slime who would probably know what had happened in the city. Bob's father looked at Mr. Foster and suddenly they asked the old man to go in quickly. He refused. He said he would go and see Mr. Slime himself if they refused. They grew angry, and shouted at him to leave. He raised his voice and the neighbours could hear. He told them they must have known what was happening and he swore that since he didn't know what was meant by all this talk about fighting in the city he would find out from Mr. Slime. The men were quiet. They asked him very gently to go in. They said Mr. Slime might know what was wrong in the city, but he couldn't do anything about it. The old man refused to go. He said he wanted the facts, and he almost broke into tears when he said what a pity it was he didn't have his strength.

The men were quiet. They wanted to let him in through Mr. Foster's door, but he said he wouldn't leave Ma alone. They didn't know what to do. They watched him trembling as he spoke, and they were almost in tears. Bob's mother and Miss Foster listened. Bob's mother wanted to send Bob to call his father, but Bob wasn't there. She called him twice, and there was no answer. She thought of looking for him in the yard, but she didn't want to miss the details of this little situation. Mr. Foster and Bob's father were still remonstrating with the old man while Ma waited at the window. She seemed to understand what the old man was asking them to do, and she was sympathetic. She thought they should go and get some news from Mr. Slime. If the fight did spread to the village, Mr. Slime was the only man who could stop it. The villagers wouldn't get involved against his will. The shops were all closed, and most people must have been hoping that something would soon happen. They must have been hungry. The old man wanted the men to persuade Mr. Slime to have the shops opened. They believed he could take care of the fighting if it came to the village.

The men waited puzzled by the old man's persistence. Mr. Foster went in, and Bob's father tried again to get rid of the old man. The neighbours looked and waited to see what would happen. Mr. Foster came back and told the old man that he would go and see Mr. Slime, but not immediately. The old man refused. He turned away, and the men pretended to be closing the window when Bob came running through the road shouting for his father. Everybody looked out, but Bob's mother couldn't understand what had happened. She would have sworn that Bob was in the yard. He was panting for breath and all they could hear him say was, 'they comin', they comin'.' They asked him who were coming, but he didn't know. He put his hand to his chest and panted, 'they comin', they comin'.' Mr. Foster came out and helped the old man up the steps. He saw him safe in the house and returned home. Bob and his father went in. All the windows were closed again, and they waited frightened and quiet to see what had happened. Bob's father rushed out again to ask Mr. Foster for some medicine. Bob had fainted.

They couldn't understand what had happened, but he couldn't say more than they comin, they comin', and when his father steadied him and asked him to try to remember, he started and then stopped abruptly. He had fainted. His mother started to cry, and the neighbours cried too. Most of the women nearby were getting ready to cry. Bob's father got the medicine and went back into the house. They closed the door and the windows and tried to revive Bob. His mother kept on asking him how he had got out, but he didn't seem to hear. He fell off into a sleep, and at intervals spoke a few words. But nothing was clear except the brief choking pant, 'they comin', they comin'.'

His mother asked him what had happened to Trumper, but he didn't hear. His father asked whether Trumper had gone out too, and his mother explained. They couldn't understand. Mr. Foster held his head in his hands as though he wanted to cry, and Miss Foster burst into tears. They waited, and later all the windows were pushed open again. Trumper came running through the road as Bob had done. He stopped now and again to say what he had seen, but the people couldn't understand because he never waited long enough to explain. Some heard about bottles, and others heard about stones, and there was some mention of shooting. If they had all got together, each putting his bit with the other's, they might have been able to make a story, but they had to remain with the fragments. Trumper ran up to the house to ask whether Bob had returned, and they opened the door for him. But he wouldn't go in. He said he wanted to know whether Bob had got away, and then added that it was safer for him to go home. They couldn't understand, and Bob's mother started to cry. She wanted to know what Trumper meant by getting away. Bob lay quiet on the bed inhaling the salts Mr. Foster had lent. All the windows were closed again as his father turned the corner in search of Trumper. His mother sat beside the bed soothing his brow with Limacol. She thought of what Trumper had said, and tried all the while to give it a meaning. She would wait till Bob's father returned with some news of what had happened to them.

Trumper was seated on the bench and the overseer's brother was coaxing him to say what he had seen in the city. He insisted on explaining what had happened to Bob, and he explained that the police might come in search of Bob. Bob's father listened and tried to find out how they had got involved from the start, but it was difficult to get Trumper to give a coherent account. He kept on asking what would happen if the police came and demanded Bob. Bob's father said nothing could be done till he had said what the trouble was, and he tried to explain. He drew his breath, wrenched himself and tried to speak. He was straying again, with questions about the police, and then he started to use the words Bob had spoken, 'they comin', they comin'.' His father collared him and told him to speak or he would cut his arse in spite of what had happened. He shivered and spoke. They listened, and he went on quietly and evenly with the story.

They had taken the road down the train line that led to the city. The houses were closed and the streets deserted till they reached the park. They scaled the fence that surrounded the park and made a short cut across the playing fields. There were cars parked in the streets, but no one moved about. The cars were empty, and three were badly damaged. They were a little frightened, but they were arguing that if the fighting broke out within a few yards they could take the same road back home before they were caught. Moreover they didn't think they were in danger since they weren't involved. No one had said who was fighting, and they walked on as if they were spectators. At the park gate that led towards the city a few men were standing, but they seemed quite unconcerned. They crept along the park rails, and when they were a few yards from the park gate a squad of police attacked them from the rear. The police had followed them across the savannah and they were involved in the fighting. They ran towards the gate when the police attacked. The men who were standing at the gate ran too, and Bob and Trumper followed the men. They had got involved. They followed the men, and when the latter realized that the police were really in pursuit of the boys they waited for them, and they all disappeared in ambush for the police. They didn't understand what was happening, but the men welcomed them. The police circled the park and the surrounding area, and they were trapped. They too were fighting. They didn't understand what the fight was all about, but they had been forced into it. The men took care of them. They sat behind a fence waiting till the police advanced. One man gave Trumper a stick and he passed it to Bob. The man cut another stick and passed it to Trumper. They too were in the fight. The police had reinforced their squad and they attacked. The men fled and Bob and Trumper got separated. That was the last they had seen of each other.

Bob's father couldn't bear it any longer. He asked Trumper what he had seen and Trumper told him to let Bob relate it. He couldn't bear it. Bob's father returned to his house. Bob was sitting on the bed, trying to collect himself. His mother soothed the brow and temples with Limacol and put the bottle of strong salts to his nose. He sat erect, trying to recall what had happened. He asked whether they had seen Trumper, and his father explained what Trumper had said. His mother began to cry. His father asked him to say what had happened after he left Trumper. He said he couldn't remember. He had followed the men for a long way. They were in the public square where a bigger mob had assembled. Then the crowds multiplied and the weapons too, and he felt sick in the stomach. He followed the men through the alleys and towards the sea. There was blood in the streets, but he was giddy with the sight of the weapons and the men standing along the waterfront. Occasionally the police attacked, and the men retaliated with bottles and stones. Some leapt into the sea, and others climbed the trees. The police were continually repulsed, and when the situation was beyond control, the shooting started. That was the last he had remembered. The men fled and he was left alone. He walked to the police headquarters and explained what he had seen, and how he had reached the city. He didn't understand what was happening. He didn't know who was fighting or why, and he had simply come to see. The police drove him back to the park, and told him to find his way from there. He had got a blow in the ribs, and it pained. He put his hand to the spot, and rubbed.

His father went to the window to see whether he could signal Mr. Foster. His mother sat beside the bed soothing the bruised flesh. He lay back and was quiet, waiting for the night to come.

The windows were still closed and the light travelling through the clouds seemed to walk from roof to roof across the roads. In the houses the people waited for the fighting to reach the village. There was nothing they could do. The shops weren't open, and many were hungry, but food was not now so urgent as their curiosity about the fighting. The boys hadn't explained enough. They had related in part what had happened to them, but everybody wanted to know what the city was like. Bob's father left the house and went over to speak with Mr. Foster. They sat and talked about what the boys had related. Mr. Foster looked terribly sad as though he were responsible for what had been happening, and Miss Foster began to cry. They couldn't bear to hear her cry, and Mr. Foster told her to go and stay with Bob's mother. She went, and the men remained in the house talking.

They were trying to understand what the fighting really meant. They understood certain things about it. They knew that the strike had started on the water front the night before. There was a mass meeting in the city which Mr. Slime had attended. Three men had spoken to the people, but they hadn't said anything about fighting. They had reminded their listeners of what had been happening in Trinidad, and they were warning certain people in the audience that if steps weren't taken to remedy the situation it was possible a similar thing would happen in Barbados. One man said it wasn't his intention to make hooligans of the workers, but if you couldn't persuade certain people to be fair you were left with no alternative but to fight for what you wanted. The people had applauded and they seemed quite willing to fight if persuasion weren't possible. Mr. Slime had spoken too, but he was more concerned about the village. He gave them a brief account of what he had done for the village, and he made it clear that he would be on the side of the workers in any calamity. He didn't want to see any fighting, but if it happened in Trinidad, and certain people weren't prepared to be fair, then it would happen in Barbados. Mr. Foster and Bob's father talked quietly. They were getting nearer the truth. The men had mentioned fighting, but there was no direct suggestion. They had only cited a particular case, and probably they intended scaring certain people in the audience. That was all they remembered. The meeting came to an end and the politicians went about their business. There were three of them of whom Mr. Slime seemed to be the most powerful. The crowds had dispersed, and they thought the matter was ended. The strike would continue till they had had further words from Mr. Slime. No word came, and when the children returned from school in the morning with the stories the teachers had told they tried to put things together. It seemed they wouldn't receive any word from Mr. Slime and they wondered how long the fight would last. Mr. Foster looked sad as though he were really at the bottom of the trouble. Bob's father said he was leaving. They walked to the door, and suddenly all the windows were opened again. The people poked their heads through to see who was speaking. It was the old woman who got drunk every Saturday night. She tottered across the street as she spoke and the saliva slavered down her chin. Mr. Foster went into the street and held her by the arm. She flounced and withdrew.

'Be gone,' she said, 'coward drunken ol' bitch like you to come to hol' on to me.' Mr. Foster stepped back and waited for her to continue.

'I jus' from the city,' she said, 'while you a big stinkin' nigger man wrap up in yuh blasted bed I been in the city an' 'tis men like you they want.'

Bob's father came out and they tried to make her speak. There were tears on her face, and the saliva spouted as she spoke. They helped her to the steps and she sat. Another two or three people came out, and the place was looking lively again. The men urged her to speak, but her mouth was full of saliva and the water blinded her eyes. She was crying like a child.

'What happen to you?' Miss Foster asked.

'My heart break,' she said, 'me heart break, break, break.' The tears flowed and she retched.

'What happen?' Mr. Foster asked.

'My heart break,' she said, 'my heart break, 'cause my boy dead.'

'Who?' Mr. Foster asked.

'Po King,' Miss Foster said, 'It is Po King who is her son.'

'Dead,' she said, 'dead as a door nail.' And the water covered her face.

'How he dead?' one woman asked.

'With a bullet,' she said, 'the gun went to 'is heart.' The women started to cry. They couldn't bear the sight of the old woman. They wiped her face and tried to find out what she had seen. The fighting now seemed real.

'Who shoot 'im?' Mr. Foster asked.

'They shoot 'im,' she said; 'they shoot 'im like he was a bird.'

'Who?' Mr. Foster insisted.

'The police,' she said. 'Some say 'twas the white inspector, an' others wus the ordinary police, but he dead.'

'Where wus he?' Mr. Foster asked.

'In the tree,' she said. 'When the law declare they all run here, there an' everywhere, an' poor Po run up the tree. The police see him where he go, an' they aim all together at the top at the tree. An' they got 'im. My poor Po fall down like a bird.'

She fell back on the steps exhausted, and Mr. Foster helped her into the house. The women were crying, and the men who had heard grew suddenly fierce. The old woman sat in Mr. Foster's house. They brought her tea, and Miss Foster changed her clothes. They were wet and foul with the vomit. She had been drunk ever since she saw her son fall from the tree. No one knew where she had bought the rum since all the shops were closed, but it was possible she had it from the day before. She usually kept it in a flat bottle in her bosom, taking a sip now and again. She had forgotten the measure this time, and she drained the bottle. They dressed her in a blue kimono and put her on the bed to sit. Two or three people gathered round the house to hear more news of what had happened in the city. It would seem the old woman had gone out early in the morning and remained after the fighting broke out. She had seen the city at its worst, but she found it difficult to put the incidents together, and whenever she remembered her son she broke into tears and the story came to an end. The windows were still open, and everyone seemed quite certain that it wouldn't be long before more news was related. The streets were empty but for the few people who had met on Mr. Foster's step. Mr. Foster asked them to go away. He said he knew how they felt, but the old woman said it was safer if they went away. It couldn't be long before the fighting spread to the village. Someone wanted to know why they would come to the village and Mr. Foster explained that it had something to do with the landlord. They were perplexed. They didn't know that the landlord was a partner in the shipping company where the strike was called. They argued among themselves. The women said it wasn't fair. Mr. Creighton hadn't done anybody anything. Miss Foster left the old woman and came to the window to tell the story of Mr. Creighton and the half-crown. The women shook their heads and said 'twas true, he hadn't done anybody anything. The men were uncertain. Some said they would go to the house on the hill to have a word with Mr. Creighton and the women cried shame. They wouldn't hear of it. Whatever had happened in the city they didn't want blood to be shed in the village. They dispersed turning the question over in their minds. Mr. Foster closed the windows and sat beside the old woman. She went on talking about what she had seen and heard in the city. Outside the windows were going down to the sills again. All the houses were shut. The sun sank beneath the pile of cloud, and the day turned dull.

Mr. Foster came out to have a word with Bob's father. They sat on the bed and Mr. Foster repeated what the old woman had said. Bob turned on one side, asleep. His mother sat on the chair beside the bed and listened to Mr. Foster. In the house the people waited for the appearance of another traveller from the city. They wondered who the next would be. Mr. Foster put the incidents together as the old woman had related them.

A crowd of waterfront workers had assembled round the public square in the early morning. A small delegation, among whom were Mr. Slime and another politician, had gone to the Governor's House to get the Governor's advice on the calling of the strike. The sentry refused them entry to see the Governor and they insisted. The sentry summoned the guard of four policemen and the men were dispersed. There was a fight at the Governor's gate in which two of the workers were seriously wounded. The politicians and the other workers left, and an hour later the fight had taken place on a grander scale in the city. The workers moved to some headquarters where they had stored bottles and stones and whatever weapons they had thought of using. The police were taken by surprise. They came out in the morning on the usual patrols with their batons strung to the leather belts, but when the workers assaulted with their weapons the police fled.

It was a terrible sight. The workers moved into the main streets of the city, and when the politicians realized what might happen they came out. They warned the men not to destroy anything, above all the lives of innocent people in stores and shops. But it was too late. The word could not reach all the workers and several had already taken command of the stores. The politicians disappeared appalled and terrified. But no lives were lost. The rioters had done great damage, but they hadn't killed anyone, and so far the only instance of death was that of the boy, Po King, who had been shot by the police.

The damage took a strange form. Cars were overturned, and the bread vans making the early deliveries were stopped, emptied and turned on one side in the gutters. Some of the men ate the loaves, and others used them as weapons to throw at the police. In the main street of the city two large stores had been entered. The show windows were destroyed but the men refused to take the cloth. They trampled across the show window over the silk and satin and entered the store. At the cashier's desk in one of the large stores the men attacked the woman who sat behind the cage. In terror she threw the notes over her head and fled to the little door. The men caught her and stared at her for a while. Then one of them felt her breasts, passed a hand over and along her backside and told her to hide. The money was left untouched. The stores had become a chaos of cloth, glass, sticks and men who were neither buying nor selling. The commodities were scattered in all directions, but there was hardly an instance of theft. The men refused to take anything away.

On the second storey of one store an amusing and ridiculous incident had occurred. One of the workers had dressed in an evening suit which he had taken from the show window. He had cornered the store walker whom he forced into a room. He undressed the store walker and dressed him again in the blue dungarees which he wore on the waterfront. The store walker shivered and proceeded to do as he was bidden. The worker simply asked him to stand in a corner and let him see what he looked like as an honest hard-working man. The store walker obeyed, and in fright asked the worker whether he mightn't do other things an honest working man would do. The worker agreed, and the store walker set about shining the shoes and brushing the evening suit which the worker was wearing. The worker wrenched him in the ribs and told him that wasn't what an honest man did. The store walker shivered and tried to scrub the floor with his naked hand. The worker watched him with contempt and walked out to continue the fight in the evening suit.

They had all been taken by surprise. The stores, the police, and all who had good reason to protect themselves. The situation had grown worse. The streets were littered with clothes and food, and in the stores the wind disturbed the dollar notes on the floor. A strange terror hung over the city, and there was nothing left for the authorities to do but declare martial law. The police came out armed with bayoneted rifles, and the tide turned against the workers. They leapt into the sea and swam to the other side of the land. Bags of sugar were hoisted overboard, and the waterfront in the dull morning was a riotous waste. H.M.S. *Goliath* arrived in the harbour, and shells were fired. There was more scampering. The rioters fled the city and were moving farther and farther back to find prey in the villages. The city shook under the explosion of the shells. It seemed a war had started. The rioters were at a disadvantage in the city, and they decided to retreat towards the villages. They probably hoped to terrify some of the people whose cars were out of order and who might have to walk home. That's what Bob's words had meant. They were really forced towards the villages, and they were coming with a special mission to Creighton's village.

That was the old woman's story. She had seen some of the incidents she related and she had overheard others from people nearby. Mr. Foster asked Bob's father what they should do. No one knew what had happened to the landlord. He might have been at home, and if the rioters went up to the house on the hill it was difficult to say what would happen. The rioters might have grown more hostile because of the interference of the *Goliath*. And there were one or two men in the village who wouldn't have thought twice about skinning the landlord alive. The men were anxious. Mr. Foster wanted to get in touch with Mr. Slime to find out what they could do if the fighting reached the village. Should they join in an attack against the house on the hill or should they try to persuade the rioters that they shouldn't shed blood in the village. Bob's father had no advice to give. He was afraid. They were sorry they hadn't seen Mr. Slime when the old man Pa urged them to. They waited, and Bob turned over on his back and groaned. He said something in his sleep about the landlord and the overseer and the men tried to listen carefully. He went on speaking incoherently about the overseer, but they couldn't put the words together. It seemed he knew something about the overseer. They wondered what he might have heard the men say about the landlord and the overseer. They didn't know how much time he had spent with the rioters before he walked to the police headquarters, and they thought it was possible the men might have told him something. They listened, but nothing was clear but the words landlord, overseer, and the pant he had made earlier, they comin'.

Miss Foster knocked at the door and asked Mr. Foster to come home with her. She was beginning to feel sick in the stomach. He left Bob's father and went into the house with the old woman. Miss Foster was panting for breath, and the old woman told her she hadn't really seen anything to pant about. She should have been in the city. Miss Foster started to cry. Mr. Foster couldn't understand what had suddenly happened to her. She buried her head in the pillow and the tears flowed. He asked her to explain. He dried her face and she sat upright. It was difficult for him to follow her words. She said when she went into the yard a while ago to collect the starched clothes she saw some men run into hiding behind trees by the train line. They carried weapons, and she was sure they saw what they wanted. They were talking among themselves and pointing as though they saw what they were looking for, and she couldn't stand it any longer. She left the clothes and ran inside. She begged him not to leave the house again. The old woman looked frightened too. Mr. Foster's face turned grim. He didn't know what to do. He half opened the window and looked in the direction of the trees by the train line, but he couldn't see the men. Miss Foster started to cry again, and the old woman soothed her with a hand. Mr. Foster remained at the window, and suddenly there was a knock at the door. Bob's father had come to say that he had seen some men crouching along the line through the trees. He rushed back into the house and Mr. Foster remained at the window. Miss Foster was almost screaming. Mr. Foster couldn't bear to hear her scream, and he shouted at her to shut her blasted mouth. It was the only way to control her in that state. He swore the louder she screamed, and soon she was quiet.

He had seen the men. They crouched on all fours along the train line through the wood, talking and pointing as they advanced. They were moving towards his house. He looked in the other direction to see whether there was anyone in sight. There were no police. The men crouched and talked, holding on to their weapons. One carried a bottle and a stone, and the others had sticks and stakes. Mr. Foster couldn't understand what was happening. He moved to another window and it was clear that everyone around had seen. Heads pushed up under the half-open windows as the men crouched along the lines. Mr. Foster moved back to the window from which he had seen them. The men looked quite certain of what they would do. They crouched along the line, and when they reached the border of the canal which separated the road from the edge of the wood they stopped. They were no longer hiding. One pointed in the direction of Mr. Foster's house, and the men came nearer. Mr. Foster closed the window. All the windows were closed. The men took up a position behind the houses and the fences on either side the road. No one looked out.

The day was changing colour continually. The clouds piled up and as the light passed through each layer the day changed. The men stood waiting behind the fences as though they were sure of their prey. The houses were all shut and Mr. Foster wondered whether it was the overseer they had seen. They would have treated the overseer as an enemy. He didn't know, but the men were outside behind his fence. They were all sure the fighting had now reached the village. Every window was shut, and the streets were empty. It might have been night with the people all asleep and the full moon passing easily over the silence of the land. They all waited within the four partitions silent and sorry for whatever might happen. The fighting had reached the village. The rioters had arrived.

Mr. Foster put his head against the partition and listened. He could hear the men talking, but it was difficult to follow what they were saying. It was clear they had baited someone and the victim was in sight. He wanted to have another look in the other direction, but he was afraid to open the window. He had seen the men, but he didn't recognize them. They weren't from the village. They changed position. Two remained behind Mr. Foster's fence while the others crossed the road and took their stand behind another fence. Bob's father prised open the window and saw them. Another crossed the street and crouched behind his house. He wanted to open the window and ask what was going to happen, but he didn't recognize the men and decided against the action. The men talked excitedly, pointing in different directions. They seemed to be discussing where the victim would pass. There weren't any police in sight, and Bob's father thought it was the overseer whom they were after. Everyone who saw them was sure it was the overseer. Bob turned on his side and woke. His father put his finger to his mouth indicating that there should be silence. Bob was dazed. He couldn't understand what was happening as he watched his father crouch on the floor with his head held close to the partition. He left the bed and walked across to where his father knelt on the floor. His mother was sobbing. They prised open the window easily and asked Bob to look. He saw the men and he recognized one of the men, but he suddenly grew frightened and couldn't speak. His father asked him what was wrong, and he started to cry. They tried to help him remember what he was saying in his sleep. His mother asked whether the man he recognized had said anything about the landlord or the overseer, and Bob shook his head. But they couldn't tell whether he understood what he was doing. He crouched close to his father, and sobbed aloud. His mother took him back to the bed and soothed his brow with the Limacol.

The men shifted their position again. But each time they moved one or two remained while the others took up a new position elsewhere. They now covered three or four houses. It seemed the victim would pass that way. They were sure. Mr. Foster asked the old woman whether she had seen the overseer, but she couldn't remember. They grew terribly sorry for the overseer, and Mr. Foster wondered what he should do if the men assaulted the overseer. He wasn't sure. He had no great liking for the overseer, but he didn't know these men, and he wouldn't have entertained the idea of a man from another village assaulting the overseer. The overseer belonged to the village, and even if the fighting was carried out in the interest of the village, he didn't like the idea of the outsider assaulting one who belonged to the village. He thought for a while. Suddenly there was a scamper of feet in the road. He prised open the window and there were more men. He didn't know them. The men joined those who had been hiding behind the houses, and a rapid exchange of words passed. They pointed in various directions as they spoke, making sure that they had their bearings. The men spoke and he could hear a word now and again. A fresh gang came up the road and it seemed the village had taken over from the city. Everyone knew the men were outside. The windows were shut tight, but within the houses the people shivered with the knowledge of what went on outside.

The new men had brought more weapons. They passed the broken bottles round till everyone was well armed, and they talked as they crouched from fence to fence along the road. There were none of them from the village, and Bob's father felt ashamed. He had been thinking on the same problem that worried Mr. Foster. If a war was being waged in the village, it was right that the villagers should wage it themselves. He wanted to have a word with Mr. Foster. He thought he might suggest to Mr. Foster that they should assemble some men and demand that the strangers explain their intentions. He visualized a fight between the villagers and the intruders, but he didn't care. He felt terribly humiliated by the way these strange men carried on. They behaved as though they were in their village or wherever they lived. He made to go out, but Bob's mother stopped him. They argued quietly. She told him not to go. If the men suspected him of taking sides with the overseer they would stone him to death. She had had a glimpse of one or two of them and she dreaded the look of them. They were desperate. They had nothing to lose by their actions. Imprisonment, death by hanging. It couldn't matter to them. They had resigned themselves to the situation. Bob's mother argued with the tears on her face. Bob argued too. He told his father he had recognized one of the men, and he wouldn't like to find himself in a fight against that man. He began to cry, and his father decided not to go. He prised open the window and looked across at Mr. Foster's house. The men were quiet now. It wouldn't be long before the victim would come into sight. They had timed his approach.

Bob and his mother went over to the bed and wondered what would happen to the overseer. They were sure it was the overseer. They didn't know where he was or what he had been doing outside, but they were sure the men were in search of him. Apparently they had the streets blockaded. There wasn't any way the overseer could pass without walking into their trap. The men were positioned in every road behind the houses and the fences. They were talking faster now, and with greater excitement. Mr. Foster could hear those who hid behind his house. They poised the sticks and the stones and waited. One said something about death, and another sucked his teeth. He didn't care. They said there had been deaths in the city. Mr. Foster was terrified. Something was going to happen. He didn't know what, but he was sure of it. The feeling was sickening. The tremendous feeling that something was going to happen and he didn't know what it was or how it would affect him. He couldn't stand it. He wanted to shout at the men, but Miss Foster prevented him. The men crouched, thirsty and ravenous for blood. The man made mention again about death, and the other remained silent. The ranks were reinforced. There were about twenty men behind the houses in that road. They seemed to understand perfectly what the next step should be, and they waited, tense, desperate, and purposeful. Their heads peeped out from behind the houses looking in the direction of the main street that separated the village from Belleville. All eyes looked in that direction. They were ready. It was about to happen. They began retreating from fence to fence. The hands were poised. The broken bottles glinted, and their eyes were steady in the murderous glances. It was going to happen, now, and if not now, never. Never. Never.

*   *   *

The landlord turned the corner and walked up the road between the houses on either side. The terror of his face was indescribable. His clothes were soiled, and he stepped with the uncertainty of a drunken person. The men waited. The thought of his death was terrible. He walked up the road. He seemed to understand what might happen, but he didn't look back. Mr. Foster prised open the window to see what was happening and he saw the landlord. It was incredible. He had never seen or imagined Mr. Creighton could look like that. No one had ever seen him walking through the village. Mr. Foster broke through the door and rushed out on the steps. He couldn't stand it. Whatever the cause of the fight he couldn't stand it. The sight of the landlord was intolerable. One of the men stooped forward and pulled Mr. Foster by his pants behind the house. 'Not yet,' the man said. 'Not yet.' Mr. Foster couldn't speak. He heard the words but they didn't register. The landlord saw him disappear behind the house, but he didn't stop walking. He had resigned himself to this. He expected the worst. His expression of impotence was inhuman. Bob's father couldn't stand it either, and came out through the gateway. The men held him down. 'Not yet,' one said. 'Not yet.' They tried to explain among themselves. 'You too anxious,' they said. 'He's done you wrong, 'tis true, so you got to be careful you don't miss him this time.' Bob's father seemed to faint. They put the stick in his hand as the landlord approached. The men were waiting till he reached the next corner. They wanted to attack from the back. It would seem they

themselves couldn't bear to look him in the face as they did this deed.
They waited for him to pass. He walked shakily like a man exhausted
and drunk. He seemed not to care what would happen. His face was
white as a pebble. He approached the corner where the roads made
four and the men turned round to aim. It seemed they were intent on
killing. They waited since they didn't want to lose this chance. The
men came out. They were all behind him now. The hands were held
steady. Mr. Foster and Bob's father remained on their knees, breathless. The landlord stood. He had reached the corner where the roads
made four. He stood quiet as though he had seen his death or his
escape. The men were puzzled. They couldn't understand why he had
stopped. They came out into the streets, and now he saw them. The
enemy was there, and they advanced quietly, confidently.

The landlord looked to the right, and then walked on. The men
followed. They were some yards behind, but the landlord had a
short distance to cover before he reached the track that led through
the wood to the house on the hill. The men walked behind with
the arms raised, and the landlord walked away. They were ready
to *fire* the stones. They argued among themselves whether they
should *fire* them. Some thought they should attack without stones.
The naked hands were enough. They argued as they advanced
quiet and cautious like boys baiting crabs. The landlord walked
away and as the men stepped nearer Mr. Slime turned the corner.
He waited at the corner where the roads made four and then walked
towards the men. He had seen the landlord and the landlord had
seen him. The men weren't sure now what they could do. They
didn't know whether Mr. Slime would have wanted to give the order
to fire. The landlord didn't look back. He guessed that Mr. Slime must
have reached the corner and in sight of the men. He walked ahead,
and the men moved forward slowly, watching Mr. Slime and the
landlord. Then all eyes were fastened on Mr. Slime. His head spun
with the terror and confusion of the scene. He didn't know what he
should do. The men looked like beasts without reason. He wondered
whether he should dare risk an order not to *fire*. They watched his
face for a signal as the landlord tottered exhausted and stupid through
the wood. He had reached the track that led through the wood to
the house on the hill. He crept slowly across the weed as the men
came forward and Mr. Slime moved nearer and nearer towards them.
The landlord had entered the track and was almost out of sight. No

stone had been *fired*. Mr. Slime looked back to see how far the landlord had reached, but he was out of sight. He had escaped. Mr. Slime
sighed as he reached the men who looked disappointed, angry, and
above all obedient. 'Thank you,' he said, 'I'm glad you didn't do it.'
Some of them dropped the stones and held their heads down. Mr. Slime
spoke quietly. The windows were prised open, and the people looked
on, helpless with excitement. The men assembled round him and he
asked them to disperse. He said it was a day such as he would never
like to see again. They looked terribly penitent and disappointed as
he lectured to them. He recalled what he had said in his speech the
night before, and they nodded their agreement. They didn't intend to
kill, but the police had been hostile. There was no alternative but to
retaliate, and after the boy Po King had been shot, they were overcome
with rage. Mr. Slime looked weary. He had heard them, and he hoped
it was all over.

In the city peace had been restored, and he warned that the police
might soon move into the village. The men walked away in different
directions. Some of them pitched the stones in the canals, or threw
the broken bottles in the wood. Others pocketed the weapons. The
men separated, and Mr. Foster and Bob's father watched them walk
out of the village. The afternoon had faded away, and the darkness
was coming on. The streets were empty once more. Bob's father
walked to Mr. Foster's house and they sat quiet, wondering what
to say. Bob's mother called and the houses were all shut again. The
old woman had fallen asleep in Mr. Foster's house. It would soon be
very dark. In the houses they heard the rumble of an engine outside.
The windows were prised open, and they looked. The police had
appeared. Miss Foster shook her head and wondered whether she was
glad or sorry the men had left so soon. The car moved slowly through
the road. The police sat three to a seat with the rifles protruding, and
the bayonets shining dull and deadly in the late night. They drove
towards the street that marked the boundary between Belleville and
the village. The dust rose behind and mingled with the deepening
twilight. The houses were shut tight again, and the night thick and
heavy settled over the terror and silence of the land.

10

THE years had changed nothing. The riots were not repeated. The landlord had remained. Pa was asleep and his snore was the same. The light burnt low on the table. It was dark in the corners of the room. The old woman sat on the chair beside the bed and everything seemed the same except the sudden awareness that nothing had changed. She shook the neck of the phial against her hand and rubbed herself along the ribs and down the side. The pain shifted but was not appeased, and she lay back on the chair waiting for a relief. She wasn't going to wake Pa, but when the pain stopped she would crawl back into bed and put out the light. Pa made a loud snore and then the room was quiet except for the voice. It was Pa's voice but the words weren't Pa's. She raised herself in the chair and listened. The voice was Pa's, but not the words. She pressed her hand against her side and walked over to the bench beside the bed. The voice stopped and started again. The old man was talking in his sleep. But it was a strange way to talk. He said something about light and then silver and the old woman moved to shake his shoulder. Then the words became coherent. He was saying something in which others were involved. She decided she wouldn't interrupt. It would be better to let him get it off his mind. She kept her hand pressed to her side and listened. He seemed like a village preacher. It was fluent and coherent, but she couldn't follow the meaning, just as the people didn't always follow the village preacher. The old man stopped and then started again. The words were spoken more slowly now, but they still didn't make sense. She kept her hand pressed against her side and listened.

. . . time was I see by the sun how the season sail and the moon make warning what crops to expect. Leaf fall or blood stain by the edge of the sea was a way of leaving one thing for another. Wood work in the morning and the tale at night was the way we walk the world, and no one worry what wonders take place on the top of the sky. Star in the dark and stone in the shine of the sun sideways speak nothing but a world outside our world and the two was one. Fire heat in the daytime and the colour that come later to take light from the eye make small, small difference to my people. The children was part of the pool. Hand in water and hair 'twixt the leaves where the jungle grow great was the same same thing. And oft-times when the black colour come to take light from the eye we hold heart in the hand and wait and wonder when the sun would sail daylight into the eye again. One question remain which we answer by quiet: wherefore was Africa and the wildness around it and the darkness above and beyond the big sea? And sometimes one lay down and die with a question answered by quiet. Far and near there were neighbours who keep god's like my brother rear rabbits, and the answer was obedience to a question never asked. Sometimes they was glad and sometimes they was sad, but the gifts of the gods was always good. When life leave the body and the corpse keep contract with the grave in the jungle the soul sail away above or below as the gods find fit. And the rest who remain give praise. In the land of the tribes 'twas the way of our neighbours. 'Twas a life we couldn't follow nor me nor my brother nor my brother before, and when the corpse keep contract with the grave in the jungle we say 'twas the end of the life and the death for the fellow below. Behaviour was private and strict without rule. A man was his master and every woman her witness and death by the hand was a perfect understanding. In the land of the tribes there was numbers who keep gods as my brother rear rabbits. Only we had the habit of being alone as we walk the world from the river to the mountain and back. Strange tribe my tribe and the tribe of your father my brother's son.

And strange was the time that change my neighbour and me, the tribes with gods and the one tribe without. The silver of exchange sail cross the sea and my people scatter like clouds in the sky when the waters come. There was similar buying and selling 'mongst tribe and tribe, but this was the biggest of the bargains for tribes. Each sell his own. A man walked out in the market square and one buyer watch his tooth and another his toe and the parts that was private for the coming of a creature in the intimate night. The silver sail from hand to hand and the purchase was shipped like a box of good fruit. The sale was the best of Africa's produce, and me and my neighbour made the same same bargain. I make my peace with the Middle Passage to settle on that side of the sea the white man call a world that was west of another world. The tribes with gods and the one tribe without we all went the way of the white man's money. We were for a price that had no value; we were a value beyond any price. For the buyer and the seller 'twas no difference 'twixt these two, price and value, value and price, since silver is solution for every ready-made sorrow. And so 'tis today in the islands left and right of this your little island and for the village too that's not very important. Silver is more than what pass from hand to hand. 'Tis also a way of what you call getting on. If the islands be sick 'tis for no other reason than the ancient silver. Your motto now is price or power which mean the same same thing. Sinner and saint are alike in this matter. I see the purchase of tribes on the silver sailing vessels, some to Jamaica, Antigua, Grenada, some to Barbados and the island of oil and the mountains tops. And then as 'tis now, though the season change, some was trying to live and some trying to die, and some were too tired to worry about either. The families fall to pieces and many a brother never see his sister nor father the son. Now there's been new combinations and those that come after make quite a different collection. So if you hear some young fool fretting about back to Africa, keep far from the invalid and don't force a passage to where you won't yet belong. These words not for you but those that come after.

From part of you that's neither flesh nor bone in a sleep before your last and longest, I come to say what I say. . . . Tomorrow you won't remember the visit made by your father's forebears, for what you call a dream the morning after has quite a different meaning from what your silence made safe the night before. Now not only black nor white, but all the colours that give credit to the skin in these islands of the west. Let sackcloth be the flag they fly whatever the limits of the freedom they talk. The beginning had the best intentions. A sailor called Christopher followed his mistake and those who come later have added theirs. Now he's dead, and as some say of the dead, safe and sound in the legacy of the grave. 'Tis a childish saying, for they be yet present with the living. The only certainty these islands inherit was that sailor's mistake, and it's gone on and on from father to son 'mongst the rich and the poor: in Slime and Creighton, landlord and politician, those who play at ruling and those at being ruled, and those who are neither one nor the other: the mob that is always good but will never understand the face of the devil nor the equal smile of the deep blue sea The fate of these islands I do not know, but man must live like a god or a dog, or be a stone that is neither dead nor alive, a pool no wind will ever wrinkle. For there's always two worlds to one man if you're a man, two darknesses to one light, one light, one light. . . .

The voice trailed off and the old woman made towards the bed and the pain sharpened. She shook the old man by the shoulder, but his sleep was still sound. She shook him vigorously and the pain was sharper each time she took her hand away. Then the old man turned on one side, and the light on the table made a pale shimmer over his face. The old woman shook him again and he began to speak.

'Two darknesses to one light,' he said, 'one light one light.'

'Pa,' the old woman shouted, 'Pa.' She strained with the shouting.

His eyes half-opened and the words trailed off again, 'one light, one light.' He was half surprised to see the old woman out of bed, but he hadn't fully recovered from the dream. He looked at her without understanding what he saw. She was silent and frightened, and the pain was sharp.

'Only one light, Ma,' he said, 'one light.'

''Tis the light of the blessed Lord and Saviour Jesus Christ,' said the old woman, ''Tis the light shed for your sins and mine.'

'Only one light,' the old man said, 'one light.'

The old woman shook him by the shoulder again. She could hardly bear the pain.

'Death an' life,' said the old man. ''tis the same said thing.'

'Only for those who've put their life in the Master's hands,' said the old woman. She moved closer to shake the old man.

'In the Master's hands,' she said, and did not speak again.

There was a groan and a crash of the skull against the partition. She had fallen onto the old man and across the bed, and all the pains had stopped. The old man saw the phial on the floor and stared from the light on the table to the body on the bed, but couldn't understand.

I I

THE surface of the sand seemed much the same the day before, even, sloping and undisturbed. I watched it as though there was an image of the other day which I carried to check the details of this. But only that day had passed and the pebble had gone. It was about the same time the day before when the sun broke through the clouds and the light fell over the sea and the leaves. The sea was steady and dull as it is at dawn and the shore was deserted. It was then that I placed the pebble under the grape leaf, grouped the leaves round it in an inconspicuous heap and left it to wait my return the next morning. There was no one on the shore to see me, and even if I had been seen it wasn't likely that anyone would suspect my intentions. I didn't know myself what my intentions were, but this feeling, no longer new, had grown on me like a sickness. I couldn't bear the thought of seeing things for the last time. It was like imagining the end of my life. Now it had happened again. The pebble wasn't there. I looked again in the hope that I was wrong. I pushed the leaves back and dug my fingers into the sand, but there wasn't a trace of the pebble. Until my touch disturbed the evenness of the slope everything had seemed as it was the day before. The leaves were there in a small heap, slightly shifted by the wind, but there was no evidence that anyone had taken the pebble. I walked away from the spot circling the trees and lifting the branches of the grape vine with my feet. The small crabs crouched into hiding, and when the wind raised the vine I saw pebbles scattered about under the branches, but the pebble I had placed under the grape leaf wasn't there. I knew it, shape, size and texture. I had held it long and seen it closely before putting it away. And on the spot where I had placed it I had seen it more accurately against the bed of sand. For a moment I wondered whether the waves had washed up overnight, but I couldn't see why that should have happened. The spot which I had chosen was far up the shore. The sea was still the morning I hid the pebble and it was as still this morning. Moreover, the sea on this side never ran so far up the shore. I had no overwhelming sense of the supernatural, but I was getting a strange feeling that something had interfered. I didn't know how to relate the situation because I didn't know how I should describe this sense of the other's interference. And in any case no one might have cared to understand why I should have hidden the pebble at all. It seemed rather silly when I thought of telling somebody, and since it was incommunicable to another I got the feeling more acutely of the other's interference. Either the pebble had taken itself away, or something had lifted it from beneath the leaves. It was clear that the sea had played no part. There was nothing I could do but carry the feeling of the other's interference and resign myself to the loss. I looked again, levelled the sand and rearranged the leaves. Finally, I told myself that it was useless to search. The day before I had seen the pebble for the last time. The sun was making a retreat behind the cluster of clouds and I entered the water dull and wrinkled like a soiled sheet. I watched the light change and the waters part as I waded forward. It was daybreak.

I had no particular liking for pebbles, but I had seen the pebble at the top of a heap of others, bright and smooth in the sunlight. I passed the heap on my way up the shore and again on my way down. Each time I noticed the pebble and thought of taking it away. It seemed a little silly to be worried in this way by a pebble and I tried to think of something else. Then I went on with my exercise up and down the beach, and it seemed the pebble became more and more insistent. It was as though it stood out from the others and asked to be taken away. I ran in another direction and it seemed the heap of pebbles had shifted. I returned to that part of the shore where the real heap was and I decided to put an end to the pebble by taking it away. I spent the greater part of my time throwing it in the air and catching it as it came down. I threw it against the rocks and played with it on the shore. Then I took it into the sea and another game started. I pitched it into the moss over the sand and dived it up. I threw it a yard away and swam under the surface to meet it before it settled on the sand. And this went on until it became other than a pebble. Each time I retrieved it I held it long and felt its shape and saw its texture until it was no longer a pebble. It had become one of those things one can't bear to see for the last time. I said I would take it home and return with it the next morning, and then the thought occurred that I should hide it.

I wasn't sure why I decided on hiding it. At first it seemed that it would mean more to me if I had been separated from it for a day. When I returned to take it from the hiding-place I would choose my enjoyment would have been greater. Then I thought of the risk of losing it because it seemed to me that there were certain things one couldn't lose. Things which had grown on you could be risked since they had an uncanny way of returning. And above all I had a vague feeling that there was no reason one should see things for the last time. I selected the spot and placed the pebble under the leaf on the even slope. A day had passed. There was no change in the weather, and the waves were as quiet as ever on this side of the sea. They rode up gently, tired themselves out and receded in another form towards the sea. But the pebble had gone. The feeling sharpened. It had really started the evening before when I received the letters, and now the pebble had made it permanent. In the evening I had read the letters and it seemed there were several things, intimate and endearing which I was going to see for the last time. It was very embarrassing when my mother came in and saw me re-reading the letters. I threw them aside and walked out of the house. At my age I couldn't risk making a fool of myself, and the safest defence seemed to be a forced indifference. Yet there was little in the letters themselves to upset me. It was the feeling which came on when I saw what was going to happen.

I tried to recall when this feeling had started, but that seemed useless. I could only think of it as a sickness which had spread through the system, gradual and unsuspected, but certain and permanent. You couldn't bear the thought of seeing things for the last time, and things included all that had become a part of your affection or anger, or even the vague feelings which you couldn't corner and define. Things included people, objects and situations. Whether you were glad or sorry to be rid of them you couldn't bear the thought of seeing them for the last time. I remembered vaguely that something used to happen when as a small boy I rode in the bus and reviewed the objects and people as they glided by. The shop and that lamp-post and the man who stood at the corner blank and impersonal. It seemed that the bus was steady while they slipped past, and I wondered whether I would see them again, and it was difficult to understand why I felt as I did when I imagined that I wouldn't. But the next day I saw them, and the next, and each time the little act repeated itself. Each day the objects were new and the feeling was new, and unless I forced my mind in another direction, I received the thought that I had seen them for the last time. I experienced the feeling in a high degree when I left the village school; and in the circumstances there was no reason to be sorry. The school was a kind of camp with an intolerable rigidity of discipline. The head teacher and all the assistants carried their canes as though they were in danger of attack from the boys, and they used them on all occasions and for all sorts of reasons. Yet the feeling was there. I was seeing the village school for the last time. The teachers shook my hand and wished me the best of luck. And I left with the intolerable feeling that they had somehow gone forever. I recalled the lamp-posts and the shops and the man at the corner, and I knew that the feeling was not new. That was a situation which I recalled, although I had to tell myself that the feeling was present long before I entered the High School.

Later when Trumper came to say that he was going to America I couldn't bear to look him straight in the face. He had always dreamt of going to America and the dream had come true. He was happy and I was glad for him. He left on a wet morning three years before I left the High School; and although an important difference in our fortunes had forced us apart I went to see him off. We stood on the pier together and watched the ship which was anchored in the distance. There were hundreds of them leaving for America, and I saw them all less real than Trumper but with the same sickness which the feeling brought on. It seemed I wasn't going to see any of those faces again. Later I returned to the pier and watched the big ship sweep through the night and out of sight across the sea. They were gone. I started to think of Trumper and Bob and Boy Blue, using Trumper as a means of tracing when the feeling had started. Boy Blue and Bob remained in the village, but they had drifted into another world. None of them had gone to the High School which was the instrument that tore and kept us apart. I started to think of the High School and what had happened to all of us in the intervening years; and suddenly as if by an inner compulsion my mind went back to the spot under the grape leaf and the pebble which I had seen for the last time. I ducked my head in the water and came up again wet and refreshed.

It was a year or two after the riots and I was eleven. It probably wasn't the way all boys at that age behaved, but when the results of the public examinations were announced and I learnt that I would be going to the High School I was wild with joy. It seemed in a way the only thing I had looked forward to, and when it happened I didn't care what would happen next. It was true my mother had been preparing me for it. For three or four years she had paid for the private lessons which were a preparation for the public examination. At last I had arrived and the world was wonderful. I told Bob and Trumper and Boy Blue and they were as excited. It was as though they were going to trade on the fact that they had a friend in the High School. But my mother saw the matter from a different angle. She said it was nothing more than she expected, and hadn't it happened she would have considered all her efforts and money a waste of time. I became less enthusiastic until the books and the school uniform arrived. These were my first introduction to the High School. There were several books including some in languages I couldn't understand, and there were books that treated of the subjects which the village head teacher used to call a kind of advanced arithmetic. The books were so many and so large that it wasn't possible to put them all in the sack. When she took me to the High School on the opening day of term we were like refugees burdened with the weight of personal possessions. I strung the black and gold tie round my neck, tieing the knot so that both colours showed equally on it. Then I put some of the books under my arm, holding the sack with the others in my hand and looked at myself in the mirror. I was pleased with what I saw.

But my mother was unsparing. She kept harping on the money she had spent on books and uniform and insisted that if I didn't do well at the High School she would consider everything, scholarship and all, a waste of time. Then there was much talk about the opportunities others had had and wasted, and the opportunity which I would now have to make a man of myself. At times she seemed to take it for granted that I wouldn't do well at the High School, and there followed an unbearable monologue which described the way her money and time would flow into Maxwell pond.

I entered the High School alert and energetic. The surroundings were very exciting. To the west the orchard with its tall green hedge and opposite the playing-field where the groundsman was preparing the cricket pitch. The school was much larger than the village school, and if there weren't more teachers, there was something which made them look more prepossessing. The headmaster wore a parson's collar with a long black gown. He had a large red face with a thick neck and very tiny eyes. When he came out into the school yard with the other teachers it was obvious that he was the chief. He didn't seem to look anybody straight in the face. When they talked his head was raised towards the tree tops and when he spoke you got the feeling that he knew beforehand what the other person was going to say and was only being kind enough to let them say it. His manner was often jovial, but never familiar. In many ways he had proved very kind to me.

It wasn't long before I relaxed into an *old boy* at the High School. I grew as callous as most of the others, and played the role which the *old boys* played. You knew the school. You knew what certain masters liked and what others couldn't stand, and you behaved accordingly as you wanted to affect them. One master couldn't bear to hear the boys talk about girls because that sort of talk would sooner or later ruin them. The *old boys* knew this and made it a point of talking about girls when he was present. Another had a liking for chocolates and the *old boys* kept asking him questions about sweets. Sometimes the boys asked questions which to them seemed perfectly straightforward but which irritated the masters. Sir, what did you have for breakfast this morning? Sir, what sort of boy were you at school? Sir, do you dance? Sir, what would you do if you impregnated a girl and you couldn't marry her because you didn't want to marry her? Sir, is it true that masturbation is bad for your health? Sir, is there a God?

This world was different from that of the village school. There was no supervising minister, and although the governor and the bishop were always invited to attend the annual prize-giving, there were no inspectors who gave orders as they did at the village school. To one who was new from the other place the High School seemed a ship with a drunk crew. The restrictions were fewer than those at the village school and the boys seemed happier. And, of course, there was no contact between the two. Education was not a continuous process. It was a kind of steeplechase in which the contestants had to take different hurdles. Some went to the left and others to the right, and when they parted they never really met again. It would have been inconceivable for a teacher at the High School to take a class in the village school, and the teachers at the village school didn't belong in or out of school to the world in which the other teachers lived. The village school and the High School were not only different buildings with different teachers. They were entirely separate institutions.

The High School was intended to educate the children of the clerical and professional classes, while the village school served the needs of the villagers, who were poor, simple and without a very marked sense of social prestige. When a boy left the village school it was customary for him to learn a trade. And many of the village carpenters and shoe-makers were recruited from such boys. They left at fourteen and spent a year at the bench. Within two years they had become men with weekly wages and women of their own. If the boy was clever at the village school, he remained to become what was called a pupil teacher. After he had taken a few preliminary examinations he was given a class. Most of the village teachers were recruited in this way, and it was no wonder the village school should have received within six or seven generations the same kind of instruction in the same way. At the High School the boys never left till they were eighteen or nineteen. Then they entered the civil service or an English University where they read for one of the professions, law or medicine. Those who didn't pass the Cambridge examinations and couldn't enter the civil service or the university were heard of four or five years after they left. They usually went to live with an aunt in New York. The doctors and the lawyers returned to practise in the island and the civil servants seemed to remain all their life under the evergreen trees outside the public buildings. When the clock chimed four in the afternoon they parked on the pavement and watched the buses and the women and the sea which never had anything to say. They were smartly dressed, well groomed and on the whole quite imposing. When you saw them you didn't think the High School had done so badly after all.

Those boys who went from the village school to the High School had done so on the award of the public examinations. There weren't many, and it wasn't easy for them to cope with the two worlds. They had known the village intimately and its ways weren't like those of the world the High School represented. Moreover, it wasn't until they had entered the High School that they knew what the other world was like. They may have heard about it and seen it in buses, at dances and in the various public departments of the civil service, but it remained foreign. Gradually the village receded from my consciousness although it wasn't possible for me to forget it. I returned to the village from the High School every evening. The men sat round the lamp-post talking or throwing dice, and when it was possible I joined them. Now that I was at the High School it was easier to join them, but it was more difficult to participate in their life. They didn't mind having me around to hear what happened in the High School, but they had nothing to communicate since my allegiances, they thought, had been transferred to the other world. If I asserted myself they made it clear that I didn't belong just as Bob, Trumper and Boy Blue later insisted that I was no longer one of the boys. Whether or not they wanted to they excluded me from their world just as my memory of them and the village excluded me from the world of the High School.

It would have been easier if I had gone to live in a more respectable district, but that was beyond my mother's resources. She would have done so without hesitation, but she saw it was impossible and consoled herself with the thought that it didn't matter where you lived. The mind was the man, she said, and if you had a mind you would be what you wanted to be and not what the world would have you. I heard the chorus every day and sometimes I tried repeating it to others. The mind was the man. I remained in the village living, it seemed, on the circumference of two worlds. It was as though my roots had been snapped from the centre of what I knew best, while I remained impotent to wrest what my fortunes had forced me into. And it was difficult to say who was responsible. I didn't play cricket at the cross-roads as often as I used to because the cricket pitch at the High School seemed to me much better, and since I had a chance of selection for the school team it seemed sensible that I should get used to things like pads and gloves. Bob and Trumper thought otherwise. It wasn't safe for the High School boys to see me at the cross-roads. And we were both right. We met every day and talked, but the attitudes were different. It reminded me in a way of the village head teacher and the inspector. Hidden somewhere in each was the other person which wondered how far the physical surface could be trusted. I had had the last of a certain situation, and I knew the feeling which the letters I received the evening before and the pebble had made permanent. I saw them every day and yet I had seen the last of them. Soon I would see the last of everything.

Some time later we heard about a war in Europe. The men who assembled round the shoemaker's shop had prophesied it, and the shoemaker who had never abandoned his friend Priestley said that that writer had prophesied it too. They said it was the last of the British Empire, and it was another piece of evidence that God didn't like ugly. That was the way they put it. They said the world had become ugly and so had the village. And in fact the village had changed greatly in some ways. But at the High School we had got used to reading about wars in Europe, one of which lasted a hundred years. It seemed that Europe had taken a fancy to war since they even tried to give them decorous names. I recalled that one was called the War of the Roses. It seemed a perfectly natural thing for Europe to have war. The newspapers and the radio reported what was happening in Europe and people seemed very concerned. But at the High School the boys weren't particularly shaken. If we regretted the war it was simply because we foresaw another date added to the intolerable pile which they called history. We received the news with the same curiosity or boredom we had shown when reading Michael John's account of the Norman invasion of England. But the shoe-maker's friends were more interested and concerned because they seemed to understand the issues much better. History had quite a different meaning for them. At the High School the battles took place there and then within the limits of the text-book, and it was our business to note and check all the details. The shoemaker's friends couldn't remember many dates, so they talked in terms of vast periods. The shoemaker said once upon a time there was a thing called the Roman Empire and it didn't matter when precisely this thing was. But the thing was real for them. These things had not only happened but they happened for certain reasons. And they knew the reasons.

One morning the boys at the High School were assembled in the hall and the headmaster announced in a very slow and solemn voice that France had fallen. He said it was the greatest threat to civilization mankind had ever known. The school was quiet, and for a moment this war seemed somewhat different from those we had read of. When they were dismissed the boys speculated on the fall of France. They talked about the Rhine and Rhône and some drew small maps of the routes the Germans must have taken. I went home in the evening and told my mother and the neighbours that France had fallen. I looked terribly gloomy and spoke in a voice like the headmaster's. They were very sorry. They didn't know anything about France, but they knew that France was on the side of England, and Barbados was Little England. Three hundred years of unbroken friendship, they thought. They understood what that meant, and the fall of France became their fall as well.

One day shortly after lunch a young man called Barrow walked up the school yard and entered the headmaster's office. He smoked a cigarette as he spoke to the headmaster, and one or two boys who passed by the headmaster's study stole a glance and ran to inform the others. Some of them said they had known Barrow at school and it looked strange to see him smoking in the headmaster's presence. We were a little curious. In the afternoon the school was assembled and the headmaster talked about Barrow. He was leaving in a fortnight to join the Royal Air Force. There were several Barrows, the headmaster said and the school felt only pride for those who had the courage to follow the motto which was printed on the plaque in the hall: Greater love hath no man than this, that a man lay down his life for his friends. Some of the boys in the upper school started to get the feeling they should become Barrows.

From now on the war had become more of a reality. At the High School a course in military training was started. One of the soldiers from the local army came every evening to train the boys in the use of the Bren and Sten guns. They crawled on their stomachs for hours across the playing-field, carrying the guns pressed under their arms. Some learnt wrestling tactics which they could apply if unarmed they were attacked by the enemy. It seemed very exciting, but for most of them the exercises were intolerably strenuous. The guns bruised their arms, and their knees and elbows remained sore. Then there were parades which lasted for hours and on which some of the cadets fainted. The training seemed terribly rigid. Those who weren't cadets were taught how to conduct themselves if the school was ever bombed. When the whistle went the boys walked out from their class rooms in single file silent and tense taking the orders from a member of the imaginary civil defence. We walked towards a wood on the outskirts of the school and stood erect against the school wall. We were told how we should stoop or lie if it were necessary to lower the body. This was very frightening for it had become part of the school curriculum, and it didn't seem that these exercises were being carried out as a joke. Moreover, a rumour had circulated from the shoemaker's shop that there were Germans in the island. It was said that some speaker by the name of Lord Haw Haw who did a regular broadcast from Germany had given the name of the sugar factory in Barbados where the island's surplus food was stored. The Germans knew the layout of the land. This war wasn't history. It was real, and we walked out every morning on the civil exercises saying farewell to the class room. We expected to hear the bomb fall.

Some of the boys were hardier and tried to make a joke of the others.

They said the island was much too small, and the Germans had nothing to gain by dropping a bomb on Barbados. One boy said that although a bomb was a little smaller than Barbados it cost more than all the sugar factories and the stores put together. One bomb could have brought an end to life in Barbados, he said, but the bomb cost so much more than the island, the expense would have been incredibly extravagant. The Germans couldn't afford to indulge such waste at that stage of the war. Another said he couldn't care less, but he had always heard his grangran say that if you went on crying wolf wolf, the wolf would one day visit you, and he believed this military training and the civil exercises were just another way of crying wolf wolf. If he were right the school went on with its cry wolf wolf, and indeed the wolf did come.

Shortly after four o'clock one afternoon a large merchant ship was torpedoed in the harbour. The city shook like a cradle and the people scampered in all directions. The war had come to Barbados. Many of us flocked to the pier in the hope of seeing the submarine. The shells made a big booming noise and the spectators ran wild with hysteria. They ran a few yards away and ran back as quickly in the hope of seeing the submarine. The ship's hull sank slowly below the surface and most of us had our first experience of seeing a ship go down. She was loaded with cargo which had not yet been taken off, and the men started speculating on what would happen. The ship sank slowly. For reasons which were never understood the three or four submarine chasers which had always been active were out of order on this occasion. One was floating some yards away from the ship but the propeller, it was said, had been taken out for repairs. The others were in the dock. The people swore the Germans were advantage-takers; and one man said if he had his bathing suit what and what he would do. No one knew whether he was going to have it out with the submarine or the inactive chasers, but he kept on swearing, 'would to Jesus Christ I had on my bathin' suit.'

But it was only natural in a war that the Germans should do what they did. If Barbados said she was Little England she had to put up with what she got for being what she was. Moreover, it was rumoured that when the Prime Minister of England announced the declaration of war the Governor of Barbados, at the request of the people, sent the following cable: 'Go brave big England for Little England is behind you.' The Germans had no time to make subtle distinctions. A man started to say that it wasn't the Germans at all. He had it from the best authority that the Germans weren't operating in those waters. He was going to explain further when the police strolled up and told him that if he wanted to spend the night with his wife and children he had better shut his mouth. The people were anxious to hear the details since he had only got as far as saying that certain people were trying to get certain ships off the line for purposes of trade between the islands. The man kept quiet looking like the others towards the sinking ship.

The war went on like an exciting habit, while the village and the High School went their separate ways, each like a slow disease. At the High School the usual things were done. Cricket and football replaced the class rooms in the evening, and the inter-school athletics were never interrupted. We sank quietly into this life like a crab clawing through filth. But the village was changing in some ways, and with each change I got the feeling which the pebble had made permanent.

So many things were being taken away and the boys' activities changed with each departure. I had a feeling sometimes that the village might get up and walk out of itself. It had receded even farther from my active consciousness, but I knew now that somewhere in my heart, already riddled with fear, ambition and envy, there was a storage of love for the sprawling dereliction of that life.

One morning I walked through the wood and placed a pin on the train line. I sat beside the rails waiting for the hoot of the engine, and it was like returning to the days before the riots. There weren't any other boys around and if I had not been so excited about seeing the blade I would have tried to find out where the boys had gone. But some time had passed since I had placed a pin on the line, and in a way. I preferred to do it alone. I waited for an hour, and then rain fell in a fine clean drizzle and I went home. The train didn't come and it never came again.

It was my last year at the High School when Bob and Boy Blue were recruited for the local police force. In the village this might have been regarded as an improvement on carpentry, but it had disqualified them further from the social layer for which the High School was preparing me. Trumper had emigrated to America and no one could tell what he would become. Most people who went to America in such circumstances usually came back changed. They had not only acquired a new idiom but their whole concept of the way life should be lived was altered. It was interesting to speculate what would happen to

Trumper. Mr. Slime had continually raised the question of emigration in the local House of Assembly, and a delegation which was sent to Washington brought back the news that the United States Government would contract a considerable number of labourers for three or four years. The rates of pay seemed fantastic to people like Trumper who had never worked. We parted as friends who had overcome all the little difficulties which the village and the High School had made for us. We were all wearing long pants now, and it seemed silly that we should be worried by the things that kept us apart while we wore short pants. We had promised to forgive and forget.

Bob and Boy Blue had also come to say that they were going into the force with the jocular warning that I would have to be on my P's and Q's. They were the civil guardians of the law. I had remained at the High School.

America. The High School. The Police Force. There were three different worlds where our respective fortunes had taken us, but now it was time for me to leave my world. The feeling came back as sharp as it did when I remembered leaving the village school and later Trumper's departure. And there was little reason why I should have regretted leaving the High School. For six years my life had alternated between boyish indifference and tolerable misery. I had done badly after the first year and shortly before I decided to leave there was a request for my expulsion which the headmaster rejected. He had summoned me to the study and it was the last of several lectures which I had. He sat behind the large oak table with his head pointing upwards and his short fat fingers twiddling on his legs. And he told me what some of the masters had said. It seemed more like a conspiracy than an accusation. Then he said what I had never before been told at the High School. He said they were trying to make gentlemen of us, but it seemed that I didn't belong. Immediately I remembered Bob and Boy Blue who in different language had said the same thing. The headmaster gave me the feeling that I had made him seem a big failure. It seemed he had spilled his attention on an undeserving wretch. He said there was nothing more he could do, and passed me on to the first assistant who would probably understand me better. There were times I recalled when I wanted to hate the masters. I didn't know whether I had been more fortunate than Boy Blue and the others, but I had a feeling that I wasn't. I tried to think what would have happened had I become a carpenter or a shoemaker or a pupil teacher. It was the feeling upper-most in my mind when I was about to leave the High School. Would it have made any difference if I hadn't gone? My interest in the games and the people I had known was exhausted and my feelings were gradually moving back to the village. It is true I had learnt something of two foreign languages which I liked, but they didn't seem to apply until I met the first assistant.

This personal attachment to the first assistant was the only concrete thing for which I could be grateful to the High School. Had I not gone to the High School we would never have met. I didn't remember how we met, but it might have had something to do with a poetry lesson which he was asked to supervise. He returned three or four times and we had talked. The first assistant was a poet and actor who could scarcely have been a finer actor, but who might have been a better poet if he weren't an actor. He was a man of medium height, robust, alert and energetic. He walked like an ex-football player who couldn't forget the athletic stride. He had a large head with a receding forehead that had got lost in a shock of thin brown hair. The hair was always flying wild, dishevelled and resistant. His skin was heavily tanned and his eyes small and brown looked down at the nose that came out from beside them like a pleasant surprise. He was over fifty with the look of a man in his early forties, and his face which was capable of many expressions sometimes gave you a feeling of unease. He was versatile, sensitive and cultured. He had a large and carefully chosen library which he had invited me to use. He was always making suggestions for my reading, and he talked about the way people painted and what had to happen before he could write a poem. When visitors called who didn't know me and who might have made me feel uneasy he gave me a large album which I fingered till they had gone.

I couldn't understand what part he played at the High School for the world of his immediate interests was quite different from what the school knew. He must have been capable of living on different levels and this must have been responsible for the reputation he had of being genteel and accessible. He was a kind of legend in the High School. But the legend had nothing to do with his interests. It related to his gifts of social intercourse. Few had ever seen him angry although it was said that he could be violently angry. From the malaise of the High School I had drifted into the despair of the first assistant's world. Soon I found it difficult to cope with what I wanted. The High School had dissolved into one man who represented for me what the school might have been. It was two years since I had known him well and the keenest result of that attachment was the feeling that somewhere deep within myself or far beyond the limits of this land was a world whose features I did not know and might never grow to understand. He was the High School without the world which it prepared me for. Now I started to feel that I was going to see him for the last time.

The two letters had arrived the evening before, and the feeling was acute. One had come from Trumper who had written in a way I hadn't thought him capable of and which in fact I didn't quite understand. He had been away three years and the new place had done something to him. The language was not unlike what he was used to speaking in the village, but the sentiments were so different. He had learnt a new word, and the word seemed like some other world which I had never heard of. Trumper had changed. The other letter came from the school authorities in Trinidad. They had confirmed the appointment which I had accepted. I was going to the neighbouring island to teach English to a small boarding school of South Americans from Venezuela and one or two other republics. There was something ironical in the choice of this teacher. I thought the masters at the High School would have been a little puzzled and amused when they heard. For a moment I felt like the small boy who had won the public examination to the High School. I promised that I would start afresh, a new man among other men.

Then the pebble returned present in its image on the sloping sand under the grape leaf, and I thought of them all in turn. Trumper, Boy Blue, Bob. The High School, the village, the first assistant. They had all arisen with the pebble making the feeling of separation a permanent sickness. The thought of seeing things for the last time. And my mother? She seemed in a way too big for this occasion. I waded out of the water and walked to the rocks where my clothes were bundled. For the last time I looked at the spot where I had placed the pebble, and then quickly turned my thoughts to Trumper's letter. It was difficult to decide which was less perplexing. I repeated the sentence with which he ended the letter. 'You don't understand, you don't understand what life is, but I'll tell you when I come and I am coming soon.'

S O seldom you come to see me,' said the old man. 'I says to myself 'tis the studies keep you away. Time an' time again I call your name.'

'I always promise to come,' I said. 'But something happens and I can't.'

'The way a thing happens I know,' said the old man. ''Twus the same with me. You got the best o' intention when you promise a promise, an' then for God knows what reason you can't sort o' pay it up. The way a thing happen I know.'

He put his hand through the oatmeal mixture in the bucket, working his fingers over the bottom and along the crease at the side. The mixture splashed up on the sides of the bucket and skidded on to his hand. The hair flattened and stuck to the skin. He worked his hand round the sides and the liquid turned thin with the oatmeal making a surface of flakes and lumps. The white goat made a noise and the old man looked in her direction and said he was coming. He brought his hand up keeping the fingers together so that he might see whether there were any solids in the mixture. It made a whirlpool dance within the bucket thin and brown with the flakes settled on the surface like bits of sawdust. The day was brighter. We drew nearer to the goat and I pulled up a bench beside the old man's. The goat made a loud sucking noise and we watched her take in the oatmeal mixture. We saw the skin along the neck in a rise and fall motion as though a slit of the throat would let the mixture out again down the ribbed flanks of the animal. The old man stroked the hair along the neck and down the spine. She wagged the short stubby tail and sucked louder. The tail was like one half of a bow tie frayed along the edge. The suck grew louder and the tail shook in a rapid sideways movement. The old man was pleased.

'Poor Ma—God rest her in the grave—won't have believe the way things change. She sort o' see it comin', but not to what we see and know now.'

He stroked the goat's hair as he spoke looking over the low fence towards the houses on the other side. His face was very creased and his hands shook when he held them at a certain angle. They were large and long with the hair on all sides. His eyebrows were bushy and they came forward from the brink of his brow as though they might fall on to his bosom. The goat made another sucking noise and crouched low on her stomach. He went on stroking the hair over the head and down the side of the face.

'First you go to High School,' said the old man, 'an' then Trumper sail all 'cross the sea to America, God bless him, an' the other two Boy Blue an' Bob, they join up in the police force. An' it all happen in the twinklin' of an eye, you an' them, an' there be many more gone this place an' the next lookin' for what they ain't put down as we use to say. 'Tis change if ever any was.'

He felt for the pipe in his pants pocket and dried his hand on the canvas apron he was wearing. He lit the pipe and watched the smoke rise in a pile over his head. It was getting warmer in the yard.

'Then look how the face o' the village change,' he said. 'Take a look at it an' ask yuhself if you believe what your eyes see. Everything change.'

We were both looking over the fence through and beyond the houses on the other side. The land was bare and bright in the early morning. We could see the public bath and on the other side in the distance the large brick house on the hill. The view was unobstructed. Not a tree in sight within the village. There were no trees at all, and the old man in that steady stare into and across the houses seemed to ask himself why this should have happened. The trees had been felled. We didn't know why or where they had really been taken, but the customary explanation was the war. Everything had happened because of the war. The train had stopped coming and the lines were taken up. Finally the trees were felled. When we asked what had happened the answer was the war. This country needed this and another country needed that. The village was contributing to the victory which would be Big England's as well as Little England's. No one seemed sure whether it was a matter for pleasure or protest. But the face of the village had changed as the old man said, and it was some of the villagers who by force or persuasion had changed it. It was a week or two after I had waited by the lines to see my pin take the shape of a blade. The trucks drove up and the villagers assembled round them. The men set to work with pick and axe, and the lines were cracked and collected in pieces. Every day for more than a week the trucks drove away with their cargo of scrap iron. Certain countries needed scrap iron we were told. Some business man had bought the lines and had had them sent across the sea as scrap. We grew used to the absence of the train as we had grown used to the pleasure of having it. Then the trees were felled. These were the property of the landlord, and no one knew why he had sold them. There was a rumour that he was leaving the village. The rumour died a quiet and natural death like the trees. The landlord remained. Since the riots we had seen little of him. The overseer had been promoted and the general supervision of the roads was his concern. He was a kind of landlord himself. It was rumoured that he might move into the landlord's house. The landlord's name was hardly mentioned except in connection with Mr. Slime. There was nothing the landlord could do to reverse the other's power.

The Penny Bank and the Friendly Society had grown beyond the needs of the village. The members were drawn from all parts of the island. It had become the depository of the poor man's penny. Mr. Slime had arrived. We saw him, saluted him and let him occupy our thoughts. The landlord was present as a relic of another time. His daughter had gone to England where it was said she would spend the rest of her life. The landlord remained with Mrs. Creighton in the house on the hill. They led a quiet life inviting their friends in the evening and driving out to the country on Sunday mornings. The villagers thought they must have been very lonely. Some said they could see Mrs. Creighton on occasions in the evenings. She sat on the roof looking in the same direction for hours. Beside her the Alsatian squatted and when she retired inside the house the dog followed. In the landlord's absence it was her companion. Some said that Mrs. Creighton was sick. It was astonishing the way white people took their illness. They sat on the roof looking in the same direction for hours. Whatever they endured the Creightons remained. It was as though the village were a disease which they couldn't be rid of. They couldn't leave it any more than the shoemaker or Mr. Foster or Pa himself. It held them as it held the villagers. Everyone said it had got into the blood. It was the soil of their roots. The rumours never ceased. There were several rumours that they would soon be leaving, and when the trees were felled everyone believed. The rumours came up like a swarm of flies. Then the overseer said something and the rumours went the way of flies. The landlord and Mrs. Creighton were remaining. They would never leave.

The goat chewed the cud, its head bowed and the eyes closed. On the other side of the yard the old man had made a small garden. There was a tomato vine and a few pods of thyme. The earth was moist and black where they sprouted. A short wire fence ran round the area. It was clean, cultivated, cared. It was the face of the land held and shaped by a man's hand. The old man had dropped his glance on to the pods of thyme.

'Yet whatever happen,' said the old man, 'there be things which remain what they be, an' there ain't no changin' them. Do what you like, 'tis got to be what it is. Come rain come sun the day goes on an' that said same thing too. I watch an' wait an' sometimes I wonder why it so.' He shot his glance from the garden to the goat and back to the garden.

'Whatever Mr. Slime might do,' said the old man, 'there be nothin' he can do to make the landlord other than what he be. Whatever trouble an' tribulation he go through the landlord goin' to die in that house on the hill an' somebody else goin' to take his place. An' Mr. Slime will go on' doin' what he doin', an' we all livin' as we livin'. The changes goin' to come an' the changes goin' to go, but at the bottom the real thing'll go on for ever. Some sailing 'cross the sea an' comin' back, others stayin' where they be. As my old Ma—God rest her in the grave—used to say, "'Twill be so till time change to eternity."'

He looked at me and smiled, waiting to hear what I might say. It was my chance to say why I had kept my promise to see him this morning.

'I'm going away,' I said.

'The same thing I says,' he said, 'some'll go an' some'll stay. When your mother break the news to me earlier this mornin' I says to her what I says to you.'

'I'm sorry she told you,' I said, 'because I would have liked to be the first to tell you.'

'It makes no difference one way or the next,' he said, 'a thing that got to be told got to be told an' it ain't matter who do the tellin'.'

The bones of his face seemed almost visible under the skin and the veins spread like roots under the hair across his hands.

'Take a look by the shops,' said the old man.

The overseer who had ridden up on horseback was shouting something to a man. The man was in the canal making measurements with a tape that spooled out from a leather case. The man measured and spoke and the overseer watched him. The old man said something about repairing the roads. The man drew the tape into the leather case and the overseer rode away.

"'Tis as you see it,' said the old man, 'they'll go on repairin' an' repairin' an' the overseer will rise or fall in position accordin' to the feelin' that take the landlord, but he'll always be Mr. Creighton's overseer. Nothin' more an' nothin' less. And when Mr. Creighton dead an' gone he'll be a next one's overseer.

He laughed and raised himself from the bench. The pipe pointed downwards from the side of his mouth.

'P'raps you know more 'bout it than me,' he said, 'but tell me what you make o' your dreams?'

'I don't remember mine,' I said, 'or only in bits.'

We walked across the yard towards the door. The day was bright.

'I get strange dreams now an' again,' he said; 'sometimes they as much as make my hairs stand up.'

He refilled the pipe and lit it. We sat in the doorway looking towards the goat and the garden. I stretched my legs out and leaned back on the elbows. It was quiet as he spoke at length about his dreams.

13

Morning

AT the habitual hour the taps were turned on and life flowed as it had to when the sun came out and movement from the crossroads to the shops had started. Savory was there on the usual spot and the crowds collected round the cart shouting their orders. He had changed the white feather of the day before for one much whiter, and the canvas apron was stiffer than ever. He looked so much older now by the wrinkles on his brow, but his movement was still brisk. The gestures were the same. He scooped the sweat from his brow with the thumb, crossed the hand across his face as he had always done. The boys seldom sat on the wheels and he was spared the trouble of chasing them away. The trees were gone and the surroundings were bare. You could see for great distances in all directions the houses and trees in other parts of the island. The people talked and made their orders as they talked while the boys sought old buckets or tin pans with which they make a wicket. Behind the bath where there were once trees and wild weed they had prepared a cricket pitch, and they played at all hours of the day. They used the pavement of the bath as their pavilion, and those who couldn't play the game sat in the rail tracks where the train lines were once laid. No one looked for the whiff of steam through the trees or imagined the shape of the blade that was once a pin or a nail. Those days were gone.

The crowds had thickened round the cart and the boys had started the cricket game. It was like any other morning. And suddenly it seemed as though all the dogs had begun to bark in chorus across the land. The dogs barked madly and some of the cocks were crowing. The crowd scattered leaving Savory alone at the corner and the boys brought an end to the game. The shoemaker was clutching his pants with one hand as he spoke. They could hardly understand what he was saying for the saliva in his mouth. They collected quickly into groups that stood or squatted around the small shop. A man respectably dressed in a white suit was standing by the door outside the shoemaker's shop. The shoemaker had left the shop and stepped on to the embankment that sloped to the canal. The other man stood firmly waiting for the shoemaker to speak. The shoemaker loosed another spate of obscenities and the man took a step back.

'There's nothing I can do,' the man said. 'I wanted to help you as best as I could.'

'Help yuh mother's arse,' the shoemaker said. 'Who want any f . . . g help from you?'

The crowd were quiet. They didn't speak except to ask what was happening and who the strange man was. The dogs were still barking.

'You'll get into trouble,' the man said. 'I'll make things difficult for you if you haven't got respect.'

'Respect for who?' the shoemaker shouted. 'I've respect as when as I've got to have it, but for you, a two-colour shit-smelling bastard like you, what you talkin' 'bout respect. An' if you don't get off this blasted land before I count ten, if by the time I count ten you ain't off this spot o' land they'll hang me, the law'll hang me.'

'This is my spot of land,' the man said angrily. 'I'll go when I want to.'

'How the bloody hell it get yours?' the shoemaker said. 'Tell me straight to my face how it get yours?'

'I've told you already,' the man said. 'I haven't got breath to waste.'

'Tell me what,' the shoemaker said, 'what sort o' nancy story you tell me, 'bout you buy this lan'; how the bloody hell you can buy this, who sell it to you, where you get money to buy it from, since when you an' a white landlord is friends for him to call you in secret an' sell you a spot o' land that I been on for only God knows how long. This ol' shop been here for more'n twenty years, an' you come on a big, bright morning like this to tell me some shitting story 'bout this spot belonging to you, an' I got to get off in how many days you says?'

'In three weeks,' the man said.

'Why God blind you; the landlord whatever he be never ever come telling anybody 'bout gettin' off this land,' the shoemaker said. 'Nobody in all Creighton village ever hear o' that. We hear o' lots o' things, but never ever in all my born days I hear 'bout havin' to get off this lan', an' even if you buy this here spot from the landlor' why you should want me to get off, when the landlor' for all these years never ever tell anybody to get off.'

'Because I want it,' the man said.

'Why, Jesus Christ, you now let me see what a black landlord would be,' the shoemaker said. 'If we had a black landlord here all these years gone by, there's be more f . . . g movin' from here to there, there be more movin' than what John read 'bout.'

'I'm going,' the man said. 'I'll let my solicitor talk to you instead.'

'You can call Jesus Christ 'imself to talk to me,' the shoemaker said. 'Send anybody you like to send, you mulatto shit-smelling son of a bastard. But I'd like you to come yuhself next time. I'll keep a present for you. I'll put it in a bottle for you. Come yuhself again. I wusn't expectin' you this bright mornin' or things would 'ave turn out different. But next time, next time you can come, an' by Christ in heaven I'll make you drink what you been smellin' for a livin' all these Goddam years.'

The man had left the shop and turned into one of the cross roads. The people sitting around watched him walk away and then turned to face the shoemaker. Some were still asking who the man was, and although they had heard the shoemaker talk about the land they couldn't quite follow the story. The overseer's brother was sitting in the crowd. He said the man was a chief sanitary inspector who lived in one of the big-shot residential areas of the island. It was either Fontabelle or Worthing. They looked at the shoemaker who rested against the door staring at the ground. The overseer's brother and Bob's father walked over to him and put their hands on his shoulder; he kept his head held towards the ground winking his eyes as though they were irritated by the dust. The overseer's brother turned and asked the people to disperse. They waited for a while, asking what was the matter. There were no explanations, and soon they walked away in different directions. Savory climbed down from the top of the cart and went down the road to wait for the other customers. The women bunched together trying to find out what had happened.

The man had said it was his land, and they started to put the rumours together. There were so many rumours in recent times about the land, but no one paid much attention. The women began to make up various stories. They knew nothing about the strange man except what the overseer's brother had said. He was a chief sanitary inspector who was at some time a famous athlete. He was what they called a coloured big shot, but they didn't believe his story about buying the land. They made up their own stories, asking themselves all the while whether the strange man might not really have bought the land.

The shoemaker sat with Bob's father and the overseer's brother in the shop. The men tried to console him. They told him everything would be all right, but he sat shaking on the bench. Bob's father did most of the talking while the overseer's brother sat beside the shoemaker with his hand on the other's knee. Bob's father recalled the strike and the talk they had had before Mr. Slime drove up to say what they should do. And whatever had happened everything did turn out all right. The riots were worse than anything they had seen, but since then everything had gone as before. It was the shoemaker who had given them courage to follow Mr. Slime during the civil disturbances, and he was right. They tried to cheer him up by saying how right he was. The overseer's brother didn't say much. Bob's father asked him whether he had any stories about the land, and he said no. He hadn't seen his brother for many weeks except when he went to pay the rent. They sat silent feeling for something to say, and suddenly they couldn't believe what they saw. The shoemaker was crying. The tears fell in large drops down his face and on to his shirt. The overseer's brother took his hand away and looked at Bob's father. They closed the door and drew nearer to the shoemaker. They didn't know what to say and they didn't want to make him feel worse by saying the wrong thing. The shoemaker sobbed loudly as the men sat around wondering what they should do. He bent and took up the boot which he placed on his knee. The men moved back a little and looked around for something to occupy them. The shoemaker punched the hole through the sole and made a stitch. The tears fell on his hand and down the leather. The light came through the window showing his face bright black with the thin lines the water made on the cheeks. Occasionally he passed the sleeve across his face.

"Tisn't a day if it ain't twenty years,' he said, not taking his bowed head from the boot. 'An' to tell me that I got to move. Not that I notice what he says, but the thought of it. 'Tis the thought of it that hurt me.' He raised his head when he spoke the last sentence. The men nodded but didn't speak.

'Twenty years,' the shoemaker said, 'it ain't as if it wus twenty days. 'Tis twenty years I wus here in this said same shop not to count the years my parents live on the same spot. My ol' ma—God rest her in her grave—always beg if nothin' else to pay my rent so that I'd be comfortable in mind, an' I hear her an' do as she say, for twenty years I do no less. Every God send week, I walk up there through the wood an' pay that rent an' receive my receipt, an' to tell me after that that a stranger who I ain't know no more 'bout than the man in the moon, to tell me he could come to tell me to get off here in three weeks. Where in the name of peace would I put the ol' shop? Who going move it? What would I pay to move it with, an' even if I could where I goin' at my age with this shop? Not that I notice what he say, but 'tis the thought of the whole thing that hurt my heart. 'Tis the mere thought of it.'

'Don't worry yuh head,' Bob's father said. 'We by yuh side always.'

They opened the doors and looked out at the cross roads where the people were moving to and fro between the shops.

'I got to go,' the overseer's brother said.

'An' don't you bother yuh brain 'bout anythin',' Bob's father said. 'What good for one good for all, an' if you sink we all have to sink with you.'

They stepped across the canal and walked away together, and the shoemaker turned to make another stitch in the sole, mumbling to himself, 'Not that I notice what he say, but 'tis the thought of it, the mere thought of it that hurt my heart.'

Noon

"Course you can sit,' said Mr. Foster, 'I ain't got nothin' 'gainst you sittin'.'

The man took off his hat and sat on the chair which Mr. Foster had indicated. The sunlight came through the crevice of the roof and his face shone with the sweat that stuck in clammy patches on it. He wrenched a handkerchief from his pocket and swept it hard over his face, but the water sprouted as quickly along the temples and down the cheeks. Soon the handkerchief was drenched and he pocketed it, tired and irritated by the itch of the sweat on his face. Mr. Foster fidgeted about, watching him out of one eye but pretending not to see his face. His manner was a little sharp, but he seemed on the whole quite friendly, and Mr. Foster who might have been perplexed by a strange visitor at that hour, tried to be friendly too.

'You ain't the said gentl'man who went to the shoemaker this mornin',' Mr. Foster said, "cause I wusn't at home?'

'No,' the man said, 'but I heard what happened.'

'So far so good,' said Mr. Foster, 'but I don't understand. 'Tis alright an' good for you to say the land is yours, but what kind of certification I got to know what r'ally happenin'.'

'I had the same kind of trouble this morning,' the man said, 'not with the shoemaker but in another part. The difference is you seem more respectful.'

'It ain't so much a question of respect,' Mr. Foster said, 'as 'tis a question of gettin' yuh meanin' clear.'

'I can't make it any clearer,' the man said. 'I've told you this spot of land is mine.'

'Well, tell me then,' Mr. Foster said, 'tell me as one man to a next, how it get in the landlord head to sell the land, an' why he sell it over our head without saying one God blessed word to the people who been livin' on it for only God knows how long?'

'It has nothing to do with the landlord,' the man said.

'What exactly you mean?' Mr. Foster asked.

'It ain't the landlord's land any longer,' the man said.

Mr. Foster sat up erect and startled. He called Miss Foster who had been standing outside the door overhearing what was said. She had been sitting in the house till the strange man arrived, and when Mr. Foster asked him to take a seat she stepped outside. She entered the house and made a polite curtsey to the strange man, before taking a seat beside Mr. Foster. They looked at each other in a kind of bewilderment and then at the strange man. He sat rigid on the chair hoping he would soon be through with the matter. Mr. Foster wasn't sure he had heard aright, and he looked at the man again before he spoke. Miss Foster appeared very anxious.

'He say the land don't belong no more to Mr. Creighton,' Mr. Foster said.

Miss Foster opened her eyes wide as though she had seen the sun falling from the sky.

'I don't quite get what you mean by not belongin' to Mr. Creighton no more,' she said.

The strange man suppressed a frown. He was growing impatient.

"Tis as I say too,' said Mr. Foster, 'but he don't follow.'

'I follow perfectly well,' the man said. He raised his voice. 'You want to say it isn't possible for me to buy land you've been on for so many years, and then ask you to leave it because I want it. But that's as it is. It's perfectly legal, and that's all that matters, the law.'

'It ain't a question of what the law say is right or wrong,' said Mr. Foster, ''tis a matter of can't be.'

'This land ain't the sort of land that can be for buy or sell,' said Miss Foster. ''Twas always an' 'twill always be land for we people to live on.'

There was a silence while the strange man waited to overcome his impatience. He cracked his knuckles and quickly surveyed the house. It didn't seem that he could continue very long with the argument. He had spoken with Mr. Foster at length in the road, and when he entered the house at Mr. Foster's request it was simply to avoid a crowd which might have collected if they saw him explaining to Mr. Foster. Now he was growing impatient.

'Let's put it to you this way,' he said. 'Suppose I have a garage and you have a car.'

'Don't make jokes, man,' Mr. Foster interrupted. The man stiffened.

'He only supposin' for supposin' sake,' Miss Foster said.

'That's right,' the man said, 'just for the sake of making everything clear. Suppose what we just supposed is true. You a car, and me a garage. You rent the garage from me, and later I sell the garage to somebody else. Who is the person you going to listen to about where and where you can put that car. No matter how long you had the car in that garage, who is the man to tell you what you should or shouldn't do about that garage?'

'To speak the truth, it got a strange sound,' said Miss Foster.

'Strange sound my eye,' said Mr. Foster. The man winced.

'I beg yuh pardon, sir,' Mr. Foster said, smiling, 'but the way it strike me you can park a car anywhere 'bout. You can't do that with an old house.'

'It is a question of who owns what,' the man said, 'and whether it's a car, a house or what you like, it makes no difference.'

Miss Foster held Mr. Foster's arm, and they all looked at each other.

'If you like,' the man said, 'if you think you couldn't move the house as I told you you'll have to, then I can buy it from you. I can save you the trouble of having to carry a house on your back.'

Mr. Foster's hands trembled as the man spoke, and Miss Foster felt for a cloth to wipe her eyes. She wasn't crying, but she wasn't sure she wouldn't soon begin to do so.

'I'll tell you something,' Mr. Foster said. He put his face close to the man's. 'If there's one golden rule we all on this land got, 'tis this: if the good God give you health and strength, work till you can get yuhself a shelter over yuh head by day, and a corner to rest yuh bones at night. And when once you get it, give the good God thanks and never get rid of it.'

The man didn't know what to answer, but he burned with words.

''Tis so,' Miss Foster said. 'Take a look all round, and poor and poverty-stricken as we all look, there ain't many a one who ain't own the little hovel he live in. It may be different with the rest, but here on this same land that is the golden rule.'

'Your own,' Mr. Foster emphasized. 'Your own own house. A man ain't a man till he can call the house he live in my own. And it ain't matter how small it be once you can call it my own own house.'

The man listened resting his head on his hands and shaking angrily as the others spoke. His anger had sunk a little as they spoke, but when Mr. Foster made ready to speak again he shifted indignantly in the chair.

'An' I'll tell you something you mayn't know,' Mr. Foster said. 'Once a house a mine move off this spot. 'Twas a flood as we never ever before see, an' like a good captain I won't leave it till they force me to. I stay on the roof and sail down the river with it, and some laugh and some cry. You can do what you please, but I tell you that to let you know what a house mean to some people in this corner of God's earth.'

The man dropped his head. It didn't seem he could make any further explanations, and he seemed to be waiting for the right moment to say he was leaving. He had hoped that they would have settled the dispute among them without great difficulty, but it was the same everywhere. Earlier he had seen a woman who lived several cross-roads away, and the difficulty was the same. They treated him as though he were a lunatic. She called out the dogs, and what with the various threats he couldn't see how he would get things done without the assistance of the police. He had hoped that Mr. Foster would have been more intelligent about the matter. He came to explain. That was itself a concession, but he thought the ignorance and poverty of the villagers warranted that approach. Now he saw himself up against a frightening difficulty. He could get the matter settled by taking legal action, but that was what he tried from the start to avoid. These were days when the better educated had to go easy with the poor since the latter's will could now be felt, and no one could tell whether he might not be called upon at some time to represent that will. The law in such circumstances would have been disastrous. He had chosen the lesser of two evils. But why couldn't they understand what was said. They knew the land wasn't theirs, and he expected them to concede that since that was so it could be bought or sold without their consent. They had taken orders from the landlords for many generations, and it was difficult to understand why one who had become the lawful owner of a piece of land should not be heard as the former landlords. It was true he hadn't bought the entire estate, but it was known by all who really mattered that the land was sold. The landlord had not informed them, but he was perfectly within his right. In any case none of them had the money to purchase a spot of land. It might have seemed decent or human or whatever one liked to say if they had been informed and offered the first chance of purchasing the spots. But that was unnecessary. They were poor. They may have bought houses such as their houses were. They lived in large-sized boxes, many of them. But the question of land was immensely more difficult. Few people could ever buy land. Houses were built and houses were sold in all parts of the island at all times. But it was always different with land. This thing which stretched high and low and naked under the eye, the foot, the wind and the rain had always seemed to carry a secret buried somewhere beneath its black surface. Why did people respect land as they did? He didn't understand, but it was a kind of visitation that assisted or terrified, an infectious disease which money made imperative for the rich to inherit. The poor understood the same issue in a different way, and since they couldn't own it, they rooted themselves into it. Dirt was cheap as the villagers often said, and sand was free; but land was the land, priceless, perennial and a symbol of some inexplicable power.

Now it was his chance to own land. He understood Mr. Foster's attachment to the house because he knew his own desire for the land. He was irritated, confused and finally downright angry. He had lived in a house and on land that weren't his property, and he had had to change residence from time to time. It was a habit not altogether uncommon among the more comfortable classes in the island. They lived for a few months in one house and quickly moved into another and another always concerned about the status of the vicinity. For the less successful professional classes or those in the lower grades of the civil service the houses were extravagant, and the problem of adequate food combined with respectable appearance and an impressive shelter was often intolerably difficult. There was something nomadic about them, intransit passengers all moving within the limits of a given land. He had known this life, and he didn't understand why Mr. Foster might not be persuaded to go elsewhere. But the villagers didn't understand. Their ways had been formed, and their life like their certain death knew its roots. Mr. Foster had been very patient. At times he seemed a little shocked by the possible truth of what he had heard, and sometimes he smiled. On the whole he had been amiable. He didn't treat the strange man as entirely a huge joke, but there was something in all he said that held the quality of the unusual. There was something comic in the news. Miss Foster was less easy. She seemed to sense evil of some kind, and she didn't smile. She spoke seriously at all times, and if Mr. Foster was trying to be facetious she hastened to correct him. The strange man was exhausted. He had put an end to the explanations. He made ready to go. Mr. Foster remained seated and watched him.

'I think you'll get all this straight sooner or later,' the man said, 'but it's got to be sooner, since I've got my own plans about this land.'

'What you know 'bout this land?' Mr. Foster said. He turned angry. The man's manner had irritated.

'I don't want to know more than I know,' the man said.

'Don't be rude to me in my own house,' Mr. Foster said. The attitudes had changed. Miss Foster sensed it and she stood, pressing her arm against Mr. Foster. The strange man had had enough of the villager's ways.

'Rude to whom?' he said. 'Don't be silly.'

'For the secon' an' last time,' Mr. Foster said, 'for the secon' an' last time I tell you don't be rude to me in my own house.'

'What!' the man snapped.

'I'll pitch your arse in the street,' Mr. Foster said, and he was on his feet shaking with excitement as he spoke. He glared at the man who had fallen back by the shock to his chair. Miss Foster trembled. The strange man was amazed by the sudden change that had taken place in Mr. Foster's manner. He had understood the raised voice, the scandalous cry, but he hadn't seen before the death lurk in the villager's straight strong glance and the shake of his limbs. It was clear to all of them what had happened. The persuasive measure had had its play. The war had started, and in the richness of his feeling Mr. Foster was more than the strange man's match.

'You can't form the fool with me,' he said. 'I ain't care tuppence who you be, you got to know yuh place with me. What you take me for, a man or a mouse? Well, I'm a man to my backbone.'

He slapped his hands against his thigh and stripped open his shirt. The skin showed under the thick short hair. The man got up to leave. Miss Foster had remained in the house in case Mr. Foster attempted to do something rash. The strange man stood waiting for Mr. Foster to lead the way. There was a knock on the door and Mr. Foster opened. The overseer entered. Miss Foster retreated and stepped outside. She was taken aback by the sudden appearance of the overseer who carried a large sheet of paper folded in one hand. It wasn't the first time the overseer had gone to see Mr. Foster, but he seemed unusually rigid on this occasion. Mr. Foster looked at the paper folded in the other's hand. It was held together by a rubber band and reminded him of the handbills which Mr. Slime had stuck on the posts from time to time. The strange man had taken his seat again, and Mr. Foster and the overseer sat too. Miss Foster took up her position outside the door as she had done when the strange man entered. Mr. Foster was quiet again. He had no great respect for the overseer, and he certainly didn't trust him. The overseer was the enemy whom one watched and played with as a cat might play with a mouse. Mr. Foster made himself easy and the strange man waited to see which of the two would speak first.

'What you know 'bout all this talk of sellin' land?' Mr. Foster said. His tone was light and jovial, as though he were inviting the overseer to share the joke.

'I don't know nothing,' the overseer said. His tone was abrupt and Mr. Foster's manner changed again. His feelings veered according to the attitude of the other person. With the overseer it was a matter of contending with two persons, the one he saw and the one he knew.

'What you mean by you don't know?' Mr. Foster asked.

'I mean what I says,' the overseer said. He dropped his glance, letting his eyes move about from end to end of the paper. Mr. Foster stiffened.

'I've explained it already,' the strange man said.

'You shut yuh blasted mouth,' Mr. Foster snapped, 'or you'll think me mad as Carter's cat.'

The overseer looked up at Mr. Foster, apparently horrified. 'I'd warn you not to behave like that with certain people,' the overseer said. His voice was grave and penetrating. Mr. Foster was quiet again. Another emotion was registered. His manner changed rapidly and each change was dictated by the interpretation he gave what he had heard. He couldn't be frightened by the overseer or the strange man, but his feelings seemed to give a special value to the other's approach. And he followed his feeling till his patience was exhausted and the other's manner made him rebellious. He couldn't understand what role the overseer was playing in this game, but it seemed that he and the strange man were on the same side. That made the situation more perplexing since the overseer with his knowledge of the land was not far removed from the landlord himself. If the overseer said that the land was sold, the situation would have to be given a new meaning. It would have lost its comic element. It would be true.

'You mean to tell me that I really got to move?' Mr. Foster asked, looking at the overseer. The overseer was silent for a moment.

'I have nothing to do with it,' he said; 'it ain't my land.'

'I know as well as the world it ain't your land,' Mr. Foster said, 'but if you don't know 'bout it, how you expect me to?'

'I don't know,' the overseer said; 'my business is to take orders.'

'Well, what's yuh orders?' Mr. Foster said. 'What's yuh latest orders?

'The gentleman here says he explain,' the overseer said. 'What more you want?'

'Is this a trick or what?' Mr. Foster asked. 'All you making jokes or what? You see what happen in this island some time ago, you see the blood that shed all over the place, and all because you take stupid chances with people.' The men were quiet and Miss Foster had entered the house. She knew when it was dangerous to stay away.

'When a poor man loose control of the best in himself,' Mr. Foster said, 'it ain't his fault at all, it is the fault of you people who go round making poppits of other poor people.'

''Tis a question of what the law going to do,' said the overseer. Mr. Foster was gradually reaching the stage when the beast in himself might have its play. He watched them in a kind of desperation, and he wasn't sure what worried him more. Was it what the strange man had said, or was it the part the overseer played. Perhaps it might even have been the thought that this talk about the land was true.

'I'm going,' the strange man said, 'but as I've told you, you'll have to be off in three weeks.'

It was the first time he had spoken since Mr. Foster had told him to shut his mouth. He stood turning the hat over in his hand. Mr. Foster's manner had changed again.

'I'll come an' let you put me up,' Mr. Foster said, smiling. The overseer was tense. It was clear that he shared the other's knowledge and even the other's disappointment that Mr. Foster couldn't understand.

'I going too,' he said, frowning at Mr. Foster.

''Tis a good thing looks don't kill,' Mr. Foster said, making the smile wider.

'The Lord go with you,' said Miss Foster. She was anxious to see them go.

'And may he go with you too,' the overseer said. 'You'll need him when you see what's on this paper.'

'You can wipe your arse with it,' said Mr. Foster. His manner had changed. He thought the overseer had tried to make a joke at Miss Foster.

'Good day, Foster,' the overseer said with a sneer and walked out with the strange man following close.

'Bye-bye, massah,' Mr. Foster said and smiled.

They left the house and stood in the road for a few minutes. Mr. Foster closed the door and turned to Miss Foster. She had taken the incident rather badly. Mr. Foster asked her not to worry, but she seemed to sense evil in what had passed. She had an uncanny insight into what would happen, and Mr. Foster knew that. She could grow hysterical on occasions and he would have to control her by shouting, but at other times her expression was serious and sad, and he knew something bigger than hysteria was going on inside her. He didn't like to look at her when she wore that expression. He buttoned his shirt and went to the window. He was going to relieve Miss Foster by making some joke at the overseer and the strange man. Miss Foster sat on the bed stretching her fingers out over the sheet. He pushed his head through the window and saw the overseer and the strange man standing at the corner. A few people assembled at the corner trying to understand what they were saying. The overseer tried to send them away since they were mostly women and boys. They scampered and as quickly settled again into a small group. Mr. Foster came out on the steps and shouted to the overseer.

'An' tell me how much money I got to pay the new landlord.' He sat on the steps howling with laughter.

'This will tell you,' the overseer said, opening the paper and flaunting it high above his head.

'Black and white, by God,' Mr. Foster shouted, 'pen and ink, that's the way the Great does things. 'Tis what I call business.'

The crowds increased. Mr. Foster's voice had summoned them and in a minute they seemed a multitude met at the corner. Miss Foster came out on the steps, and watched the overseer and the strange man. The overseer walked towards the lamp-post and placed the paper against it. He tried it several times to see what position was best for reading. The people left the houses and shops and flocked to see what it said. Many of them had witnessed the incident by the shoemaker's shop, and some had heard Mr. Foster's voice when he shouted at the strange man. The strange man walked away while the overseer stuck the bill onto the post. The people came from all directions. They prattled excitedly as they ran, but when they reached the corner they turned silent. The overseer saw the bill safely stuck and ran towards the strange man. They walked away together towards the boundary that separated Belleville from the village. The shops were deserted and the shop-keepers came out on the steps to hear what was written on the paper. Mr. Foster brushed his pants and walked towards the lamp-post. Miss Foster followed. He was struck by the people's silence. They read and occasionally someone turned a head in surprise or asked quietly for an explanation of some word. But on the whole they were quiet. Mr. Foster forced his way through the crowd and read the words printed on the paper.

This land (or estate) formerly the property of John Nathaniel Creighton, Esq., has been sold. Tenants will continue to pay rents as usual into the offices of the Creighton's estate although certain lands called spots have already been disposed of. Information regarding the purchase of such spots must be had from the Managing Director on behalf of the Poor Man's Penny Bank, or the Secretary-General of the Help Your Brother Friendly Society.

Signed, WATSON AND PETERS,

Solicitors of Creighton's Offices.

'What is it it say?' Miss Foster asked. Mr. Foster turned away without speaking. He moved away through the crowd and walked to his step. Miss Foster followed. The others looked lost as they buzzed quietly, repeating the words.

'What is it it say?' Miss Foster asked again.

'It say we got to see Mr. Slime,' one man said.

They didn't know what that meant. It was a strange man whom they had seen by the shoemaker's shop and later in front Mr. Foster's house. Some remained standing by the lamp-post reading and re-reading the bill while others walked back towards the shops. They all seemed giddy with the echo of the words in their minds. It say we got to see Mr. Slime. See Mr. Slime. Mr. Slime. Mr. Slime. Mr. Slime.

Night

The old man lay back deep in the chair which the old woman had always used when she was alive. He stretched his feet out over the small bench and sucked the stem of the clay pipe. The lamp burnt low on the table beside the bed. The head teacher struck a match and lit his cigarette. The old man looked up and said something about the chair. His face was drawn and more wrinkled than ever, and the teeth which held the pipe had turned dark brown. He was looking askance at the chair the head teacher sat on. It was his chair, the one he used when the old woman was alive. He had thought of getting rid of it since there was no need for more than one chair, and it always reminded him that someone was absent. At the table in the morning and in his bed at night he couldn't escape the reminder. He had put most of the old woman's things in the coffin beside her; the little things like pins, and her communion badge and one or two pieces of clothing. And he had never stopped thinking how he might get rid of the rest. And yet there was little consolation in throwing things away. He had understood that. If you put new things in their place you were always reminded why the new things were there, and if you left the space empty you couldn't forget that something was absent. That's what had happened with the birds on the glass pane in the door. After the old woman's death he painted the panes black, and the picture of the birds perched on the twigs was lost beneath the mourning surface. But it didn't help. The black splodges at the top of the door were neither black nor splodges. When he watched them in the sunlight at morning he saw clearly what was hidden. It was useless. There was no way of forgetting what you didn't want to remember. Once you were alive there was no death for other things till you yourself had died. A man's memory, it seemed, was the penalty he paid for his own existence. He remembered the dream and quickly turned his thought elsewhere. The head teacher was drawing at the cigarette like a novice.

"Twas a good good thing I din't dump the old chair,' the old man said, "cause you wouldn' 'ave had nowhere to sit yourself. 'Twas in my head to dump her.'

The head teacher took another draw of the cigarette and looked down at him. He looked straight ahead as he spoke as though the listener were posted somewhere in the yard. Sometimes the head teacher looked towards the partition in the direction of the yard. It made him feel more at home.

'An' 'twas so good after all's said an' done,' the old man went on, "twas so good of you to come. Makes me wonder for a minute what could get in yuh head to do what you do.' The old man paused but the head teacher didn't speak, and soon the old man continued to speak. 'People has a way of not rememberin' that old people alive. They sort o' take you for granted as if you wus a chair, no more good for using an' just put out o' harm's way in the corner. An' when you's as old as me an' that ever happen you get the feelin' that you trespassing, that you's somewhere you ain't got no right to be, an' you ain't belong no more.' He chuckled when he had finished speaking the last words, and the head teacher was relieved. He was beginning to feel a little queer, but then the old man seemed not to be worried and everything was all right.

'I don't think anyone in all this village forgets you, Pa,' the head teacher said. 'Neither you nor Ma, and no one ever will.'

"'Tis better'n winning the Sweepstake,' the old man said, smiling. 'To know that you's sort of in other people's remembering even when you ain't in sight, 'tis a good feeling.'

The head teacher shifted in the chair and recalled two or three stories he had heard the children relating about the old man. Some of the bigger boys recalled incidents with the goats. He kept three or four goats before the flood, and the boys often went in the evening to take them out grazing. And what happened to the goats was not the old man's business. He knew that they grazed well, and were always in good condition. And on more than two occasions the younger goats produced young long before he had thought them ripe for the ram. These boys who had remained in the village remembered all that happened in the evening when the goats were taken out. The head teacher finished the cigarette and lit another.

'P'raps 'tis as you says,' the old man said, 'but 'tis still good of you to come. There ain't many who as takes it upon themself to come, an' I wait sometimes till all those lights put out and I go for a walk round the corner. 'Tis a joke to hear how the ol' bones crack, but the stick keeps me up.'

'You must be careful,' said the head teacher. 'I don't think you should go out after dark.' The old man chuckled and watched the smoke leave the bowl of the pipe.

'Well, thank my spirit,' said the old man, 'thank my spirit I ain't got no excuse for goin' out tonight, 'cause 'twas so good of you to come.'

'I don't know if you will like what I did,' the head teacher said. There was a momentary hitch in their intercourse. The old man showed no sign of nervousness, but the head teacher had sensed a change in the quality of the other's feeling.

'What you do, my son?' the old man said. He seemed unmoved by anything he might have suspected. It seemed that he suspected nothing except the head teacher's visit. It wasn't really a suspicion. It was a surprise, but after they had sat and talked it seemed quite normal. The old man sat quiet, puffing his pipe and watching the smoke curl upwards. He was waiting for the head teacher to say something. The head teacher seemed more uncertain now. He played with the cigarette on the edge of his lips, and suddenly brought his head down close to the old man's. They were silent. Then he rested his hand on the old man's chair and waited.

'I saw the landlord about you this morning,' he said, and waited as though he expected some special reaction from the old man.

'Which of them?' the old man asked. 'They make me to understan' there's new landlords and more'n one o' them.' He had heard of the incident by the shoemaker's shop and he had followed much of what had happened at the corner at noon. But no one had yet come to tell him the details. And in a way he thought the head teacher had made that task his responsibility.

'I mean the old landlord,' the head teacher said. 'I mean Mr. Creighton.' He paused, and the old man for the first time seemed a little unsure of what was coming. Anything could happen now, but he didn't try to guess.

'Go on,' said the old man, 'what about Mr. Creighton?'

'We arranged to send you away,' said the head teacher.

'Where to?' the old man asked. He was more concerned now, but his tone was still neutral and a little grave. The head teacher fumbled with the cigarette and the old man had to urge him.

'Where to?' the old man asked again.

'To the Alms House,' the head teacher said. He let go of the chair and sat upright. The old man went on puffing at the pipe, watching the smoke fall through the light and on to the bed.

'Somebody buy my spot too?' he asked. The voice was steady. He took the pipe from his mouth while the head teacher watched him. More closely than ever.

'Yes,' said the head teacher, 'your spot was sold.'

They had reached the stage when each wonders what is going on in the other's head. The words are spoken and the gestures made, but they give no clue, and each knows that the other person is hidden somewhere. The body with its stupid sprawling limbs and its meaningless noises is just a relevant response in a given situation. But no clues are given. The old man made himself more comfortable in the chair, and turned to face the teacher.

'An' my house,' he said, turning his head again to face the yard, 'what 'bout my house?'

'I said to myself you might want to sell it,' said the head teacher. 'You couldn't move it, Pa, I'm sure you couldn't, and that's why I went to see the landlord about you.'

They were silent. The head teacher closed the window and put the stick in the corner where the partitions met. The wind was making the flame skip up and down in the chimney. The smoke from the old man's pipe flattened out and fell over the lamp and the bed. The head teacher lit another cigarette. He watched the old man who steadied himself again in the chair. He was looking round the house as though he were about to make the bargain or as one who wasn't going to leave what he valued most. His eyes moved from corner to corner, and the head teacher watched him, wondering what he was thinking. On occasions he dropped his head, and his change of expression seemed to indicate a certain change of feeling. He puffed at the pipe, and cleared his throat, and went on puffing more and more strongly. The head teacher watched him raise his head and waited for him to speak.

'The Alms House,' said the old man, and it wasn't easy to understand what he meant by that exclamation. He took the pipe from his mouth and rubbed the stem along his chin. 'This ol' house ain't got no age,' he said, looking from corner to corner along the ceiling. 'An' my dear Ma—God rest her in her grave—always say to me that if there be one thing on this God's earth I wasn't to do when she wus dead or alive wus to get rid o' the ol' house. She din't have no liking for the things o' this world, but there wus something that sort of tell her always stick to yuh house.'

He looked ahead as he smoked as though the listener were in the yard. The head teacher didn't know which worried him more, the sale of the land, or the thought of the Alms House. He tried to forget for a while what the Alms House meant. Then it seemed it was the old house which worried the old man. He talked coherently but as though there wasn't anyone listening, and then he poked his thumb into the bowl of the pipe, levelled the ash and refilled it. The smoke coiled upwards again, and he fell into a long silence.

The head teacher sat quiet in the chair wondering what he was thinking. He would have given anything to get into that bald brown skull if that would help him to understand what went on in the old man's mind. The old man went on puffing the pipe and watching the smoke drift about the room. He hadn't betrayed any feeling about the Alms House. The head teacher wanted to know what he felt about that, but even when he exclaimed 'Alms House' a while ago it wasn't possible to say what he meant. He had turned quickly to the thought of his own house and what the old woman had said. The head teacher understood that. He was one of the villagers who had done well, and although he might have learnt different ways he knew what affected them most. When he heard the stories about the strange men in the morning and at noon, he understood. He understood what the strange men couldn't understand as well as what had seemed meaningless to the shoemaker and Mr. Foster. He had shared both worlds, and in a way it was this double understanding that had urged him to see the old man. He wanted to prepare him for the shock, and in a way he wanted to help feel it with him. But it was difficult to gauge the old man's feeling. He hadn't exploded as Mr. Foster and the shoemaker had done, and it didn't seem that his age was totally responsible for his failure to do so. He seemed to feel on another level altogether.

The head teacher recalled what he knew of the old man. He had been comfortable some years ago, and although much of what he had earned in Panama had been spent in one way or another, he had never been dissolute. He never seemed to regret anything, not even his present poverty which seemed tolerable. He had always carried himself tidily with the air of a man who reminded others that he knew better times. Everyone remarked his tidiness, and they often said that the old man was great once. He had money and he had also that air of dignity which they associated with the Great. The old man had a mind, and the mind was the man. The head teacher recalled what he knew about the Alms Houses, and he tried to put these accounts together. What did the old man think of going to the Alms House? That was the question that bothered him. He would have been greatly relieved if he knew for certain how the old man regarded the suggestion. But he hadn't spoken on the matter. He had simply mentioned the word and quickly turned his attention to his own house and all the old woman had said.

The head teacher knew what the Alms House represented. Everyone knew what the Alms House represented, although no one might have known what the Alms House was. The Alms House was a house of charity. But this was charity of a certain kind. This charity had nothing to do with love or compassion, a human compulsion to offer where the offering met a definite need. The Alms House was a kind of appointed State burden. It was the unwelcome task of preventing old age, poverty and disease from spreading into the nuisance that was inevitable if certain people were left unattended. Everyone knew that. Those who served at the Alms Houses as well as those who were the victims of that service. The residents often seemed reduced to so many bundles of bones held together and covered with what might once have been flesh. The head teacher recalled his visits to certain Alms Houses and the state of the objects he had seen stretched out on beds. Those who were strong enough walked about in the yard, but the paralysed or acutely tubercular remained inside caged in their impotence. Certain sections of the Alms House had become the refuge of those tubercular cases which would not be admitted to the general hospital. This was the disease that carried the greatest social stigma. He had seen many of them during his visits. There were also the deaf and dumb, the blind, those who were swollen, sore stricken and in some cases apparently leprous. When they heard your approach they would try to raise an arm to receive the customary copper. If the nurses were around they would try to make signs. On such occasions the nurses were their greatest enemies, and he often wondered why the nurses grudged them the pittance. And sometimes it seemed strange, too, that they should care to ask for money. They couldn't leave the beds, but it seemed that begging had become a habit which they substituted for some other activity. He had seen them often and in different stages of dying, and he had often wondered why some of them hadn't been helped in the effort to get out of their pain. They were an incredibly shocking sight. They were no longer men, but objects capable of certain gestures, cries, and with an apparatus that could register pain in extreme.

That in a way was the Alms House. It wasn't a prison, which could become part of a man's experience. It was the final stage of human degradation, the grave of those who though dead had been allowed to go on living, and the point at which no noble human attribute could be claimed by the victim. The old man hadn't spoken nor had he shown any sign of fear, anxiety or anger. He sat puffing the pipe and watching the smoke float in all directions through the house, and the head teacher wondered what he felt. Each, it seemed, had retreated farther away from the other. The head teacher lit another cigarette. He wondered whether the thought of the Alms House mightn't have struck the old man as altogether humiliating. It might have been different with Pa since he had a past to draw on. And he wasn't destitute in the way the ordinary resident was. If he went to the Alms House it would be for the simple reason that there was no one to take care of him. In such circumstances he stood a chance of much better treatment. If he went to the Alms House retaining a certain status it was likely he would be treated differently. The nurses might make a pet of him. The old man shifted in the chair and the head teacher put an end to the speculations. He played with the cigarette and watched the old man. He finished the cigarette and watched the old man take the pipe from his mouth. Soon the air was clear of smoke and the lamplight fell clean and clear on the naked skull. The old man turned and looked at the head teacher. He made an attempt to speak, but the words didn't come at first and he cleared his throat. The head teacher was anxious to learn what he had been thinking.

'There ain't much that can take me by surprise now,' he said, 'there ain't much at all, but 'tis one thing I'd like to know, just one thing or two.' His voice was now even and very controlled.

'Tell me,' the head teacher said, appearing to coax him.

"Tis this,' said the old man, 'why first of all did Mr. Slime leave the teachin', an' how an' why he come to buy this land since there wus no love an' harmony 'twixt 'imself and Mr. Creighton?'

The head teacher wasn't sure what he should say. Mr. Slime had resigned from the school for reasons which were generally accepted as laudable. Most people had followed his rise to power with great interest, and he had created certain things like the Penny Bank and the Friendly Society which were all they needed to be satisfied with his work. There were few who hadn't been helped by these two concerns. They deposited their pennies and in turn they received modest sums which pleased them. It might have been a novelty, but it was certainly useful to many. They learnt thrift. The old man was waiting for the head teacher's explanation, but the latter wasn't sure what he should say. He said simply that Mr. Slime had resigned, and when he said the word it seemed to carry a special meaning. It didn't quite mean leave, but it also didn't quite mean resign. The old man didn't worry much about that since he had his own notions about Mr. Slime. He believed what he had always told the old woman about Mr. Slime. 'I as much as always says to myself,' he said, 'that he leave the teachin' in the school 'cause he want to do a teachin' of a bigger kind. My own feelin' wus that the sort of teachin' he wus giving the big people wus sort of bigger than what he give in the school. An' in a sort of way the two don't go together. The education he wus givin' to the children studyin' the books an' so on don't go hand in hand with the education he wus givin' the big people from the platform every night. He had to choose one o' the other, an' it seem to me he choose the most important.'

'The school is very important,' the head teacher said. He was glad the old man hadn't probed further about Mr. Slime's resignation, and he thought he should keep the question away from the subject.

"Tis true,' the old man said, 'that's too true, but he wus strikin' a bigger blow; p'raps he wus sayin' you could leave the children till they grow up a little when the education would mean more, but 'twus the big ones he want to teach a lesson.'

'I don't know exactly how or why he bought the land,' the head teacher said. The old man watched him steadily as though he might find sooner or later an answer to his question in the other's eyes. The head teacher was growing more and more uncertain of what he should say. He wanted above everything to keep the old man's attention from the question of Mr. Slime's resignation.

'I really don't know how or why he bought the land,' he said again.

'Some says they know how,' the old man said, ''cause the paper on the post tell them.' The paper say something 'bout the Bank and the Society. 'Tis with the money o' these two he buy it.'

'That may be so,' the head teacher said, 'but I think lots of other people put money into it.' It seemed now that he was trying to evade the question of the land as much as that of the teacher's resignation. If he were a stranger it would have been different. But he understood what the old man felt, and whether or not he wanted to he was forced to share a measure of that feeling.

'He always did say way back,' said the old man, 'way way back in the first days he says he would make us owners.' He turned his head away from the head teacher. ''Tis that I don't understand how he could let the strange men come in.'

'The strange men you hear of,' the head teacher said, 'they put money in the Bank and the Society. They're what you know as partners. Mr. Slime is the boss all right, but they're others who put money in, and they got the first choice of buying any spot they wanted.'

'How many o' them put in this money?' the old man asked.

'I don't know,' the head teacher said.

'Seems to me,' said the old man, 'there be as many with first choice as there is people livin' in the village.'

'I don't think so,' said the head teacher. He was growing more and more uneasy by the old man's questions. The old man had said that he wanted to ask one question, or probably two, but it seemed he had asked thousands. And the head teacher couldn't understand what he was thinking. His expression was strange. Sometimes he looked in another direction as though he didn't want to see certain things. It was often very uncomfortable for the head teacher. He couldn't cut short the questions because he understood. In a way he was paying for his understanding. He knew how the old man might feel, although he didn't quite understand what he was thinking. The old man was very controlled, but it seemed he managed only with effort. When he turned his head away it was clear sometimes that he couldn't stand what he thought he saw. He shifted in the chair and looked at the head teacher again.

'An' why the landlord go an' sell it without tellin' us?' the old man said. 'Why he do that?' His tone had changed, and there was a kind of desperation creeping into his voice. The head teacher was about to speak but the old man interrupted. It seemed he was angry.

"Course me an' Ma know he wus goin' to sell it,' he said, 'but 'twusn't right for him to leave us like stray dogs without a owner. He always say he wus responsible for the villagers. That's what he always say. He had a responsibility which we mayn't quite understand. An' now, look, look what he do.'

The head teacher was feeling for the right thing to say. He sensed the change which had come over the old man, and it made him feel uncertain of what he might say. It also gave him a feeling of guilt. He still would have liked to know what the old man had thought about the Alms House, but nothing had been said. The old man had stuck to the land. He wanted to get certain principles regarding the land clear. He was worried by the sale of the land, and particularly concerned about all that might have happened. He remembered the promises which Mr. Slime had made. He would help the villagers to buy the land. He had told them time and time again that they should own it, and if he had his way they certainly would. At first he wasn't perturbed about the sale of the land. He had told himself that it had given Mr. Slime a chance to do what he always wanted to do. If Mr. Slime had made himself the new landlord, there was no one to prevent him from passing the land over to the villagers. The sale of the land was the first step on the way to the promised land. Yet he couldn't understand why the landlord had chosen to sell the land to Mr. Slime. Surely it wasn't out of love or friendship for Mr. Slime since the latter had made himself the enemy of the landlord. He was responsible for the first strike, and he played a great part in the riots. He recalled what had happened to Mr. Creighton during the riots. He had come as near to death as any man who had done so and escaped. He was worried about this. Why did Mr. Creighton sell the land to the teacher? He wasn't forced to do so, since the owner of property had the right to dispose of it as he pleased. He wanted the head teacher to help him through this difficulty. Other things could be left for a while, but this was urgent. This strange relation between Mr. Slime and the landlord.

The head teacher played with the cigarette between his lips, waiting for him to speak. He was struggling to put these things together.

'Wus it p'raps,' he said, 'wus it p'raps the landlord say to 'imself Mr. Slime wus one of us, and seeing how he raise up the Society and the Bank—'cause the landlord did have a sort of respect for that—seeing all this, p'raps he say to himself Mr. Slime wus the right man, an' if 'twus so, why bring in the strange men, 'cause I don't think Mr. Creighton expect to see what going to happen?'

'I don't know,' the head teacher said, 'I don't know.' He could hardly speak. He was finding the old man more than he could manage.

'But p'raps you could find out,' the old man said, 'you's in a position to find out, an' I too old to find out. I too old for that.'

The head teacher let his hands rest on his knees. He couldn't return the old man's glance, and later he couldn't bear the shake of the old man's voice. The old man sat shaking a little in the chair. It was unbearable, his failure to understand, his sense of disappointment and his suspicion of the possible disaster that was ahead.

'I'm not crying,' the old man said. 'I'm too old to cry.'

His face was wet. The head teacher put out his cigarette and wondered whether he should go. It was late, and he couldn't bear the sight of the tears on the old man's face. They ran freely into his mouth. But he went on sucking the pipe, and watching through the mist of his eyes the smoke drifting through the room. The head teacher held his hand for a while. The old man tried to say something, but his voice was choked with a kind of grief deeper than anything he had known. He was like a child in the shake of his limbs with the tears on his face. The head teacher stood, but the old man paid no attention. He looked at the partition towards the yard.

'I must be going,' the head teacher said, 'but you mustn't bother your head about anything. I'm not going to hurry you off, and I'll buy the house if you want to sell it. You mustn't worry.' He didn't know whether he had said the right thing, but he was sure he didn't want to stay any longer. He couldn't bear it. The old man didn't seem to hear. He made no answer. The head teacher patted him on the shoulder, and walked through the door, closing it quietly behind him. The room was full of smoke, and the lamp burnt low on the table beside the bed.

14

THE grease had soaked through the cover of the exercise book making a faded yellow patch on the opening pages. It had lost its odour, but the colour seemed to come between me and the words on the sheet. I turned the leaves until I found a page that wasn't soiled, and I read.

January.

When the year ends and a new year begins I make the same promises, above all to keep a diary. I am occupied till about May and then it seems there's no longer an excuse for writing and the diary comes to an end. I put the notes away on the shelf and they are never heard of again except someone rescues them from the garbage. But I have made the promise this year, and since it doesn't matter what has happened in the previous years I start the diary. We brought the year's festivities to a close with Christmas and the annual Agricultural Exhibition, but it was the latter which I really enjoyed. Every year these farmers and peasant folk select the choicest specimens of their crops for display in Queen's Park, and those who don't live in the country get an idea of what it means to work on the land. We are used to sugar cane and the vegetables, but we have never really known them this size. All these exhibits are three times larger than what we have known in the city. And so are the animals. In the shed there were thousands of pigeons of all shapes and sizes, and opposite rows of kennels where the dogs sat waiting for the judges. I have never seen a stall for cats. I don't understand why cats shouldn't be exhibited. And there are the women, in a way the most exciting of the exhibits. They haven't got owners like the animals, but they too have come on exhibition. It seems a shame they should use the same dresses on the last night. When it turned dark I saw them like sentries sitting on the grass. Then the clock chimed and the keepers said everything had come to an end but the people on the grass didn't go, and I knew the dresses would be soiled. Crossing the bridge at midnight with the

girl whom I had just left still clinging to my memory I thought something should be done. There should be a place where we could change
into tougher garments for the night. Every year I wonder whether I
haven't seen the last, and so I make no plans for the next. But it will
probably come again, and we shall return to see the earth's produce
on show and to show ourselves as well.

*   *   *

My mother called from the kitchen to say that she would soon be
ready. I interrupted my reading and waited to hear whether she would
speak again. It wasn't wise not to hear her when she spoke. She didn't
speak and I turned the pages and read.

March.

The men were sitting round the table at the Miami Club. There were
four, two of whom I didn't recognize. One was the village head teacher
and the other who sat nearest me with his back turned was Mr. Slime.
They were drinking rum and soda. I was having falernum in coconut
water, and I was trying to avoid them. I didn't want Mr. Slime or the
village head teacher to see me. Not that I was afraid, but I thought it
would be difficult to talk with them. They were discussing the land
and the conditions they would create for the villagers. After the
privilege spots had been sold they were going to sell the other spots
to the villagers. One man said it wasn't likely that the villagers would
be able to buy. The spots were about three hundred dollars each, and
I forget how much interest the purchaser would have to pay if he
couldn't deliver the money cash. Someone said they would make about
five hundred dollars on each spot if they got the interest they expected.
The man was certain the interest would increase since the villagers
couldn't pay more than three or four shillings a week. There would
be weeks when they couldn't pay at all. Mr. Slime didn't speak, nor
did the head teacher. They called for another rum and soda, and when
the waiter passed I asked to have a double falernum poured into my
glass. Someone said you had at least to make the villagers an offer
although you knew they couldn't make use of it. The head teacher
wondered what the villagers were thinking, and one of the men said
jovially that the head teacher was probably thinking about going into
politics. Mr. Slime agreed that they had to think of what would happen
to the villagers, but there wasn't much they could do to help them

directly. He would make them the offer. It seemed the head teacher wanted to ask Mr. Slime something, but he didn't have the courage. He made two attempts to speak and suddenly said it didn't matter. They finished another rum and soda and collected their things. I kept my head bowed. Then Mr. Slime asked the head teacher whether he had found someone to move the old man's house or whether he was going to buy it. I wondered whether they were thinking of Pa. The head teacher was slow to reply. Mr. Slime was puzzled. He didn't seem to understand what was worrying the head teacher. They said something about the Alms House and I got frightened. One of the men whom I didn't recognize seemed to know what the head teacher was talking about. He said something about the old man, and then he added that it didn't matter since he had men who could do the job. I asked the waiter for a rum and soda and hurried out of the club. It sounded like murder.

*   *   *

My mother called to say that she would soon be ready. I waited to hear whether she would speak again, but she didn't and I re-read the last sentences on the sheet. My mother was stirring madly in the kitchen and I wanted to finish reading the notes before she came in. This didn't seem possible so I turned to the last pages of the book and read what I had written the day before. She called to say she was coming, but I didn't answer. I would close the book when she arrived.

April.

No, it isn't likely I shall see the exhibition again. And I am certain now I shall be seeing most things here for the last time. The tickets came this morning, and I shall be leaving by plane early on Wednesday. Until the tickets came I thought there might be a chance of staying. Now I shan't be staying except I lose the tickets. But I don't want to stay. That is not altogether right. It would be more accurate to say I want to go. I have been wondering what the other place will be like. As far as I know no one knows me there, so I can start with a clean record and try to make an impression. If you aren't native to a place you have an excellent chance of becoming a gentleman in it. My mother has been packing for almost a week. One would think she was leaving too. Tonight I shall be cock in the yard at a farewell party, and two days later I see them for the last time.

I don't remember anything except the singing. They shouted 'for he's a jolly good fellow' which, of course, I have never been. When I review these relationships they seem so odd. I have always been here on this side and the other person there on that side, and we have both tried to make the sides appear similar in the needs, desires and ambitions. But it wasn't true. It was never true. When I reach Trinidad where no one knows me I may be able to strike identity with the other person. But it was never possible here. I am always feeling terrified of being known; not because they really know you, but simply because their claim to this knowledge is a concealed attempt to destroy you. That is what knowing means. As soon as they know you they will kill you, and thank God that's why they can't kill you. They can never know you. Sometimes I think the same thing will be true in Trinidad. The likenesses will meet and make merry, but they won't know you. They won't know the you that's hidden somewhere in the castle of your skin.

On my way home the prostitute intercepted me. She was well dressed and smelling to high heaven. We went to the house and when she fingered me I belched. She laughed like a circus clown and said she had never made anyone do that before. She sat on the bed naked and the skin was thick and creased. I didn't know whether it was ugly or beautiful, but I had never seen that kind of black before. Wet and shiny. I belched again and she shouted that I could go if I didn't want to do it. I said I didn't want to do it, but I would pay her nevertheless and tell her a story. She dressed and listened. When I was a little boy I knew another little boy who was in the habit of accumulating birds' shit. When he got the right quantity he cut a stick and painted it with the birds' shit. He hid the stick till it was dark, and when he went out, unseen and hardly seeing, he would make conversation with another boy. Then he would ask the boy to hold the stick, and when the boy held he pulled the stick through the clenched fingers, and the paint came off in a solid little pile on the other's hand. She said it was very, very funny, but she didn't understand why I told her. I couldn't wait to explain.

I had my last engagement last night. I shan't write in this book again, because I say the same things over and over. Tomorrow I leave. The likenesses will meet and make merry, but they won't know you, the you that's hidden somewhere in the castle of your skin.

*   *   *

'Two things happen,' my mother said, clamping the dishes on the table. I was re-reading the last sentence of the diary. She made a noise with the dish before setting two large white plates beside it. The room was bright. 'Two things happen,' she repeated and I looked up from the exercise book and asked what had happened. It didn't seem important and I wasn't very interested. She sucked her teeth and swept out of the room. I went on re-reading the diary. In a minute she returned with a bowl and another plate. The room was full of steam. There was a silence while she arranged the things on the table. Then she banged a hand on the table and shouted, 'If you think you can treat me as you like you make a sad mistake.' I dropped the exercise book and looked up to ask what had happened. She had stalked out of the room again. I wanted to go on reading the diary but it wasn't safe to provoke her further, moreover I didn't understand why she spoke as she did. She returned to the room carrying a jug filled with water and two glasses. She balanced the jug in the palm of one hand while the glasses scotched between the fingers of the other hand. It was like a circus stunt. She set the jug and the glasses on the table and turned to the door.

'I won't stand for it, I tell you,' she said, "cause you ain't no man yet. You just gone past seventeen an' you ain't see a star pitch in this world.' I had put the exercise book under the chair and I had an urge to retrieve it and go on reading. I didn't want to annoy her further, but during these chastisements I felt very uneasy unless I had something to occupy part of my attention. It was difficult to sit and stare through the rising steam while she rebuked. The mist rose from the table and spread across her back which was turned to me as she stood at the door looking out into the distance. I wanted to ask what had happened, but it seemed difficult to speak. She left the room and I sat back in the chair wondering whether I should ask what had happened. She returned with a small bowl of salt and a bottle of black peppers soaked in vinegar. The meal was ready and I thought I should begin eating. She put the things on the table and took a step back towards the door. The cloud of steam was thinning out in its drift through the room. I took a look at the meal and another at my mother.

'You hardly out the eggshell an' you come to treat me as if I was a maid 'bout the place.' She spoke quietly but with a certain aggressiveness. 'What you take me for?' she asked and turned to face me as she repeated the question. 'What you take me for?' she asked again and seemed to be waiting for my answer. Now I wanted to speak, but it wasn't clear to me how I had offended and the offence might have seemed greater if I asked what I had done. I wondered how I should meet her question without causing her further annoyance. She drew a chair and sat at the opposite end of the table, keeping her eyes on the floor. The light was thickening into the early darkness of the village night. Through the door I could see the clouds gathering into a heavier pile, and the light of the sun was leaner on the galvanized sheets that roofed the houses. It was half-light in the room with the steam rising from the bowl and the plates. The atmosphere of the room reminded me of the mist breaking over the hills in the early morning. You expected the sun to plunge through it at any moment, or it might be smothered by a sudden descent of darkness. I was glad to have the mist of steam in the room, but it was drifting outside and the room was becoming clearer.

My mother kept her head down staring at the floor and I waited for the right moment to strike a reconciliation. It was difficult to judge what was the right moment. This wasn't a new experience, for I had grown used to these sudden explosions of anger. They seemed to me uncalled for, but they had become so frequent in recent times that I thought my mother couldn't help it. She wasn't naturally quarrelsome, but in the last three or four years she had grown terribly anxious about everything. When the quarterly reports came in from the High School she would be kept busy for a week. She didn't understand why the masters should say what they had to say. She didn't think I was as bad as all that, and she didn't believe the masters would tell lies. Sometimes she wept to think that everything had been wasted. Sometimes she visited the headmaster or asked to see the master whose condemnation had been the least sympathetic. She became very nervous, and everything, it seemed, was on my account. I watched her staring at the floor with her chin cupped in the palm of one hand. It was as though she had seen a new sorrow. I made up my mind to say something, then I waited till the last cloud of mist had drifted outside the door. The room was almost clear again. I looked at the food and the table and finally at my mother. It was not only difficult but sometimes unwise to speak on these occasions, and I didn't know how to say I was sorry. Even when I felt a genuine guilt about something I had done I didn't know how to say I was sorry. I expected the other person to judge my feeling from the quality of my response. I was going to speak. She relieved her left hand by bringing the right up to the line of her chin. The room was clear of the mist and the silence passed when she spoke:

'You never miss the water till the well run dry,
'You never miss a mother till she close her eye.'

This was unbearable. She hadn't directed the words to me, but she spoke as though they would be applicable to me were I sensitive enough to understand. I got angry and confused and asked outright what I had done this time. I had committed another error. This time! She seized on the words like one who had been waiting for the wrong thing to be said. This time meant, I had never done anything at any time. I never did anything: and when people heard her voice raised it was simply because she was stupid and had nothing to do but wake up the whole neighbourhood. I wanted to give her a bad name. It was unfortunate I should have said 'this time.' I hadn't expected her to give the words such a meaning. She seemed to make them mean so much more than they said. Her hand had fallen from the chin and she was red in the face. It wasn't the first time I had regretted having spoken. I could expect the worst. "Course you think I have no right to speak to you,' she said. Her voice was raised so that it might be audible to the neighbour. 'You're a man now, but you better remember what the old people always say. What sweeten goat's mouth burn his tail. You can play man when you cross the sea tomorrow but not now. You're my child now, an' I don't care how old you be, once I'm alive you got to have the right and proper respect for me. If you grow to one hundred you're my child. So you just put that in your pipe and smoke it, and when you see the others playing man, an' doing as they please, just tell them you sorry, 'tis different with you, 'cause your mother ain't that sort o' woman. Let them know I don't play, an' that a child is a child for me. Nothing more an' nothing less.'

Now I had been bombarded with words. I sat silent waiting for the other silence to return, but it didn't seem my mother would be very brief. She spoke with a fluency and rapidity which were astonishing. There wasn't a break between the sentences, and sometimes I recognized what she said because I had heard it several times before. Although her accusations changed I didn't think there was much change in what she ever had to say. She hadn't stopped talking. Each silence was a breathing-space before renewing what she had said several times before. The room was quite clear again with the half-light filling the corners. The bowl and the plates gave off no steam. I watched the food and wondered whether I should start eating. This was always a difficult decision. It was likely that my mother might grow more exasperated if she thought I turned to the food because I didn't want to hear more of her. If the food grew cold she might charge me with not caring a damn that she had spent her time cooking all evening, I wasn't sure what I should do, and it wasn't likely she would start to eat first. I waited and then she spoke again, but her tone had changed. She wasn't apologetic. It seemed she was simply trying to make her position clear. She always did this. After she had tired of rebuking you, she went on to explain why she had to do what she did. Then she was very charming and you forgot what she had really said previously.

'I'm not sayin',' she said, 'I'm not sayin' at all there ain't going to come a time when you got to make your own decisions all by yourself, and then I can't have nothin' to say. But even then you got to respect me. 'Tis all I ask that you show me the right an' proper respect that a chil' should have for a mother, an' particularly you for me. I had no easy time bringin' you up. 'Tis all I ask you. Remember me an' you won't ever forget your respect for anybody else.' She had shifted her position in the chair and I knew she was looking at me, but I didn't want to return her glance. I thought I had had enough. Whether she was rebuking or explaining I told myself I had had enough of this and I wanted to find a way of escape. She had stopped speaking for a while, then she went on in the same tone. She told a story of someone who had caused the parents so much grief, and she said it was the parents' fault, but she wasn't going to let the same thing happen to her. When I left whatever I became no one would be able to say she hadn't tried. That's why she had taken to speaking at length and in this manner. I bent forward and held the spoon. She was still speaking, but I didn't listen. I poked the spoon into the food and the steam flew up like a spurt of water. She had stopped talking. Then she mumbled something which I didn't hear. I had taken the fork and was going to eat. The steam rose and I heard her mumble again, but I didn't look up because I didn't want my eyes to meet hers. She had raised herself from the chair and moved back towards the door. I watched her from the side, but I didn't want her to think I was noticing. Apparently she didn't want me to see why she had got up from the chair. She felt with one hand in the corner and when she turned I saw her standing over me with the stick raised. She held it like a fence, making the threat. I pushed the chair back and retreated. She came forward ready to strike. 'You think I'm 'fraid of you,' she said, 'or you think I makin' fun.' 'I know you're not making fun,' I said, and I was unsure what I should say next. But it did seem ridiculous. I was amused, but I couldn't laugh. She held the stick high. 'What right you have not noticing me when I'm speaking to you?'Tis the same thing I sayin'. What you take me for at all, tell me?'

'The food was getting cold,' I said.

'Let it get cold,' she rejoined. 'If I speakin' to you you have a right to pay me some attention.' She made an attempt to strike and I ducked. I caught the stick and held it tight while she tried to wrench it away. She was like a fencer who had the odds against her. I was taller and much stronger. She let go of the stick and turned to find another weapon. It was very amusing. The laughter burst from my throat and she returned to retrieve the stick. I let the stick fall on the table and she raised it again, coming forward.

'I not laughin',' she said, 'I not laughin' at all at all.'

'I'm not laughing either,' I said. 'I mean I'm not laughing at you.'

'How you mean you not laughin'?' she said. She kept the stick raised. 'What you laughin' at if you not laughin' at me?' She was insistent. 'You think you got tricks.' She had gained another inch. I was half-standing. ''Tis a long time I ain't hit you, but I'll let you have it good an' proper this evening if you give me cause to.'

She had relaxed. I made to sit down and she took a step back. She turned away and I giggled. She didn't hear and I tried to be serious. If I appeared defenceless I thought she mightn't want to strike. She placed the stick in the corner and returned to the table. She looked exhausted but I noticed she was about to break into a grin. I pretended not to see; suddenly the laughter burst again and she looked up. She too was laughing. I started to eat, and the steam rose from the plate. It was such a long time since she had threatened to beat me that the spectacle of her approaching me with a stick was almost ridiculous. At first I thought she was joking. Then I knew she was serious, and finally I wondered which was right. She was laughing quietly as she ate. The steam rose from the plate and it was almost dark in the room. I was still laughing, but she had turned serious again. I kept my head down to avoid her stare. 'I not laughin' at all,' she said; 'you think I laughin', but I not laughin' at all at all. An' if you think I makin' jokes I'll show you that you ain't too big for me to take your pants down and roast you tail alive.'

I stopped laughing because I wasn't sure that she wouldn't try what she had said. She had levelled the food on to her plate. I kept my head bowed and waited for the storm to pass. The steam from the food kept rising with each cut, and the light was getting darker. We would soon need better light. She cut and ate and I watched her small jaws move in a rapid up-and-down exercise. She ate very fast as though she wanted to get through and go on to something more important. We were both eating, easy and quiet.

'The trouble is,' she said looking up from the plate, 'the trouble is I give you too much rope, an' 'tis the same said rope you goin' to hang yourself with. But I not responsible. God in Heaven knows I not responsible; 'tis your own own life you got to live, and I suppose you can do what you like with it. I not goin' to bother myself further, take it from me.' After she had spoken it was quiet. We heard nothing but the occasional clang of the wares and a fine chewing sound of the food in the mouth. In the silence I could think of a way to appease her. She ate rapidly, without looking up, while I ate slowly, making little patterns with the food on the bottom of the plate. I piled small parcels of food into a little heap and then crushed it with the back of the fork. It looked like half-chewed food in the mouth. Occasionally she looked up to see how I had been getting on with the food. Suddenly she dropped the fork and leaned back in the chair. She kept her eyes on the plate. I thought I should say something.

'You said something happened,' I said. I made a noise with the fork against the plate as I spoke. She looked up from her plate as though I had surprised her. She brought her elbows down on the table and propped her face in her hands. I didn't look up because I didn't want our eyes to meet.

'You now remember to ask what happen,' she said. 'Well, that won't do for me. When I talk to you, you have a right to stop whatever you doin' and listen. 'Tis my privilege.' It seemed she was going to repeat all she had said before, but the difference was she was more at ease now she spoke. She felt I had realized what was wrong, and was making an effort to say I was sorry. I hoped she wouldn't say too much about her privileges.

'You said something,' I said again, and thought there was too strong a note of insistence in my voice. She didn't seem to notice.

'It ain't matter now,' she said, 'but if I didn't get back there in time you wouldn't have had a thing to eat the food with.' She took another mouthful and shifted her position in the chair. She was getting angry. "'Tis that same black cat again,' she said. 'It comes from wherever it come from, and only God knows who the owner is, but when I get back in the kitchen from the yard, there it was climbing on to the kitchen table to walk off with the fish I just finish frying. An' fish five for the bit.'

I laughed quietly and waited for her to continue. It was a great relief to know that I wasn't the target of her anger. She took another mouthful. 'It ain't nothin' to laugh at,' she said, "'cause I had five minds to break his back whoever it belong to. 'Twus only the hand o' the Lord that stop me, I tell you, or I would have let him have the piece o' walloba wood right across his back. 'Tis a high burnin' shame people can't get a thing to eat these days an' when they do try, that thieving wretch should come wherever he come from to walk off with it.'

The black cat which seemed to have no owner had been the plague of the village for several weeks. He was hardly seen in the day, but every morning there was a fresh complaint. Chickens were stolen as well as food which had been left from the day before. Some people thought they knew who the owner was, but they never said in public. It was believed that the owner was ashamed to say he owned the cat and had no intention of getting rid of it. Once some of the boys had set a snare which caught the cat, but he escaped when they were seen. They had taken him in a bag under one of the trees and were about to tie him up by his testicles when the old man Pa appeared. They ran and the cat fled in another direction. When the villagers heard, they didn't know whose side to take. The thought of the cat's death in that manner was horrible, but the thought of their losses was hardly more bearable. My mother couldn't bear the sight of that black cat.

'An' when I think to myself,' she said, 'that it is probably the last good meal I'll give you in this life my heart hurt me to think that that vagabond nearly walk off with my fish. 'Cause when you'll get a meal like this again only God knows.' She sat back in the chair and surveyed the room.

'I think they cook in Trinidad,' I said. I was uncertain of the result, but the strain between us had passed and I took the risk of speaking frankly. 'They cook all over the world,' she said, 'but 'tis how an''

what they cook. If you think cookin' is putting a pot on the fire an'
leavin' it till it tell you to come, you make a sad mistake. There be
people who eat all sort o' jumble up mess and they call it cookin' too.
An' once they got a hole in their face to stuff, they couldn't care less
what an' what they stuff it with. But if you think that's cookin' you
make a sad mistake.'

'I suppose they have their own kind of cooking,' I said. 'Those I
see look quite healthy, and when they come here to play cricket sometimes they win.'

''Tis a different thing,' my mother said, 'as far as I gather they eat
out in restaurant an' cook shop and only God knows what. But when
it comes to cookin' a good an' proper meal in their own own home
they don't know how to start. An' on the back of it, they call that
modern. That's what they say. They say they more modern than the
others in the other islands.'

'How do you know that?' I think my questions had become teasing.

'Ask Dave,' she said. 'You forget Dave just come back from there.
Let Dave tell you what an' what go on in that place. He say they're
nice people an' all that, but there be certain things he can't understand
at all at all. Most o' them, an' particularly the young ones, don't know
what an' what a home mean. If they want to give you a rippin' good
time, Dave say they'll never invite you home. They ask you to go to
the Chinese restaurant, or this hotel or that hotel, an' they eat their
guts full. But you never get one o' them to say come home, let my'
mother or my wife prepare you a meal. Never, never, Dave say. An'
you know full well 'tis just the opposite here. Here the first thing we
do to a stranger is give him something to eat home, an' no matter
how bad the old home look, you want him to eat something you cook
your own own self. 'Tis the opposite with them, an' all because they
got a generation o' damn lazy young women who can't do one God
blessed thing but expose themself in front a mirror an' go out like
a cat baitin' a rat. They don't know what the inside of a kitchen look
like. But they just sit on they backside all day whether or not they
workin', an' when night come they pick up their heels and go 'bout
they business. When they get in all hours o' the night, they askin' for
this, that an' the next as if they put down something. 'Tis what Dave
say 'cause he been down there four years and he knows who is who
and what is what.'

My mother sat forward in the chair and took a deep breath. This was her last chance to tell me all that she had heard about Trinidad, and her intention was to warn me against the pitfalls. This was perfectly natural, but I didn't understand how she had come by all this information. I had known Dave vaguely. He had joined the army and was stationed in Trinidad for some years. We never spoke for any length of time since his return, but one evening my mother told me she had been having a talk with Dave. It seemed this was when she got the information about Trinidad. She said Dave was reliable and since he was in the Army and had to go here and there he had learnt the place thoroughly.

"'Tis a thing I can't understand,' my mother said, 'the way we can be so different though we so near. Dave say, for example, they have a way of praisin' the things we won't hear 'bout for a minute. If a man is a thief, whether or not he's politician or priest, we won't forget to say what we think, and what we think won't be nice, but Dave say 'tis the other way round. They think a man a hero the bigger thief he is, and Dave say you can hear them sayin' now an' again, "Boy, that man know how to get away wid money," an' 'tis something they take a drink on. 'Tis something to make a joke 'bout.'

'I don't believe it,' I said. She didn't seem to respond.

'I say to myself it can't be true or how people live at all,' she said. 'Dave say it happen in all circles, not only the poor who may got a good cause for stealin'—though I think stealin' at any time is wrong—Dave say it happen in the highest places where you would expect if nothin' else a kind o' respect and honesty, 'cause the public watching you.'

'Did Dave say anything about the libraries?' I asked. I was very curious to know whether the libraries were as good as ours.

"'Tis that that take the wind out my sail,' she said. 'He say that one day he wus standin' in a certain library, an' a couple of English people come in, an' the lady turn to the gentleman an' say how pleasing the atmosphere was and the gentleman say, yes it's one o' the few libraries in the world that have everything except the books you want! An' in the same said library he say he know for a fact things that go on there could never happen here in Kirton's rum shop.'

'Dave has something against Trinidad,' I said. My mother was on the uptake.

'That's the thing,' she said. 'He likes it. He say he like it ten times more than he like here, but it got a kind of corruption which he couldn't stand, an' 'tis that make him come back. But he like his friends. He say if there's one place where people live an' let live 'tis Trinidad. 'Tis only the corruption that stink in some places that he couldn't stand.'

'What about the carnival?' I asked. Apart from the library there was nothing that excited my curiosity like the carnival.

'I was comin' to that,' my mother said. 'Dave say that if you see those people jump in the street like wild cats for two days, you think the devil horse kick you. They ain't got no care for nothing on this God's world, an' that kind o' playing hooligan go on for two whole God blessed days. They jump all 'cross the street as if some demon inside them get away, an' what an' what they don't do for those two days Dave say never happened.'

'I'm dying to see this carnival,' I said. I was glad she had spoken with Dave.

'Dyin' to see it,' she said. 'Well, I tell you something, the day I hear you jumpin' up in any street like a bloody hooligan, the day I hear—— Well, I tell you boy, I'll come for you if I got to walk the sea to an' fro. With the help o' the Lord I'll come for you.'

'But the law allows it,' I said.

'I have nothing to do with the law,' she said. 'The law is like the people who make it. I bring you up in the fear of God and the love o' your fellow-men. An' if after all that you come to tell me that you goin' to Trinidad to jump all 'bout the road like a lunatic, well I tell you I now see where all my time an' money gone, in Maxwell pond.'

'But I'll have to make friends,' I said. She had turned very serious.

'Which bring me to a next thing,' she said. 'This question o' company. Have a care the company you keep. Dave say since the Americans been there you don't know who is who. The Americans turn everything upside down. An' they make the decent indecent and the indecent decent, an' now you don't know who is a lady an' who ain't, for all the stories that going round. If they ever wus a judge o' character 'twus the yankee dollar, an' what some o' those women who play their foot can't touch earth, Dave say what some o' them didn't do wus what they didn't know. So you watch out. Everything in a skirt ain't clean. An' you know I always warn you 'bout your health. Nothin' frighten me more than what an' what can happen to a young boy who ain't know where an' where he pushing himself, an' when you're in a strange land you don't know who is who till you find out. You got

to think 'bout your health, that's all I got to tell you. You may say
I am a big botheration to you, but for all I know I may never ever
bless my eyes on you again, so I take this opportunity to remind you
o' one or two things. An' whenever you see temptation comin' your
way, just bear in mind all I tell you 'bout your health an' so on. I
won't put you wrong.'

'You don't know why Dave came back?' I asked.

'I don't know,' she said, 'but whatever happen to Dave he ain't the
only person I hear say,

> Trinidad is a nice place,
> But fire, fire down there.

'course I know there must be decent people there as they are all over
the world.' She dropped her head as though this wasn't quite so
important as the unpleasant facts. I was a little anxious to hear who
the decent people were, for it seemed Dave hadn't spared anyone.
Yet she said he liked it. I was surprised when she said that, and I was
getting a feeling some of the things he said must have been true. I had
a prejudice in favour of the library. I didn't think the comparison of
the library with Kirton's rum shop was a fair one. But she insisted
Dave had said things which she didn't care to repeat. She didn't know
which library it was because Dave hadn't said. I was at sea because
I didn't know which library I should avoid, and Dave said there were
several. I couldn't find out whether it was a public library, but Dave
had had no time to explain.

'I know people from Trinidad myself,' she said, 'and there be people
who nobody could ask to trot. They're proper and respectable as any
here, but I only warn you 'cause I know you. An' you have a way of
behavin' as if you don't have sense. The hell an' botheration you cause
me at the High School won't ever let me forget, an' I tell you I get
to know you as never before. If you're left all on your own not the
devil in hell self can keep up with you, 'cause all you want is a little
encouragement, an' it don't matter what they encourage you to do. If
they tell you do good you'll do better than all o' them put together,
and if they tell you do bad you do worse than all them put together,
'cause you seem to me a kind o' machine that ain't got no brakes, an
when you start you don't know how or when to stop. That's why I
take this last chance the good God give me to try an' call you to your
senses, 'cause 'tis never too late to save a soul.'

'This was very good,' I said, finishing the meal. I smacked my lips and smiled.

'If they ask you what you eat at home you can tell them,' she said. She wanted to smile but she didn't. She got up and closed the door. What would I tell them I wondered. I had seen the last of the meal disappear through the hole in my face. I sat quiet thinking on what she had said.

'You mustn't say,' she said, 'you mustn't say I say. Don't say your mother say anything 'bout Trinidad, 'cause as I say I meet many o' them who nobody here could ask to trot. I know for a fact 'tis so.'

'The meal was very good,' I said. She seemed very pleased to hear that.

'You think they know how to turn cuckoo down there?' She had hardly finished speaking before she cleared the table and swept out of the room. The plates were piled on top each other. She put the glasses one in the other and placed them on the plates, while she carried the jug in the other hand. The room was clear of the steam but the darkness had come on. There were four pieces of furniture in the room including a large larder with netted wire that filled the spaces between the wood. It stood in one corner with dishes and other wares on top. These were the things we never used except on very special occasions. The wares which my mother had just cleared from the table had been taken from the top of the larder, but this was the last big meal that she would be giving me for a long time, so she had treated it as a special occasion. They would be washed and put back till Christmas or Easter or the unexpected arrival of an old friend. There were cups and saucers on the larder which I could never recall her using. This meal had been an occasion. Judging from what she had said it wasn't likely I would eat the same kind of food in Trinidad. I didn't know what food they ate except a vegetable muddle called callalloo cooked with crab. I liked to catch crab, but eating them didn't strike me as an altogether pleasant pastime. It seemed I had a chance of introducing a new dish to that island. Even if they knew cuckoo it wasn't likely from all my mother said that they would know how to cook it.

In the first place they didn't have flying fish in their seas, and cuckoo wasn't cuckoo if it weren't prepared with flying fish. It was a common question in the village. If someone asked whether the other was cooking cuckoo, the answer came back, 'What I going to eat it with?' You expected this answer when flying fish were out of season. During the flying fish season, the question would simply have been, 'Have you any corn meal? Lend me some.' But we had eaten cuckoo with flesh other than flying fish and I didn't see why I couldn't try preparing the meal with some other kind of fish.

I recalled what I had seen her do before the meal could be considered finished. I didn't want to ask her, so I remained silent in the early dark, arranging the order of the meal. Earlier I had seen her sifting the corn flour and it seemed a very tedious undertaking. It was a yellow powder almost as fine as dust. Before it had passed through the sieve there were lumps and bits of extraneous stuff that belonged to the sack from which the shop-keeper had taken it. My mother had sifted it till the powder fell on to the plate leaving the lumps at the bottom of the sieve. It formed a pointed little heap on the plate with a slope from top to bottom. Meanwhile she had kept the fire going under the pot that contained the water. The water boiled and she added the ochroes which had been cut into thin round slices. Slicing the ochroes was almost as painstaking as the sifting of the meal. The prickly surface irritated the skin, and the slices fell off on the hand in a slimy mess.

When the ochroes had been thrown in the pot the water quickly became a thick boiling slime. The flour remained in the plate on the table. Meanwhile she had put the slab of wood which we called the cuckoo stick to soak in a bowl of water. She left the pot open as the slime boiled. Then she took out half the water and slid the flour in very gradually. The mixture thickened and she applied the slab of wood. From now on the cooking took the form of a vigorous stirring. Occasionally she threw in the water to moisten the mixture. The flour quickly stiffened into a coarse mixture which mellowed and softened as the slime was thrown on. The stirring went on till the mixture in the pot had turned soft and without resistance to the cut of the stick across the surface. Then she removed the stick and scraped the cuckoo point downward and the lump of cuckoo gradually slid from her finger into the hearth. It was the surest test that the meal had been well stirred. She added the remaining portion of slime and left the food simmering in the pot. The cover was put on so that there was a wide-open space through which the steam rushed upwards. The mixture steamed while she prepared the fish. On the tables she had put out two plates. She removed the pot cover, and took half a calabash from the partition. She passed the calabash through the bowl of water, wiped it and then used it to scoop the cuckoo from the iron pot.

It was a delight to watch her serve the food on to the plate. She filled the half calabash and shook it sideways before turning the mixture onto the plate. The steam rose in a thick pile from the calabash. Then she turned it face down and emptied the cuckoo onto the plate. On the plate the cuckoo looked like a fruit that had been pulped from the skin and left untouched. The calabash had given it a smooth even curve all round. It was like a visitor waiting to be shown in. Then she applied a thin paste of butter. The heat melted it and the mixture seemed to shine. The ochroe seeds were a dull pink and all over the surface of this curve you could see them pushing up like dots that decorated the mixture. Here and there were the bits of green that edged the slices of ochroe. Whether or not you liked to eat cuckoo it was something you could look at and feel a quiet satisfaction from. The colours were sharp in contrast. Yellow and pink and the green of the sliced ochroes. When you cut it the steam flew up so that the colours became indistinct. The steam rose like a white cloud over everything, and you waited till it passed and the colours of the cuckoo came out again.

The flying fish were a separate dish. You had to mix them later. She had the fish buckled in a plate and in the small blue bowl the seasoned gravy in which the fish had been soaked. With the wings and head removed the fish looked much smaller than usual. But these weren't wasted. The wings and head with the back and side bones were boiled and eaten on another occasion. Sometimes they were left overnight, but the black cat had cut a way through the kitchen and the plates were found empty next morning. My mother asked God to give judgement. The neighbour had told her to poison the bones and let them all be rid of the cat. She thought it over and decided she couldn't. God knew best.

'P'raps they can make this,' my mother said entering the room, 'but I don't think they can turn cuckoo down there. I don't think so at all at all.'

She was laughing like one who had sprung a surprise on his host. She swept the table cloth away and set the glass of ice cream before me. I understood why she laughed. . . . I knew she was cooking the cuckoo, but I hadn't been prepared for the ice cream. It was pink coconut cream with large black currants sticking out from the top.

She had flavoured it with essence of vanilla. I plunged the small spoon into the surface and watched the cream melt. I didn't like ice cream hard as I had seen others eating it. I chopped the spoon into it, scraped and turned till it had melted into a still cold pool. The currants floated on top like bits of burnt wood. I drank it slowly with a sucking noise. This meal was an occasion.

The light went on and the room was bright. The furniture showed up and from one corner the larder cast a shadow across the table. The netted wire in shadow across the table was like the bottom of the sieve. I had another glass of ice cream which I allowed to turn liquid. It was very quiet outside and the night through the spaces of the door was thick. My mother sat at the other end of the table with a sheet of paper and a pen. She looked much happier now bent over the table and reading the paper. I didn't know what it was and I didn't care to interrupt by asking. I wondered what I would do before going to bed. I had fulfilled all my appointments the night before and I was a bit exhausted. My mother had warned that I should go to bed as early as possible since one needed a special resistance for a plane flight. That is what Dave had said. I finished the ice cream and took another look at her. She had raised her head from the paper.

'This is the list,' she said. 'You can see for yourself what an' what clothes you got an' where an' where you can find them. When you reach Trinidad if there ain't nobody to do it you can take them out yourself an' put them on hangers. An' there ain't no need to rumfle them if you take them out as they stand. An' above all, for God's sake check by your list all the time.'

I understood what the paper meant. She remained seated revising the list. She had made it herself and made also brief instructions for finding what I wanted. Shirts . . . at the side. Suits . . . at the back. Handkerchiefs and underwear . . . at the bottom. It was very simple. But there were certain odds and ends which she had omitted and she was making this an opportunity to include them. She read the list carefully while I watched her. I played with the glass on the table as an object to which I could turn if she suddenly looked up. The exercise book was still on the floor under the chair and I thought for a moment I should re-read the diary. I might have made another note about the list she had made. I was very touched by this methodical sense she showed. Everything had to be in order, and she made it easy for you to keep order. Bent over the list in the light I had a chance to see her well. Her hair was long and thick falling in black coils round her face, and in her steady concentration she was like a recluse. I preferred seeing her in this attitude. When she rebuked she grew red in the face and the hair flew wild like leaves in the wind. Now she was very still. Her small eyes winked quickly and briefly and her hands which were small but strong shook when she put her weight on the elbows.

I tried to remember what she was like before I left the village school, but nothing was clear to me. I remembered she had grown thin after I entered the High School. Her neck was small and the collar bones were prominent so that a space like shallow saucers had formed between the bones and the shoulders. The line of her mouth was sharp and her expression had hardened into a schoolmaster's rebuke. But when she laughed her austerity disappeared like a mask which had been removed. Her laugh was clear and loud and long like a fowl's cackle, and her face lit up. Her face could change colour very quickly, from its ordinary half pallor when nothing was happening to a flaming red when she was angry or excited. She had never lost the fine brown freckles which were hardly visible. Her nose was like a brief index finger pointing downwards, sharp and straight and strong. I recalled shortly after my ninth birthday she had taken me to see the doctor. A village carpenter had died of blood poisoning caused through a nail puncture in his foot. The woman who brought the news had also told us of another man who died from similar causes. It was the strangest coincidence that I should soon get punctured by a nail. I had been walking across broken shingles when it happened; and I swore by all the gods that my blood was poisoned. I had all the symptoms the woman had related, so I was taken to the doctor. He said the blood wasn't poisoned and my symptoms disappeared, but when we were leaving he asked what I would do when I grew up. I didn't know. I watched him with his short stiff hair like a pig's and his soft dark face, and it seemed appropriate to say I wanted to be a doctor. He told my mother to save her pennies, and then he added it was a pity I didn't have her skin. With my hair and her skin everything would be all right. I could get a permanent appointment at Barclay's Bank. We were all very pleased. I never wondered how my mother had come by her skin. She was what they called a very fair mulatto. I was brown.

She raised her head from the table and I let my eyes fall on to the glass. The list was longer than I had thought. She spoke something which I couldn't hear and I got up to see what the night looked like. I closed the door and went back to my seat. The room seemed brighter and cosier and I watched her closely again as though I had been looking for the last time at something I couldn't do without. The feeling came on, and then there was the image of the pebble under the grape leaf. I didn't want to encourage this, but it seemed impossible to escape it. She had bent over the list again and the light fell full on her. The face was beautiful in its quiet concentration. I wished she wouldn't talk till it was necessary to do so. She made a note with the pencil and looked up.

'Remember,' she said, 'you must keep an eye on the things all the time, 'cause you never know what happen in these places, an' you can't afford to lose one blessed thing. Dave say you never can tell what happen in the Customs. He had friends, Customs officers, an' he say they honest alright but there ain't no telling what an' what can happen.'

As she had said earlier it was her privilege to speak, but I would have preferred to watch her in her silent perusal of the paper. I thought it safer to let her have her way. She had returned to the paper.

'Two things I want to tell you,' she said, 'don't go 'bout drinkin' rum. 'Tis not only a wicked waste o' money, but it dangerous too, an' when you in a strange country you don't know who is who. Not that anybody will get it in their head to do you anything, but it just ain't the right an' proper thing to do. There's a right an' a wrong in every God blessed thing.' She made another note on the paper and looked up. I dropped my head and looked at the glass. I turned it round so that the spoon made a noise at the bottom. 'An' above all,' she said, 'shake your pyjamas at night. Before you slip yourself in them give them two good an' proper shakes. Don't you ever get in your bed without giving them a shake 'cause Dave say they have all kind of snakes in that place.'

I laughed and she added quickly that she wasn't making fun. She had turned very serious and had started to say what and what would happen to me, if I didn't hear what she said. Then she related a story of a man who never took the trouble to see what he was wearing, and once at a big party when he wasn't expecting he had felt a centipede crawling up his pants.

'He was no use to himself afterwards,' she said and dropped her head. Outside the night had turned black and we couldn't see anything beyond the window. She went on checking the list and I watched her. The feeling had come again. The feeling you were seeing something for the last time. For a moment it seemed bigger and more penetrating than I had known it. At the sea in the morning and even in the intervening days I had expected this. I put it off because it was difficult to carry it long, but the things I did as a substitute reminded me most vividly of what I wanted to forget. There was a lump in the throat and a strange constriction of the muscles along the neck. The ice cream was finished and there was nothing to occupy my attention fully. I couldn't return to the exercise book. She gave me another piece of advice and another warning and started to re-read the list. It seemed she had forgotten to include something on the list which she had probably put in the trunk. She read it slowly. Then she interrupted with another warning. Bent over the table with her small bright eyes in a rapid sideways movement she was like a hen clucking the brood to safety. I saw the pebble and the sloping sand beneath the grape leaf. The village and Trumper and the first assistant. Yet the feeling seemed somewhat different now. With the others it was no less intimate and immediate, but somehow it seemed different. When I looked at her and the pebble came back the feeling was like being a tooth which had been taken from its snapped roots, leaving the gum a space to occupy the probing tongue. I was hoping something would interrupt. She remained bent over the table revising the list. I didn't know how many times she had read it. She put the pencil on the table and held the list up to the light. There were marks on both sides of the paper. Then she turned to speak, keeping her eyes on the list. I watched the glass as I listened.

'An' at the top of everything,' she said, 'I put the little book. I didn't put it with the other books in your box, 'cause I say to myself you might like to read it in the plane, an' 'twould be difficult to get at it. P'raps you might care to put it in your pocket. 'Tis safest there I'd say.'

'Which book?' I asked her. She hadn't looked up from the list. I hadn't been reading any little books except a small paper-bound copy I had seen on one of the shelves.

'The Gospels,' she said. ''Tis the little blue back paper-cover book with the gospels. I put it 'cause I always hear you readin' chapter fourteen o' St. John's Gospel. 'Twus only yesterday I hear you reading aloud to yourself.' She paused and looked up from the list. I kept my eyes on the glass. 'It please my heart to hear you readin' it,' she said, "cause although I hear the others say what they say 'bout you, that you don't believe a word of what the church stand for, I say to myself that if you can still find time to read that chapter as I hear you readin' it, I know you ain't turn an outright heathen yet. There's probably still a little room in your heart for what's worth while.'

I was hoping she would not linger on this subject. She was a convert of one of the evangelical bodies, and she regarded the salvation of a close relation as her special concern. Yet she was very considerate and never pressed me to join the church or attend the meetings. She said what she thought was right and wrong, and she told me I could choose. It seemed I hadn't chosen as she would have wished, but I never let her know what I might have thought about her choice. She never asked.

'You never ever tell me what an' what you believe,' she said, 'but I hear what an' what your best friends have to say. An' it don't please me at all at all. 'Tis the reason why that master at the High School didn't like you. Haynes come here the other morning an' he wus relating to the other boy what happen between you an' the master, an' I wish I wus there to put you in your place. When the master ask the class whether they believe in God you had to get up with your mannish self an' say, "Gentlemen, let sleeping dogs lie." ' She paused and I wondered what this would lead to.

'Had I known it before I would have cut your tail, I tell you.'

I offered no resistance. There was silence. If I attempted no answer in my defence the storm would pass. I kept quiet. She remained still looking at the list. Then she folded it and put it on the table before me.

'I'll keep the little book in my pocket,' I said. She hadn't raised her head, but her manner had changed. She seemed more at ease.

"'Tis a good chapter,' she said, 'John 14. Let not your heart be troubled.' She had taken the pen from the table. In the silence it fell from her hand. Then she spoke, and the new quality in her voice brought on the feeling more intensely than I had known it. I kept my eyes on the glass. 'Let not your heart be troubled: ye believe in God, believe also in me. In my Father's house are many mansions: if it were not so, I would have told you. I go to prepare a place for you. And if I go and prepare a place for you, I will come again and receive you unto myself; that where I am, 'there you may be also.'

The tears had tumbled past her lips and on to the paper. There was a knock on the door. She wiped her face and went out.

'Gracious goodness!' my mother shouted. Then she called to me. There was a low laugh like a male grumble, a sudden silence and then my mother shouted, 'God bless my eyesight!' She called again. Then the other voice spoke, and I rushed from the table to make sure I had recognized it. It was Trumper. There was a sudden silence as though we had seen the worst or the best. Then the laughter rang through the house. My mother was beside herself with excitement. One or two boys who had followed Trumper to the house remained outside staring. They couldn't understand what the fuss was all about. My mother wiped her face and stared at us. Trumper was smiling. A big, confident, self-assured smile. His assurance puzzled me.

'When did you get here?' I asked him. He held his head back as though he were uncertain of the hour. I noticed his clothes and was even more puzzled.

'This mornin' 'bout eleven-thirty,' he said. His voice was deeper, and he spoke more slowly and with greater care. The accent hadn't changed. 'Just in time,' I said. I didn't know whether he knew that I would soon be leaving. My mother was about to speak. I could trust her to break the news. 'I know,' said Trumper. 'You're leaving to-morrow.' I didn't know how he felt but he seemed to treat it as a perfectly natural occurrence. It was as though people left every day, every week, every year. He showed no surprise. 'What a pity you didn't come a minute ago,' my mother said. 'You could have got something in your stomach.'

'I'm alright,' Trumper said. 'I been eatin' too much these last few days.'

I wanted to laugh. I couldn't imagine Trumper eating too much, and it was almost a kind of revelation to hear him refuse. My mother seemed puzzled too although she knew there wasn't anything to give him. Although we were always told to say no, we hadn't been used to an actual refusal. My mother laughed, and Trumper went on smiling. Big, confident and self-satisfied.

'Well, sit down an' tell us somethin',' my mother said. 'How you spend your time. What you do an' so on. You must have a lot to tell.' She bombarded him with questions and the smile broadened. He gave her his hat and sat in the best chair. I sat opposite while my mother remained standing against the sill. I watched him closely as he sat back in the chair smiling. He looked happy and prosperous. My mother closed two windows and the room seemed cosier and brighter. She returned to the window and remained standing.

'I see one or two things change round this joint,' Trumper said. He turned serious as though he didn't like the change. It was astonishing how rapidly expressions changed in the village. He smiled again as my mother spoke.

'What joint?' she asked. She didn't understand joint. Trumper laughed.

'I mean the village,' he said. We smiled and Trumper understood. One or two words had changed for him, and it was only when he used these words that one detected a change in the manner of speech. My mother laughed and repeated joint. She seemed quite fascinated by the word joint as a substitute for the village. We wondered how many new words Trumper would use.

'Well, tell us something 'bout America,' my mother said. She remained standing against the sill watching Trumper smile. Each time she spoke the smile broadened, and it seemed that each time he was about to speak she put a new question. She was insistent and Trumper seemed to enjoy it.

'We hear so much 'bout America,' she said, and drew a chair. We were all seated. Trumper drew his legs up and put his hands over the back of the chair. He never stopped smiling. Sometimes my mother laughed aloud.

'There ain't much to say,' said Trumper, 'except that the United States is a place where a man-can-make pots-of-money.' The smile broadened and he sat back throwing his legs out. My mother waited anxiously to hear how they made the money. She was always suspicious of people who made a lot of money.

''Course 'tis what they all call high life,' said Trumper. 'Seems a next kind o' world. When I tell you I use to have two telephones and three 'lectric fans in a small place o' mine, you can sort o' get my meanin' clear.'

My mother bent forward with her mouth open. In the village we classified people according to their possessions. If a boy had a bicycle we knew what sort of parents he might have, and people with telephones and electric fans were automatically called the Great. The landlord would have those things. My mother waited for Trumper to continue. He was enjoying it. 'Things goin' on all the time over yuh head an' under yuh foot,' said Trumper, 'an' if you come from a small place like this you sort o' don't know where you is sometimes. Nothin' ain't small in the United States.' He paused and drew his legs up. My mother kept her mouth open. "'Tis p'raps the only place in this God's world where there ain't got night an' day,' Trumper said. 'In the-united-states you-dont-know when-its-night-or-day.'

'Are you going back?' I asked him. It seemed a stupid question. But I found it difficult to make questions because there was an assurance about Trumper that silenced me. He didn't seem to think the question silly.

'I-want-to-go-back to-the-united-states,' he said, 'but I-want-to-go-in-a-sorto-different circumstances if you know what-ah-mean. I want-to-go sort-of-on-my-own.'

Whenever he spoke about the United States he quickened his speech, and the words followed without a break as though the whole sentence were a single word. But the syllables were distinct and we understood him. My mother looked very serious now. She didn't seem to like the sound of America. I was expecting her to tell Trumper to make his peace with God and settle down to a quiet life in the village. He went on speaking about America and the other boys he had seen there. My mother and I took a look at his clothes and he knew we were looking at him. He kept smiling. He wore a thin brown suit with a bright tie and suède shoes. The jacket was long and deep and the pants were very narrow at the bottom and unusually wide at the knees. I wondered how he got his foot through the bottom of the pants. He was wearing a silver chain round his wrist and on the lapel of the jacket a small badge with stars and stripes. We looked at him well.

'You really look sweet,' my mother said, and he laughed. He sat in the chair, easy, almost nonchalant, and sometimes it seemed to me he had all the answers for any questions you would ask. He was still smiling a lazy, prosperous smile. Sometimes he turned serious, but suddenly the smile had come back and you hadn't noticed the change. It happened twice and I thought it strange. I wondered whether there mightn't be something unpleasant going on in his mind. He was smiling now.

'You don't know when you'd go back?' my mother asked.

'I don't know,' he said, 'but I want-to-go-back different. The emigration scheme might be all right for some people, but it don't give you a kind of freedom you want.' My mother didn't understand what more Trumper could want. He looked healthier than she had ever known him.

'An' I like to do as I please when I please,' he said. 'I like to be free.'

My mother didn't press for an explanation, but I saw she was puzzled. I wanted to ask something, but I wasn't sure what I wanted to ask. At times it seemed difficult for me to make conversation. Trumper seemed so different from the person I had known. I wanted to find out what this new person was. He slouched back in the chair and his legs slid forward. We could see the cut of the pants. I didn't understand how he got his legs through the narrow space at the bottom. He looked very much like the well-to-do at the annual exhibition. My mother went on saying how pretty everything was. She commented on the handkerchief in his pocket, and she liked the way he kept his collar. Nothing pleased her more than a collar that was spick and span.

'How you feel the first time you see the place?' she asked.

'I wus sea-sick couple-days,' Trumper said. 'So I didn't see the place from the sea, but I hear the rest talkin' 'bout the statues o' liberty an' all the rest. 'Tis one thing 'bout statues, you know, they make a place look like if the people who live in it really belong to it. 'Tis a funny thing the way those statues make me feel.' He drew up his legs and smiled. 'But the first night I walk down Broadway,' Trumper said, 'that wus something out o' this world. I don't exactly recall what kind o' feelin' I had, but nothing seem real to me. 'Tis one thing you always feel 'bout America. Although everything goin' on round you for you to see, nothing still seem real. There wus just light an' light an' more lights. I start to get a headache when the lights go on an' off till nothin' seem but one set of light. An' the noise! When I tell you noise, boy, I mean noise. If America is anything in this world, 'tis a country o' noise. People, motor car, aeroplane, bus, train, everything mornin' noon an' night seem to talk an' talk; an' if there's one sort o' talkin' machine you can't control, 'tis the American woman. When a American woman start to talk not even the dead can count themself safe. That first night I walk an' walk an' when I couldn't stand the noise no more I get in a vehicle and drive back to my camp. When the car stop, I'd land up some two hundred miles from the camp. They couldn't find me for two days.'

My mother laughed and wiped her eyes. Trumper was amused by his recollection of the first night. He made himself more comfortable in the chair and continued:

'America make you feel,' he said, 'it make you feel that where you been livin' before is a kind of cage. Then there's a lot of loose livin', an' girls in galore. Sometimes you only got to snap your finger so, snap, an' you see a beauty tellin' you to get in. No trouble at all at all.'

'Get in where?' my mother asked. She didn't like this aspect of America.

'Get in her car,' said Trumper. 'In America every woman got a car like civil servant with bicycle 'bout this place. An' when you get in a car, you don't know what happen next, 'cause you get up next mornin', God knows where, with your eyes comin' out your head. An' it ain't cost you one cent. Believe it or not. People talk 'bout giving. Well, I tell you something. Americans is people who give like they ain't got no sense. If an American want to give you a good bigtime, the biggest biggest insult you can insult him is to put your hand in your pocket, saying you goin' help spend. They won't hear 'bout it. They spend money like little boys who ain't know what it mean not to have it. 'Tis a kind o' big bad habit.'

'Where they get all this money from?' my mother asked. She was curious.

'Work,' said Trumper. 'In America everyone work. Man, woman an' chil'. If nothin' else, America is a country o' work an' a country o' noise.'

'P'raps it make you feel quite lost here?' my mother said. 'It's so small.' The smile had disappeared and Trumper sat erect, serious. I had this feeling that there was something else he wanted to say. It was as though the talk about noise and lights was an attempt to obscure another issue. I didn't know what he had thought about the village. It had changed considerably since he left. The wood, the train lines: these had disappeared since Trumper's departure, and I had a feeling they affected him. I didn't know whether he had heard of the sale of the land. I didn't know what he would say. He was very quiet now, almost grave; and then I tried to speak.

'It's all been very sudden,' I said, referring to the village. 'The lines went first, then the wood. Now it's all talk about the land.'

My mother had broken her silence. She couldn't remain silent when the land was mentioned. It was like taking the name of the Lord in vain. 'We couldn't believe our ears,' she said, 'an' even those who read the paper don't sort o' understand what happen. 'Twus like an earthquake.'

'I suppose you can buy a spot?' I said. I was smiling. He was serious.

'I could if I want to,' he said, 'but I won't. I got something 'gainst doin' it. If you buy a spot then you make the people who sellin' it think they doin' the right thing, an' by Heaven I know they ain't doin' the right thing. I say to myself not one blind cent o' mine.'

My mother was serious at first, but when Trumper finished the last sentence she laughed aloud. Trumper remained serious. He had strong feelings about the land. I didn't know what I should say because my feelings were still confused. When I heard the land was sold something happened to my thinking, and I didn't think I had quite recovered. But I understood how Trumper felt.

'Yet it's a question of buy or go,' I said. I wanted him to speak further on the matter. My mother seemed very anxious to hear him.

'You think they dare move all these houses?' he asked. 'If every one o' you refuse to pay a cent on that land, and if all o' you decide to sleep in the street or let the Government find room for you in the prison house, you think they dare go through with this business o' selling the land?' He was angry now, and I thought I heard him utter an obscenity. My mother held her head down listening. She didn't know what to think about Mr. Slime, but she seemed to think there was sense in what Trumper had said.

'And above all, they want to send the old man Pa to the Alms House.'

'What?' my mother was shaken. She had brought her head up quickly and stared at Trumper. Then she said in a kind of despair it wasn't true.

'The Alms House,' said Trumper. ''Tis a place he would never ever go on his own accord in this life. He wus too decent, Pa. Slime couldn't look Pa in the face if it's a question o' dignity we talkin' 'bout. But that's life. 'Tis the way o' the world, an' in a world o' Slimes there ain't no way out for those who don't know how to be slimy.'

''Tis really hard,' my mother said, keeping her stare on the ground.

'Hard ain't the word,' said Trumper. 'There be times when it seem a kind o' crime. Nothing more or worse than a nasty crime.'

'You mustn't say that,' my mother said. ''Tis what Job says too, but he wus wrong. There's always a way out if you wait an' pray.'

'I tellin' you,' said Trumper. 'I just back from the United States of America an' I know. There be people there in the hundreds o' thousands who would have give anything not to get out their mother's guts.'

His manner had changed greatly. My mother didn't contradict although she knew he was wrong, and I knew she felt the change that had come over him. For a while we were silent, thinking about the land. In the last few days there was hardly anything worth talking about but the land. It was the topic at all times and in all places. At the open-air meeting the preacher had used it as the basis for a sermon. They had said prayers in the big church for those who might be gravely inconvenienced by the change. The villagers met at the street corners and in the shops, and always the question was the same. How you goin' to manage, chil'? If I could only move the old house I would, but I know it ain't strong enough. It ain't safe for me neither. So and so tell me to sell an' get the few cents an' then go live somewhere else. But where you goin' at this age? How long you been here? Only God in Heaven knows. I born an' find the ol' house there an' I's nearly sixty. I wus tryin' to move mine but I don't see how I'll put it up again. But why they sell it at all when they know what would happen to we? Four hundred dollars, they say. And with interest, p'raps five hundred. You think anybody'll ever be able to pay it off? I don't know. I wonder what'll happen in the end? I don't know. Boysie start to drink, he say he can't stan' the thought. An' look how the shoemaker change. Who you think responsible for all this? I don't know. Bye-bye, chil', see if you get any more news. Land is botheration, chil'; 'twus so from the beginning o' the world. God make His big mistake when He turn to the earth. 'Tis the only flaw in creation. You mean the land. Yes, the land. Oh the land!'

'So you leavin' tomorrow,' said Trumper. ''Twill be a good change.'

My mother had left the room. She had related two stories about the land and we had a hearty laugh, but Trumper's manner hadn't changed. He remained as he did. We were all involved in the sale of the land, but Trumper was the first person who had given me this feeling of tremendous injustice in the transaction. I had no particular feelings about Mr. Slime. He had taught me at the village school, and as far as I could remember he seemed perfectly decent. I didn't know what had happened since he left the school. He might have changed. But Trumper spoke with an almost criminal contempt of Mr. Slime, and my mother was puzzled. She had known Mr. Slime, too, and she didn't see the matter in this light. She became suspicious. Trumper had done something to give us a new slant on the sale of the land. We were

worried about what would happen to our spot, and we had even dis-
cussed the possibilities of buying it. My feeling had changed, and
my mother was less certain. Mr. Slime had become suspect. Trumper
had no doubt. He felt contempt for the very name. His face registered
the disgust it evoked. 'I don't know much 'bout Trinidad,' he said,
regaining his composure. 'But you might got to go further one day
an' there be quite a few things you got to learn. The things you got
to learn in this life you never see and will never see in the books
you read at that High School. 'Tis p'raps what the ol' people call
experience, but take it from me, barring learning to count an' write
your name there ain't much in these schools that will help you not to
make a blasted mess o' your life when you get out in the world. You
can count on that from me.'

'What do you think about Mr. Slime?' I asked. I wanted to hear
him further on the land. Perhaps I wanted to form an opinion myself.

'I don't have to think much 'bout him,' said Trumper. 'An' I not
at all surprised that he do what he do. 'Tis what I learn in the States,
an' I know how to handle all the Slimes that come my way. Way back
he promise that he'd make these people here owners o' this land. He
tell them there wasn't nothing to prevent them buying this lan', and
he wus right, 'cause I know for a fact that the very money that go in
that Penny Bank an' Society buy this land in his name. That's what I
know. Nothin' he do ain't surprise me.'

'There are others involved,' I said. 'I know some of them.'

''Course there is,' said Trumper. 'There's always more'n one in
this kind o' deal. They ain't surprise me. The man who set me thinkin'
is the landlord. I don't quite understan' why he take that risk. He take
a good risk.'

'What risk?' I didn't see any risk in the sale of the land.

'The risk he take,' said Trumper. 'There ain't no reason under the
sun why he should 'ave sell this land to Slime.'

'I don't understand what you mean by risk,' I said. 'I don't see any
risk.'

'I don't know,' said Trumper. 'P'raps I use the wrong word. You
call it what you like, but why the landlord sell that land to Slime we'll
find out one day. But remember this: this world is a world o' camps,
an' you got to find out which camp you're in. And above everything
else keep that camp clean.'

This was all very cryptic. I hadn't understood the risk. But Trumper was confident in his supposition. He didn't explain and I decided to leave it at that. He stood beside the chair turning his hands about his pockets. My mother returned to the room and closed another window. The night was thick.

'We goin' take a little stroll,' said Trumper. 'If you don't mind, I mean.' My mother shook his hand and said good-night. I walked ahead through the door and down the steps, and he followed close behind.

The gas lamps at the cross roads weren't lit, but there was a light in one of the shops and light flickered through the windows of one or two of the houses. The sky was like a big black canvas hoisted over everything. The moon was under cloud and the stars were hidden. The darkness had come on early and it had thickened quickly. We walked side by side in silence. It was Trumper who suggested that we should walk, and I waited for him to say something. There was low talking in some of the houses and in the distance the sound of several voices raised in singing. There weren't any children in the street, but it might have been the village choir in training for the Easter competition. They had changed their headquarters from the shoemaker's shop to a spare room under the grocer's shop in the main road. Until recently they met at the shoemaker's in the part of the building he used as his living quarters. But since the news of the land and particularly since the notice he had been given he was hardly seen. No one knew whether he was going to move the shop, or whether he had been planning to purchase a spot of land elsewhere in the village. But the choir had taken up a new training centre. The voices stopped abruptly and were suddenly raised again. Beyond the houses and towards the house on the hill the blackness was bare. In other days there would have been the shapes of trees to give you your bearings, but we knew the village and there was no danger of taking the wrong road.

I didn't know where Trumper intended going, but I guessed that we might have walked through the roads and finally had a drink at Kirton's. It wasn't likely that we would have time for a similar walk before I left. Trumper's shoes were making a creaking sound as though they were new. Occasionally we stumbled over a shallow ditch where the surface of the road was worn, but no rain had fallen and no pools were formed. There were several such ditches. The boys made them with their bats or the sticks they used as a wicket at cricket. The light in the shop went out and the night seemed thicker. The streets were empty but for stray animals, mostly cats scampering between the fences on opposite sides of the road. I wondered whether the black cat was anywhere around, and I had a feeling I might get Trumper to co-operate in trapping him. I wanted to suggest it, but Trumper hadn't spoken and I felt uneasy. Ever since we mentioned the land his manner had bewildered me. I thought I had seen the clue to his letter although I didn't know what the clue was. We passed Mr. Foster's house and Pa's, but there wasn't any noise inside. In Pa's house the lamp burnt low and the window where he sat was still open but we saw no one. I had a feeling he had fallen asleep. We reached the track where the train lines were once laid and Trumper raised his feet high in anticipation. Then he brought one leg down in a jolt and we laughed. I didn't know whether he had forgotten that the lines were taken up, or whether he was trying to be funny. It was the first time he had made any noise since we left the house. I didn't know what Trumper was thinking, but he had taken this change in the village very seriously. We had felt it too, but no one had shown the same kind of concern. Most of the villagers didn't know what to say. They talked incoherently, patching together thousands of rumours. There were some who didn't believe Mr. Slime had bought the land. A new Mr. Slime had been invented, and for days the rumour went around. The new landlord wasn't the politician. The rumour didn't last. Some of them had seen Mr. Slime, but nothing had been forthcoming. He had arranged to speak in public on the fate of the village. It seemed there were still plans going ahead for their safety. But on the whole they were hopeless and bewildered. I wasn't sure that Trumper's bitterness hadn't started before we talked about the land. Although he had profited greatly by living in America, he had been very critical. My mother couldn't understand whether he wanted us to believe that America was a good place or a bad place. We were simply glad to see him again.

A cat crossed us and scurried through the bush. Then there was a scream and it seemed the cats were at their fun again. Trumper made a noise which seemed more like a grunt than a noise. He said something about the cats and the frogs and the night we had entered the landlord's yard. I was glad he had started to talk. We entered the path that led to the landlord's house, and he was quiet again reminiscing, I thought, on the past. Once there was a wood where we walked, thick and cool in the afternoon. The trees blinded you to everything beyond

the landlord's house. Now there wasn't a tree left. The space was
open, bare and black. On a hill a light came from the landlord's house,
but there was no light in the yard. It was later than I had thought. I
wondered what the landlord was thinking about the land. No one
had heard much of him. No one knew how he felt except perhaps the
old man Pa. He told the others that the old woman had seen him
before she died, and he had talked with her. They knew he would sell
the land, but they didn't expect it would have happened so suddenly.
The old woman hadn't lived to see. Trumper didn't speak. There was
a time when we walked together in a similar way, unspeaking but
taking note of each other's physical responses. But that was different.
The High School had done that. But there was a sense in which the
village had restored what the High School had destroyed. This silence
was quite different. It had nothing to do with the High School.

We reached the road which marked the boundary of the village, and
we stood wondering which route we should take. It was much livelier
here. The street lights were on and the buses were passing up and
down. This was the main road from which the village stretched to
meet Belleville on the other side. It was really the boundary of the
village, but it had become a part of the village like any of the other
roads which were the property of the landlord. At a public stand
people were filling buckets with water. They collected round the
pipe pushing and shouting. Occasionally someone shouted that it
would be better to make a queue so that they might fill the buckets
more quickly. They agreed and pushed more fiercely. No one knew
whose turn it was. The buckets wrangled in the scramble, and the
voices yelled and the water made its noisy spurt against the ground.
When they placed the buckets under the pipe, three or four at the same
time, the water skidded off the sides and flew in a thick spray over
their heads. It was ugly but amusing. We stood on the other side and
watched. Trumper didn't speak. The policeman arrived and there was
an instantaneous silence. The pushing ceased, and they lined up one
behind the other. Then there was a low grumbling and above it the
splash of the water in the bucket. They were getting things done. The
policeman turned away and entered the shop and the shouting rose
again. He returned to the scene and the silence was complete.

We walked ahead towards the rum shop. Trumper said something
about Kirton still going strong. We walked up the steps and entered the
shop. It was almost deserted. Trumper pushed back a chair and asked

me to sit. We sat in the small room where as boys we had seen the village teacher enter. It was a kind of reserved place for those who bought the better brand of rum, or those who didn't want to be seen on the other side. I didn't think Trumper cared which side of the bar we used, but there weren't any chairs on the other side. The men who went on that side never sat to have their rum. They asked for it in a small glass, and threw their heads back tossing the liquor down the throat. Then some of them ate a pepper, made an ugly, twisted face from the burn of the pepper and called for another rum. There was no time for sitting. We sat at opposite ends of the table, and Trumper took off his hat and put it on a chair. The man brought the rum and we tilted the glasses. This was a farewell drink. Trumper sipped the rum and set his glass down on the table. He was going to speak. I took a sip of the drink and waited.

'You don't know much 'bout politics?' he asked. He looked me straight in the face as though he wasn't sure I would answer truthfully. It seemed a strange question.

'What do you mean?' I asked him. He seemed as puzzled.

'How you mean what I mean?' he said. 'You got education better than me.'

'I know what politics means,' I said, 'but I don't understand what you mean.'

'I mean what I mean,' he said. 'There's a kind o' big game which go on in public.'

'I don't know it as a game,' I said. 'That's why I asked you what you meant. It calls for a kind of responsibility which I wouldn't like to undertake.'

'You really won't?'

'Of course,' I said. 'I don't like the idea of being responsible to hundreds of people. It frightens me the thought of being called on by every Tom, Dick and Harry to explain why I did something.'

He sipped the drink and set the glass on the table. One of the lights went out, and the room was half dark.

'You got a lot to learn,' said Trumper. 'Time wus I had a right an' proper respect for certain people. But now my head get giddy with a kind o' big confusion. There be only one thing I sure 'bout under the sun, an' that I'll tell you in a minute or two. There be things you got to learn.' His eyes were getting brighter. I took another sip of my drink.

'There be people who always get hurt,' he said, ''cause they got all sorts o' ideas 'bout this life except the right ones. An' it ain't their fault. There's a part o' those people which can't sort o' cope with what you call life. That's what I was trying to say in my letter. 'Cause I know you be one o' those people. This business 'bout a thing be what you make it an' think it is. 'Tis all well an' good for the nursery. It won't do for what we call life.' He sipped the drink and wiped his face. The drink was having its effect. 'I know a man in the States wus like that,' he said. 'He had one funny theory 'bout politics. Said you should leave politics to certain people, 'cause there wus other things to worry 'bout. He had a kind o' theory that the politics only belong to one place and that politicians couldn't do much for the real man. He use to use a phrase I never ever forgot. Says the politics has to do with one external relations. 'Twus his phrase: external relations. Things like shopping, buyin' this, an' payin' for that. Politics wus these things, a kind o' high-grade housekeeping. Every politician had a little o' the housekeeper in him, he say. But these things wus all external relations as he say. They didn't have nothin' to do with people like you an' me and he an' she. Then he give illustration. I have shoemaker an' tailor an' grocer an' such people who do things for me, but apart from my size an' measurement an' my appetite he say these people ain't know nothin' 'bout me. An' 'twus the same with the politics. 'Twus a kin' o' shoemaker and tailor an' housekeeper all put together. 'Twus external.'

He drained the glass and signalled the bartender to refill them. I was very interested in what he had said. He had wiped his face again.

'The last I hear o' him,' said Trumper, 'he wus in a home for dypsos. He take to the bottle an' now he's a gonner.'

'Why did he take to the bottle?' I asked.

'Things wusn't as he see it,' said Trumper, 'an' he get hurt. He get a shock one time an' he never recover. He wus like a monk with a rotten cock who ain't know how he come by the said same infirmity.'

Another light went out in the shop and it turned dark in the room. The bartender had refilled the glasses. We knocked the glasses and set them on the table. The bartender came over to say that it was closing time, but if we cared he would close the doors and let us stay for another few minutes.

'We'll finish this an' have another for the road,' said Trumper.

I drank quickly, and the bartender came over with a bottle from which he filled the glasses. Another light went on in the room. Trumper was feeling inside his jacket pocket.

'I'll show you something before you go,' he said. ''Tis my little box.'

He took the small box from his pocket and set it on the table. It was the size of a box camera with two knobs to the front and a wire running back to front on all sides. Trumper touched a piece of wire and a light went on in the box. I took a look inside at the small intricate mechanism of wires and bulbs and switches. Trumper turned the plug and there was a click, then a low spooling wheeze and finally music. We sat silent and listened to the music. It was a Negro spiritual sung by several voices. I knew the tune but I couldn't remember the title of the words. The singing lasted three or four minutes, and then there was another click, and the low spooling wheeze repeated. At the side the light had registered one, and Trumper turned another switch and the light registered two. Another spiritual was sung. This was a solo and the voice was a woman's. Trumper hadn't spoken and I didn't care to interrupt. I thought I would ask him about the spirituals later. This solo went on for about five minutes and then we heard the click and the spool and the light registered three. It was very fascinating. We took another sip of the drink, and the bartender came over to hear the music. He was very excited and it seemed he wanted to call Mr. Kirton, the proprietor, but Trumper interrupted him. The man remained behind the counter watching the small box. Then Trumper turned the plug, and it was time to hear the third piece. The spool went on longer than it had with the other two. Trumper sipped his drink and set the glass down firmly on the table. 'This is my favourite piece,' he said. 'An' the singer my favourite singer.'

The spool finished and the music followed low and sad at first but rising gradually to a kind of ecstasy. Then the music thinned out and a voice came through deep and beautiful in its controlled resonance. Trumper sat steady, his head bowed close to the box. I had never heard anything like it before. I couldn't remember this spiritual, but I was more concerned about the voice. I tried to follow the words, but I couldn't, and then Trumper started to speak them through the singing. It seemed even more beautiful. There was the click and the light at the side which registered the numbers went out. The singing was at an end, but Trumper went on reciting the words in a low, grave voice. I tried to memorize them as he spoke:

Let my people go.

'I like it,' I said. 'That was really very beautiful.'

'You know the voice?' Trumper asked. He was very serious now. I tried to recall whether I might have heard it. I couldn't.

'Paul Robeson,' he said. 'One o' the greatest o' my people.'

'What people?' I asked. I was a bit puzzled.

'My People,' said Trumper. His tone was insistent. Then he softened into a smile. 1 didn't know whether he was smiling at my ignorance, or whether he was smiling his satisfaction with the box and the voice and above all Paul Robeson.

'Who are your people?' I asked him. It seemed a kind of huge joke.

'The Negro race,' said Trumper. The smile had left his face, and his manner had turned grave again. I finished my drink and looked at him. He knew that I was puzzled. This bewilderment about Trumper's people was real. At first I thought he meant the village. This allegiance was something bigger. I wanted to understand it. He drained the glass and set it on the table.

'I didn't know it till I reach the States,' he said.

'Didn't know what?' I insisted. I understood the Negro race perfectly, but I didn't follow how I was involved. He hadn't spoken.

'Know what?' I insisted. 'What did you know there?'

'My people,' he said again, 'or better, my race. 'Twus in the States I find it, an' I'm gonner keep it till thy kingdom come.'

There was a pause and we had the glasses refilled. The bartender left us.

''Twus what I mean when I say you don't understan' life,' Trumper said. 'An' I didn't understan' it myself till I reach the States. If there be one thing I thank America for, she teach me who my race wus. Now I'm never goin' to lose it. Never never.'

'There are black people here too,' I said. I hadn't quite understood him.

'I know,' said Trumper, 'but it ain't the same. It ain't the same at all. 'Tis a different thing altogether. 'Course the blacks here are my people too, but they don't know it yet. You don't know it yourself. None o' you here on this islan' know what it mean to fin' race. An' the white people you have to deal with won't ever let you know. 'Tis a great thing 'bout the English, the know-how. If ever there wus a nation in creation that know how to do an' get a thing do, 'tis the English. My friend in the States use to call them the great administrators. In America I have see as much as a man get kick down for askin' a question, a simple question. Not here. That couldn't ever happen here. We can walk here where we like if 'tis a public place, an' you've white teachers, an' we speak with white people at all times in all places. My people here go to their homes an' all that. An' take the clubs, for example. There be clubs which you an' me can't go to, an' none o' my people here, no matter who they be, but they don't tell us we can't. They put up a sign, 'Members Only,' knowin' full well you ain't got no chance o' becomin' a member. An' although we know from the start why we can't go, we got the consolation we can't 'cause we ain't members. In America they don't worry with that kind o' beatin' 'bout the bush.'

'What's the difference between us an' the black people over there?' I asked.

''Tis a great big difference,' said Trumper. 'They suffer in a way we don't know here. We can't understan' it here an' we never will. But their sufferin' teach them what we here won't ever know. The Race, our people.'

I took a sip of the drink and tried to ferret things out. I recalled the letter he had written and understood why the meaning wasn't clear. It seemed my last chance to find out. I understood the village, the High School, my mother, the first assistant. There was a sense in which I would have called all these mine. I understood my island. This was more impersonal, less immediate, but not altogether outside my claims. I spoke of my island. But this new entity was different. The race. The people. Trumper was right when he said certain things weren't mentioned at the school, but I didn't see what the High School could say about this. They couldn't teach me how to belong to this thing which Trumper called race and people. On that account I had nothing to be angry about. The Race. My people.

'Am I one of your people, Trumper?' The question was almost desperate. I was beginning to think that another world infinitely more vast than the High School was coming between us.

'You're one o' my people all right,' said Trumper, 'but you can't understan' it here. Not here. But the day you leave an' perhaps if you go further than Trinidad you'll learn.'

'I have heard stories of cruelty to black people in America,' I said, 'but I don't understand what you mean by different.'

'There ain't the same people,' said Trumper, 'an' as a matteroffact there ain't goin' to be ever.'

'Why?'

He paused and took a sip of the drink.

'You know here,' said Trumper, 'we call a man a nigger man. Sometimes if you get vex you say so an' so is a blasted nigger man. Sometimes here the whites talk 'bout the Negro people. It ain't so in the States.'

'What do they say?' I was more anxious to hear than he was to explain.

'There they simply say the Negroes,' said Trumper, 'an' sometimes this nigger or that nigger an' so on.'

'What's the difference?'

''Tis a tremendous difference,' said Trumper. 'One single word make a tremendous difference, that's why you can never be too sure what a word will do. I'm a nigger or a Negro an' all o' us put together is niggers or Negroes. There ain't no "man" an' there ain't no "people." Just nigger an' Negro. An' little as that seem 'tis a tremendous difference. It make a tremendous difference not to the whites but the blacks. 'Tis the blacks who get affected by leavin' out that word "man" or "people." That's how we learn the race. 'Tis what a word can do. Now there ain't a black man in all America who won't get up an' say I'm a Negro an' I'm proud of it. We all are proud of it. I'm going to fight for the rights o' the Negroes, and I'll die fighting. That's what any black man in the States will say. He ain't got no time to think 'bout the rights o' Man or People or whatever you choose to call it. It's the rights o' the Negro, 'cause we have gone on usin' the word the others use for us, an' now we are a different kind o' creature, but we got to see first an' foremost 'bout the rights o' the NEGRO, 'cause it's like any kind o' creature to see 'bout itself first. If the rights o' Man an' the rights o' the Negro wus the same said thing, 'twould be different, but there ain't 'cause we're a different kind o' creature. That's what a simple little word can do, an' 'tis what you goin' to learn sooner or later. You'll hear 'bout the Englishman, an' the Frenchman, an' the American which mean man of America. An' each is call that 'cause he born in that particular place. But you'll become a Negro like me an' all the rest in the States an' all over the world, 'cause it ain't have nothin' to do with where you born. 'Tis what you is, a different kind o' creature. An' when you see what I tellin' you an' you become a Negro, act as you should an' don't ask Hist'ry why you is what you then see yourself to be, 'cause Hist'ry ain't got no answers. You ain't a thing till you know it, an' that's why you an' none o' you on this island is a Negro yet; but if they don't know, you goin' to know 'cause if my mind tell me right you goin' to go much further than Trinidad, an' that's why I bring you here for this talk, 'cause it frighten the life out o' me to know what's goin' to happen. Now you won't be able to say Trumper didn't tell me. Let's have the last drink.'

We had the glasses filled and Trumper reached for his hat and stood behind the table. I remained seated for a moment. I had nothing to say because I wasn't prepared for what had happened. Trumper made his own experience, the discovery of a race, a people, seem like a revelation. It was nothing I had known, and it didn't seem I could know it till I had lived it. He put his hat on the table, and we stood at opposite ends, silent with our hands stretched out. The glasses touched.

'I wish you from the bottom of my heart the best of everything.' His voice was firm, assured and yet very tender. I gulped the drink, unspeaking. The lump had come to my throat and then the feeling came on. It was the last drink.

We left the shop and took the road that led to Belleville on the other side of the village. And we were silent again. All the shops were closed. The night had grown thicker, and I thought it would soon rain. It was a long time since I had seen such a black night. The streets were deserted. Trumper didn't speak, and although I wanted to say something I didn't try because I knew that it would have been difficult to give the words sound. He understood and remained quiet. Whatever he suffered his assurance was astonishing. He had found what he needed and there were no more problems to be worked out. Henceforth his life would be straight, even, uncomplicated. He knew the race and he knew his people and he knew what that knowledge meant. Here in the village and even throughout the island we had known differences between the well-to-do blacks and the simpler less prosperous ones. I had known both. There was a difference between the village school and the High School. There was a difference between Trumper and Bob and the friends I knew later at the High School. But this difference revealed to Trumper was in another category. This was something vast like sea and sky all wrapped up in one. To be a different kind of creature. This was beyond my experience. The subterfuge the whites employed to keep a club for themselves was clear to me, but I also knew that certain blacks employed a similar subterfuge to exclude other blacks who weren't equal to their demands. I didn't know why this was so. There was a kind of possessive prejudice between whites and blacks, and blacks and blacks, but it couldn't have been for the reasons Trumper had given. Whatever we had known we hadn't known this difference. To be a different kind of creature. It was difficult to think. To be a part of something which you didn't know and which if Trumper was right it was my duty to discover. It was much too late for me to ask further questions, and in any case I thought I knew how Trumper would answer. I wasn't worried about my duty. I had a lot of time to find what Trumper had already known, but a new thought had registered. Suppose I didn't find it. This was worse, *the thought of being a part of what you could not become*. It was only Trumper's assurance that made it seem less frightening than it might have been. I envied that assurance. He had found something to cradle his deepest instincts and emotions. He was a Negro and he was proud. Now he could walk in the sun or stand on the highest hill and proclaim himself the blackest evidence of the white man's denial of conscience. And if there was a God in heaven or any possibility of justice on earth the revelation of this new difference would have been a justification for this existence. To be a different kind of creature.

We turned the fence and kept straight ahead. In the distance there was a light that looked like candlelight or the burning wick that stuck out from an oil can. Trumper said something about the light but I didn't hear. There were several voices raised in a confusion of orders and rebukes. We drew nearer and the voices were more distinct. The light came from an oil can tied with string to a cart. It was one of the large handcarts which had to be drawn by several men at a time. The cart was parked at the edge of the road and the men stood on the embankment in twos and threes around the house. It was the shoemaker's shop. We didn't hear him, but I thought I knew what was happening. Trumper hadn't known about what had happened recently between the shoemaker and the strange man. I didn't speak. The voices were raised again, and there was a fall of wood and shingles. Then everything was lost in the shouting.

'Ready,' one voice said, and a chorus came back, 'Now, now.'

'Lift,' another voice shouted, and the chorus came back, 'Up, up.'

The noise was terrifying. One or two windows were opened, but no light came from them. Then the voices were raised altogether as though it were the final effort. The scream was terrifying. They lifted quietly, not speaking a word while the house was raised from the groundsel. Then suddenly there was a crash from within and a mad scamper of feet. The partitions and roof had collapsed. The shoemaker's shop became a bundle of wood heaped on stones. The men ran out from all directions, and we stood opposite, silent, almost humiliated. There was nothing we could do.

"Twus the same thing, I say,' one man said. 'You couldn't move that shop. It been there more'n thirty years.'

'Would have been all right to make a patch here an' there,' said another voice, 'but to move the whole thing, I thought to myself 'twus dangerous.'

'There wusn't nothin' he could do,' said another. 'He had to get off.'

'He won't be the shoemaker he wus again,' said another.

'Nor you won't ever get one like him again,' said another.

They sat on the cart helpless. A few more remarks were made about the shoemaker and then they were quiet.

We walked away unspeaking. This was the first house they had tried to move, and it wasn't going to be the last. The rumour had already gone around that Mr. Foster would be leaving. He had found a piece of land in another part of the island, and it was said he would work on the land in payment for keeping his house on it. The produce went to the owner. It was difficult to think what might happen to Mr. Foster's house. Then there might be four or five more. They might all have to go sooner or later. What could Trumper do? What could I do? What could any one of us do who knew the village, lived in it, loved it? What could any of us do about it? There was nothing I could do.

'Trumper,' I had spoken but I had already forgotten what I wanted to say. I wasn't sure I would see him in the morning. He was listening. I couldn't remember for a minute what I wanted to say. I believed it was an attempt to escape thinking about the village. He asked me what I wanted.

'You remember,' I said, 'a long time ago we spent a day at the beach? You and me and Bob and Boy Blue.'

He answered yes, but there was a strange quality of irrelevance in his voice. I wondered whether he, too, had been thinking about the village.

'You remember you were saying about a feeling,' I said, 'a big bad feeling in the pit of the stomach. A feeling you were alone in a world all by yourself, and although there were hundreds of people moving round you, it made no difference. You got giddy. Boy Blue said it made him giddy to think about it.'

'You ever feel like that now?' he asked. Again I thought there was that quality of irrelevance in his voice. It was as though he knew what I wanted to say and it didn't matter because he knew what was wrong. It was this assurance I couldn't penetrate, but I wanted to explain what I felt.

'A man who know his people won't ever feel like that,' said Trumper. 'Never.' He took my hand and shook it strongly, repeating the wish he had made in the shop. We promised to meet the next morning and walked away in different directions.

The men remained on the cart grumbling. Most of the houses were shut tight. When the shoemaker's shop crashed to the ground the noise must have awakened some of the neighbours. A few windows were opened, but there was no light coming from them, and no one spoke. The men went on grumbling. No one had seen or heard of the shoemaker. And if he was nearby he didn't speak. It was very still but for the occasional rise and fall of the men's voices. They didn't know what they should do. The house had collapsed and their problem was to find a place to stack the broken boards. No one knew how the owner of the land would view the shoemaker's misfortune. The house couldn't be carried to another spot, nor could they think of setting it up again where it had crumbled. There was nothing to restore. One man went on saying he had warned them not to touch the house. They shouldn't have attempted to move it. There was a quiet altercation. The house had to be moved and they were being paid to do it. Another man said they had two more jobs in the same road. They were going to remove two more houses the following night. They argued quietly whether they should make the attempt. I didn't know how many houses were going to be removed. I tried not to think about it since there was nothing I could do. I left the men behind and quickened my pace. I didn't realize that I had been standing listening to their altercation. I turned to the left where the roads made four. Mr. Foster's house was shut tight. There was no light at all here, and the night seemed thicker and heavier. This was the last I had seen of the shoemaker's shop, the road, the men grumbling their annoyance and confusion. Then I heard a voice as though it had come like an object out of the dark. It was ahead of me but I couldn't see. I moved forward on tiptoe and listened.

'Whatever it be make such a sound?' the voice said. I gathered that was the question I hadn't heard at first. I drew nearer and when the voice spoke again I recognized. It was the old man Pa.

'What are you doing out?' I was quite surprised to see him at that hour. He didn't seem to hear what I had said. Apparently he didn't know who it was.

'Taint a right an' proper hour o' the night to make such noise,' he said. I went closer and asked him again what he was doing out so late. It was likely he couldn't find his way. I had seldom known it so dark.

'Whoever it be?' he asked and I got the feeling he had turned to face me. We were very close now.

'What are you doing out so late?' I asked again, and he recognized the voice. He had touched me with the stick.

'Takin' a last look at the place,' he said.

The remark escaped me. I thought he was making a joke since he knew that I was leaving the next day.

'Why a last look?' I asked him. I was prepared to continue the joke.

''Cause I leaving tomorrow,' he said. His tone was decisive.

'I know it in my heart o' hearts I won't set foot here again,' he said. He had rested a hand on my shoulder. Then he took it away and as quickly put it back. I had an idea what had happened but I wasn't sure he would have liked me to talk about it. The Alms House wasn't the kind of residence one admitted. I knew that. I wanted to find out what he thought about going, but it seemed silly to ask him. What could he feel? Moreover, I didn't want to arouse any unbearable emotions. I didn't know how long he had lived in the village, but I was sure it was longer than any of the villagers I knew. He had known the shoemaker as a boy.

'We both settin' forth tomorrow,' he said. 'I to my last restin'-place before the grave, an' you into the wide wide world.'

I decided I wouldn't question him about the Alms House. But I wanted to say something that would sound cheerful. We stood outside his house waiting to tell each other good-bye.

''Twus a night like this,' he said, 'nine years ago when those waters roll without end all over this place. 'Twus a flood as I won't want ever to feel for nothin' in the world.'

He paused and tapped the stick on the ground.

'P'raps you won't remember much 'bout the flood,' he said. 'You wus scarcely out the eggshell.' I said I remembered it.

'You wus small then,' he said, 'too small to care much 'bout the calamity that happen. But it wus the beginnin' o' so much in this place. 'Twus strike an' then 'twus riot an' what with one rumour an' a next, now 'tis the land. We see Penny Bank an' Society an' now 'tis the end.'

'What do you think about Mr. Slime?' I asked him. I wanted to respond in some way to all he had said.

'I don't know,' he said. 'A man make a promise an' a man change, an' the man who make a promise ain't the same said man as the man who change, an' I don't know, I don't know who got the right to judge why he change or whether he should have change at all. I don't know.'

He paused and then a cat scampered across the road. It seemed to run from one side to the next, but we couldn't see anything. We drew nearer the house. And he felt for the steps with the stick.

'You must be good to yourself,' he said.

He passed his hand over my head and then bent forward and kissed me on the brow.

''Tis the last thing the old man can give,' he said. 'A kiss of blessing. P'raps you'll remember Pa 'cause you won't ever see him again.'

I was going to speak.

'You won't see me again, my son,' he said, and felt his way up the steps. The door closed gently behind him.

I stood for a moment waiting to see whether he might put on the light. The feeling had seized me again. You had seen the last of something.

''Twus a night like this nine years ago when those waters roll.' The village/my mother/a boy among the boys/a man who knew his people won't feel alone/to be a different kind of creature. Words and voices falling like a full shower and the old man returning with the pebble under the grape leaf on the sand: You won't see me again, my son.

The earth where I walked was a marvel of blackness and I knew in a sense more deep than simple departure I had said farewell, farewell to the land.

Ann Arbor Paperbacks